# SISTERHOOD
*of the*

# SQUARED CIRCLE

*The*
# HISTORY
AND **RISE**

*of*
# WOMEN'S
# WRESTLING

# PAT LAPRADE AND DAN MURPHY

Published by ECW Press
665 Gerrard Street East
Toronto, Ontario, Canada M4M 1Y2
416-694-3348 / info@ecwpress.com

Editor for the press: Michael Holmes
Cover design: Michel Vrana
Cover photos: Sasha Banks; Trish and Lita © 2017
World Wrestling Entertainment, Inc. / WWE
Melissa © Yan O'Cain Collection; Fabulous Moolah
© Linda Boucher; Charlotte © Bill Otten; Becky
Lynch © Ricky Havlik

LIBRARY AND ARCHIVES CANADA
CATALOGUING IN PUBLICATION

Laprade, Pat, author
Sisterhood of the squared circle :
the history and rise of women's wrestling
/ Pat Laprade and Dan Murphy ;
foreword by WWE Superstar Natalya.

ISSUED IN PRINT AND ELECTRONIC FORMATS.
ISBN 978-1-77041-307-8 (paperback)
also issued as: 978-1-77305-015-7 (PDF)
978-1-77305-014-0 (EPUB)

1. Women wrestlers. 2. Wrestling—History.

1. Murphy, Dan (Journalist), author
II. Title.

GV1195.L37 2017    796.812082    C2016-906364-X
C2016-906365-8

The publication of *Sisterhood of the Squared Circle* has been generously supported by the Canada Council for
the Arts, which last year invested $153 million to bring the arts to Canadians throughout the country, and by
the Government of Canada through the Canada Book Fund. *Nous remercions le Conseil des arts du Canada de
son soutien. L'an dernier, le Conseil a investi 153 millions de dollars pour mettre de l'art dans la vie des Canadiennes
et des Canadiens de tout le pays. Ce livre est financé en partie par le gouvernement du Canada.*

PRINTED AND BOUND IN CANADA          PRINTING: MARQUIS   5   4   3   2   1

MIX
Paper from
responsible sources
FSC® C103567
www.fsc.org

*In memory of Stewart Allen,*
*cofounder of Ringbelles.com*

FOREWORD
  BY WWE SUPERSTAR NATALYA 7
INTRODUCTION 11

CHAPTER 1 *The Origins: From Amazons to*
  *Wrestlers* 15

CHAPTER 2 *The Pioneers* 19
  Cora Livingston 22
  Clara Mortensen 26

CHAPTER 3 *When Millie Met Billy:*
  *The Billy Wolfe Era* 29
  Mildred Burke: The Queen
    of the Ring 33
  June Byers, G. Bill, and the Split
    between Wolfe and Burke 37
  Nell Stewart 46
  Cora Combs 50
  Mae Weston 52
  The African-Americans 54
    • Babs Wingo 55
    • Ethel Johnson 56
    • Marva Scott 56
    • Louise Greene 56
    • Kathleen Wimbley 58
    • Ramona Isbell 58
  Ida Mae Martinez 62
  Gladys Gillem 65
  Penny Banner 67
  Johnnie Mae Young 73

CHAPTER 4 *From Slave Girl to*
  *Women's Champion: The Rise*
  *of Lillian Ellison* 80
  The Complicated Legacy
    of the Fabulous Moolah 84
  The Moolah Girls 89
    • Rita Cortez 89
    • Ella Waldek and the Story
      of Billy Wolfe's Ward 92
    • Ann Casey 97
    • Betty Jo Hawkins 100
    • Judy Grable 102
    • Princess Little Cloud 105
    • Vivian Vachon 107
    • Donna Christantello 109
    • Joyce Grable 112
    • Bette Boucher 114
    • Susan "Tex" Green 116
  The Independent Women 119
    • Evelyn Stevens 119
    • Kay Noble 122
    • Betty Nicoli 125
    • Beverly Shade 127
    • Donna Lemke 129

CHAPTER 5 *The Rock 'n' Wrestling*
  *Connection and the 1980s:*
  *Girls Just Wanna Have Fun* 141
  Wendi Richter 147
    • The Original WWF Screwjob 150
  Leilani Kai 153

Judy Martin 157
Velvet McIntyre 159
Sherri Martel 161
Rockin' Robin 163
Debbie Combs 165
Misty Blue Simmes 167
Candi Devine 168
Madusa/Alundra Blayze 170
  • WCW: "Where the
    big girls play" 172
GLOW: Gorgeous Ladies of Wrestling 175

CHAPTER 6 The Attitude Era: The Revival
  of the WWF's Women's Division 179
  Sable 180
  Chyna 183
  Trish Stratus 189
  Lita 194
  Ivory 198
  Jacqueline 201
  Jazz 204
  Molly Holly 206
  Luna Vachon 209
  Torrie Wilson 212
  Stacy Keibler 215
  Victoria/Tara 217

CHAPTER 7 Total Nonstop Action:
  A New Frontier 221
  Gail Kim 224
  Awesome Kong 228

The Beautiful People: Angelina Love
    and Velvet Sky 231
ODB 234
Daffney 238
Mickie James 240
Jade 244

CHAPTER 8 The Rise of the Divas 247
  The Bella Twins: Nikki and Brie 250
  Michelle McCool 254
  Melina 258
  Beth Phoenix 261
  Naomi 264
  A.J. Lee 267
  Natalya 271

CHAPTER 9 International Report 275
  Mildred Burke and the Introduction of
      Women's Wrestling to Japan 276
    • The Beauty Pair: Jackie Sato
      and Maki Ueda 280
    • The Crush Gals: Chigusa Nagayo
      and Lioness Asuka 283
    • Jaguar Yokota 286
    • Devil Masami 288
    • Dump Matsumoto 290
    • The Jumping Bomb Angels:
      Noriyo Tateno and Itsuki
      Yamazaki 292
    • Bull Nakano 294
    • Akira Hokuto 297

- Manami Toyota 300
- Aja Kong 303
- Megumi Kudo 306
- Monster Ripper 308
- Reggie Bennett 312
- Ayako Hamada 317

Mexico 319
- Irma Gonzalez 320
- Lola Gonzalez 320
- Lady Apache 321
- La Diabolica 323
- Sarah Stock 323
- Sexy Star 326

United Kingdom 328
- Saraya Knight 328

Australia 331
- Madison Eagles 332

**CHAPTER 10** *Dave Prazak's Crazy Idea:*
*SHIMMER* 335
The Women of the Independents 339
- Allison Danger 339
- Mercedes Martinez 343
- Malia Hosaka 346
- Lexie Fyfe 349
- Cheerleader Melissa 353
- LuFisto 357

- MsChif 367
- The Canadian Ninjas: Portia Perez
  and Nicole Matthews 369
- Jessicka Havok 373
- Santana Garrett 376

**CHAPTER 11** *NXT, the Revolution, and*
*the Return of the Women's Title* 379
The Death of the Divas Title 382
Charlotte Flair 385
Sasha Banks 389
Bayley 392
Becky Lynch 395
Paige 398
Emma 401
Asuka 403
Sara Amato 406

**CHAPTER 12** *Stephanie McMahon:*
*Holding the Future of Women's*
*Wrestling in Her Hands* 409
Ronda Rousey: The Biggest Prospect
  Who's Not Even a Wrestler Yet 411
What Does the Future Hold? 413

**SELECTED BIBLIOGRAPHY** 416
**ACKNOWLEDGMENTS** 421

# Foreword

Not a day has gone by when I haven't thought of or spoken about wrestling. My grandfather, Stu Hart, had so much passion for wrestling that when he was a young man he hitchhiked to Ottawa to become the amateur wrestling champion of Canada. Many didn't know that at the time, Stu was homeless.

Stu would later open up western Canada to professional wrestling, with the biggest stars performing there. But there were also women who wrestled for my grandfather.

In the late '50s it was Johnnie Mae Young. In the early to mid-'60s there were Penny Banner, Lorraine Johnson, Marva Scott, Ethel Johnson, June Byers, Fabulous Moolah, Bette Boucher, and Princess Little Cloud. In the '70s there were Marie Vagnone and Susan Green. In the '80s there were Wendi Richter, Joyce Grable, Velvet McIntyre, Judy Martin, Rhonda Sing from Calgary, Debbie Combs, and a couple of pretty famous Japanese girls, Devil Masami and Chigusa Nagayo.

*Natalya and her uncle Bret, from the famous Hart family.*
NATTIE NEIDHART COLLECTION

Now that is some *girl power*.

Professional wrestling has always been the backdrop of my life. I grew up in this very crazy world with some of the most unique people on the planet. There was never a dull moment in our house ... And there was always Gene Okerlund's voice in the background on our TV.

Once I started training with my uncles in my grandfather's basement — a.k.a. the infamous Hart Dungeon — I was hooked. It was so much fun and a great outlet to be creative and escape reality. Wrestling is a form of self-expression; it's an art.

Five years later, after wrestling in Canada, Japan, Europe, and the United States, I was hired by WWE. I was so grateful I had been able to learn and work with so many awesome women, like Sara Del Rey, for example. But I couldn't believe I was actually going to work for the company I grew up watching my dad and uncles wrestle for. It felt like a dream to work for WWE. I almost forgot how to do a headlock I was so damned excited. The butterflies *never* went away. I realized I liked those butterflies, especially before each match, because they told me I was living my dream.

I have shared the stage with so many strong women. I feel proud of every match I've ever had, even if some of them left me in tears for all the wrong reasons. I've grown so much from the bumps, bruises, and "trainwrecks" as well as the rare moments of glory where I felt like I was floating and no one could touch me.

In wrestling, as in life, you fall down and you have no choice but to get back up and keep fighting. There are no victims — only survivors who live to tell their stories. And what grand stories they are. Some of the greatest survivors are women.

Girls like Beth Phoenix taught me so much about inner strength. The Bellas taught me to embrace my inner beauty when I didn't always feel so beautiful. In Charlotte Flair during our infamous 2014 NXT TakeOver match, I learned so much about myself. She was a girl who, like me, felt she couldn't fill her family's big boots. What she later realized mattered most was blazing her own legacy.

Because of all the things I've learned from wrestling, I feel like there's *nothing* I can't conquer. I'm happy so many women of the next generation are also going to experience this surge of strength.

Only a handful of women on the planet can do *this* — and I'm damned proud of that.

I'd like to thank my dear friend Dan Murphy and his coauthor, Pat Laprade, for asking me to be a part of this book. Thank you, Dan, for believing in me and women's wrestling for all these years. You rock.

Nattie Neidhart
#womenswrestling

# Introduction

It all started in the carnivals. You had the bearded women. You had the clowns. You had the feats of strength. And then there were the wrestlers who would take on (and defeat) anyone from the crowd. Sometimes, that wrestler happened to be a woman. And most of the time, *she* could beat a man in a heartbeat.

By the 1930s, women's wrestling had graduated from the carnival sideshows to popular (albeit often controversial) attractions presented alongside men's matches. For some adventurous women, professional wrestling was a way to travel, to earn money, and to live a life of excitement. These women wanted something different from settling down, starting a family, and doting on a husband who "brought home the bacon."

There were perks to a wrestling life. Some women were able to see the world, from Los Angeles to New York, Paris to Tokyo, and all points in between. But it was also a life filled with unscrupulous promoters, some of whom felt entitled to sexual favors in exchange for presenting women's matches on their cards, always trying to pay as little as possible. It was a world of backstage politics and squabbles, of constantly moving from town to town, and of perpetual aches, pains, and injuries.

It wasn't just a job. It was a vocation, a lifestyle that was completely different from the norm. It was a profession that presented women as major-league athletes and entertainers at a time when a woman's place was supposed to be in the home.

In the '40s and the '50s, Billy Wolfe, Mildred Burke, and the Fabulous Moolah helped women's wrestling expand into an international attraction. The advent of television turned wrestlers — both male and female — into TV stars, bringing them out of the arenas and into viewers' living rooms. If this was the golden era of women's wrestling, the next two decades weren't. But when Vince McMahon Jr. broke all of wrestling's unwritten rules and took his World Wrestling Federation national in the mid-1980s, he put women's wrestling once again in the forefront, turning a shy young girl named Wendi Richter into a household name.

That didn't last long though, and with an edgier product on its way, the presentation of women's wrestling in the 1990s changed a great deal. Women were presented purely as sex objects, competing in bra and panties matches or other novelty matches designed to show as much skin as possible, an act women's wrestling still has trouble getting rid of today. At the same time, in Japan and on the indies, women's matches outshone the men at times, and women displayed unmatched athleticism, intensity, and showmanship. The new millennium brought a mix of all this, with women being portrayed as divas or being part of a revolution.

This is a look at the history of women's professional wrestling, from the carnivals to that so-called women's revolution. It's a look into the lives of some remarkable women whose dedication, talent, and hard work have made a lasting impact on the world of wrestling — women who struggled hard to be more than just an attraction or a novelty act.

Vince McMahon once approached Trish Stratus backstage and complimented her on her match. Stratus pantomimed dialing a phone and said, "Hello, 911? I'd like to report a robbery. It looks like the women have stolen the show." That's what this book is all about. Women's wrestling, finally rising back to its rightful spot: in the main event.

# The ORIGINS
## From Amazons to Wrestlers

Although wrestling was commonly practiced by men, the male sex didn't have a monopoly on grappling. According to folklore, the Mongol princess Khutulun was a respected warrior and wrestler. She would consent to marry only a man who could defeat her in a wrestling match. Many tried; no one succeeded.

The most famous of the fighting women of antiquity were the Amazons, the mythical warrior women who maintained a matriarchal society and were regarded as some of the finest warriors of the era. There is little physical proof that the Amazons ever existed, but they became the stuff of legend among the Greeks, who depicted them in sculptures, pottery, friezes, jewelry, and poetry.

Interestingly, some etymologists have examined the term *Amazons* and theorized that it originated from the combination of *a* (meaning "without") and *mazos* (meaning "breasts"). This interpretation led to the theory that Amazonian warrior women either cut or cauterized their breasts in order to maintain better control of the bow, the Amazons' weapon of choice. Yet, Greek art of the era strove to represent impossible physical perfection, and the supposedly breastless or small-breasted Amazonian women were depicted as busty and beautiful female forms. It represents a paradox that still survives today; even female warriors were held to idealized and often unobtainable standards of physical beauty.

In any case, women learning the art of wrestling as a form of hand-to-hand combat and self-defense was more commonplace than it might seem. Reports of women's fighting as an entertainment spectacle can be found as far back as the 1700s, when historian William Hickey wrote that he had witnessed a battle between two "she-devils . . . engaged in scratching and boxing" in London. In the 1720s, boxer Elizabeth Wilkinson was billing herself as "the Championess of America and Europe" for women's fighting, similar to what Hickey observed. The prize awarded to the winner of an 1876 boxing match between two women in New York City was a silver butter dish, a prize both valuable and practical for the fashionable dinner party hostess. Male fighters were awarded cash or free beer.

In the American Midwest, wrestling became a staple of traveling circuses and carnivals, which also featured a variety of sideshows, attractions, and games of skill and chance. Fairgoers were encouraged to challenge the carnival's star wrestler. Anyone who could beat the champ — or last a set amount of time without submitting or being pinned — would receive a prize.

Like many of the attractions on the carnival midway, these contests weren't necessarily on the up and up. Sometimes the plucky carnival-goer who accepted the challenge was in on the act and just trying to drum up business and encourage others to try their hand. It was wrestling with a dose of showmanship. It was an attraction designed to sell tickets and manipulate audiences . . . and it wasn't exactly what it seemed to be on the surface.

The modern "sports entertainment" spectacle known as professional wrestling grew out of those carnival sideshows, where gullible "marks" were fleeced of their money, and turning a profit at the gate was more important than winning or losing on the mat. By the latter half of the 1800s, professional wrestling was one of the most popular attractions in Europe and North America, although its legitimacy was frequently called into question by critics and sportswriters, even in the infancy of the sport. And women were getting into the game.

In American saloons and carnivals, these fighting women usually wore black tights and flashy, form-fitting leotards. A large part of the appeal of women's wrestling was the implicit sexuality inherent in the bout. This was an era in which modesty ruled the day; Victorian-era swimsuits were knee-length affairs worn over bloomers, complete with stockings and ornate caps. In carnival and circus attractions, the audience was invited to gawk as two women in provocative outfits maneuvered into some rather suggestive positions, either with the intent to outwrestle an opponent or with the intent to titillate the paying customers. It was part athletic competition, part carny swindle, and part sexual fetish, and spectators were lining up to pay good money to watch it unfold.

In 1875, Jackley's Circus, a traveling circus featuring performers from Europe, toured the United States and included female wrestlers from Vienna as part of the act. "Large crowds would gather to watch the highly publicized all-female wrestling competition, the prize of which was jewelry, presented in front of the crowd on a pillow," wrote L.A. Jennings in her book *She's a Knockout!: A History of Women in Fighting Sports*.

Women's wrestling even became popular in France, where exhibitions were held in fashionable Parisian nightclubs and featured in the famous Folies Bergère in 1889 and 1890. Similar exhibitions were later held at burlesque halls in the United States.

One of the first female American wrestlers to gain notoriety was Grace Hemindinger, who stood six feet tall and weighed in at 275 pounds. A mountain of a woman, she wrestled primarily against male challengers from 1875 to 1878, when she gave up wrestling and focused on performing feats of strength on the circus circuit.

Wrestling women were defying societal norms and changing notions of femininity. Strong women with powerful and defined muscles were becoming sex symbols. As suffragettes pushed for voting rights in the United States, a small group of women were showing that "the fairer sex" could compete athletically against men and were challenging established gender roles.

Women's wrestling received national attention in the *National Police Gazette*, a tabloid newspaper that specialized in true crime stories that more conservative newspapers avoided. By the late 1880s, the *Gazette* was known for its lurid engravings, drawings, and photographs, often depicting burlesque performers, dancers, and prostitutes, skirting the ever-so-fine line between news and smut. The spectacle of women's wrestling was a natural subject for the *Gazette* to cover, and it became a popular topic among readers.

In 1891, under publisher Richard K. Fox, the *Gazette* sponsored the first recognized women's wrestling championship, which would be awarded to the top wrestler in the game. The championship marked a recognition of the growing appeal of women's wrestling and a first step toward legitimizing it taking it from a sideshow attraction to a sporting event that could be presented side by side with male wrestlers.

# The PIONEERS

The *National Police Gazette* crowned its first women's wrestling champion at the Bastille of the Bowery, a sporting house owned by Owney Geoghegan, a former bare-knuckle boxer in his native Ireland. The hall was located in a rough-and-tumble section on the south side of Manhattan known for its numerous gay and lesbian bars. Josie Wahlford was the *Gazette*'s first champion.

A native of Elizabeth, New Jersey, Wahlford (née Josephine Wohlford) had come up through the carnival circuit. By the age of 24, she was touring vaudeville stages, performing a strongwoman routine. Billed as Minerva (after the Roman goddess of wisdom), Wahlford was allegedly able to deadlift 700 pounds, which, if true, would still hold up as a world record today. She stood 5'8" and tipped the scales at 165 pounds, although she weighed much more than that as her career really took off.

Wahlford was the real deal — a capable wrestler with remarkable power and balance. She was trained by her husband, "The Professor" Charley Blatt, a powerlifter and wrestler from Hoboken, New Jersey, who took Wahlford under his wing.

"The Professor taught Josie all the tricks and she became invincible," wrote wrestling historian Nat Fleischer in a 1966 article in *Ring* magazine. "I would say that Josie Wahlford was the first generally accepted champion among the fair wrestlers of the USA."

Wahlford may be generally accepted as the first women's champion, but she wasn't the undisputed champion. Alice Williams also staked a claim to being the champion, by virtue of her win over Sadie Morgan at the Bastille of the Bowery that same year. However, Wahlford continued to defend her championship and had a lengthier career, pushing Williams's claims into the murky shadows of history.

Wahlford defended her championship in the back rooms of taverns in clandestine bouts that were not regulated by any governing body or commission. She defended the title against both men and women, but male challengers were limited to amateurs who could not outweigh Wahlford by more than 20 pounds, maintaining a common stipulation that was used during the open challenges from the carnival circuit.

Although reliable records of the era are hard to come by, it seems that Wahlford relinquished the title to Alice Williams, who subsequently lost the title to Laura Bennett in 1901. Bennett had made her name as one of the Bennett sisters, a group of touring siblings who put on boxing exhibitions. Bennett successfully defended the title against former champion Wahlford on multiple occasions. Those were the last matches that Wahlford had in her attempt to return to wrestling. After a worldwide career, Wahlford retired from the feats of strength competition in 1910. She died on September 1, 1923.

But the *Gazette*'s championship was just a small step toward legitimizing women's wrestling, which continued to thrive on the carnival and burlesque circuits, but was still outlawed by some state athletic commissions and kept wholly separate from men's wrestling events, which were presented as legitimate athletic contests in arenas, gyms, and boxing halls.

Another American woman to make a name for herself on the carnival circuit was Marie Ford. Born in New York in 1900, Ford took up marathon running, acrobatics, boxing, and wrestling. As an adult, she stood 5'6" and weighed 132 pounds — certainly not the stereotypical Amazon. Ford was a legitimate athlete, and she toured North America issuing open challenges for wrestling or boxing. Challengers could be women or men (provided the men were not professional fighters and did not outweigh her). If challengers were slow to come forward, she would insult the audience, challenging their masculinity and goading them out of hiding, demonstrating a key component of modern professional wrestling: the art of cutting a promo.

A quick-pin specialist, Ford wore down opponents with body blows (in bouts where combined wrestling and boxing rules were in effect) or simply threw them to the ground and into an immediate pinning combination. She was a pioneer of what would later be known as mixed martial arts, combining the striking punches of boxing with submission grappling. Many opponents were so surprised they had been taken down that they simply could not recover their sense in time to avoid a speedy pin. Although she was never recognized as champion, Ford built a reputation as a carnival attraction.

Caricatures and paintings of women wrestlers of this time often depicted them as obese "housewives from hell," looking to smother hapless men, or pulchritudinous giants in battle. Female wrestlers were portrayed as sideshow freaks, analogous to the bearded ladies, geeks, and assorted other oddities occupying the midway. But as photography grew in popularity and cameras became more widely available, these caricatures were replaced by promotional photographs showing physically fit and attractive specimens. In Europe, especially in Russian circuses, many women were both wrestling and performing feats of strength, such as Marina Lurs (billed as the strongest woman in the Russian empire), who began wrestling in 1907; "The Ukrainian Hercules" Agafia Zavidnaya, who was billed as "the most dangerous woman in the world who is able to topple any man"; Masha Poddubnaya, who was proclaimed the "lady world wrestling champion" six times between 1889 and 1910; Anette Busch, who also did some sumo wrestling later in life; and the Irish-born "Miss Vulcana" Kate Roberts, who evoked a combination of strength and physical beauty a century before Beth Phoenix would embrace both of those same qualities and dub herself the Glamazon.

## CORA LIVINGSTON

Back in the United States, Laura Bennett would end up dominating female wrestling for the first decade of the century, only to be surpassed by Cora Livingston. Many of the details of Livingston's early life have been lost to the mists of time — and generous amounts of promotional hyperbole — but one unassailable fact rings true: Livingston (whose name was also spelled as Livingstone in some reports) was the premier female grappler of the first two decades of the 20th century.

According to L.A. Jennings in her book *She's a Knockout!*, "at the time that Livingstone earned the right to declare herself the female champion wrestler of the world, the American press was displeased with female wrestlers because, up until the early 1900s, there had never been a particularly skilled one. This was perhaps because most of the women billed as wrestlers were either actresses pretending to be competent fighters or untrained women looking to fill a particular niche." Ironically, in the 1920 U.S. Census, Livingston would declare herself an actress, although by that time she had been a wrestler for more than a decade.

Livingston is believed to have been born in Buffalo, New York, anywhere between 1886 and 1893, although it has also been reported that she was born somewhere in Canada. According to the 1920 and 1940 U.S. censuses, she was respectively 32 and 52, and born in the state of New York, meaning she would have been born in either 1887 or 1888. According to most sources, both her parents died when she was young and she was placed in a convent school where she was raised by the nuns.

The nuns weren't likely to have approved of Cora's eventual vocation, but as a professional wrestler, the orphan from Western New York went on to tour the country and earn national acclaim as an athlete and attraction.

With her hair cut in a short and fashionable bob, Livingston somewhat resembled Hollywood's original It Girl, Clara Bow, but

*A true pioneer, Cora Livingston.* RING MEMORABILIA COLLECTION

whereas Bow evoked girlish femininity, Livingston had the strong, sturdy build of a woman accustomed to a life of manual labor.

Livingston stood a reported 5'5" tall and weighed in at a stocky 138 pounds in her prime. As a girl, she reportedly excelled in track and field before turning her attention to wrestling. According to some sources, she was trained early on by two former American heavyweight champions, the late greats Dan McLeod and Dr. Benjamin Roller.

Livingston's first documented wrestling match took place on March 19, 1906, at the Lafayette Theater in Buffalo. A March 18 preview article in the *Buffalo Evening Times* stated that "Miss Cora Livingstone, 110 pounds, champion featherweight of Buffalo, and Mrs. Hazel Parker, 110 pounds, champion featherweight of the United States, will meet all comers in their class and offer $25 to any lady either fails to throw in 15 minutes. During the week Miss Livingstone and Mrs. Parker will contest for the featherweight championship of America, best two falls out of three, one bout a night to a finish. Both women are clever wrestlers and hold records."

Parker won the first contest on March 19. Livingston evened the score with a pinfall win on March 20. On March 23, Livingston won the third and deciding bout. From that point forward, Livingston was billed as a world champion, a title she defended throughout the East Coast and the Midwest.

She eventually caught the eye of Paul Bowser, a talented middleweight wrestler from Western Pennsylvania. The two met in 1910 and were married in 1913, Livingston legally using the name Cora B. Bowser from that point on. Bowser also helped train Livingston, further adding to her reputation as the most well-rounded technical female wrestler of the era.

Livingston toured throughout the United States and Canada, facing opponents like Canadian champion Celia Pontos and British champion Bessie Farrar, giving her further credibility as a world champion. Bowser would go on to become a wrestling promoter and would stake his claim to the Boston territory, which Livingston would call home.

Livingston suffered her first loss in suitably controversial fashion. On September 7, 1910, the champ faced local challenger May Nelson in Pittsburgh, Pennsylvania, at the Academy of Music before a reported crowd of 2,000 spectators. Livingston took the early advantage, and the crowd quickly turned nasty. The match was stopped by the police at the 13-minute mark when ringside fans attempted to storm the ring because of Livingston's rough treatment of the challenger. The match was postponed, and when it resumed two days later, Nelson pinned Livingston. Livingston's championship was not at stake. The riot was averted and the fans went home happy. Nelson reportedly received a purse of $100 for her win.

On October 28, 1910, Kansas City promoter H.M. Donegan arranged a match between Livingston and Laura Bennett, who was one of Livingston's early trainers, with the winner earning the right to be called the undisputed women's world champion. Donegan had an extravagant title belt made for the occasion, believed to be the first time such a belt was awarded in the women's division. Livingston won the match in two straight falls.

"The Livingstone girl tore into the Bennett girl right from the start and pinned her in 12 minutes," wrote Nat Fleischer. "Miss Bennett's morale was shot to pieces by that fall. The second part of the match was no contest. Cora threw Laura in three minutes. When I say 'threw' I mean it. A half Nelson and crotch hold proved to be the Livingstone media for victory. Cora was recognized everywhere as the greatest female wrestler in the world." More than 90 years later, in March 2004, that same belt was sold on eBay for US $1,677.00.

Livingston's win helped elevate the prestige of the women's title. Although it was still a rarity, Livingston was booked to defend her world title on the same card as men's matches, rather than compete in back rooms of taverns, burlesque halls, and carnival sideshows. That's not to say that Livingston abandoned the side show circuit entirely. She and her husband continued to tour carnivals and theaters, where the champ offered $25 (an impressive sum in those days) to any woman who could last 10 minutes with her. She occasionally accepted challenges from men — usually her husband, although that relationship was usually kept hidden from the audience.

Livingston competed in Decatur, Illinois; Boston, Massachusetts; Columbus, Ohio; Washington D.C.; Charlotte, North Carolina; Montreal, Quebec — in markets large and small. Livingston proved to be a marketable attraction and was often featured in newspaper advertisements promoting upcoming shows. She had the look, the attitude, the showmanship, and the substance to be a star. In some advertisements, she was billed as "the Gotchess of the Mat," a reference to legendary world champion Frank Gotch. Another ad saw her billed as "Miss Cora Livingston: World Famous Physical Culture Beauty and Champion Woman Wrestler of the World." Interestingly, her beauty took top billing over her credentials as a champion wrestler.

"'Bring on your champs, I can throw them all,' is what Cora Livingston toots," read ad copy from a 1915 Boston newspaper display advertisement, featuring a headshot of Livingston, looking serious. "She's got the idea into her loft that she can pin the shoulders of any girl wrestler in Boston to the mat in short order. Pretty loud talk but she stands ready to deliver the goods. 'The heavier they are the harder they fall,' says Cora. Run in this afternoon and watch the champion at her best."

On Thanksgiving Day 1923, Livingston successfully defended her title against Virginia Mercereau, a former basketball player from Appleton, Wisconsin, who wanted to try her hand in wrestling. Although the *Boston Globe* reported that Livingston had won that match, Mercereau began billing herself as the world champion, claiming she had defeated Livingston. Without a national media to contradict her claim, several outlets failed to question the validity of Mercereau's story and recognized her as champion. But Mercereau was unable to find enough female opponents whereas Livingston was married to one of the most influential promoters in the nation. Mercereau mainly defended her "title" against men and then vanished from the scene, and Livingston was again recognized as the rightful champion.

Livingston retired from the ring in 1935. After retiring, she helped her husband run the New England wrestling territory, which became one of the nation's top wrestling circuits. She also became a mentor to her title successor, Mildred Burke. She died on April 22, 1957, in Boston. Her husband, Paul Bowser, died three years later following a heart attack. He was 74.

Although overlooked by many historians and left out of the major wrestling halls of fame, Livingston was a true pioneer and the first true American women's wrestling champion.

## CLARA MORTENSEN

One of the most popular women on the carnival circuit was Clara Mortensen, the daughter of wrestler Fred "Mart" Mortensen, a former light heavyweight champion. She wrestled her first professional match at the age of seven, when her father put her in the ring against her brother, Leo, at an Elks Club picnic in Portland, Oregon, in 1925. Mortensen had been wrestling all her life, having been trained by her father. She adopted the nickname the Eternal Woman and laid claim to the women's championship, asserting she had won the title by beating Barbara Ware in

1932, following the retirement of recognized champion Cora Livingston. Of course, with no sanctioning bodies, championships were purely promotional tools; if Mortensen claimed she was champ, then she was champ until someone beat her for the honor.

Starting at the age of 16, Mortensen performed with a California-based touring circus called Crafts Big Shows, becoming a feature attraction. A pretty young girl who wore her hair in a fashionable bob, she may not have looked like a champion grappler, but she knew how

One of the first recognized women's champions, Clara Mortensen. PRO WRESTLING ILLUSTRATED

to shoot. At the same time, she was described as being a little drab, too mechanical and boyish in the ring. She later accepted bookings outside of the circus, touring with her brother and a manager called Bluebeard Bill Lewis, a dapper gentleman who stood at ringside in an expensive business suit.

In 1933, Mortensen competed in front of a reported 31,000 fans in Honolulu. A 1937 article in the *Washington Times* described her as "a classic Nordic beauty" with a "lithe, supple, shapely body of classic sculpture." Because she was a good draw in places like California, Florida, Montana, and Washington, D.C., she was featured in an article in *Time* magazine in 1937.

Unbeknownst to her at the time, Mortensen would play a pivotal role in the evolution of women's wrestling, helping to clarify the title picture and "giving the rub" to a young claimant to the women's crown. Years later, she would retire from wrestling, her in-ring career coming to a virtual finish when the state of California banned women's wrestling in 1939. Following her retirement, she became an actress, appearing in the exploitative film *Racket Girls*, a 1951 gangster movie set in the world of women's wrestling, appearing alongside fellow female wrestlers Rita Martinez and Peaches Page. With an assist from promoter Billy Wolfe, Mortensen would help move women's wrestling off the dusty carnival circuit and into arenas. The game was about to change.

# When MILLIE Met BILLY
## The Billy Wolfe Era

He was an over-the-hill journeyman wrestler on the carnival circuit; his best-known move was licking the palm of his hand and delivering a loud, smacking slap to his opponent's chest. She was a 17-year-old single mother from Coffeyville, Kansas — a waitress with no prospects and an irresistible desire to be somewhere else, *doing* something else.

Together, Billy Wolfe and Mildred Burke became women's wrestling's power couple. They would take women's wrestling from the grimy carnival midways to athletic arenas worldwide. They would be featured in *Life* magazine, adorn themselves in diamonds, introduce their version of women's wrestling to exotic countries, and control women's wrestling from the Great Depression through the baby boomer era.

And for most of their partnership, they despised each other. The marriage was marked by open affairs and violence. Their inevitable divorce sent ripples through the wrestling industry and had everyone choosing sides.

Burke was born Mildred Bliss on August 5, 1915. The youngest of six children, her parents divorced when she was 11 years old. Bliss was an athletic girl, excelling in soccer and track. She was 14 years old when the stock market collapsed on Black Thursday. She dropped out of high school and picked up odd jobs, working as an office stenographer and as a waitress on an Indian reservation in New Mexico. At the age of 17, she married a man nearly twice her age, Joseph Martin Shaffer. "I would have married anyone to get off that reservation," she later said in her unpublished memoirs.

Shaffer took his betrothed to her first wrestling card at the Midway Arena in Kansas City. It was an experience that would change her life. "Watching these bouts fascinated me, absorbed, and excited me in a way that I had never known before," she later wrote. "Something deep in my core had been tapped awake. Immediately I began fantasizing myself in the ring, applying those grips, holds and throws. A desire and a drive to fill in those fantasies with flesh and blood came surging to life." After the show, she told her husband that she wanted to become a wrestler herself. He laughed in her face. She would never forget, nor forgive, that reaction. She became pregnant and Shaffer left. She moved back in with her mother and took a job waitressing at the small restaurant her mother owned. They renamed it Mom's Café.

Mildred met Billy Wolfe in the summer of 1934 when he happened into Mom's Café with Kansas City promoter Gust Karras. Wolfe was 37 years old, a former wrestler who started when he was in the army during World War I, and both his ears were cauliflowered. He wore thick black-rimmed glasses and wore his hair greased back. He had an eye for the ladies, and Mildred Bliss had caught his eye.

Born on July 4, 1896, in Wheaton, Missouri, Wolfe had previously been married, but he'd left his wife and run off with wrestler Barbara Ware. He and Ware wrestled the carnival and small-venue circuit together, with Ware often taking on challengers from the audience. He also ran a wrestling gym stationed above a garage just a few blocks away from Mom's Café. Bliss told Wolfe of her dream to become a wrestler. Wolfe became a regular at the restaurant, seducing the mother-to-be with stories from the road and the wrestling lifestyle.

Mildred gave birth to a son named Joseph on August 4, 1934. When she recovered, she begged Wolfe for a tryout at his gym. Wolfe gave her a chance. She showed up at the gym and climbed into the ring, wearing a black swimsuit and boys' black sneakers, feeling nervous and self-conscious. Wolfe later told the story of what happened next to the *National Police Gazette.*

"I had this little girl figured dead wrong," Wolfe said. "Geez, I hired a kid and paid

**BOOKER AND MANAGER OF 95% OF ALL GIRL WRESTLING ATTRACTIONS IN THE ENTIRE WORLD**

*A controversial man, to say the least.*
JACK PFEFER COLLECTION/UNIVERSITY OF NOTRE DAME

him a quarter to get into the ring with Mildred. I said to him, 'You give it to her so good, that she'll never come around here bothering us again.' Well, this little boy gets into the ring and does his level best, but she knocks him out so fast that it leaves me thinking that maybe she's got something that I didn't see before."

Wolfe dumped Ware and brought Mildred into the fold as his new attraction. Against the advice of her mother, Mildred took her son and hit the road with Wolfe for a carnival tour in 1935. Without her daughter to help, Mildred's mother sold the restaurant.

Once Wolfe and Mildred got on the road, the reality of her situation quickly became apparent. Wolfe demanded to know how much money she had made from the sale of Mom's Café. Mildred told him she had not been part of the sale. For the first time, she saw Wolfe's ugly side. He became infuriated. He had expected to get his hands on

*Billy Wolfe teaching his girls.* PRO WRESTLING ILLUSTRATED

some of that cash. He then informed her that he would not marry her (thereby providing a sense of financial security) for a period of one year; essentially, she had to audition for him and prove herself worthy. And if she left him for any reason, he would report her to federal authorities for violating the Mann Act, crossing state lines for immoral purposes.

Their carnival act had Burke take on all comers, offering the respectable sum of $25 to anyone who could beat her by pin or submission. Men had to be within 20 pounds of her weight of 115 pounds. Each contest had a 10-minute time limit. Wolfe was the hype-man, the carnival barker selling tickets. One day, he changed her name from Mildred Bliss to Mildred Burke — perhaps to play up to, or against, Irish sentiment of the day. The name stuck. From that day, Bliss was Burke.

In the fanciful promotional biographies they later produced, Wolfe claimed Burke had taken on more than 150 challenges and never lost one. This wasn't true. Some of the matches were "worked" (against a planted member of the audience and choreographed). Other matches had her stall to run out the clock. In the end, though, the only "official" record book was the one being kept by Wolfe.

Less than two weeks into the carnival tour, Burke caught Wolfe having sex with another carnival worker. That's when she realized with clarity that her relationship with Wolfe was a professional partnership; it was all business. Weeks later, she learned that Wolfe had beaten her infant son, whose crying had interrupted another romantic liaison with a different carnival girl. She walked out on the carnival with the baby in tow and tried to hitchhike away, but she eventually called Wolfe to come get her. In her memoirs, she wrote that she gave him a warning she meant with all her heart: if he ever hurt her son again, she told him, "I'll wait until you're asleep and I'll cut your head off your body."

## MILDRED BURKE *The Queen of the Ring*

When the summer carnival season concluded, Wolfe and Burke began looking for bookings at wrestling arenas. Matches between male and female wrestlers were still outlawed in most of the country, and with only a handful of women wrestling, finding a capable female opponent was a challenge.

They pleaded with Gust Karras to book her for a match. They then took out advertisements in the local newspaper: "CHALLENGE any man my own weight, 121 pounds, to a wrestling bout. Mildred Burke."

The challenge was accepted by a man named Cliff Johnson; Burke defeated him in seven minutes. They took out ads issuing open challenges in other cities. Her opponents proved to be reluctant, embarrassed about wrestling a woman and afraid of being humiliated if they lost. But the ploys brought in curious fans. In an era when men's wrestling was waning, Burke proved to be a draw.

On April 24, 1936, Wolfe and Burke were married in Abilene, Texas, with no party being held, just the two of them in front of a judge. "There was no question of my being in love with Billy Wolfe," she later wrote. "He had become physically and sexually repulsive to me."

*Two great champions: Lou Thesz and Mildred Burke.*
PRO WRESTLING ILLUSTRATED

This certainly proved to be the case when Joe became ill and Burke told her new husband she needed to take time off to nurse the baby back to health. He punched her in the face. She left him and went to stay with a friend in California. Wolfe begged her to come back. He knew she could be the box office draw that he never could. She knew she didn't have the contacts or experience to land bookings without him. "What I told myself in the dark nights when I lay awake pondering my next move was that I would have to suffer Billy Wolfe — put up with the bastard — in order to get what I wanted in life." Again, she went back to him. As much as Wolfe saw Burke as a paycheck, she saw him the same way.

Wolfe realized that the key to long-term success would be to find a female opponent for Burke. That's when he found Clara Mortensen.

Wolfe persuaded Alabama promoter Chris Jordan to book Burke against Mortensen, claiming they would draw the biggest gate he had seen in a year or else he wouldn't have to pay them. Wolfe was right; the curiosity bout drew a sellout. Jordan ran the match around the circuit, and Burke and Mortensen consistently drew full houses. As the senior attraction, Mortensen was put over, which Burke resented. Bad blood and jealousy soon developed between the two. Burke began threatening to "shoot" and beat Mortensen for real. On January 28, 1937, Burke finally defeated Mortensen in Chattanooga, Tennessee, in front of 6,157 fans, in what was then the most-publicized women's match ever. Many believe it to be the start of modern women's wrestling. With the win, Burke had a claim of being women's champion.

Wolfe had masterfully timed the title change. The news story and photos from the match were picked up by national wire services. Articles about the new women's champion ran in sports pages around the country.

Burke and Mortensen had a rematch in April 1937 in Charleston, West Virginia, drawing a capacity crowd of 2,500 and turning away another 500 at the door. By this time, the two women had developed an intense hatred of each other. Mortensen always claimed that she had won a rematch over Burke, but Wolfe's presence in the media was just too strong for her claim to be considered. More than 40 years later, when the Cauliflower Alley Club invited both women to its annual reunion, each refused to attend if the other would be there. As Burke's career took off, Mortensen's crumbled. Not being friends with Wolfe or Burke didn't help her.

In the meantime, Wolfe struck up a relationship with Ohio promoter Al Haft, one of the most influential wrestling promoters in the country. Haft promoted a tournament to name a new Midwest Wrestling Association women's champion. Burke won the tournament, adding more credibility to her claim as women's champion. Haft and Wolfe presented her with an expensive championship belt made of gold and inlaid with diamonds and gems.

Wolfe eventually made Columbus, Ohio, the base of his operations, establishing a women's wrestling school there. He also made himself Burke's personal P.R. man. He would bring his champion to newspaper offices for interviews with the sports writers. He would encourage the writers to feel the champion's biceps or Burke to show off her six-pack abs, which earned her the nickname "Muscles." Reporters were smitten. Sometime before they got married, Burke had injured her knee and Wolfe wanted to let her go. She begged him, and he finally agreed to keep her until they could train another woman. That first recruit was

Wilma Gordon. Wolfe began to sign other women to his troupe to work with Burke, including Gladys Gillem and Gordon's sister Mae Weston, who both became his mistresses.

Although women's wrestling was gaining popularity with fans, it was also generating a formidable backlash. Women's wrestling was banned in California for being "improper and vulgar." Clergyman the Very Rev. W.E.R. Morrow declared: "To my mind, nothing is more calculated to degrade human nature to its most bestial depths than the sight of an apparently healthy pair of young women, wearing nothing more than a bathing suit, indulging in the repugnant postures of 'all-in' wrestling to the accompaniment of the jeers and promptings of a mixed crowd of onlookers."

By 1938, Burke was a star. That same year, she wrestled Wilma Gordon in Akron, Ohio, in the first women's "Hindu style" match — mud wrestling, in other words. Believe it or not, men had been wrestling in these bouts for years, where the participants grappled in a mixture of mud. But the obscure specialty match took on a new dimension when women competed, as the mud covered them, making it hard to know where their swimsuits ended and where their flesh began. *Life* magazine ran a seven-page photo spread.

Burke developed her signature look: white tights and white boots, which stood in contrast to her deep tan. Her opponents (most notably Gillem) usually wore black. Burke had a rhinestone-encrusted robe made for $1,100, designed to sparkle under the arena lights, along with her gold belt. Mink coats and diamonds were her trademarks outside the ring. Wolfe wasn't nicknamed "Diamond" Billy for nothing.

When the New Jersey Athletic Commission green-lighted women's wrestling in 1940, promoter Jack Pfefer wanted to get in on the game. An eccentric Polish immigrant, Pfefer promoted wrestling as a spectacle, heavy on the freaks and midgets — exactly the kind of "performers" NWA champion Lou Thesz and others would rail against. But his vision is what drew in the Northeast. Burke and Gillem tore down the house at the Meadowbrook Bowl in Newark, drawing plenty of press from the New York media.

As a publicity stunt, Pfefer staged a picket line by Wrestlers

Association 1234, to protest the "unfair invasion" from women, outside the Laurel Garden in Newark. It was all a goof, but it generated publicity.

Years later, Al Haft would write to Pfefer, discussing the top draws in both men's territories. "The girls had a big night here last night. Looks like the public likes the puss." But in the end, Pfefer's attempt didn't work. Only Wolfe seemed to know what to do with women's wrestling and how to do it.

## JUNE BYERS, G. BILL, and the Split between Wolfe and Burke

Although Wolfe and Burke were drawing crowds in the late 1930s, the breakout of World War II would prove especially lucrative. As millions of men joined the service following the bombing of Pearl Harbor, wrestling promoters struggled to retain talent and keep their cards filled. Similarly, the war threatened to shut down Major League Baseball, leading to the creation of the All-American Girls Professional Baseball League and inspiring the movie *A League of Their Own* starring Geena Davis and Madonna. As in America's favorite sport, women helped fill the void in pro wrestling too. Even California, which had banned women's wrestling outright, relaxed its standards in 1943, allowing women to appear twice every six months. But a year later, it was banned again. Although their business was flourishing, Wolfe and Burke were never able to establish themselves in the biggest states. A decade later, when more than 40 states allowed women's wrestling, the four most populous still didn't. It didn't seem to matter, though. By the early 1940s, 40% of the national audience was women, and more women wanted to become wrestlers.

Back at the school, Wolfe was accepting new students, as long as they were 18 to 24, weighed 130 to 150 pounds, and stood between 5'2" and 5'7". They also had to be "photogenic" and were required to fill out an application assuring they were "single, intelligent, physically agile, and sound of character." Essentially, it was a dating profile for Wolfe's benefit. He once asked a young girl who wanted to wrestle if she was a lesbian, and, if not, if she would sleep with him. She refused, and Wolfe told her she would never be champion. The girl worked for him anyway. "The thing they were interested in was getting bookings and they didn't have the brains enough to know they could have got them without screwing that old fart," said Mae Young, in her own unique way.

In a newspaper interview, Burke claimed she had earned $22,000 in 1943, which would have made her one of the highest-paid pro athletes of the era, with almost 10 times the average income. As years went by, Burke's claimed income, always compared to the highest-paid baseball players or male wrestlers of the time, grew exponentially. It may have been just another way for Wolfe to make the news with his champion. Wolfe's stable of female wrestlers had grown. The couple was no longer traveling together; Wolfe would travel with his newer, younger girls (Nell Stewart had been the most recent to catch his fancy) while Burke would travel with Wolfe's son, George William, known to all as G. Bill. When she had to travel alone, Burke drove with a snub-nosed .38 in the glove compartment for protection.

Described by Gillem as "a big sloppy boy," G. Bill was in his early 20s when he began traveling with Burke. He was an alcoholic who was cowed by his father, sensitive where Wolfe was cutthroat, accommodating where his dad was unyielding. He was also closer in age to Burke than his father and was kind to her. He was helping her on the road better than his dad and was more than a brother to her son, Joe. G. Bill eventually fell in love with Burke. Although she claimed in her memoirs that she never loved G. Bill ("I was fond of him, grateful for all he did for me daily, and I had love for him without being in love with him," she wrote), the two began an affair of their own. It didn't matter to Billy.

As the war was coming to an end, Burke's popularity was reaching new heights. In 1944, she defended her women's title in front of 12,000 fans at Arena Coliseo in Mexico City. In 1948, she finished sixth out of 16 candidates in the Associated Press poll for female athlete of the year, in an era mostly dominated by another Mildred, golf player and arguably the greatest female athlete of the 20th century, Mildred "Babe" Didrikson Zaharias.

It seems as if it didn't really matter to Wolfe, who had found, in Houston, another young girl that he brought into the fold. Born DeAlva Eyvonnie Sibley, she had begun training with Wolfe and wrestling under the name June Byers. At 5'7" and 150 pounds, she was a tough, fast, muscular, strong, and beautiful brunette, who Wolfe had taught his patented palm-lick chest slap. Trained by Mae Young, she made her debut in 1944. Wolfe was grooming her for the women's title and pushed her as heavily with the media

*June Byers, one of the most dominant women in the 1950s.*
CHRIS SWISHER COLLECTION

as he had Burke a decade earlier. He would eventually have an intimate relationship with her as well. It was a known fact that when Nell was in town, he would be with her, and when June was in town, he would be with her. Each was in charge of a different group on the road.

Wolfe's sexual appetites had become well known within the industry. "His orgies and trafficking in the sexual favors of some of his girls were infamous in the business," Burke wrote. "Some promoters happily took part in this lavish whoring, envying Wolfe his access to so much female flesh."

Wolfe was successful, but many of the male wrestlers still saw him as an outsider. "Even though Billy had been a wrestler, he kept away from us and we kept away from him," wrote Freddie Blassie in his autobiography. "He wasn't one of the boys as far as we were concerned. We thought of him as a pimp."

In his book *The Queen of the Ring: Sex, Muscles, Diamonds and the Making of an American Legend*, author Jeff Leen wrote that "only Hollywood moguls and their casting couches in sunny Los Angeles, and a few years later Hugh Hefner and his Playboy bunnies in Chicago, could compare to the operation Wolfe had established."

In 1948, a group of wrestling promoters throughout the United States looked to lock down control of the business, better regulate member territories, and consolidate many regional championships while recognizing one world championship. Therefore, those promoters established the National Wrestling Alliance, a governing body that would control the business for the next 40 years. Although he was a controversial figure, Wolfe was invited to become a member of the NWA, and he did so late in 1949. That being said, the NWA never officially recognized Wolfe's women's title. But it didn't matter to Wolfe. The organization would promote his girls through its channels, and would give him better access to all kind of promotions. If a girl wanted to leave, he could easily blacklist her.

Women's wrestling even had its critics within the business itself, including "Strangler" Lewis and the NWA world champion himself, Lou Thesz. "One dispute I didn't win involved the NWA's decision that the champion should not appear on cards that featured women wrestlers, midgets, wrestling bears, or any kind of carnival act," Thesz later wrote. "Everyone agreed credibility was critical whenever the champion appeared, and even then the promoters who used a lot of those acts conceded they didn't exactly enhance their chances for projecting a first-class image, so the rule was adopted unanimously. It died almost immediately, though, when Sam [Muchnick] booked me with promoter Al Haft in a small town in Ohio where the show was being held in a high school gymnasium. As I was walking through the lobby on my way to the dressing room, I spotted a poster announcing the night's lineup, and noticed there were women wrestlers on the card. I found the matchmaker . . . and told him I wouldn't be wrestling. I had nothing against the idea of women wrestlers but it's a fact I never actually met one — a wrestler that is — during my career. Every single one of them were performers, and their whole act was designed to titillate the males, so I was happy when the NWA ruled I didn't have to appear with them."

Haft, however, was a member of the NWA in good standing, and women's wrestling was becoming an important part of his business. Thesz was talked into competing that night, but he never warmed up to women's wrestling.

*Millie and Billy Wolfe's son, G. Bill.*
JACK PFEFER COLLECTION/UNIVERSITY OF NOTRE DAME

Around that time, G. Bill went to his father and asked for permission to marry Mildred, since it was obvious that Wolfe was no longer interested in her. Wolfe refused and mocked his son for becoming attached to Burke. Rejected and unwilling to stand up to his father, G. Bill's drinking worsened and his health deteriorated.

In September 1951, Burke was driving (she didn't trust G. Bill anymore because of his drinking problems) from California to a booking in Oklahoma; her 17-year-old son, Joe, was following behind in his car. Burke's tire blew. She spun out and was T-boned by a car in the oncoming lane. Burke suffered five broken ribs, an injured neck, a dislocated sternoclavicular joint, and lacerations; G. Bill suffered a fractured skull and several broken bones and would require a full-body cast. That was the end of their relationship.

Burke was told she needed at least six months to recover, but Wolfe pressured her to return to the ring sooner as he was anxious to put the title belt on Nell Stewart. Wolfe met Burke at a restaurant and told her she would be losing the belt to Stewart. She refused. "If you think she's good enough to beat me, just let her do," she told Wolfe, challenging Stewart to a shoot fight. Burke knew that once she lost the belt to Stewart, Wolfe would stop booking her entirely. Her career would be over. The title was her only insurance policy.

When Burke refused to relinquish the title, Wolfe and G. Bill (who was unable to stand up to his domineering father) savagely beat her outside of a liquor store, in front of her son, Joe. They left Burke bleeding in a heap on the sidewalk. She was treated in a hospital in Pasadena, having suffered broken ribs and lacerations to her face. When she failed to show at an NWA convention as she recovered from her injuries, Wolfe spread rumors that she had cancer and that her career was over.

In 1952, after eight years without living together, Burke had Wolfe served with divorce papers. She asked for no property or alimony, looking to avoid a lengthy legal battle. Burke wanted to apply for an NWA membership, which was denied to her since the alliance wasn't allowing any women. Still, the NWA held a meeting to try to arbitrate an agreement between the two regarding the future of the championship. As a woman, Burke was forced to sit in the hotel lobby as the matter was being discussed. The solution that the other promoters came up with was that one had to sell to the other. Wolfe agreed to sell his right to the title for $30,000. Burke accepted the agreement, although she had to scramble to find investors willing to give her the cash she was required to turn over to Wolfe.

Less than two weeks after the agreement was made, Burke turned over a briefcase containing $30,000 to Wolfe, in front of witnesses G. Bill, Sam Muchnick, and Lou Thesz. Wolfe agreed to refrain from promoting women's wrestling for a period of five years, and Burke founded a company named Attractions, Inc.

But there were loopholes in the agreement large enough to make it essentially worthless. In March 1953, Wolfe established Girl Wrestling Enterprises, Inc., with Nell Stewart as secretary and June Byers as treasurer. The address of the business was Al Haft's gym in Columbus, where Wolfe ran his school. It was a shell game; Wolfe had no inclination of leaving women's wrestling, and Stewart was his handpicked champion.

"Mildred Burke has been the champion of the Women Wrestlers for more years than some of us have lived, and it is our opinion that her sun is setting," wrote *Boxing and Wrestling* magazine, in a story likely heavily influenced by Wolfe himself. "If she is still champion when the last day of 1953 is here, we'll be the most surprised people there are."

In June 1953, because Burke had gone public saying that Stewart was going to win the tournament, Byers, now G. Bill's wife, won a 13-woman tournament in Baltimore to take the women's title, as recognized by Girl Wrestling Enterprises. Burke sold her diamonds and furs to wage war against Wolfe, continuing to tour with her title and maintaining that she was still the rightful champion. All those expenses didn't do her any good. Some of her girls were leaving for Wolfe, her business was forced into receivership, and the court had to choose a receiver able to manage the company for the company to pay its debt. In August 1953, a judge appointed none other than Billy Wolfe as the new administrator of Attractions, Inc. Wolfe didn't lose any time, sending a letter to all promoters, asserting that he was the booker for Burke and the 27 female wrestlers from Attractions, Inc. Burke sent letters to NWA's officers and to promoters she thought were friends, asking that her status as champion and booker of the women's division be resumed. At the annual NWA convention in September 1953, it was decided that Wolfe would have to pay for Burke's $30,000 debt in order to take control of her promotion and, in return, she'd have to continue working for him for another two years before calling it quits. But even more important, the NWA members, even though they didn't have any problems working with Wolfe and accepting Burke's blacklisting, decided to eliminate official supervision of women's wrestling. "Wrestling's old-boy network had had enough of Wolfe's marital discord," wrote Jeff Leen. The split took a heavy toll on all involved, especially Burke, who was left with no money. Although popular enough to be invited on some game shows, Byers did not draw as Burke had drawn as champion. It became obvious that in order for women's wrestling to survive, there needed to be one undisputed champion.

On August 20, 1954, in Atlanta, Georgia, Burke faced Byers in what was scheduled to be a shoot match; the winner would walk away as the recognized champion. The fans had no idea this match would be a rarity in pro wrestling — a match where the winner wasn't predetermined. Byers had trained heavily for the match with former NCAA champion turned pro wrestler Ruffy Silverstein, adding noticeable muscle mass; she was announced at a fighting weight of 180 pounds to Burke's 140 pounds. Byers, who was athletic and had good ring psychology, would be known for the rest of her career as one of the toughest women in the sport, sometimes breaking her opponents' noses.

For six methodical minutes, Burke and Byers circled for an opening. Byers began landing shots to Burke's ribs, and at the 16-minute mark, Burke's knee buckled and she fell to the canvas. Byers collapsed on top of her and managed to pin her shoulders to the mat for a three-count to win the first of three falls.

Burke worked her knee back into place in the break between falls, then came back with renewed energy. While Byers's added mass had given her an early advantage, it started working against her, affecting her stamina as the match passed the 30-minute mark. The slow-paced bout wasn't what the fans had come to expect from the women; they had no way of knowing that this particular match was real and that all the others had been spectacle. The crowd grew restless. As the match neared the one-hour mark, the athletic commissioner announced he would stop the bout if there wasn't a fall in the next five minutes. There wasn't; the match was stopped after 63 minutes.

The match designed to end the controversy actually created more controversy. Two falls were required for the title to change hands. There had been only one fall, so Burke believed she had retained the title. However, Byers had scored the only pinfall in the match and had cleanly pinned the champion. She and Wolfe took that to mean her own claim to the championship had legitimacy. Immediately after the match, Wolfe sent telegrams to his national media contacts, explaining his version of events. Even though the ring announcer said that Burke had kept her title, the Associated Press's headline, thanks to Wolfe, was "June Byers gets moral victory over Miss Burke." In a sense, Wolfe was doing to Burke what he had done to Clara Mortensen two decades earlier. Meanwhile, Atlanta promoter Paul Jones was so angry about the lackluster match that he refused to pay Burke; her son had to hock a diamond ring so he and his mother could get home to California. Nevertheless, both Burke and Byers would later consider this match the greatest of their respective careers.

As much as Wolfe wanted to get the title off Burke, Byers was not the draw he was hoping for. Millie tried to open another office, but bookings were tough to find. Burke and Wolfe had lost tons of money during their war.

Wolfe continued promoting women's wrestling until his death. After his divorce from Burke, he married Nell Stewart. He divorced Stewart and got together with 18-year-old Mercedes Waukago, a Native American who would wrestle under the name of "Princess" Tona Tomah. The relationship was short-lived though, and he then married 20-year-old LeeChona LaClaire (he was 60). He divorced LaClaire and married 17-year-old wrestler Lola Laray, although she divorced him after just two months. He then married Karen Kellogg once she turned 21 — so she wouldn't require a note from her parents. They had a son together in 1961. The only other known female wrestler he had a child with was Ann Laverne. Born in 1942, Marie Laverne grew up to be a wrestler herself and admitted years later that Wolfe was her biological father. He died following a heart attack on March 7, 1963. He was 66.

In the shadow of the Fabulous Moolah, Byers still found success for the next decade, but she had to retire on January 1, 1964, following a car accident. Divorced from G. Bill, she was also running a wrestling school with her new husband, former wrestling promoter Sam Menacker. Eight months later, her ex-husband died, like his dad, from a heart attack at age 42. He had been sober since 1956 and happily married to an ex-wrestler named Betsy Ross; both were retired from the business. Byers died of pneumonia in Houston in 1998.

Burke continued as a wrestler, trainer, and booker, through a new company called International Women's Wrestlers, Inc. She helped get women's wrestling reintroduced in California in 1966 and successfully introduced women's wrestling to Japan, where it took on a life of its own. Since she was based on the West Coast, she tried to work with Moolah, who was on the East Coast, but the latter never got back to her. Eventually, because most of Millie's girls were not seen as good enough, Moolah took over Millie's territory as well. Burke died following a stroke on February 18, 1989, at the age of 73.

Somehow, Wolfe was able to maintain balance (or at least keep the peace) within his stable of women, even while bouncing in and out of bed with several of his wrestlers. But when he became smitten with the 15-year-old Nell Stewart, Wolfe's delicate balancing act came crashing down around him.

## NELL STEWART

Verdie Nell Stewart was working as a waitress in a diner in Birmingham, Alabama, when she met Johnnie Mae Young. Stewart was captivated by the glamor of the wrestling lifestyle and the diamonds and flashy outfits worn by Mildred Burke. Stewart was a slightly heavyset country girl, but Young was won over by her enthusiasm and passion and introduced her to Wolfe, who took her under his wing.

Stewart's father had passed away a year earlier. Wolfe, no doubt, came across as a father figure, a man who promised her she could make much more money as a wrestler than pouring coffee in a diner. He put her to work training under Gladys Gillem, who eventually left Wolfe's troupe when she saw that the relationship between her boss and Stewart was becoming physical.

Stewart made her wrestling debut in Mexico City in 1944, at the age of 15, for promoter Salvador Lutteroth. "I was so scared she whipped me in five minutes," Stewart later remembered of that first match.

Wolfe put Stewart on a special diet, helping her trim down and tone up. He had her dye her hair blonde and reinvented her in the image of movie starlet Betty Grable, even going so far as to bill her as "the Betty Grable of the mat" in promotional clips.

"Nell Stewart wasn't glamorized in Hollywood but by wrestling," Wolfe wrote. With her big bust (38 inches — a detail that frequently found its way into magazine articles on her) and blonde hair, Stewart was an instant sex symbol.

"Nell boasts a superb figure and a complexion that would make a Dresden China doll frantic with envy," reported the August 1952 edition of the NWA Official Wrestling Program. She may have been beautiful, but she was happy to wrestle ugly. Stewart was a natural rule breaker and favored an aggressive, brawling style.

*Nell Stewart, the Betty Grable of the mat.* CHRIS SWISHER COLLECTION

"Miss Stewart's tactics at times are not too becoming a lady and usually after her opponent has taken considerable hair-pulling, finger-biting and the like from the quick-tempered blonde, they proceed to return in kind, much to Nell's dismay," wrote a reporter in the *Bismarck Tribune* (North Dakota) in 1949. Stewart's heel tactics earned her another, more appropriate nickname: the Alabama Assassin.

Stewart was the heir apparent to Burke's championship, but she never managed to claim the title, despite coming close on a few occasions, like when she wrestled Burke to a one-hour draw in Columbus,

Ohio, in 1952, in what was described as a classic. In the early 1950s, she was named NWA Texas and Ohio women's champion, a way for Wolfe to keep her happy since he couldn't give her the main title.

Despite her sexual relationship with Wolfe and some of the signs of favoritism Wolfe exhibited toward her, Stewart was well liked and respected by many of the women in Wolfe's group, helping to train them on the road.

"She was beautiful and I thought she was a helluva good wrestler," her frequent in-ring opponent Ida Mae Martinez later remembered in an interview with author Jeff Leen.

"Once I saw Nell Stewart, I said that's exactly what I want to do," Belle Starr said. "She was so pretty and beautiful, I just wanted to be like her."

However, the increasingly tenuous marriage between Wolfe and Burke came apart at the seams with a divorce. With Wolfe and Burke forming divided factions, Stewart remained with Wolfe and was named secretary of Girl Wrestling Enterprises, Inc., the promotion Wolfe ran from behind the scenes in order to avoid a non-compete agreement included in his divorce from Burke.

Preparing for a promotional war with Burke's stable of wrestlers, Wolfe upped the promotional hype on Stewart, advertising her as "the Queen of Them All, [the] Greatest Box Office Attraction of Girl Wrestlers." With prodding from Wolfe, Baltimore promoter Ed Contos lobbied NWA president Sam Muchnick for the right to hold a tournament to crown the rightful NWA women's champion, claiming that Burke had previously suffered losses to Clara Mortenson and to other women, including Slave Girl Moolah in New York. Muchnick approved Contos's request. Stewart was positioned as the clear front-runner to win the tournament and claim the title without ever having to beat Burke.

A furious Burke fired off a telegram to the office of the *Baltimore Sun* to weigh in on the legitimacy of the title tournament. "Congratulations to Ed Contos for promoting a tournament in which Nell Stewart is to win from nobody," Burke wrote. "I wrestled Nell Stewart last year in seven matches for the title and defeated her seven straight falls. These were the last matches she wrestled me. No champion in history has ever defended his title that many times in succession against one opponent. This wire is dated and timed before the Baltimore Tournament."

Once Burke's letter was published in the newspaper, Wolfe was compelled to change his presumed booking plans, so June Byers defeated Stewart in an upset finish in the finals.

On May 1, 1953, Stewart, 24, married Wolfe, 57. It was a marriage of convenience, not of love, and again, a way for Wolfe to smooth things out with her for not giving her the belt. According to Martinez, Stewart loved another man — NWA board member Joe Gunther of New Orleans. But Gunther was married to another woman. Although Stewart never got the storybook wedding of her dreams, she ended up living with Gunther after her career was over.

Two weeks after marrying Wolfe, she won the WLW TV title by beating Martinez in Cincinnati, earning a $2,000 prize and a championship belt. But Stewart never fully recovered from being politicked out of the NWA women's championship. There were talks of a Hollywood motion picture based on her life, but they never materialized. Stewart finally parted from Wolfe in 1954. She came back to wrestling three years later, taking care of one group while Byers was taking care of another one, just like the old days. But she would eventually leave Wolfe's promotions again to settle in New Orleans. She had memorable rivalries with Martinez, Ella Waldek, Gloria Barattini, and Penny Banner, among others. She retired in the mid-1960s.

Stewart slipped into anonymity following her retirement. After a while, Martinez took it upon herself to try to track her down.

"When Nell was hiding out from everybody, I found her in the mountains. I flew into Birmingham and rented a car, asking around phone companies, gas, electric," Martinez said. "I went to a liquor store and said, 'Would you happen to know Nell Stewart?' This girl popped up and said, 'That's my cousin!'"

Stewart died on January 2, 2001, after a lengthy battle with cancer. She was 71.

In a testimony to her popularity among her peers, Banner and Martinez established a benevolent fund to help assist Stewart with her medical bills. She was awarded the Posthumous Award by the Cauliflower Alley Club in 2002.

"She was beautiful," Cora Combs said. "She was one of the prettiest girls there was. She was really a sweet person. In the ring, she wasn't. She was a villain."

## CORA COMBS

Before she was belting opponents with haymakers, Cora Svonsteckik (later shortened to Szestecki) was belting out tunes with a country music band called the Trail Raiders. She certainly had the pedigree for that gig; after all, she was a real-life coal miner's daughter, born and raised in Hazard, Kentucky.

Born on St. Patrick's Day, 1927, she grew up in Kentucky, playing a little basketball and competing in the high jump in school, but music was her primary love, and she took up the bass fiddle. She and her family moved to Nashville, and Music City was an ideal home for a music-minded young woman. She joined the Trail Raiders, performing at clubs and honky-tonks throughout Tennessee. But her career took a dramatic turn when she decided to check out a wrestling show promoted by Nick Gulas at the Hippodrome.

"My sister went all the time and I never went, so I went with her and I fell in love with it right away," she told SLAM! Wrestling. She approached Gulas, who directed her to Billy Wolfe. Wolfe invited her to Columbus to train.

At the age of 21, she moved up to Ohio and spent six weeks training to become a wrestler. She wrestled her first match in Jacksonville, Mississippi, in 1945, participating in a seven-woman battle royal. She was paired up with June Byers on the road, and Byers became a mentor. She began wrestling under the name Beulah Szestecki before changing it to Cora Combs (or Miss Cora, as she was frequently called).

Remarkably, Combs would wrestle for 50 years. She was one of Wolfe's featured women right up until 1954 when she got married. "Combs was probably the second tier of woman stars of that era, known for being a good worker and glamorous looking for the standards of that era. She was a name wrestler, but not a superstar for that period," Dave Meltzer, founder of the *Wrestling Observer Newsletter*, the *Wall Street Journal* of professional wrestling, wrote.

Combs continued wrestling as an independent, booking herself after leaving Wolfe's group. She made tours of Florida, Georgia, the Carolinas, Tennessee, the Central States region, the St. Louis territory, Indiana, Ohio, Michigan, Amarillo, Oklahoma, Louisiana, and Arkansas. She also worked internationally, completing tours of Mexico, Japan, Cuba, Fiji, and Nigeria.

*Cora Combs wrestled for 50 years.* CHRIS SWISHER COLLECTION

"It's very lonely on the road," she told SLAM! "Back then, you couldn't go to a bar by yourself or they'd think you were trying to pick up somebody. What I did, or what most all of us did, we'd just go back to the hotel and stayed because we had to wrestle the next day."

Combs won the NWA U.S. women's title and was a four-time NWA Southern (Florida) women's champion. She was crowned California state women's champion in 1966, after California finally legalized women's wrestling.

She also made history on March 8, 1972, when she wrestled what is believed to be the first women's match in New York State after the ban on women's wrestling was lifted by the New York State Athletic Commission.

When her daughter, Debbie, began wrestling in 1975, Cora became one of her frequent opponents and her tag team partner. As late as 1995, at the age of 68, she was working matches against her daughter under a mask as Lady Satan. That way she could hide her age. Cora settled into semi-retirement in 1985 and dabbled in acting, making some small appearances in movies and country music videos, and even an appearance on *The Jerry Springer Show*. In 2007, she was inducted into the Professional Wrestling Hall of Fame. She died on June 21, 2015, at the age of 88.

## MAE WESTON

Mae Weston wrestled her first match at the age of 15 in a carnival sideshow and wrestled her last match at the age of 71 in Las Vegas, Nevada, a longevity very few women enjoyed in the business.

Weston was eight when her mother died, leaving her father to raise three children on his own. Facing a custody dispute with the children's grandmother, her father moved the children from Leavenworth, Kansas, to a small mining town in Missouri.

Born Betty Mae Garvey on January 30, 1923, she completed the sixth grade (the end of the local education system) and found herself looking for work. Her older sister, Wilma Gordon, had joined Billy Wolfe's contingent of wrestling women to escape a bad marriage, and Weston was enamored with the glamor of the wrestling lifestyle. At the age of 13, she decided to follow in her sister's footsteps, joining the carnival as a traveling acrobat. She also trained in boxing and would later face all comers in carnival boxing and wrestling exhibitions.

She trained with Wolfe and her sister, making her wrestling debut in 1938 at the young age of 15. In homage to the biggest screen siren of the era, Mae West, Wolfe dubbed his young protégé Mae Weston, looking to capitalize on the sex appeal of the Hollywood starlet.

A 1943 article in the *Washington Post* colorfully (if somewhat chauvinistically) described a bout between Weston and Mae Young at Turner's Arena. Describing Weston as "a beefy brunette in a very skimpy black bathing suit [who] could double for Superman's little sister," sports reporter Oscar Elder reported that Weston defeated Young with an airplane spin at the 19-minute mark. "Both gals started off in a whirl of mascara like a pair of bargain-basement commandos at a remnant sale with the 1600 fans loving it," Elder wrote.

Weston was a persistent challenger for Mildred Burke's championship. Her career in wrestling — as a wrestler and later as a manager — extended through seven decades.

Wrestling became a

*Mae Weston training her headlock like Strangler Lewis.*
JACK PFEFER COLLECTION/UNIVERSITY OF NOTRE DAME

family affair. Weston's younger sister, Rose Evans, also took up wrestling, as did her niece, Marie Vagnone. Weston eventually married Bill Murphy and settled in Columbus, Ohio. She worked as a hotel credit manager when not competing in the ring.

"When Champion Mildred Burke popularized girls' wrestling I knew that was the sport for me, and I entered it," Weston said in a 1951 interview with *Wrestling and TV Sports: The Fan Magazine.* "I was a click from the start because I had had all types of athletic experience and it didn't take me too long to learn the many grips in wrestling, and how to break them in a crisis. What I learned in boxing came in rather handy — footwork, blocking and countering. Of course, [Professional Wrestling's Hall of Famer] Everett Marshall taught me many wrestling tricks, too. I owe a lot to him for his patience."

Weston's final run came in the Gulf Coast Championship Wrestling territory as the villainous Maw Bass, the matriarch of the rule-breaking Bass family (made up of her "sons" Ronnie and Donnie). She was known for passing her boys a loaded purse to use as a weapon. She had so much heat in the early 1970s that they brought Fabulous Moolah to work as a babyface against her. Moolah would defend her title and the two of them would main-event all the cities in the territory.

Weston wrestled her final match in June 1993, competing in a Golden Girls Extravaganza battle royal at the Ladies International Wrestling Association convention organized by the Fabulous Moolah. She became one of Burke's best friends, and the pair operated a small restaurant together in the 1960s. Weston was a member of the Cauliflower Alley Club and enjoyed attending various wrestling reunions in her later years. She died in 1999 at the age of 76.

## The AFRICAN-AMERICANS

Billy Wolfe didn't see black and white . . . he saw only dollar-sign green.

Although segregation was the rule of the day in much of the country, Wolfe had no problem signing African-American women to his troupe. "Negro men have been competing in pro wrestling almost since the origin of catch-as-catch-can matches in the United States, 63 years ago," he said in a wrestling program.

"They have met with success in such faraway places as Thailand (Siam), Burma, and Indonesia. Then why wouldn't the Negro girl athletes stand an equal chance of making the grade? That's the way I figured it. And from the tremendous fan support given the Negro girls' matches I have not been wrong in my figuring."

In 1951, he brought on several African-American girls, usually booking them against each other in tag team bouts. Before booking them against his white wrestlers, he would pull the white women aside and ask if they had any issues working with a black girl. All of his girls were willing to do it; after all, they had all faced discrimination themselves and didn't want to be guilty of treating others the same way. The black girls found wrestling could offer a decent paycheck. Female African-American wrestlers were earning an average of $300 per week, according to a *Jet* magazine article in 1952.

"Billy should get 100 percent credit for integrating women's wrestling," said black wrestler Kathleen Wimbley. "He was the first one to have the chance to do it. I broke many color lines. He took a chance where nobody else would."

Finding accommodations for the black girls was difficult. They were frequently turned away from hotels and forced to stay with other black families on the road.

"It wasn't an easy time," Ethel Johnson told the *Columbus Dispatch* in 2006. "The white girls who would go down there with us, they'd go to jail for being in the same car with you. You couldn't even be on the sidewalk. If a white person was on the sidewalk, you had to get off."

Long before Jacqueline and Naomi, black women were stars of the mat. Here are some of the most well-known female African-American wrestlers of the 1950s and 1960s.

## Babs Wingo

The 5'3", 150-pound New Orleans native favored a roughhouse style and frequently squared off against her little sister, Ethel Johnson, wrestling against her in more than half of her recorded matches. Born Marva A. Goodwin on November 21, 1937, she was billed as the Mississippi State Negro Girl Champion. "Babs Wingo was the reason why I first became a rulebreaker," Penny Banner told *LadySports* magazine in 2011. "We were wrestling down in Mexico and I was still a rookie and working 'clean,' while Babs was well known as being really mean in the ring. Anyway, the promoter told us we'd have to switch styles and I had to fight dirty. When I asked why, he said it was because the fans would riot if a black rulebreaker beat a pretty blonde 'good girl,' so I had to become the villain so the fans would cheer Babs." Babs died on August 13, 2003.

## Ethel Johnson

Babs Wingo's little sister started wrestling in 1951 and became one of the most popular African-American wrestlers of the era. A fan favorite, she was billed as "the biggest attraction to hit girl wrestling since girl wrestling began." A very attractive young woman, she was the first African-American sex symbol in wrestling. She usually posed in pinup girl–style publicity photos. She competed in Mexico, in Puerto Rico, and in Calgary's Stampede Wrestling promotion before retiring in 1977.

"Without a doubt, the number one lady was sultry Ethel Johnson, who was a huge fan favorite in her day," said historian Jim Melby. "Ranking close to her in popularity was Babs Wingo and Kathleen Wimbley. Louise Greene, usually booed as a villainess by the crowds, also ranks as a star in her own right. Last but not least, teenage sensations Marva Scott and Ramona Isbell rank among the top six of their era."

## Marva Scott

The Detroit native also wrestled under the name Marva Wingo and was promoted as Babs Wingo's sister, usually in tag team matches against Ethel Johnson. Also known as the African Black Cat, she added the flamboyant touch of dyeing her hair peroxide blonde. She wrestled into the late 1970s.

## Louise Greene

The statuesque Greene primarily wrestled as a heel and was a frequent foil for Ethel Johnson. She was described as a "sturdily-built grappler of great promise."

*Babs Wingo.* CHRIS SWISHER COLLECTION

*Louise Greene.* CHRIS SWISHER COLLECTION

*Marva Scott.* CHRIS SWISHER COLLECTION

*Ethel Johnson.* CHRIS SWISHER COLLECTION

*Kathleen Wimbley and Ramona Isbell.* JACK PFEFER COLLECTION/UNIVERSITY OF NOTRE DAME

## Kathleen Wimbley

A former high school basketball standout and model in Columbus, Ohio, Wimbley contacted Wolfe and asked for permission to wrestle. But Wolfe also had to get permission from her parents. Wolfe visited her home and had dinner with her family, promising he would take care of her on the road. She started wrestling in 1951 and was reportedly earning $10,000 a year by 1953. Her signature move was the airplane spin. After her wrestling career ended, she became a supervisor at a Manhattan banking conglomerate.

## Ramona Isbell

Born June 20, 1939, the Columbus, Ohio, native was known for her acrobatic skill and her vaunted monkey flip out of the corner. She began wrestling in 1950 and continued to wrestle into the late 1970s, when she wrestled for Verne Gagne's AWA.

# LIPSTICK & DYNAMITE, PISS & VINEGAR

Women's wrestling was so fascinating in that era that in 2004, film-maker Ruth Leitman released the critically acclaimed documentary *Lipstick & Dynamite, Piss & Vinegar: The First Ladies of Wrestling*. The film broke through kayfabe and provided a fascinating insight into the personalities of the Fabulous Moolah, Mae Young, Gladys Gillem, Penny Banner, Ida Mae Martinez, and Ella Waldek, shining a light on the world of women's wrestling in the 1940s and 1950s.

Leitman came upon the idea of doing a documentary on women's wrestling by chance. A friend was working as a publicist for World Championship Wrestling and was traveling through Texas with wrestler Terry Funk when Funk introduced her to Kay Noble.

"When my friend came back from that trip, she called me and said, 'Ruth, did you know that women wrestled in the 1940s and 1950s?' I didn't know about it until connecting with Kay," Leitman said. Leitman was between projects at the time, and she soon found herself researching the subject.

"I found that it was this fascinating subculture. There were these women who were traveling around the country. Men usually stayed in one territory for a while, while the women moved around, facing a lot of danger on the road, and in the ring, and in their lives. I found them to be incredibly strong and resilient, and I wanted to tell those stories," Leitman said.

Leitman set out to find wrestlers who had gotten their start during the Billy Wolfe era, focusing primarily on the 1940s and 1950s. Several women — such as Gillem, Martinez, and Waldek — were eager to cooperate and tell their stories. The Fabulous Moolah, who was still associated with WWE and had maintained kayfabe for her entire life, proved to be more elusive.

"Moolah and Mae were actually the last ones I got to interview the first time around, then I got to spend more time with them afterwards,"

"EXCELLENT!"
-IndieWIRE
"A FASCINATING TREAT."
-The Slammer, NY DAILY NEWS

THE FABULOUS MOOLAH

THE GREAT MAE YOUNG

GLADYS "KILLEM" GILLEM

IDA MAY MARTINEZ

ELLA WALDEK

PENNY BANNER

*Lipstick & Dynamite*

THIS SPRING GRAB
LIFE IN A HEADLOCK

A RUTHLESS FILMS AND 100-TO-ONE FILMS PRODUCTION "LIPSTICK & DYNAMITE" EDITOR M. CONNIE DILETTI
A FILM BY RUTH LEITMAN CAMERA RUTH LEITMAN & NANCY SEGLER SOUND LIZ STUBBS
SOUND DESIGN JASON WELLS DIGITAL FILM FINISH CINEMA CONCEPTS FEATURING MUSIC PERFORMED BY LOS STRAITJACKETS, KELLY HOGAN & NEKO CASE
ASSOCIATE PRODUCER ERIN FAITH YOUNG CO-PRODUCER M. CONNIE DILETTI PRODUCERS DEBBIE NIGHTINGALE & ANNE HUBBELL
EXECUTIVE PRODUCER LYDIA DEAN PILCHER PRODUCER JAMES JERNIGAN
WRITTEN, PRODUCED AND DIRECTED BY RUTH LEITMAN     FILM NOT YET RATED

KOCH
LORBER

*The best film ever done on women's wrestling.* RUTH LEITMAN COLLECTION

Leitman said. "I packed up my daughter, flew to Atlanta to pick up a crew, left my daughter there with some friends, drove to Columbia, South Carolina, with the crew and we got to Moolah's compound and she was not there. I ended up making this little thing called 'Chasing Moolah' [released as an extra on the DVD] which was about the year that it took me to get her to be in the film. I tried everything and she blew me off. If you're filming somebody and you have people flying and renting equipment, it's really a problem for somebody to not show up. I couldn't yell at her because she's Moolah and I needed her. But when I spoke to her, I asked what happened. She responded in her perfect, charming Southern drawl, she said, 'Oh, Vince [McMahon] called. I had to go.' Maybe you could have told me?"

Leitman finally got Moolah to appear when she laid things on the line. "I told her everyone else is going to talk about you. You should be able to talk about yourself. Then she did it," Leitman said.

Between researching, shooting, editing, and fund-raising, Leitman said she spent about four years working on *Lipstick & Dynamite*. It premiered on the film festival circuit in 2004, with a small theatrical release in 2005.

"We brought all of the girls to either the Tribeca Film Festival or Hot Docs in Toronto," Leitman said. "Traveling around with them — of course, we got really great press because everyone wanted to talk to Moolah and Mae, which rekindled the animosity with the other wrestlers who already had issues with Moolah anyway. It was like traveling around the country with six grandmothers who all hate each other."

Among other shows, the film was promoted on *Late Night with Conan O'Brien* and on *The Tonight Show with Jay Leno*. Rotten Tomatoes, the best-known film review website, scored the film a 62 percent. Liz Braun of the *Toronto Sun* said that "*Lipstick & Dynamite* is a glimpse of the wild and woolly pre-feminist world these capable women inhabited," while SLAM! Wrestling stated that the documentary "was one of the hotter tickets at Toronto's Hot Docs documentary film festival, attracting an eclectic following of hip movie-lovers and wrestling geeks."

*Lipstick & Dynamite* provided a star turn for the underrated

Gillem, in particular, who has some of the most memorable scenes in the film when she shoots from the hip in her inimitable style. Sadly, less than 10 years after its release, all six of the stars have died: Moolah in 2007, Banner in 2008, Gillem in 2009, Martinez in 2010, Waldek in 2013, and Young in 2014.

Leitman currently lives in Chicago and has become a fan of the Chicago-based SHIMMER independent promotion.

"The idea that I can go to this small arena [the Berwyn Eagles Club] that seats maybe 300 to 400 people, and I can see the most talented women wrestlers from all over the world and see them up close and working so hard, that's really pretty incredible," she said. "The spirit of that is so close to the camaraderie and the sisterhood and the relationships between the wrestlers that I saw from the early days. It feels so connected to what it was like back then on the road. I've been fortunate to get backstage at SHIMMER. You pull the curtain back, and I see what it looked like to be backstage from the scrapbook pictures that I got from Ella Waldek and Penny Banner. There's still that same feel. It was a subculture back then and it's still a subculture now."

# IDA MAE MARTINEZ

Being a female professional wrestler wasn't the most unique item on Ida Mae Martinez's resume ... she was also a professional yodeler! Toward the end of her life, she was known in her hometown as "the Yodeling Grandma from Baltimore."

Born Ida St. Laurent on September 9, 1931, she grew up in the care of relatives in North Stonington, Connecticut. Her mother abandoned her as a child, and she never knew her father. Her last name came from her mother's first husband, who had already parted with her mother by the time she was born.

In an obituary published in the *Baltimore Sun*, her longtime friend

Wally Shugg said that she was abused at an early age.

"Her mother hung out in bars, dating sailors, and abandoned her to her aunt's care after the first few months," Shugg wrote. "Yet being raised in her aunt's household brought emotional and physical hardships and — at age seven — sexual abuse. Instinctively, she fought back against the boys and girls on the streets in her neighborhood. The strenuous life naturally came to her and continued into high school, where she went in for acrobatics."

*Ida Mae Martinez, the yodeling lady.* GREG OLIVER COLLECTION

She eventually dropped out of high school. She married at the age of 17, and she and her husband ran off to Houston, Texas. She took a job as a waitress.

According to Shugg, she discovered wrestling when local pro wrestler Larry King (not the CNN one) came into the restaurant and the two started talking. She went on to check out the matches and was enthralled when she saw Johnnie Mae Young battle Gloria Barattini.

"I don't know why," Martinez later wrote in a profile published on the G.L.O.R.Y. Wrestling website. "I didn't realize it, but I had always been wrestling with life, the guys at school or anybody who wanted to fight."

She tracked down Billy Wolfe and asked if he could train her to become a wrestler. Her youthful, rebellious marriage had already crumbled. Wrestling presented a new opportunity.

She moved to Columbus (selling her cherished guitar for bus fare) and learned the craft under Adele Antone, making her pro debut in August 1951. A petite young girl with a sultry appeal, she was christened Ida Mae Martinez and began wearing red, white, and blue ring gear, which became her calling card.

"My first match was against Mars Bennett. She was my first opponent in a little town in Ohio, and I was scared stiff. I had worked out and worked out. I was wearing one of Mildred Burke's robes, and her boots, because I didn't have anything."

Martinez proved to be particularly popular in the Southwest. She was recognized as Mexican champion on tours south of the border in 1952 and 1953. She had notable in-ring rivalries with Barattini, Nell Stewart, Ella Waldek, and Mildred Burke. She also unsuccessfully challenged the Fabulous Moolah for the title in 1957.

"I threw a lot of dropkicks like Rocca. Cora Combs said she was hit in the chest by my feet harder than anybody's ever hit her in the chest."

Martinez wrestled from 1951 until 1960, when she retired after marrying Herbert Selenkow (the two later divorced). She moved to Baltimore and earned her GED in 1971, followed by an associate's degree in nursing in 1975 and a bachelor's degree in nursing in 1980. She attended school part time while raising two daughters, earning her master's degree in nursing in 1990. She became one of the first nurses in Baltimore to care for patients suffering from AIDS.

Martinez became involved with the Cauliflower Alley Club in the 1980s and was awarded the Senator Hugh Farley Award by the Professional Wrestling Hall of Fame in 2006, in recognition of her achievements as a wrestler and a nurse; the award is given to "well-known wrestlers who made significant societal contributions outside of the squared circle." She was also awarded the Pioneer Award from the Gulf Coast Wrestling Reunion, and she regularly attended CAC and Gulf Coast reunions to reconnect with her brothers and sisters in wrestling.

In 2004, Martinez released a yodeling CD titled *The Yodeling Lady Ms. Ida,* and she was even invited on *The Rosie O'Donnell Show* to showcase her talent. She was featured in the documentary *Lipstick & Dynamite* alongside longtime friend Penny Banner and Mae Young, her inspiration for getting into wrestling decades earlier.

She died following complications from a stroke in 2010 at the age of 78.

## GLADYS GILLEM

Gladys "Kill'Em" Gillem may have wrestled back in the days of black-and-white television, but she was a colorful character in her own right.

Born on January 16, 1920, Gillem grew up in Birmingham, Alabama. A standout softball player in high school, she was booted out of Catholic school when she got caught putting minnows into the holy water. She also got into hot water for making homemade wine.

After her father died when she was 19 years old, Gillem cared for her disabled mother, but she yearned to do more with her life. She never wanted to be a nurse. That's when she saw Mildred Burke in action at a wrestling show in Fairfield, Alabama.

Gillem was captivated. After Burke's match, she approached Billy Wolfe and asked if she could become a wrestler, too.

"You're too fat," Wolfe replied flatly.

Gillem was undeterred. She promised to get into wrestling shape. And if quarters were tight traveling, she said, "you can put me on top of the car, I'm going to be a lady wrestler," Gillem recounted in a 2006 interview with journalist Jamie Melissa Hemmings.

Wolfe was in need of fresh opponents for Burke, so he brought Gillem on board and set her up to train under Wilma "Babe" Gordon.

Gillem made her debut in 1942 and quickly became one of Burke's top challengers. With the terrific nickname "Kill 'Em" Gillem, she was a natural heel with a keen understanding of her role and the nuanced psychology of wrestling.

"She was not beautiful and she was never allowed to win," wrote

*"Kill 'Em" Gillem was one of the best nicknames around.*
CHRIS SWISHER COLLECTION

Leen. "But she was a terrific performer and she played a key role in Mildred Burke's rise. With the addition of Gillem, Wolfe took a major step in the direction of building a stable of women who could make Burke look good and at the same time draw fans of their own. This would be the linchpin of their success."

Gillem was an unorthodox wrestler. She took awkward, unpolished bumps. She could be hot tempered — on one occasion she bit into Burke's thigh and latched on, only relinquishing her grip when Burke broke her nose. But Gillem proved to have a lengthy career in the ring, wrestling for about 20 years, largely as Burke's villainous foil.

Adding to the dynamic between Burke and Gillem was the fact that Gillem became one of Wolfe's several mistresses, a fact she candidly discussed on camera at the age of 85 in the documentary *Lipstick & Dynamite*. Outspoken and unrepentant, Gillem stole the show in the film.

"He couldn't get a good hard-on," Gillem told Leen. "If you weren't very nice to him, you couldn't get good bookings."

"He was a lousy lay and he was a promoter. People take advantage of you," she told Hemmings.

Gillem left Wolfe's troupe when he asked her to lose matches to 15-year-old Nell Stewart.

"I spent 10 years traveling with Mildred Burke and Billy Wolfe, put diamonds on his fingers after giving him 50 percent of what I made, had my nose broken twice by Mildred, didn't dare hit her back or I would lose my job," Gillem said in a 1965 letter published in *Ring* magazine.

After her split with Wolfe, she found work riding horses at a race track and began studying to become a circus trapeze artist. Instead, she discovered lion taming and became a freelance lion tamer, working with several touring circuses, including Ringling Bros. and Barnum and Bailey.

"I was looking for something easier [than wrestling], so I tried lion taming," Gillem later cracked.

While working with the circus, she met and married John Aloysius Wall. The couple had three children and settled in Jacksonville, Florida. Now a mother, Gillem gave up lion taming in favor of something a little safer . . . alligator wrestling!

She wrestled 'gators at Casper's Alligator Farms in Jacksonville. She told people the key to wrestling 'gators was to tickle their bellies — apparently the alligators liked it.

Gillem had emergency bypass surgery in 2003 and her health began to deteriorate. She died of Alzheimer's disease on August 12, 2009, at the age of 89.

# PENNY BANNER

Born Mary Ann Kostecki on August 11, 1934, in St. Louis, Missouri, Penny Banner was a small-town tomboy who went on to achieve some pretty incredible things, including becoming the AWA women's champion, publishing her autobiography, and dating the King himself, Elvis Presley.

She also become one of women's wrestling's most iconic figures, thanks to a leopard-print bikini and a pinup that circulated all over the country.

Kostecki was helping a friend waitressing when a former boxing hustler came in. Struck by her athletic figure, the hustler issued a challenge.

"If you can do 200 sit ups, I'll give you $20," Banner recounted the man saying in her autobiography, *Banner Days*, cowritten with Gerry Hostetler. "I took him up on the challenge. After the lounge closed I did the 200 sit ups for him. I was only making $15 a week at the governess job and the 20 dollars was welcomed."

The boxing hustler put in a call to St. Louis wrestling promoter Sam Muchnick, the acting president of the National Wrestling Alliance. Muchnick was looking to recruit new women. He had Cyclone Anaya and Killer Kowalski call and ask Kostecki if she was interested in traveling to watch women wrestlers in action. Kostecki hung up on both of them, figuring they were crank calls; she didn't believe there was such a thing as *women wrestlers*.

Finally, a call directly from Muchnick piqued her interest. Kostecki met with Muchnick and agreed to travel to Billy Wolfe's school in Columbus, Ohio. She insisted on a written agreement that she would be paid $50 per week, that her train fare would be paid, and that she could leave after two weeks if she didn't care for it. Muchnick agreed to her terms, and she was off to Columbus.

She trained under Wolfe and dyed her hair blonde. She had her first match by answering an open challenge issued by June Byers.

"Billy said he wanted me to go [to the matches] next weekend and challenge her," Banner wrote. "'What do I have to do?' I asked. 'Just do whatever you have to do, but don't let her beat you.'"

"Each time she took me down and got on top of me, I kicked and ended up under the ropes," Banner wrote. "She got up and pulled me back to the middle, not letting me get any breath or rest before she was all over me again."

Kostecki survived to the time limit and was presented with a crisp $50 bill for her efforts. "You are now a professional lady wrestler,"

Wolfe told her as he handed over the prize money. "And your next match is next week."

She adopted the ring name Penny Banner — Banner after a character played by Charlton Heston in the movie *Arrowhead*, and Penny "because a penny was so insignificant and that was how I thought of myself; so small out here in this huge world and in a sport I knew nothing about."

Banner wrestled primarily in tag team bouts, starting out in Calgary, Alberta, teaming with Bonnie Watson. She stayed with the Hart family, with Stu chauffeuring the girls all over the territory.

One of the greatest woman wrestlers of her time, Penny Banner. JACK PFEFER COLLECTION/UNIVERSITY OF NOTRE DAME

On July 8, 1955, Banner teamed with Mille Stafford to wrestle the first women's tag team match ever presented in Chicago. "The Commissioners were very strict and insisted that the girls must have a physical prior to wrestling. We had to bring a paper with us, stating [we] were healthy in every respect. Before that, they insisted on the girls having a 'pap smear,' which was totally unreasonable. The promoter, Leonard Schwartz, managed to get that ridiculous requirement squelched fast," Banner wrote.

Banner wrestled primarily as a heel for most of her career. She won the NWA women's tag team title on three occasions (with Bonnie Watson, Betty Jo Hawkins, and Lorraine Johnson) between 1956 and 1960. "Penny Banner's late 50s tag team with Lorraine Johnson is generally considered the best female tag team ever in North America," wrote Dave Meltzer. "She was one of the first women to work in a two-piece outfit, in 1958 when teaming with Johnson."

Banner's blonde locks and fit figure caught the attention of Elvis Presley, known for being a huge pro wrestling fan and for having a thing for female wrestlers. Presley set up Banner with tickets for a concert at the Kiel Auditorium, and the two rendezvoused for a party at the Chase Hotel after the show. "I left and drove to the Chase Hotel, and sure enough, they let me go up to the penthouse and I was let in," Banner wrote. "It was full of guys and girls and drinks for all. They offered me a beer as I waited for Elvis to come out. . . . We talked and we talked. . . . He was really impressed at my being a lady wrestler."

The newspapers caught wind of the celebrity couple and linked Presley and Banner in gossip items, but other than a few dates, nothing came of the relationship. "With the two of us constantly on the road travelling, we didn't contact each other at all," Banner wrote. "We had no way of knowing where the other would be. I suppose we could have found out, but we didn't. I went my way and he went his."

Banner ended up marrying wrestler Johnny Weaver in April 1959, and 11 months later, she gave birth to a 7-pound, 11-ounce baby girl. Her relationship with Weaver quickly deteriorated as he became verbally and physically abusive. Banner feared he was having an affair.

She returned to the ring just four months after giving birth and quickly worked her way up the ladder of contention. In the summer of 1961, Banner received a call from Indianapolis promoter Jim Barnett asking her if she was interested in facing June Byers in a world title match. Banner had taken Byers to a draw in their only previous singles meeting, so she quickly accepted the opportunity for a rematch.

The title bout was scheduled for August 26, 1961, at Buck Lake Ranch in Angola, Indiana, but on the day of the event, Byers failed to appear.

"Balk [Estes], the booker, was upset but he made several calls to James Barnett," Banner wrote. "He returned and called all of us out of our dressing rooms into the large center foyer behind the stage and made his announcement. . . . 'There was to have been a women's championship match, and there will be one with one big change. After I called the office, we decided to change you nine girls from the two four-girl tag team matches to a nine-girl battle royal. Since Penny's opponent didn't show, she'll also compete in it. The winner will be named the first AWA women's champion. OK, now you have it. Get ready. You'll get your instructions in the ring.'"

The battle royal set the stage for a series of singles bouts, concluding with Banner against Theresa Theis

*The queens of the tag team division: Lorraine Johnson and Banner.* WRESTLING REVUE ARCHIVES/WWW.WRESTLINGREVUE.COM

(the wife of Ray "The Crippler" Stevens) in a best of three falls bout for the new championship. After splitting the first two falls, Banner won the third and deciding fall to become AWA women's champion — although it wasn't the same AWA that Verne Gagne promoted, leading to all kinds of confusion over the years.

To publicize her new title, Banner had a series of publicity photos taken at Franklin Studios in Charlotte, North Carolina. The session yielded the iconic shot of Banner in her leopard-print bikini, her right arm folded behind her head and a flirtatious smile on her face.

The image ran in newspapers and magazines, heralding the arrival of the new women's champion.

Between Banner, the Fabulous Moolah, and June Byers, three women were claiming to be the world champion, and promoters walked delicate political high wires in booking talent, unwilling to make enemies or get blacklisted by the National Wrestling Alliance.

"While Banner continued to be highly respected as a worker, due to politics, the places she could work narrowed," wrote Meltzer. "With no organizational backing, as Barnett had moved to Australia, the AWA title she held was forgotten, and Moolah was booked by most NWA promoters as world champion and since Banner didn't play ball with her, a lot of her booking opportunities dried up, although by that time she was already in her late 30s."

In addition, she was raising a child, and her marriage was on the rocks. When she decided she couldn't find a balance between wrestling and family, she vacated the championship, although she continued to wrestle periodically until her retirement in 1977.

Banner was also known for keeping kayfabe to a degree that very few people actually do. She claimed that all of her matches were real and that the first time she learned about men's matches being worked, it was through reading Ole Anderson's book . . . published in 2003!

In 1994, she left Weaver, ending a tumultuous 35-year marriage, although they were never legally divorced. In her later years, Banner became involved with the Senior Olympics, competing in swimming (butterfly and backstroke), shot put, and discus. She was enshrined in the Professional Wrestling Hall of Fame in 2005. She also received the Art Abrams Lifetime Achievement Award from the Cauliflower Alley Club in 2007 and the Frank Gotch Award from the George Tragos/Lou Thesz Professional Wrestling Hall of Fame in 2008.

She died on May 12, 2008, at the age of 73 after a lengthy battle with cancer.

"She probably never got as much respect and credit as she deserved. Her work was stiff, and no different than the men of that time," said St. Louis historian Larry Matysik.

"She would have to be high on any list of the greatest woman wrestlers ever to work in North America. She was considered one of the top five women wrestlers in the world for more than a 15-year period," concluded Meltzer.

## JOHNNIE MAE YOUNG

They don't make 'em like Mae Young anymore.

It's impossible to imagine Young being anything *but* a wrestler. She was brash, tough, and confident, and she lived to perform. Even into her late 80s, she was still popping the crowd.

Young claimed to have wrestled in nine different decades (from the 1930s to the 2010s), although that claim has been disputed. She said she began wrestling in 1939, although most historians believe her first match was in 1941 for Billy Wolfe. Her sole match in the 2010s (a handicap match against Michelle McCool and Layla El in 2010 that never even made it to the ring) was more of a skit than a match.

"In reality, Young is believed to have competed in seven decades, matching the record held by Lou Thesz, who debuted in the '30s and had his final match in 1990 in Japan," said Dave Meltzer.

In any case, Young's career spanned generations, with her starting as a women's wrestling pioneer and growing into the role of wrestling's most beloved sex-obsessed, whiskey-swilling great grandma.

Born March 23, 1923, just west of Tulsa in Sand Springs, Oklahoma, she was the youngest of eight children. She was raised by a single mother during the Great Depression and grew up to be a strong young woman, excelling in softball and wrestling. She joined the boys' wrestling team in high school in an era when the concept was virtually unprecedented. She was also a field goal kicker for the football team and worked at a cotton mill after school.

According to legend, Young got her start in pro wrestling when she attended a wrestling card in 1939 and, being an accomplished amateur wrestler and not having been "smartened up" to the wrestling business, tried to issue a challenge to Mildred Burke. Young claims she received a shoot match against Gladys Gillem (although it was most probably a try-out), which she quickly won, prompting Billy Wolfe to offer her a job. Young's story has never been officially verified, but given Young's confidence and toughness, it's entirely plausible to imagine her showing up at an arena and challenging the champion.

In any case, Young started wrestling for Wolfe at the turn of the 1940s. Like Gillem, Young was a shooter. Young, Burke, Gillem, and Mae Weston were the core of Wolfe's group of female grapplers, with Young surpassing Gillem as the leading heel. Young was a capable and respected worker who spoke her mind and never backed down, even from the men who tried to have their way with her or the other women on the road. Women's wrestling was so popular that in 1944, she main-evented an all-women's show, something of a rarity at the time, in Des Moines, Iowa, for promoter Pinkie George.

In 1949, she was acquitted of a first-degree robbery charge in Reno, Nevada, after the victim (a 200-pound man) was found beaten on the road. The jury later ruled the man "the victim of his own amorous advances," according to a *Los Angeles Times* article. Mae Young could take care of herself.

In the documentary *Lipstick & Dynamite*, Penny Banner remembered the first time she met Young. "All I know is, I saw Johnnie Mae Young — she had men's shoes on, men's pants with a zipper up the front, a cigar hanging out of her mouth. Back in 1954 you didn't do that — and she looked at me and says, 'Hi, Fuckface.'"

Being a blonde pinup wasn't for her; wearing gold was more like it. She became the inaugural NWA Florida women's champion, beating Cora Combs for the vacant title on October 15, 1951, in Tampa. She and Ella Waldek were also recognized as the first NWA women's tag team champions before dropping the belts to June Byers and Mille Stafford in Mexico City, Mexico, on October 4, 1952. She also briefly held the NWA U.S. women's title in 1968.

"Wrestling, it's my living, my profession," she said in a 1949 interview with the *Nevada State Journal*. "It's just as respectable as pounding a typewriter and a lot more profitable."

Although she was known as a tough broad who smoked cigars and wrestled almost exclusively as a heel, Young also had a spiritual side. She became a Christian evangelist, joining her sister who was very active in the church. At one point, she was looking to earn enough money from wrestling to sct up a church of her own. She later gave up on that dream and lifestyle entirely.

"There is little doubt she was among the toughest of any of the women wrestlers who were in the so-called golden age in the 40s and early 50s, when Wolfe had a huge stable of women all over North America," wrote Dave Meltzer.

*They simply don't make them like Mae Young anymore.*
JACK PFEFER COLLECTION/UNIVERSITY OF NOTRE DAME

By the late 1940s, she became one of Wolfe's top trainers, and she was largely responsible for training Lillian "The Fabulous Moolah" Ellison when she joined Wolfe's group in 1949. It was the start of a lifelong friendship for the two women, a friendship that would survive all of the bizarre politics of wrestling and would still be running strong more than a half century later.

When Burke and Wolfe parted ways, Young stayed on with Burke and embarked on tours of Japan (where she frequently wrestled Burke on the top of the card) and Canada. She won the respect of Stampede promoter Stu Hart by being one of the few women who would go downstairs and shoot in his notorious Dungeon.

Ed "Strangler" Lewis once told Mae Young, "I don't like women's wrestling, but if ever there was a woman born to be a wrestler, you're it," according to SLAM! Wrestling producer Greg Oliver.

She also put her friend Moolah in touch with Vince McMahon Sr. "I was one of the first girls to work for Vince Sr. when he opened up Joe Turner Arena in Washington, D.C.," Young said in an interview with James Guttman's *Radio Free Insanity* show. "At that time, Lil [Moolah] had never worked for Vince Sr. She had been calling me and writing me to use some of her girls. Mildred and Billy had split up at that time, and Vince asked me what I thought about getting Lil and her girls. I told Vince that would be the greatest thing that ever happened."

"These were wild times — and there were a lot of wild girls on the road back then. Mae was one of them," Moolah later wrote in her autobiography. "She used to like to go out drinking 'til all hours, smoking cigars and picking fights with big, bruising men in dark honky-tonks. She'd always laugh later about that expression on their face, a mixture of surprise and shame, just before they hit the floor after she'd conked them upside the head."

Young had a few brief retirements but always found her way back to wrestling, even though bookings were drying up by the 1970s as women's wrestling was falling out of favor. She stepped away from the ring to take care of her ailing mother in California. When her mother passed away, she moved in with Moolah in Columbia, South Carolina, in 1991. Also living with Moolah at the time was Diamond Lil, who became the best-known female midget wrestler of all time.

Young wrestled with Moolah's Ladies International Wrestling Association in Las Vegas in the 1990s, where she continued to take bumps and wrestle in a physical and competitive style. She was alternately billed as "the Great Mae Young" or simply as "the Queen."

"She'd play poker with the boys, and lift up her leg and let out a big fart," recalled Freddie Blassie in his autobiography. "If a guy did something to piss her off, she'd try to provoke him into a fight. She knew how to take a punch from a man, then kick his ass."

Young was introduced to a new generation of wrestling fans

in 1999 when she and Moolah were seated at ringside during a *SmackDown* event and got into an altercation with Jeff Jarrett. Jarrett had been feuding with Chyna and was on a misogynistic streak in the storyline. He invited the women into the ring and proceeded to smash his trademark guitar over Moolah's head and put Young in a spinning toe hold.

Moolah and Young began doing more comedy bits for the Attitude Era WWF, and Young showed she was game for any storyline pitched . . . no matter how bizarre. In September 1999, she and Moolah wrestled Ivory in a handicap evening gown match that saw the 76-year-old Young get stripped down to her bra and panties.

And believe it or not, it wasn't the first time she got down to her bra and panties in public.

"One night around 1 a.m., I heard banging on my door," recalled Pat Patterson in his book, talking about the time he was in Boston in the early '60s. "It was Mae Young wearing only her bra and panties with a martini in her hand. What the hell?"

"Patterson, let me in."

"What's the matter?"

"Don't worry, Pat, I just want to talk bullshit with you."

Young also won the Miss Royal Rumble bikini contest at the 2000 Royal Rumble, when she removed her bathing suit top, revealing a remarkably realistic looking pair of sagging prosthetic breasts. She was also on the receiving end of a pair of frightening power bombs from Buh Buh Ray Dudley — one off the top rope through a table and the other off a staging area off the entrance ramp through another table.

Dudley said Young was adamant that she didn't want any special treatment for those dangerous stunts. "Hey, hot shot, if you're gonna slam me, you slam me like one of the boys,'" Dudley said in an interview for the book *World Wrestling Entertainment Unscripted*. "I was like, 'Holy crap, yes ma'am, no problem. Whatever you need."

"By far, that was the toughest person, pound for pound, we've ever been in the ring with," D-Von Dudley agreed in that same interview.

Young also did an infamous angle where she announced she was pregnant (at the age of 77) with Mark Henry's baby and later "gave birth" to a rubber prosthetic hand on television. She continued making sporadic appearances on WWE programming up until March 4, 2013, when she celebrated her 90th birthday on *Raw*. She was presented with a customized WWE Divas championship belt by Vince McMahon and Triple H on that telecast.

She had her feet fondled by Gene Snitsky, performed a bronco buster on Eric Bischoff, and smooched with the Rock ... she was willing to go to any length to entertain the fans.

"Mae planned out a spot where she should be in the ring with Crash and I'd sneak in behind her," said Hardcore Holly in his book. "She would turn around and I'd clothesline her. I said to her, 'Mae I've got all the respect in the world for you but if you're asking me to clothesline you, you need to know that I lay it in there.' She said, 'Sure I know that, I want you to clothesline me.' I said, 'No, you don't understand — when I clothesline somebody, I try to rip their head off. It's TV, I don't want it to look bad but I don't want to hurt you.' This nearly 80-year-old woman just looked at me and said, 'Bring it, motherfucker.' In Gorilla just before the match, I gave her a hug and thanked her in advance for the match, then asked if she was sure about the clothesline. She said, 'If you don't bring it, when we get back, I'm going to kick your ass.'"

For Dave Meltzer, that second career made her a much bigger star. "It was that career that got her into both the WWE Hall of Fame and the Pro Wrestling Hall of Fame, and created the image of she and the Fabulous Moolah as the grand old ladies and respected pioneers of women's wrestling. During her prime, she was never ranked as one of the elite stars on the level of Moolah, Mildred Burke, June Byers, Nell Stewart, Penny Banner, or even later like a Betty Nicoli or Vivian Vachon. During her prime she was sometimes regarded as among the top ten women wrestlers in the country."

Regardless, she was inducted into the Pro Wrestling Hall of Fame in 2004 and the WWE Hall of Fame in 2008. For several years, she maintained that her goal was to wrestle a match on her 100th birthday against Stephanie McMahon. Sadly, it never happened.

Young died at the age of 90 on January 14, 2014.

"She was an inspiration, a true trailblazer.... And one of the toughest SOB I ever knew. I used to say to her, 'When I grow up I want to be just like you'," recalled WWE Hall of Famer Trish Stratus to SLAM! Wrestling upon Young's passing.

"There will never be another Mae Young," said Vince McMahon after she passed away. Her longevity in sports entertainment may never be matched and I will forever be grateful for all of her contributions to the industry."

Without a doubt, a whole generation of wrestling fans associates Mae Young with the woman who would take the next era of women's wrestling by storm, pretty much replacing Mildred Burke as world champion and Billy Wolfe as promoter.

# From SLAVE GIRL to WOMEN'S CHAMPION
## The Rise of Lillian Ellison

When Billy Wolfe and Mildred Burke parted ways, Lillian Ellison was perfectly positioned to fill the void and take control of the women's wrestling world. Best known as the Fabulous Moolah, Ellison established herself as the premier power broker in women's wrestling for more than three decades.

Respected by her allies and feared by her enemies, Ellison was a master politician and a shrewd, calculating businesswoman. As an in-ring competitor, she was widely considered the most well-known female wrestler in the game for 30 years. Her career as a trainer and promoter extended even further. And, in 1999, at age 76, she had one final run as WWF women's champion, during a peak period in wrestling's popularity.

"When I was coming up, it was unheard of for a lady wrestler to be strong and independent," Ellison wrote in her 2002 autobiography *The*

*Fabulous Moolah: First Goddess of the Squared Circle.* "We were the valets for the men stars, and we had men — promoters, other wrestlers, husbands, or boyfriends — telling us exactly what to do. I did what I wanted to do, ever since I was a little girl and defied my dear daddy's wishes by entering the ring."

Mary Lillian Ellison was born on July 22, 1923. She grew up in the tiny town of Tookiedoo, outside Columbia, South Carolina. She was the youngest of 13 children and the only girl. She grew up roughhousing with her brothers, fishing in the nearby creek, and riding horses on the family farm. She was eight years old when her mother — the biggest female influence in her life — died from cancer at 40 years old. She went to live with her grandmother and worked on the family's cotton farm, lugging heavy bags of cotton in from the fields under the hot Carolina sun.

"My daddy saw me for who I was. And he saw what I was going through. So he tried to come up with things for just the two of us to do, ways for me to spend special time with him and preoccupy my mind," Ellison wrote. "He was a wrestling fan like you wouldn't believe; he loved it. So one of the things he did was get us ringside seats every Tuesday night for pro wrestling in Columbia. I was ten at the time. At first, I was just excited to be sharing something special with my daddy, without all my brothers hovering around."

On one fateful day, Mildred Burke came to Columbia as Ellison was watching from the front row. It was the first time Ellison had even seen a woman compete in the ring. She became obsessed with the idea of becoming a pro wrestler herself. Her father disapproved. Wrestling was not a ladylike line of work.

Still a teenager, Ellison eloped with Walter Carroll. The young couple had a baby girl they named Mary who would end up wrestling under the name Darlin' Pat Sherry. Shortly after the baby was born, Walter and Lillian parted ways. Married life had left her unfulfilled; she was determined to try her hand in wrestling.

Still, it took her six years before she approached Billy Wolfe and asked to join his group. Ellison took an instant disliking to Wolfe. "To

*Boxing legend Rocky Marciano and Slave Girl (Not Fabulous Yet) Moolah.* CHRIS SWISHER COLLECTION

my way of thinking, he was a despicable human being," she wrote. "Even so, I knew I had to deal with him — at least at first — to realize my dream."

Wolfe told Ellison she was too small to be a wrestler and advised her to "go home and get yourself a job as a secretary so you can sit on some lawyer's knee," Ellison recalled. But the girl from Tookiedoo wasn't about to give up on her dream that easily. Wolfe ended up bringing her on board, and she wrestled her first match on July 20, 1948.

"We traveled in two separate groups," Ellison wrote. "So when Bill would go with Mildred's group, he'd sleep with her. But sometimes he would go with June's group [June Byers], and that's when he'd get her or Nell [Stewart] in bed. June and Nell wanted the best bookings, so they slept with Billy whenever he liked."

Ellison rebuked Wolfe's advances, so she never got the push as one of Wolfe's top girls. She balanced bookings with regular visits to her daughter and to see her father, who was suffering from lung cancer. She was in Columbus, Ohio, when on her birthday in 1949 she received a call telling her that her father had died. She went to Wolfe's hotel room and asked for a $100 advance so she could get home for her father's funeral.

"His exact words were: 'You just left home two days ago. What do you want to do, go home and hold his hand?'" she wrote. "I knew he was no good, but this was even below him. . . . Through clenched teeth, I managed to blurt out: 'I hope you die in the damned gutter and the worms eat your body before they find you!'"

This was the end of Ellison's partnership with Wolfe.

Ellison had begun dating wrestler Johnny Long. In addition to training with Ellison and helping her refine her wrestling skills, Long introduced her to New York promoter Jack Pfefer. Pfefer loved promoting larger-than-life attractions and the opportunity to work with the women. He wanted to create a new money-making gimmick for little Lillian Ellison.

"He started asking me questions, like 'Vy do you vant to vestle all the time?' Finally, annoyed, I blurted out, 'For the money! I want to wrestle for the moolah!'"

Pfefer decided to pair Ellison with one of his top stars, "Nature Boy" Buddy Rogers. Ellison was to be Nature Boy's "slave girl" — Slave Girl Moolah. She began wearing a tiny leopard-print skirt and waiting on Rogers as he entered the ring.

Ellison and Long married but Long's infidelities put the marriage on rocky terrain. At the same time, Ellison was being pressured into a sexual relationship by Rogers. Ellison shot him down, then went and reported Rogers to Pfefer. It was a risky move — Rogers was one of the biggest draws in the game. She had already burned her bridges with Wolfe. She knew she was risking her career by reporting Rogers's conduct.

Instead of firing her, Pfefer paired her up with the Elephant Boy, Tony Olivas, a big, dark-complexioned Mexican billed as hailing from "darkest Africa." Slave Girl Moolah and the Elephant Boy had chemistry . . . in fact, they may have had *too much* chemistry. The sight of a scantily clad white woman catering to a dark-skinned man who was easily mistaken for a black man was too much for the racial climate of the time. At one event in Oklahoma, a fan rushed the ring and slashed Moolah with a knife after Moolah had kissed the Elephant Boy on the cheek.

"I saw something glitter in his hand as it came toward me, and the next thing I knew I heard the tearing of my dress — that's when it dawned on me that he had a knife and was trying to stab me!" she wrote. "Well, if it hadn't been for the bra that I had on, he would have cut me good. As it was, he cut through the straps of my bra and I had nicks all the way down my side."

Ellison developed a relationship with wrestler Buddy Lee. She left Long and married Lee, and the couple left New York to settle in Columbia, near Ellison's childhood home. That's where Moolah and Lee started training female wrestlers. To help pay the bills, Lee found work as a handyman; Ellison sold cosmetics door to door. They moved to the Bronx, but the country girl wasn't cut out for living in a tiny apartment where the train shook the walls as it passed by throughout the day, and they settled back in South Carolina.

Having parted from both Wolfe and Pfefer, Moolah lobbied Boston promoter Paul Bowser to use her and her trainees. Bowser brought Moolah's girls on board. "Once we started wrestling in Boston, other promoters came out of the woodwork," Ellison wrote. "Atlanta, North Carolina, Seattle all called."

And so did Vincent James McMahon. McMahon had established control of New York, New Jersey, and Baltimore. Moolah began working for him in 1955.

On September 18, 1956, those promoters created their own world championship, when Moolah competed in a one-night tournament, Moolah beat Judy Grable in the championship match, and she was awarded a gorgeous new title belt. Needless to say that women's champion June Byers wasn't invited to participate in that tournament.

Now that Moolah was the champion, McMahon dropped the Slave Girl moniker and rechristened her with a term he considered more appropriate. The Fabulous Moolah was born.

## The COMPLICATED LEGACY of the FABULOUS MOOLAH

Moolah would end up controlling women's wrestling for three decades, and she wielded considerable political power. She could make a career or break one. In many ways, Moolah was women's wrestling's version of Don Corleone ... and her tactics could be just as ruthless and cutthroat as those of "the Godfather."

Jeannine Mjoseth had a brief wrestling career in the mid-1980s as Mad Maxine. At 6'2" tall and sporting a spiked green mohawk, she had a perfect look for the era, looking like a female Road Warrior. Mjoseth was referred by Beverly Shade to Moolah for training, but she doesn't have many good things to say about Moolah.

*Fabulous Moolah held that title for most of the next 28 years.*
JACK PFEFER COLLECTION/UNIVERSITY OF NOTRE DAME

"She was an evil person," Mjoseth said in an interview with SLAM! Wrestling. "I understand why. She came from nothing. Her mother died when she was just eight and she was never going to be poor again."

Mjoseth said Moolah exploited her trainees, who were obligated to rent a room at Moolah's compound and were charged room and board and for training, essentially making them indentured servants for the length of their training. With Moolah controlling the bookings and taking a cut of the payoffs (anywhere from 25 to 50 percent, according to various sources and depending on who it was), Moolah could keep her trainees in debt to her for as long as she liked.

Barbara McCoy, the sister of Susie Mae "Sweet Georgia Brown" McCoy, said that her sister was not permitted to have her own bank account when she started at Moolah's school. It was a concerted effort to control the trainees by managing their earning potential.

"Moolah did send girls out to this guy in Arizona and pimped them out," Mjoseth said. "I actually spoke to him on the phone and asked him what he was looking for. He said, 'If I'm spending all of this money, you know what I want.' That was part of Moolah's way of making money. She was just a bad person. She didn't have a good bone in her body."

Some people have condemned such criticisms of Moolah as sour grapes. Mjoseth's wrestling career never panned out; maybe she has an axe to grind (although Mjoseth had a successful career out of wrestling, becoming the acting chief of communications for the National Human Genome Research Institute).

Following Moolah's death, Penny Banner felt the need to speak out, posting the following comments online.

"Let's get this out of the way first, so I don't have to dance around the subject — Moolah was a pimp," Banner wrote. "From her sprawling 42-acre estate in Columbia, South Carolina, Moolah would send out her half-trained underage female wrestlers to 'photo shoots' that by the standards of today would be considered pedophilia and pornography. She sent trainees to wrestling promoters in set numbers. Renting them out to promoters in bulk, with the understanding that the girls would have sex with the promoter and all the wrestlers on the roster who wanted them. Promoters liked free sex, but what they also liked was for [the] boys not to go outside looking for it and possibly running into trouble. Sex on [the] road with a steady and pliant group of semi-attractive women in return for money, that is what Moolah offered. The women that were sent on these tours were not told of this 'arrangement' ahead of time. They found out about it on the road. Those that refused to have sex with promoters and wrestlers were raped."

Allegations like these persist about Moolah, but the truth is difficult to determine. Kayfabe was a powerful mind-set during that era. A female wrestler who reported rape could have been blackballed from the wrestling industry, which may have left them in debt to Moolah and without the means to pay off that debt.

In a 2006 article in *Metro Spirit*, Ida Mae Martinez verified that some promoters "demanded personal services" before they handed over pay to female wrestlers. But it could be argued that those promoters acted on their own, and that Moolah (or whoever booked the girls for that promoter) could have been unaware of those overtures. Even though Moolah was repulsed by Wolfe's tactics, as a promoter, she had some things in common with him.

"She was trained by him so I guess you know she got it from him. What goes around comes around. She got it done to her and she was doing it to everyone else," said Judy Grable in *Lipstick & Dynamite*.

"Women's wrestling was shady throughout history. It's no surprise that Moolah was dishonest, greedy, etc. since one of her first mentors in the business was Billy Wolfe — the king of all those traits," said wrestling and baseball historian Tim Hornbaker. "Moolah, however, could have changed things by running an honest syndicate, training and booking women on the level. She could have broken the patterns established by Wolfe. She chose not to. Maybe it was just too deeply ingrained."

It was an environment rife with opportunities for abuses; whether or not those abuses occurred — or to what degree — remains speculation. Moolah was never charged with any crimes, and she remained in good standing with the McMahons throughout her life.

Canadian wrestler Sandy Parker trained under Moolah and said Moolah openly played favorites.

"Everyone knew that if you weren't on Lillian's good side, you got crappy bookings," Parker told SLAM! Wrestling. "I wasn't on her good side because I wouldn't do what she wanted me to do."

Parker says she also got heat from Moolah because Parker was a lesbian, and Moolah wanted her to avoid gay bars and date her nephews. "Lillian was two-faced because she had her own little dalliances that we all knew about," Parker said.

In addition to those allegations of sexual abuse, Moolah also garnered criticism for her wrestling abilities and her training methods.

Moolah was never a premier technical wrestler. Most of her repertoire consisted of hair-pulling, kicking, and brawling tactics. Although she ran the most well-known women's wrestling school in the United States, Moolah handled very little of the training, leaving it in the hands of Buddy Lee, Donna Christantello, Leilani Kai, or other students. Moolah was a trainer in name only.

"During the period Moolah controlled women's wrestling, the popularity and product didn't evolve," said Dave Meltzer. "The women in the 1940s and the 1950s, even the late 1950s in some places like Florida, they were headlining shows. The idea that women can't headline came years later because they used to headline and they were successful. Women's wrestling under her tutelage, and I don't know if it's her fault, went way way down. By the 1980s, the version in Japan grew [and] was light years ahead in every way possible. Some of that was due to the differences in culture and being on network television weekly. But a lot was also due to progressively evolving the style to make it more exciting and appealing, creating far stronger heel and face characters, and making wrestlers into rock stars. But Moolah was there before them and stood the test of time. And Moolah remained a name in our culture long after those women had become culturally passé."

Moolah also earned heat from her contemporaries in the 1990s when she and Mae Young spearheaded the Las Vegas–based Ladies International Wrestling Association. The organization collected donations, ostensibly to help build a retirement home for wrestlers in need, but nothing ever came of it, leaving some supporters feeling they had been swindled.

Her involvement in the 1985 screwjob match against Wendi Richter also somewhat tarnished her reputation among some of her peers.

Although Moolah has her detractors, she also had many powerful supporters and maintained a positive reputation within the industry. Moolah protected kayfabe with her life. She was loyal to her allies. She didn't write tell-all exposés or grant "shoot" interviews. When booking her wrestlers with various promoters, her word was her bond — if she promised that a wrestler would be somewhere, she would make sure she was there, on time, and ready to wrestle, and if something came up, she would substitute in for the wrestler, ensuring that the promoter wouldn't be out a match.

There was resentment over her tactics, her death grip on the championship, and her success, but Moolah managed to have a long and successful career in wrestling, becoming one of the most famous (and wealthy) female wrestlers of all time. A true icon in wrestling, Moolah's death warranted an obituary in the *New York Times*, a tribute on WWE programming, and a mention on ESPN's *Pardon the Interruption*, a sign of her fame with mainstream audiences.

## *The* MOOLAH GIRLS

Although women's wrestling would never gain back the popularity it had enjoyed up until the early 1950s, a lot of aspiring women went to South Carolina in the late '50s and the '60s hoping to become wrestlers one day. They were of all shapes and sizes, coming from all over the United States and even Canada. Many of them succeeded, and the cornerstones of the women's scene in the '60s and '70s became known as the Moolah girls.

### *Rita Cortez*

The media dubbed her the Mexican Spitfire.

The Fabulous Moolah had another name for Rita Cortez: homewrecker.

Born Yolanda Gutierrez, Cortez enrolled in Moolah and Buddy Lee's school in the late 1950s, dropped off by her mother at Moolah's door. Moolah took a personal interest in the petite and charming 19-year-old Mexican girl and took her on as a pet project.

"Rita was a dark-skinned Mexican girl, and I just loved her to death," Moolah wrote in her autobiography. "Like a lot of the girls, she had idolized me and kind of wanted to be me. She was always trying to help me around the house, and I took her under my wing like she was a daughter or sister. Whenever I would go shopping for myself, if I bought myself a pair of panties and a bra, I'd buy Rita the same. In my mind, by treating her so well, I was making up for how cold Mildred Burke had been to me all those years before."

Before long, Moolah was hearing reports from promoters that Rita was adopting many of Moolah's signature moves and mannerisms in the ring. Cortez's appreciation for Moolah had turned into mimicry. Then one day, Moolah said, she received a phone call from another wrestler who said that Rita and Buddy were having an affair behind her back.

"I decided to make an unexpected trip home," Moolah wrote. "Well, there was no more doubt when I walked in my house that day. Let's just say that what I saw left little to the imagination. I just stood there, looking at this scene, my blood boiling."

Moolah booted Lee from the house and divorced him. Lee married Cortez in 1967. The two moved from Columbia to Nashville and remained together until Lee's death in 1998.

With Cortez as his top star, Lee attempted to run in opposition to Moolah, but Moolah's girls remained loyal to her, and Lee struggled to attract students other than Cortez.

Lee formed country music promotions company Aud-Lee Attractions with Audrey Williams (the ex-wife of his longtime friend Hank Williams Sr. and mother of Hank Williams Jr.) in 1964. He took full control of the company in 1968, renaming it Buddy Lee Attractions, and Cortez later took an active role in assisting Lee. Now run by their daughter, Donna Lee, Buddy Lee Attractions remains Nashville's oldest and largest privately owned talent agency, having represented such acts as Willie Nelson, Garth Brooks, George Strait, and the Dixie Chicks. With their country music business doing better than their wrestling business, they left the latter, leaving Moolah with the monopoly of the division.

As Moolah's power and influence grew, Cortez's bookings waned. On March 21, 1964, Cortez helped reintroduce women's wrestling to the state of Michigan, wrestling Olga Martinez in the first women's bout held there in 25 years. "She was a pivotal figure in the history of U.S. women's wrestling," stated Dave Meltzer.

"Rita Cortez's career didn't get into high gear until near the end of the golden age of women's professional wrestling, otherwise her exciting ring personality might have had an even greater impact on the profession," noted the 2001 CAC awards program when she was honored by the group. "Even as it was, this one time protégé of the Fabulous Moolah prompted plenty of excitement with her dark come hither good looks and sparkling personality. By the mid-1960s, Rita Cortez was a name prominent enough to rank with Moolah, June Byers, and Penny Banner as the premier headliners of the game. And she, of course, is still remembered by many as the luchadoress of Mexican wrestling history."

*Rita Cortez, Moolah's rival . . . outside the ring.*
CHRIS SWISHER COLLECTION

She died in 2012 at the age of 73. Moolah and Cortez never spoke again, and the latter never hesitated to take a shot at the champion, mostly saying that stealing Lee from Moolah was the biggest conquest of her life. In reality, Moolah became more successful after parting ways with Lee, and Lee found newfound fame and success in the country music world. Cortez's romance with Lee affected both wrestling history and the history of country music.

## *Ella Waldek and the Story of Billy Wolfe's Ward*

A farm girl from Custer, Washington, Elsie Schevchenko became one of wrestling's most notorious characters because of a freak accident.

On July 27, 1951, her opponent, Janet Boyer, collapsed during a tag team match and died later that night. The cause of her death was unrelated to the match, but Schevchenko was tried and convicted in the court of public opinion. For the remainder of her career, she would hear catcalls of "Murderer!" and "Killer!" in every arena she competed in.

But she was no murderer. In fact, as a young girl, she planned on becoming a nun.

Born on December 2, 1929, Schevchenko, the daughter of a German mother and a Russian father, grew up on a farm in rural Washington, living in a converted barn. Her father left when she was three years old. As soon as she was able, Elsie's mother put her to work on the farm out of necessity.

"I was raised on a farm driving tractors and throwing around 50-pound bales of hay," she told Jeff Leen in an article for SLAM! Wrestling. "I went to school as Elsie the Cow. I was always bigger than everybody, more mature than everybody."

By the time she was 11, she was hired as a waitress at a drive-in diner, where she worked with her mother. She was eventually reported to the police for working underage and was given a choice of going to reform school or a convent. She chose the convent. As a girl, the religious life appealed to her. By the time she returned to her mother's home, her mother had remarried a man who had two lecherous sons of his own.

"I overheard my stepfather say if the sons didn't get me, he would. And I said, 'That's it. I'm gone,'" she told SLAM!

Looking more mature than her 15 years, she found a man and got married to get out of that house, but the marriage was doomed from the start. She left her new husband and took a job as a mechanic for the Air Force. She left that job after suffering a severe chemical burn on her leg. She found work selling magazines, then waiting tables. At the age of 16, she ended up in Columbus, Ohio, where she found work competing in roller derby.

While competing on the derby circuit, she met wrestling promoter Tommy Ward, who introduced her to wrestling. Wrestling presented a big opportunity to a corn-fed farm girl.

Ward put her in touch with promoter Jack Pfefer, who sent her on to Lillian Ellison for training in 1950. Schevchenko trained under Ellison for a year, but there was no regular work to be had. "There wasn't a whole lot of matches because she was an outlaw [running against the NWA and Billy Wolfe]," Schevchenko said.

*Wrestling wasn't easy on Ella Waldek.* CHRIS SWISHER COLLECTION

The final straw came when a male wrestler attempted to rape her before a match in Toledo, Ohio, she said. Some other male wrestlers saved her, but she made up her mind about leaving Moolah and got in contact with Billy Wolfe. Wolfe put Schevchenko in the ring against two of his best shooters — Johnnie Mae Young and Dot Dotson. The 21-year-old held her own and impressed Wolfe.

Wolfe gave her the ring name Ella Waldek. At 5'5" and a muscular 140 pounds, she trained in shoot fighting and submission grappling and quickly became one of Wolfe's enforcers. She specialized in a short-arm scissors lift, a move that showcased her impressive upper body strength.

She said Wolfe took a hefty fee for his booking services, including

50 percent of her $600 payout for a match in Cuba. "He would never allow me to make any money so I could get away. He made sure if I made any money he'd make me stay off wrestling for a couple of weeks. He never wanted me to make any money so I could leave."

Wolfe also limited the number of title shots Waldek had against Mildred Burke. She says it's because Wolfe and Burke were afraid she might go into business for herself and pin Burke for the title.

In early July 1951, she won the NWA women's tag team title with Mae Young in Marion, Ohio. Then came that fateful night on July 27, 1951, at the Patterson Field Stadium in East Liverpool, Ohio.

Janet Boyer had come to Billy Wolfe through a recommendation from Minneapolis promoter Tony Stecher. When Wolfe met her, Boyer was a 16-year-old girl living with her widowed mother and working in a stocking factory to support the family.

Wolfe was initially reluctant to sign the petite 5'3" teenager, but Boyer was persistent. Over the next year, she added more than 50 pounds to her frame, bulking up to 180 pounds. Wolfe acquiesced.

Because Boyer was under 18, Wolfe was required to become her legal guardian in order to train her to become a wrestler. He signed the guardianship papers with the blessing of Boyer's mother, Selma. Boyer took the name Janet Boyer Wolfe.

For several weeks before that night in East Liverpool, Boyer had privately complained of excruciating headaches to several of the girls, but she refused to tell Wolfe, fearing that she would lose bookings. Wolfe had big plans for his adopted daughter, grooming her as a potential successor to Mildred Burke down the road, and Boyer didn't want to jeopardize her spot. Like many other athletes of the era, her mind-set was simply to work through pain.

On July 27, the then 18-year-old Boyer wrestled in a singles match against Ella Waldek, losing in seven minutes. In the locker room after the match, she complained of a "bursting headache" to Waldek. Waldek suggested she tell Wolfe and pull out of a scheduled tag team match later in the evening. Boyer refused. The tag team match went on as scheduled.

Boyer teamed with Eva Lee against the team of Waldek and Mae

Young. Boyer started the match with Young, wrestled for a few minutes with Waldek, got body-slammed, and tagged out. But as she stepped through the ring ropes to the apron, she went weak in the knees and collapsed suddenly to the canvas, losing consciousness. She was rushed to East Liverpool Osteopathic Hospital, with both Young and Waldek doing the ambulance ride with her, where she was pronounced dead at 4 a.m., having never regained consciousness.

The police detained Waldek, Young, and Lee for questioning, to determine if there had been any foul play during the match.

"They locked [us] in a hotel room because they had no prison facilities for women," Waldek later said in an interview in the documentary *Lipstick & Dynamite*. "And we were going to be accused of manslaughter in the first degree."

But Wolfe, either because of anger, sadness, or greed, called Waldek out publicly.

"When I got through with the matches, I contacted the hospital and they still hadn't found out anything," Waldek remembered. "But on Monday the newspaper came out. Billy Wolfe had released an article to the newspaper that I had killed her, that I had dropped her on her head. I tried to straighten this out with Mae Young in New York. She said she was accused of killing her; the hell she was. She was never accused of killing her, I was."

Ultimately, no charges were filed. Boyer died of natural causes — a traumatic rupture of the stomach and a subdural hematoma in the brain. Although she should not have been wrestling in her condition, no one had dealt the proverbial death blow. Boyer simply collapsed and died in the ring.

"I had already had publicity all over the United States and maybe further that I had caused Janet Wolfe's death," Waldek said in *Lipstick & Dynamite*. "I went into the ring sometimes and everybody was calling me a murderer. I had to have guards, sometimes. But, boy, I was doing houses. Everybody wanted to see this stupid blonde that killed Janet Wolfe."

Women's wrestling suffered a black eye following Boyer's death in the ring. Cleveland councilman Harry T. Marshall called for a ban on women's wrestling, citing Boyer's death to argue that "the sport is too much hazard for women." Editorialists came out against women's wrestling as well.

Wolfe was devastated by Boyer's death. He had bought a diamond ring he planned to give his adopted daughter following a tournament he had scheduled in Columbus to crown a new junior champion, a tournament Boyer was likely scheduled to win. He gave the ring to Boyer's mother, instead. Mildred Burke never issued a comment on Boyer's death.

"My daughter's death was an accident that could have happened in any sport," Selma Boyer told the Associated Press. "She was doing what she wanted, and what happened was God's will. Janet was always a strong, healthy girl, so I didn't stand in her way. If a girl wants to do something and really has her heart set on it there is no sense standing in her way. It will only make her bitter."

Still, Waldek was haunted by Boyer's death for the rest of her career, wrongfully blamed by fans for killing Boyer in cold blood.

"Right after that, Mille Stafford broke her leg in Dayton, flying out of the ring while we were training. I was the one who threw her. And she didn't fall right. That was another hit on me. Anytime anybody got hurt, [the magazines] wanted to know if I was the one in the ring."

Not too long after that, Waldek felt intense pain when she took a kick to the abdomen from Cora Combs. She suffered severe damage to her ovaries, her stomach, and her Fallopian tubes. She was unable to ever have children. The injury caused her to go through early menopause in her mid-20s.

She returned to wrestling following surgery, and when Wolfe split with Burke, Waldek said Wolfe asked her if she wanted to be the new women's champion.

"I have a letter he wrote me asking me if I would take the world's title," she told SLAM! "I was shocked as hell."

Wolfe eventually went with June Byers instead. Waldek continued wrestling, moving to Florida where she worked for promoter Cowboy Luttrell. She won the NWA Southern women's championship three times from 1957 to 1969 and captured the NWA Florida women's title in 1971.

With the wrestling business in a downturn, Schevchenko took a job as a security officer. She worked as a security guard for 17 years. While in the line of duty, she suffered a severe neck injury when she confronted a group of shoplifters and was slammed against a plate glass window. The injuries suffered in that attack officially ended her wrestling career.

"That's one of the nicest ladies you'd ever want to meet and one of the toughest ladies . . . in and out of the wrestling business," said Beverly Shade. "She trained me. She's tough, but also just as sweet as can be."

She later opened a greenhouse with her third husband, James Mecouch. She joined the Cauliflower Alley Club and reunited with some of her former wrestling compatriots.

Waldek was featured in the documentary *Lipstick & Dynamite* in 2004. She died on April 17, 2013, after a lengthy battle with lymphoma. She was 83.

## Ann Casey

If a cat truly has nine lives, then Ann Casey has certainly lived up to her nickname of Panther Girl. In September 1973, Casey was shot six times. She not only survived, she was back in the ring just a few months later. In 2005, she suffered a stress-related heart attack and was taken in for emergency surgery. Her heart stopped; she died on the operating table. But she came back once again, making a full recovery.

Born September 29, 1938, Lucille Ann Casey was born in Saraland, Alabama. Her father was of Irish descent; her mother was a Creek Indian. She grew up working the fields on her family's cotton farm in Mississippi, working long hours and performing strenuous manual labor. At the age of 16, she married her boyfriend, falsifying her age in an effort to start a new life away from her rugged existence on the family farm. The marriage was later annulled but yielded a son.

*"The Panther Girl" Ann Casey.* CHRIS SWISHER COLLECTION

She found work as a ticket-taker for the Fields Brothers' wrestling promotion in Mobile, Alabama. In 1962, she met the Fabulous Moolah at the wrestling arena. The two struck up a conversation, and Moolah offered Casey a chance to train at her school and become a wrestler. Casey turned it down at first, since she was unwilling to relocate from Mobile to Moolah's training school in South Carolina. But bills needed to be paid, and her meager wages she earned as a ticket-taker and as a barmaid were not enough to provide for herself and her son.

Casey packed up and moved to Columbia and trained at Moolah's school. Moolah gave her the Panther Girl nickname that she would keep throughout her career. With her leopard-print one-piece bathing suits and her jet-black hair, Casey could have passed as Bettie Page's sister. In the fall of 1962, Casey made her pro debut in a tag team match, partnering with Judy Grable against Rita Cortez and Brenda Scott.

Casey was a natural fan favorite (although she did have a few stints as a heel throughout her career). She was agile and frequently came off the top rope, which was still extremely rare in women's wrestling. She adopted the airplane spin as her signature finishing move, usually set up by a flying dropkick.

But Casey quickly tired of Moolah taking 30 percent of her pay and also allegedly dipping into her payouts for unspecified "expenses."

During a tour of Hawaii, Casey told Moolah she was leaving her employ, creating a deep rift between the two women.

Casey remained in Hawaii for a time, then returned to the mainland where she accepted bookings throughout the United States and Canada, including matches in Vince McMahon's territory in the Northeast, where Moolah reigned as queen. She turned down out-of-town bookings in the winter months so she could remain home with her son. "I was a mother first, and wrestler second," she would later write in a sprawling autobiography totaling more than 1,000 pages. The boy would do his homework in the locker room during shows.

In 1972, Casey made a startling discovery: a cache of drugs hidden in her son's belongings. "There were drugs in there I didn't even recognize," she later wrote. "Marijuana of course, but also some powders."

Fearful that her son might have been dealing drugs, she went to the police. According to Casey, she and the authorities worked out a deal where she would use her wrestling connections and heavy travel to gather information for the police. If she saw something shady at a truck stop on the road, she said she would take down license numbers and report back to the police.

This work apparently made her some very serious enemies. One night, a man Casey later believed to have been a drug kingpin walked up to her car with a Luger pistol in his hand. When Casey saw him, she hit the gas, but the man emptied his clip firing at the car. She was struck multiple times as she drove off, eventually stopping at a gas station for help.

Casey suffered life-threatening injuries to her liver and lung as well as significant blood loss. She was rushed to a hospital and underwent emergency surgery. Against all odds, she survived the surgery but was told she would likely never walk again without the aid of crutches. Her wrestling days were over.

Casey had different plans. She would not only walk without aid, she would also wrestle again. She went back to Moolah and helped train some of her students. Moolah persuaded Casey to return to wrestling, and her comeback took her to the next level of stardom. She challenged Moolah for the championship in March 1975 and was named Girl Wrestler of the Year by *The Wrestler* (the precursor to *Pro Wrestling Illustrated*).

She won the vacant NWA U.S. women's title with a win over Toni Rose and held that title for four years, dropping it to Joyce Grable in 1978. Her little sister, Jo Casey, briefly took up the sport, using the nickname Black Cat, and the sisters had a string of catfights.

Casey went into semi-retirement in the 1980s after a 20-year career. "One tough woman," said fellow wrestler Susan Green. Truly a super nice person, but she was tough in the ring."

Casey wrote and self-published her life story, titled *Autobiography of Professional Woman Wrestler Ann Casey: The Lady, the Life, the Legend*. An abridged version was printed in the sports magazine *Victory Journal* in 2014 with the more lurid, pulpy title "The Legend of Panther Girl: She Fought to Win. They Shot to Kill."

### Betty Jo Hawkins

She might be remembered as the beauty who married the Brute, but Betty Jo Hawkins was much more than that.

Born Bettie J. Floyd on October 22, 1930, in Boyd, Kentucky, she suffered from rheumatoid arthritis from an early age, which was originally misdiagnosed as childhood polio. The arthritis caused pain and swelling in her joints and curtailed much of her athletic development until it subsided when she was in her teens. The arthritis would return in her 30s and would contribute to the early end of her wrestling career.

She began wrestling in 1948, according to Penny Banner, who became Hawkins's tag team partner and one of her closest friends. Ella Waldek helped train her in Columbus, Ohio.

"She was always the nice, clean country girl. She could give you back what you gave her but she stayed a fan favorite," Waldek told Jamie Kreiser in a 2007 interview. "She was very friendly and outgoing. No drinking and carousing, which some of [the girls] did. She was dedicated to her family and her occupation. She was a very quiet, loveable, happy-go-lucky person."

But Hawkins was no pushover. In her autobiography, Banner

remembered an altercation Hawkins had had with a bar patron who refused to take no for an answer.

"'Don't you like boys?' Then he looked over at his friends at the bar. 'You girls like each other, what are you, queer?' Well, that was the wrong thing to say. Betty's bottle of beer was almost half full . . . she grabbed the bottle by its neck, stood up in front of him and slung it at his head. It didn't break but the bartender quickly came over and asked him to leave us alone," Banner wrote.

*Betty Jo Hawkins, the beauty who married the Brute.*
CHRIS SWISHER COLLECTION

Hawkins became a mentor to Banner and taught her the nuances of the game. "She told me how the 'little things' in a match mean a lot. Such things as how to throw my whole body into a really powerful 'forearm blow,'" Banner wrote. "Other things she taught me [included] how to get in and out of the holds legally [which wouldn't matter to a heel wrestler]. All of these things and more tricks took years to 'come natural' to me."

Hawkins and Banner were the recognized NWA women's tag team champions in 1956. That was good enough for Stu Hart, who then billed the team as the Canadian tag team champions on their first tour through his territory in Alberta. Hawkins also had success teaming with Cora Combs (her third cousin) and Toni Rose. Although she won the NWA Florida championship in 1953, Hawkins primarily competed in tag team matches. Banner said she preferred tag matches because her arthritis caused her severe pain, and tag matches gave her an opportunity to tag out for brief rest periods. "She was so healthy looking and strong, no one would ever expect how handicapped she was," Banner wrote.

"She had the guts to get in there. That's the biggest thing about her. She had the intestinal fortitude to do what she wanted to do and she stuck with it," added Waldek. Hawkins retired from wrestling to marry wrestler Brute Bernard (James Prud'homme). She and Bernard had a son, and her health deteriorated a short time later.

"[From when] I was four or five years old, my mother was really sick," her son Tony Prud'homme told Kreiser. "She was amazing. She would lay in bed at night . . . and you would hear her crying from all the pain. I never heard her complain. The only complaints that would come out were in her sleep. She was always one of those who said, 'Hey, my legs are bad, but I'm better than someone who has no legs.'"

Her husband died in 1984 of an accidental self-inflicted gunshot wound. Betty Jo died three years later on December 4, 1987, at the age of 57.

## Judy Grable

Hollywood had "The Pinup Girl" Betty Grable; the wrestling world had "The Barefoot Contessa," Judy Grable.

Judy Grable was born Nellya Baughman on August 21, 1935. It was Moolah who renamed her Grable, after the beautiful 1940s film star and pinup girl. With blonde hair and legs as lovely as her namesake's (Betty Grable's legs were once insured for $1 million as a publicity stunt), Judy Grable became one of wrestling's top stars of the 1950s and 1960s.

The youngest of six children, she grew up in Tennessee and then moved to Florida. A tomboy who enjoyed the outdoors and sports, she eventually found work as an acrobat with Ringling Bros. Circus.

"Every day after school, I would hurry over to the grounds and watch the [circus] performers going through their routines," she said in a 1964 newspaper interview. "It wasn't too long before the group sort of adopted me. Those circus performers are wonderful people. You have to be close to them and learn just how wonderful they are."

She decided to leave the circus after a scary incident where she fell off a high wire. Wrestling proved to be a career where she could utilize her balance and athleticism and still perform in front of a live audience. "After all, in wrestling you have something to grab hold of, unlike a high wire act," she said.

She moved to Columbia and trained under Moolah and Buddy Lee, making

*"The Barefoot Contessa" Judy Grable.*
JACK PFEFER COLLECTION/UNIVERSITY OF NOTRE DAME

her wrestling debut in 1953 as Peaches Grable, before changing her name to Judy Grable. She was a curvy 5'6" and 137 pounds, with piercing blue eyes and an easy smile. She chose to wrestle barefoot, which added to her sex-symbol mystique.

That appeal wasn't lost on the media, either.

"In addition to possessing natural beauty, some wrestlers like Judy Grable and Dottie Carter are as curvaceous as old Route 40 between Cumberland and Hancock," wrote columnist J. Suter Kegg in the *Cumberland (Maryland) Evening Times*. "In as much as they do an excellent job of 'filling' their skirts and blouses, these gal grapplers are frequent targets of second glances from the men folk when they walk along the street or appear in public."

In 1958, Grable appeared on the TV game show *What's My Line?*, where a panel of celebrities tried to guess her occupation. Her blonde hair and pretty face got the celebrity panelists flummoxed, particularly after Grable admitted that her profession involved "touching other people" ("For how much?" panelist Groucho Marx quipped).

Fellow panelist Dorothy Kilgallen had a memorable Freudian slip, asking "Would you say that you deal with more sex — *more with one sex* [than the other]?"

"You think I'm the only one obsessed with that subject, huh?" Marx responded.

Grable was known for her high dropkick and "the kangaroo flip," which she developed. Considered by some the female Antonino Rocca, Grable proved to be a perfect babyface opponent for Moolah, and the two of them had a lengthy in-ring rivalry. Indeed, Grable and Moolah were the final two participants in the battle royal to crown a new NWA women's champion in 1956, with Moolah pinning Grable to start her epic title run.

"[Grable] was a shy, naïve girl out of the ring. But inside the ring, she had some talent," Moolah wrote in her autobiography. "They called her the 'acrobatic blonde with the educated flying feet.' They called me a lot worse than that, never mind that I'd taught Judy a lot of those flying moves."

Grable had two runs as NWA Southern women's champion (Georgia version), from 1958 to 1959 and 1961 to 1963. But her high-flying wrestling style took a toll on her physically. She broke both ankles and dislocated several vertebrae during her career, and she made the damage worse by wrestling through the pain, including wrestling on a broken ankle for several months.

Grable went into semi-retirement in 1966 and married and settled down near Seattle. She wrestled sporadically up into the early 1970s, including a brief stint in the Super Star Wrestling promotion in Spokane in 1974. She went back to school, graduated in 1978, and became a certified nursing assistant in a veteran's home.

When her daughter, Debbie, looked to get into wrestling, Grable adamantly opposed it. Debbie eventually tried wrestling years later, after her mother had passed away.

Grable died on May 11, 2008, at the age of 72. She had been in ill health for several months, living with diabetes and the early stages of Alzheimer's disease. She was posthumously inducted into the Pro Wrestling Hall of Fame in 2011.

## Princess Little Cloud

Dixie Jordan's wrestling career lasted only six years, but as Princess Little Cloud, she proved to be one of the most memorable female performers of the 1960s.

Jordan was born on November 11, 1946, in Falling Waters, West Virginia, and grew up in the small town of Williamsport, Maryland. She had Native American roots; her father was San Carlos Apache and her mother was Cherokee.

A conscientious student and athlete (excelling in basketball and track), Jordan was the undergraduate valedictorian for her 11th grade high school class. But instead of going on to senior year, and perhaps college, she left school to become a pro wrestler.

"I grew up in a small town in Maryland and there weren't a lot of opportunities," she said in a 2013 interview on the radio show *Rasslin' Memories*. "I was a very physical person, very strong and active. There weren't a lot of sports activities available for girls, and I knew that's what I wanted to do. I was leafing through a wrestling magazine in a doctor's office one day and I saw an ad saying 'Come Be a Professional Wrestler,' which was an ad for a new wrestling school being run by a woman named Slave Girl Moolah. So I wrote to her, and I went to South Carolina and never looked back."

Moolah called her personally and invited her to move onto Moolah's estate to train. "Moolah was really looking toward building a career for herself in promotion, so she bought two houses," Jordan said. "I lived in the house next door to her. The backyard consisted of a garage where we trained and a cage that contained her wrestling bear that she and Buddy [Lee] got from the circus. We worked out on mats in the back."

*Princess Little Cloud had real Native American roots.*
CHRIS SWISHER COLLECTION

Moolah gave her the name Princess Little Cloud, playing up Jordan's American Indian heritage. She made her wrestling debut in 1963 at the age of 16. Young and athletic, Little Cloud was a colorful character, wearing an ornate Native American headdress, moccasins, and fringed ring gear that made her look as if she had walked right in from the set of *Gunsmoke*. Little Cloud was a major draw in the American Wrestling Association and throughout the Midwest. She also proved to be a popular draw on international tours, including tours of Australia, Japan, Puerto Rico, South America, and Central America.

Aside from Moolah, she had some run-ins with some promoters along the way, including Tennessee promoter Nick Gulas.

"There were some really truly ex-circus folk who became [wrestling] promoters. One of them was Nick Gulas," she said on *Rasslin' Memories*. "As weird as he was, his desire was to have a circus-like atmosphere around wrestling. He would make up names for the girls. So if we went into a territory, he might change our names and make it something more risqué, more stripper-like. When I encountered him in 1964 for the first time, he had given me this name, something like

'Luscious Beauty.' And I told him I would kick him in the balls if he ever said that to me again and that I wasn't going to go on the card that night unless they corrected my name."

She retired from wrestling in 1970 and married wrestler and wrestling trainer Eddie Sharkey. Her departure from wrestling was hastened somewhat by a falling out with Moolah after Jordan negotiated her own contract for a tour of Australia, infuriating Moolah, who had been handling all of her bookings. Despite that flare-up, Jordan said she still had the utmost respect and admiration for Moolah. After almost seven years of living out of a suitcase, Jordan was ready to hang up the boots.

She occasionally assisted Sharkey in training young wrestlers (particularly the women) but mostly vanished from the wrestling scene, wrestling rare spot shows here and there in the early 1970s.

"The only really notable rivalries I had were with Bette Boucher and Toni Rose, and a very old hand named Johnnie Mae Young — who in my estimation was the toughest woman in the business by far, and the strongest."

In an interview with Mike Mooneyham, Bette Boucher named Princess Little Cloud as her all-time favorite opponent. "We executed so well together. It was a pleasure working with her. We'd have the crowds crazy," Boucher said.

After she ended her wrestling career, Jordan became a professional advocate, representing children with disabilities and advocating mental health services. In 2005, she received the Outstanding Advocacy Award from the Midwest Symposium for Leadership in Behavior Disorders, in recognition of her contributions on behalf of troubled children and their families. She has written several articles and training curricula related to special education law, services, and outreach to diverse families. She also does public speaking.

### Vivian Vachon

Although she was born in Newport, Vermont, Vivian Vachon (whose real name was Diane) didn't grow up in the United States. She was born on January 23, 1951, at a hospital five minutes away from the

*Mad Dog and Butcher's sister, Vivian Vachon.*
PAT LAPRADE COLLECTION

Canadian border, and she spent her childhood in the Eastern Townships of Quebec, where the Vachon family lived. "She's the only one in the family who wasn't born at home," says her brother Paul.

She started her career when she was still a teenager, in the late 1960s. Her brothers Paul and Maurice didn't want her to wrestle, but Vivian was determined to succeed. Maurice sent her to train with the Fabulous Moolah, and her career started from there.

It was actually Maurice who found the ring name for his sister. "Marilyn Monroe was very popular during her days. Her initials were M.M. Maurice wanted to find something similar for his sister. So he came up with Vivian Vachon, so that the initials were identical, like those of Marilyn," says Paul.

In the 1970s Vachon wrestled in the United States, Japan, Australia, and, of course, Canada. On February 26, 1971, she won the California women's title, and on November 4 of the same year she won the AWA championship. At the time she was considered one of the best female wrestlers in the world; the public dubbed her "the Queen of Wrestling."

An article published in *The Wrestler* magazine in December 1972 debated who could wrestle the world women's title away from the Fabulous Moolah, saying: "Vivian Vachon, of course, is the most likely. A dynamic wrestler, Vivian has the size, speed, and savvy needed for the rigorous schedule the women's champion must follow. She can be brutal when necessary yet is a master of scientific wrestling. Her best facet, however, is that she seems to have no flaws at all. In fact, if anybody upsets Moolah for the championship, it's likely to be Vivian Vachon."

According to the newspapers and magazines published at the time, Vivian was more popular in the United States than in her own province. "Vivian was very strong and wrestled like a man," her niece Luna remembers. During those years she wrestled in small towns, but not in Montreal, where women's wrestling wasn't accepted by the Athletic Commission until the mid-1980s.

In spite of her popularity, Vivian was famous as one of the best heels in the business. She performed in the movie *Wrestling Queen* in 1975, after having retired one year earlier. "I wanted to have a family," Vivian explained in an interview in 1986 — the year she returned to the ring for her brother Mad Dog's retirement tour, wrestling mainly against The Lock and Candi Divine.

The 1980s also saw her return to Japan. Unfortunately on August 24, 1991, she and her daughter were killed in a car accident. "The accident occurred in Mont-Saint-Grégoire. Vivian was about to turn on road 104 on her way to Mansonville when she got hit by a drunk driver. He was going twice the speed limit," remembers journalist Ghislain Plourde, who was at the scene. Vivian had retired again from wrestling in 1987 and was 40 at the time of the tragic accident.

## Donna Christantello

Donna Christantello was working as a waitress in her hometown of Pittsburgh, Pennsylvania, but the lure of fame, fortune, and travel to faraway places enticed her to leave the steel city behind and start a new beginning in Columbia, South Carolina.

Born Mary Alfonsi on May 23, 1942, she was a wrestling fan since childhood and would attend events to cheer on Bruno Sammartino and jeer Buddy Rogers. When she saw her first women's match on TV, she was determined to give it a try herself. She and a friend began training locally; the friend gave it up after her first match. Alfonsi wanted to continue, and Waldo Von Erich and Klondike Bill recommended she look up Moolah.

In 1963, she moved to Moolah's home to train; she would remain there for the next 35 years. She began wrestling as Donna Christantello (although her surname was spelled a variety of different ways in different territories, including Christianello, Christian, Christenello, and Christanello). She also wrestled under the name Princess White Cloud for a time, passing off her Italian ancestry as Native American ancestry.

Christantello had a natural aptitude for wrestling and a conscientious work ethic. She eventually became one of Moolah's top trainers and went on to train many of Moolah's students, including "Sensational" Sherri Martel. She was widely considered to be Moolah's right hand, overseeing the school while Moolah was away.

Christantello was one of Moolah's top students and earned bookings all over the world, including tours of Australia, Japan, and Hawaii and all over the continental United States and Canada.

She formed a tag team with Toni Rose, and the pair was named NWA women's tag team champions in November 1970. Christantello and Rose kept those belts through most of the decade; they lost the belts to Joyce Grable and Vicki Williams in 1973, regained them in 1975, and held them until losing them back to Grable and Williams in 1979, when Rose retired.

"The girl had done so much for Moolah. She always took a backseat to everybody. She was Lil's right-hand person. When Vince Sr. decided he wanted tag team champions, he chose Donna and Toni Rose," said Mae Young during Donna's introduction speech at the PWHF in 2009.

After being a regular for the WWF until 1984, her last major appearance came at the age of 45 at the 1987 Survivor Series, when she teamed with the Glamour Girls, Martel, and Dawn Marie to face the Jumping Bomb Angels, Velvet McIntyre, Rockin' Robin, and Moolah. Christantello was the first participant eliminated as she got pinned by McIntyre after a victory roll.

She continued wrestling sporadically until retiring in 1991. In 1999, she left Moolah's estate and returned to Pittsburgh, finding work in the accounting department of a local Walmart. She was inducted into the Pro Wrestling Hall of Fame in 2009.

"This is one of the greatest things to happen in my career in wrestling. I would do it all over again," said Christantello during her acceptance speech.

*Pittsburgh's own, Donna Christantello.*
JACK PFEFER COLLECTION/UNIVERSITY OF NOTRE DAME

Unfortunately, she died not too long after, on August 23, 2011, at the age of 69, due to chronic obstructive pulmonary disease.

"Donna was like a second mother to me and most of the girls," Princess Victoria posted in a memorial on LadySports Online. "If you had a problem, you talked to her. If you were sick, she came to take care of you. If you were stuck on a move, she was the most likely person to walk you through it and figure it out. She was my roomie for two years or better, and there is a hole in my heart that will not be filled."

### Joyce Grable

Much like Dino Bravo and Gorgeous George, two women wrestled under the name Joyce Grable. The first was Barbara Nichols (who also wrestled as Joyce Fowler and Joyce Becker, and was married to wrestler George Becker), who wrestled from 1963 to 1974. She was an early advocate of lifting the ban on women's wrestling in New York State and Ontario.

The second, and more widely known, was Betty Wade-Murphy, who adopted the name as a tribute to her trainer and childhood hero, Judy Grable, as well as for her resemblance to the original Joyce Grable.

A native of LaGrange, Georgia, Wade graduated from Moolah's school and started wrestling in 1971. To hear her say it, Moolah picked her out of obscurity after one of her friends pulled Moolah aside and inquired about taking up the grappling arts.

"Moolah saw me sitting at ringside and she said, 'That's a pretty blonde-headed girl there. Do you want to be a wrestler?'" she said as she was being inducted into the Pro Wrestling Hall of Fame in 2013. "I weighed 120 pounds. I didn't wrestle. She said, 'Bring her with you, and I'll train the both of y'all.' I stayed there with her for almost 15 years."

She became one of the trainers at Moolah's school in the 1970s and helped train, among others, Sherri Martel and Wendi Richter. She and Richter would go on to form a championship tag team, winning the NWA tag team title on two occasions. She also held the NWA tag title with Vickie Williams twice, the NWA U.S. title, and the NWA Texas title. Grable was cut from the classic cloth — she didn't fly around the ring much, preferring to work holds and overpower opponents with body slams, and in 1973, her hard work paid off as she was named Girl Wrestler of the Year by *Sports Review Wrestling*.

Life on the road had been exciting when she was a young girl, but the appeal wore off quickly, even if the tour was meticulously planned.

"We tried to avoid crisscrossing the country," she said in a 2009 interview on the Cauliflower Alley Club website. "A typical tour would start out in New York, and from there we'd go to Minneapolis, Calgary, California, Texas, into Louisiana for Bill Watts, Alabama, and then home. It could be tough, because you couldn't have a dog, or keep any plants, because they'd turn brown! For everything you got, you had to give up something."

In addition to the domestic tours, she also wrestled internationally, competing in Canada, Japan (her appendix was removed while on tour in Tokyo), Mexico, New Zealand, and San Salvador.

In November 1980, she teamed with Judy Martin to face Steve O and Jerry Roberts (Jacques Rougeau Jr.) in a heavily promoted "battle of the sexes" tag team match at the

*Joyce Grable helped the careers of many women who followed her.* CHRIS SWISHER COLLECTION

Omni Arena in Atlanta. The male squad won that match, but Grable and Martin won considerable respect for taking on male opponents.

She wrestled through the 1970s and into the 1980s before taking time off to start a family. "I thought, 'I'm getting older, I want a baby.' I decided that I'd better quit, especially if I was going to have a baby. I shouldn't be out there taking bumps." She officially retired in 1991.

Grable earned a reputation for her willingness to go the extra mile for storylines. "What I really liked was if they asked me to do something that was new and different. My thought was 'let me try one time,'" she said. She wrestled a match where both women were blindfolded.

She worked "boxing matches" wearing gloves. She did an angle in Tennessee where she was packed inside a box as Boris Malenko agreed to wrestle whoever — or whatever — was inside the box (an angle World Championship Wrestling recycled years later when Madusa Miceli was put inside a mystery box presented to Sting; Kevin Sullivan was the brains behind both angles).

In 2013, Grable was diagnosed with cancer but beat it with the help of a bone marrow transplant using stem cells donated by her sister. That same year, she was inducted into the PWHF by her former tag team partner Wendi Richter.

"I have to say that I feel that she's one of the greatest professional wrestlers, man or woman, of all times," Richter said at that event. "She helped train me as well as a hundred other ladies — without compensation. When we went on the road, most of our first tours were with Joyce Grable. I learned so much from that, and I am so grateful that I was able to have that experience and learn from this. We all paid our money to be trained, and they gave us Joyce Grable."

## Bette Boucher

Even though Moolah billed herself as the women's champion for 28 years, she had put some of her girls over for the title on four occasions, something she — and the WWF, for that matter — would never admit in interviews later in life. The first time was on September 17, 1966, when Bette Boucher scored the biggest win of her career, defeating her mentor Moolah to win the NWA women's title in Seattle, Washington. Boucher's reign was brief as she dropped the belt back to Moolah just 13 days later. Moolah most probably put Boucher over because she was her sister-in-law at the time and Moolah knew she would return the favor. Nevertheless, for Boucher, it was a validation of her career and her abilities.

"It was the highlight of my career," she said. "I loved wrestling for wrestling. But that title was the thing."

At barely 5 feet tall and 110 pounds soaking wet, the skeptics said Barbara Boucher was too small to be a wrestler, let alone the champion.

When she showed up at Moolah's training school, Buddy Lee gave her the once-over and urged Moolah to put her on the first bus back to her hometown of Webster, Massachusetts. But Boucher's passion and natural athleticism won Moolah over, and eventually Bouncing Bette became one of her top pupils . . . and a world champion.

She was born on July 29, 1943, and grew up one of seven children. As a girl, she excelled in softball and track. She discovered wrestling on television at the age of 10 and took an immediate

*Bette Boucher, one the few women to win the NWA women's title.* CHRIS SWISHER COLLECTION

liking to the sport. "I'm going to be like them one day," she recalled telling her parents on more than one occasion in a 2006 interview with Mike Mooneyham. Although her parents didn't realize it at the time, Barbara was dead serious.

"I knew there was good money in it, and the traveling was very enticing. I wanted to get out and go. I wanted to see things and do things. All that appealed to me," she said.

She attended wrestling shows in nearby Worcester, Massachusetts, and eventually befriended wrestler Pat Patterson. Like Patterson, Boucher had French-Canadian roots. She begged Patterson to tell her how to join wrestling's secret society and get in on the action.

When Patterson determined that she was serious, he made arrangements for her to meet with the Fabulous Moolah following a card in Worcester. Moolah accepted Boucher as a student, and in 1962, she caught a bus to South Carolina to train at Moolah's school.

Boucher trained for about six months and eventually took on the role of a trainer herself. Moolah changed her first name from the common *Barbara* to the exotically French *Bette*, and Boucher was on her way. She made her pro debut for promoter Jim Crockett in North Carolina in 1963.

Boucher adopted a ring style that included gymnastics and aerial attacks — a stick-and-move strategy that was necessary against larger and stronger opponents. In an era before terms like *workrate* were part of the common parlance, Boucher was a wrestler's wrestler, a fleet-footed athlete who worked twice as hard to prove she wasn't too small for her chosen craft.

Boucher completed tours of Australia and Japan and stints in the NWA, the AWA, and Vince McMahon's fledgling WWWF in New York.

"The women had to stick together because there simply weren't that many of us," she said. "We were all fighting to strive and survive because we were up against male domination. We had to band together and let it be known that this was our profession, too, and we loved it. We just wanted to do our thing."

Her younger sister, Shirley, took up wrestling and briefly competed as Rita Boucher, and the Boucher sisters became a popular tag team act. Rita retired after just a couple years, and by 1970, Barbara was ready to retire, too.

She married and settled down in Columbia, South Carolina, where she worked at a Lowe's department store for several years.

## Susan "Tex" Green

Susan Green was 15 years old when she had her first professional match . . . and she required a note from the governor to make it happen.

A wrestling fan since she was old enough to talk, Green regularly attended the matches promoted by Joe Blanchard near her home in Corpus Christi, Texas. By the time she was 10 or so, she had made up her mind that she wanted to give wrestling a try. The youngest of five children, sports had appealed to her, but there were few opportunities in professional sports for women, whereas wrestling could allow her to travel the world. She regularly begged Blanchard to train her for the ring. After years of pleading, Blanchard agreed to train her, but first she needed to get a wrestling license.

Green's parents met with Texas governor John B. Connally and lobbied to have him personally approve her application for a wrestling license. "He had to interview my parents and me to make sure I wasn't being forced into child labor," she said in a 2006 interview with Jamie Kreiser of SLAM! Wrestling. "They assured him that whatever money I made was going to be my money to do whatever I wanted to with. And I would only be wrestling during holidays and weekends, I would not be doing this through the school weeks."

Her request was approved and Green started her new career, wrestling her first match in 1969 on her 15th birthday. She wrestled throughout Texas and into Mexico on weekends and school holidays, and she participated in swimming (she competed in the Junior Olympics and had aspired to compete in the 1972 Olympics) and tennis during the week. She grew to a height of six feet tall, which made her appear older than her true age; few fans realized they were watching a high school student in the ring.

When she graduated from high school, she went on to college on a swimming scholarship but decided wrestling was more to her liking. She left school and moved to South Carolina to work for the Fabulous Moolah. Green was both athletically gifted and a strong study and quickly became one of Moolah's top girls, receiving bookings throughout the United States and making international tours of Hong Kong and Vietnam. Her signature spots included leaping over the top rope into the ring and her trademark Texas bulldog finisher.

Green was part of Moolah's stable through the 1970s. During that time, she won the NWA women's tag title with Sandy Parker in 1971 and became the NWA women's champion, defeating Moolah for the

*Susan Green won the NWA title in her home state of Texas.* CHRIS SWISHER COLLECTION

title on February 2, 1976, in Houston.

"Beating Moolah was one of my favorite moments, one of my highlights," she told Kreiser. That win in 1976 allowed her to be voted Girl Wrestler of the Year by the readers of *Sports Review Wrestling*.

"Susan spent a lot of time with me in the ring and had to take me on the road as a new student. I know it was not easy for her," Leilani Kai recalled. "But I learned fast and she kept it simple with me and never lost her cool, struggling with me as a new student in front of the fans. She is a good trainer and a good friend. I give her and Ann Casey a lot of credit for my start in the pro wrestling circuit."

In addition to performing and helping rookies learn the ropes, Green and other female wrestlers had to put up with a different set of standards than their male counterparts, and from Moolah herself.

"I made money, I cannot argue with Moolah," she told Kreiser. "Yes, I paid her a lot but I made money. I have a home in Texas that is paid for. I've got this home out here in South Carolina. I was able to buy what I wanted and spend what I wanted when I was on the road wrestling with her. The 10 years I was with her I had a new car every two years. Would I have liked to have the money I paid her? Yeah. Was it fair that I was taking all the bruises and getting the concussions and she got as much as she got? Was it right that promoters didn't always give the females the same treatment they gave the guys? If you didn't work, you didn't get paid but if the guys got hurt — whether it be a car wreck or in the ring — they would pay them a weekly salary, not what they would have made if they wrestled, but they got something. Where the females, if we didn't climb through those ropes, we got nothing."

In August 1979, she was involved in a catastrophic boating accident. The boat slammed into a dock, and Green broke her back and neck; her skull was fractured in 13 places. The doctors said her wrestling career was over. They were wrong. She was back in the ring just two years later.

She continued to wrestle periodically throughout the 1980s and into the 1990s. When the Professional Girl Wrestling Association launched in 1992, she became one of the company's top stars and was recognized as the first PGWA champion. Although age and injuries took their inevitable toll, she continued wrestling into the 2000s. She was honored by the Cauliflower Alley Club in 2004 and inducted into the NWA Hall of Fame in 2011.

## The INDEPENDENT WOMEN

At that point in time, the Fabulous Moolah was the premier power broker of women's wrestling, but some women decided they didn't want to partner with her and hand over a percentage of their booking fees. These women relied on networking with promoters and fellow wrestlers and made their way by booking themselves, proving they could enjoy a long career nevertheless.

### Evelyn Stevens

The highlight of Evelyn Stevens's wrestling career was on October 8, 1978, when she scored an upset win over the Fabulous Moolah and won the NWA women's wrestling title in Dallas. The low point

— both in her career and in her life — was in December 1986, when she got arrested and convicted of killing her live-in boyfriend after shooting him in a lover's spat.

A pretty girl with blonde hair and a statuesque body, Stevens played up her sex appeal in and out of the ring. In the prevailing spirit of the kayfabe era, Stevens reportedly wrote an article in the magazine *The Wrestler*, in actuality penned by a staff writer, provocatively titled "Sex and the Girl Wrestler." The fanciful piece proclaimed, "In this most outspoken article ever written by a girl wrestler, one of the sport's greatest and loveliest stars tells it exactly as it is." Accompanied by a photo of Stevens wearing a frilly white bikini and showing off her toned posterior, the text described the difficulties of dating and the creepy stares from some dirty old men at the arenas.

"What makes these old guys feel like boys again, I suppose, is the sight of two shapely young women dressed in scanty bathing suits clawing each other and being forced into rather suggestive positions," Stevens wrote. "Often times these positions can be downright embarrassing. But we can't help that. When your opponent catches you just right and pulls your legs apart there isn't much you can do about it. But you can never convince that old man in the first row of that. He has the idea, as he stares up at the ring with eyeballs popping, that the girls are trying to stir him up."

Although it reads like a precursor to the apartment wrestling approach *Sports Review Wrestling* would later adopt, the tone of the piece captures the prevailing attitude about women's wrestling of the era. The sexualized component was never far from the surface, something you could actually still see in recent years.

When Stevens wasn't lending her name to wrestling erotica pieces, she was one of the top female stars in Texas. Born in Tampa, she was raised in Nashville, Tennessee. She was a cheerleader and basketball player growing up. In newspaper interviews, she claimed she first picked up wrestling by roughhousing with her brother.

She made her wrestling debut at the age of 23 in 1963, a lightweight at 5'4" and barely 110 pounds. "They told me I was too light so I took the falls, body slams, and punishment. Then I came back for more and now I am doing well," she told the *El Paso Herald Post* in a 1968 interview.

Although she was with Moolah's stable in the 1960s, she passed most of her career as an independent. Wrestling primarily as a heel, she competed in Missouri, the Midwest, and the Great Plains before settling in Texas, where she won the women's title, thanks to Dallas booker Gary Hart.

"In October 1978 I had Moolah booked in a couple of matches against Evelyn Stevens, and I thought it would be fun to do a quickie title switch," said Hart in his book. "There

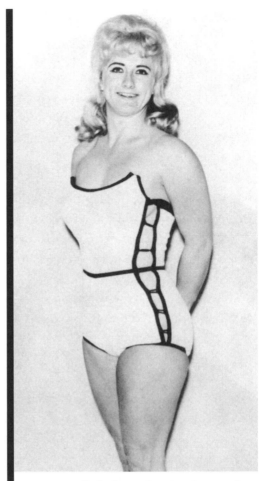

*Evelyn Stevens, from champion to murderer.*
CHRIS SWISHER COLLECTION

were a couple of problems with that, however. First of all, Moolah first won the belt in 1956, and she didn't like losing it. Second, Evelyn wasn't one of Moolah's girls — she was considered an independent. It was rare enough that Moolah was getting in the ring with someone she didn't control, and now I was asking her to drop her belt to that person! Moolah had a lot of trust in me, though, so when I asked her if we could do a title switch, she agreed."

Stevens's reign as NWA women's champion lasted only two days before Moolah regained the belt in Fort Worth. Still, Stevens is one of just a handful of women who can boast of having a pinfall win over Moolah, especially for a title.

She married and divorced wrester Don "The Spoiler" Jardine and kept his surname following the divorce. She dabbled in acting and stunt work in the 1970s. In the early 1980s, she began dating Frank Riegle, a fitness club owner in San Antonio and a former powerlifting champion. The two lived together for almost two years before the tragedy occurred.

In December 1986, Jardine allegedly shot her boyfriend three times at point blank range during an argument. Police found a hand-written confession, and she subsequently pleaded guilty to murder.

"May God in Heaven forgive me for what I have done," the letter stated. "I have reached out to everyone for help. I love [Frank] enough for us to die together."

It was a sad end for a woman who — if only for two short days — had been on top of the women's scene.

## Kay Noble

"To this day at the Funkin' Conservatory Wrestling School, we are still teaching techniques invented by Kay Noble."

Dory Funk Jr. made that remark in a 2010 interview with the *Miami Herald*, four years after Noble's death from inoperable stomach cancer. With her legendary toughness, her agility (she was one of the first female wrestlers to execute a nip-up), and her creativity in the ring, Noble was one of the most universally respected female wrestlers of her era.

Born October 15, 1940, in St. Joseph, Missouri, Mary Charlene "Kay" Noble was determined to become a pro wrestler by age 15. However, the local promoter, Gust Karras, wasn't interested in taking a gamble on a 15-year-old girl (even though she already stood an impressive 5'7" tall), and she had to wait until she turned 18 before Karras had her begin training with Sonny Myers and Laura Martinez. She had her first match in 1957, losing to Rose Roman in Leavenworth, Kansas. She was paid $25 in crisp five-dollar bills for the bout.

One year later, she was already making headlines when she, Martinez, Lorraine Johnson, and Penny Banner were arrested and charged with inciting a riot during a tag team match in Amarillo, Texas. Knowing that kind of publicity could spur ticket sales for the inevitable rematch, the promoters happily paid the fine.

She wrestled throughout the Southwest for the first few years of her career, often competing in mixed tag team matches, which became one of her specialties. "I remember in Amarillo a mixed tag team match with my brother, Terry Funk, and Betty Nicoli vs. Kay Noble and Sir Nelson Royal. In a four-way mix-up, Kay Noble caught Terry by surprise with a back bodydrop," Funk told the *Herald*.

*One of the Kansas City girls, Kay Noble.*
CHRIS SWISHER COLLECTION

Wrestler Tom Andrews told SLAM! Wrestling about a time when Noble came to his rescue and saved him from a beating from angry fans. He was hobbled by a broken leg at the time. "I was out there at ringside like a manager [for Ox Baker] and . . . we really got the heat going. Ox jumped out of the ring and took off. I had these people swarming me, and of course, I'm on crutches. Kay Noble came out and saved me. I'm not kidding you. She came out. . . . I was swinging punches just like her. Boy, she led me back to the dressing room, just knocking guys on their butts."

In the 1960s, she competed primarily in the Minneapolis area for promoter Verne Gagne. She frequently wrestled mixed tag team matches, teaming with her husband Doug Gilbert (Doug Lindzy), whom she married in 1959.

"Perhaps her most famous program was a battle of husband and wives as a gimmick where she and Gilbert in the early '60s would face Roy "Ripper" Collins and then-wife Barbara Baker," remembered Dave Meltzer.

She defeated Kathy Starr to win the vacant AWA women's title and was recognized as AWA women's champion for six and a half years. She was named Girl Wrestler of the Year for 1971 by the Wrestling Fans International Association. She also won the NWA Texas women's title twice and the NWA Central States women's title for promoter Bob Geigel; she also worked as a bartender at Geigel's bar at the time.

"She was the leader of a troupe of Central States and Midwest women's wrestlers, who usually didn't wrestle against Fabulous Moolah's South Carolina based troupe, although there were exceptions and they were not considered warring camps," said Meltzer.

Noble competed in Japan and throughout Canada and had a series of memorable bouts against Vivian Vachon. She also trained Ed Wiskoski, who went on to wrestle as Col. DeBeers.

"She didn't want to go to Moolah or work with Moolah," said Wiskoski. "She had a good enough name at that time that she could call up and get herself booked. She's the best woman worker I've ever seen and I have a great respect for her."

Noble was known as a wisecracker. Donna Lemke remembers a funny story involving a referee. "We were in Louisiana and the referee wore a toupee. And he always told the guys, leave it alone, nobody touches the toupee. Well, that's all she had to hear. There were four girls in a tag team match and she told Sandy Parker and the two of them pulled the toupee off the ref's head. I was laughing so hard, standing like this with my legs crossed, afraid I was going to pee my pants. And they're kicking this thing across the ring and hitting it and throwing it around, and the poor referee is so red, and he's lying there on the mat trying to cover up his head. That's the kind of stuff Kay would do."

Noble split her time between wrestling and raising children. She continued wrestling periodically all the way up until 1987, when she wrestled her final match against Marie Laverne and announced her retirement at the age of 46. After leaving wrestling, she went into the pest control business and, later, into the upholstery business. Noble passed away on April, 27, 2006, and was posthumously inducted into the Pro Wrestling Hall of Fame in 2010.

## Betty Nicoli

At barely 5'1" tall, a lot of people thought Betty Jo Nicoli was too small to be a wrestler. But, as she never tired of reminding people, "dynamite comes in small packages."

Born in 1946 in Kansas City, she saw her first wrestling match at the age of 12 in St. Joseph, Missouri, where promoter Gust Karras told her she might make a good wrestler someday. That's all Nicoli needed to hear. She began training at the age of 18, learning the ropes from Jessica Rogers and midget wrestler Lord Littlebrook. Littlebrook proved to be a major influence.

"He trained me more than anybody," Nicoli said in a 2006 interview with SLAM! Wrestling. "He had ring psychology. He made a statement to me one day. He goes, 'Betty, you're a short girl. Let's face facts. Unless you get in there and kick ass and make a name for yourself, you're just going to be known as a loser.' So he basically told me that if I wasn't going to get in there and fight like a pitbull, I might as well get out of wrestling."

Nicoli made her pro debut in 1963, competing in a battle royal in Sedalia, Missouri. She and Jean Antone, a good, fiery babyface trained by Ella Waldek and coming from Laurel, Missouri, wrestled a lot together as the two of them were booked through Bob Geigel's office. "One time, one of the wrestlers said, 'If I didn't know any better, I'd think ya'll were married.' We were in the ring together so much," Nicoli said. "It just happened to work out that way because we worked, basically, out of the same office. Promoters in other areas would ask specifically for us." They were such fixtures in Kansas City

*Former AWA and NWA U.S. women's champion, Betty Nicoli.* WRESTLING REVUE ARCHIVES/WWW.WRESTLINGREVUE.COM

and wrestled each other so many times that they could almost read each other's minds in the ring. "They worked for us, and we made sure they stayed booked," said Geigel. "They worked here, they worked for Verne in Minneapolis, Verne and Karbo, they worked in Tulsa, they worked for Joe Dusek out of Omaha, Max Clayton when he was there." Nicoli vs. Antone is believed to be one of the biggest pairings in wrestling's history.

Nicoli also frequently worked with Kay Noble, both as tag team partners and opponents. She defeated Noble for the AWA women's title on November 9, 1969, and was named NWA U.S. women's champion in 1970, although she vacated that title later that year. She lost the AWA women's title to Vivian Vachon in November 1971 but regained the title in August 1973, holding it until the AWA deactivated the title in 1975. In 1974, she toured Japan, winning the WWWA tag team title with Sandy Parker four times in a six-week span. Nicoli married wrestler Akio Sato (Sato from WWF's Orient Express) and retired from the ring in 1976 to start a family. "I walked away from wrestling practically unscathed," Nicoli said. "I had broken fingers, I can't count how many concussions, broken nose. Moolah busted my nose. I had to have it rebuilt. I figured I was one of the lucky ones. I got out and had everything intact." She was honored by the Cauliflower Alley Club in 2007 and inducted into the Professional Wrestling Hall of Fame in 2008.

Geigel was an important part of her career. "I really look up to Bob. He took care of me when I first started wrestling. He just made it clear, him and Gust, be professional and don't be ridiculous. He made sure I got booked, got good bookings. If I had a problem with any of the other promoters, money-wise, he always stepped in. He just took care of his people. He was a good promoter, he was an excellent wrestler. You couldn't ask for a better man to be in your life."

## Beverly Shade

A wrestling fan since childhood, Beverly Shade, born March 21, 1936, remembers the first time she discovered women's wrestling.

"I had been a wrestling fan ever since TV came out. As kids, we would sit around and watch wrestling every Saturday night," Shade said. "One Saturday, they had women wrestlers on. I had never seen women wrestlers before. I turned to my girlfriend and said, 'Hell, I can do that!'"

A self-professed tomboy, Shade played baseball and basketball growing up, and wrestling appealed to her. She was living in Alton, Illinois, and ventured across the Mississippi River to check out the wrestling scene in St. Louis, Missouri.

"I went up to St. Louis promoter and NWA president Sam Muchnick and told him I wanted to wrestle. He told me I was crazy. But I pestered the hell out him," she said. Muchnick eventually introduced her to June Byers, who also tried to dissuade Shade from getting into wrestling. When it was made clear that Shade wasn't going to be talked down until she at least gave it a shot, Muchnick had her get some promotional photos taken. He would get back to her about training.

"He was going to send me to Billy Wolfe's school in Ohio, but then about two and a half weeks later, he called and said he wanted me to go to see Cowboy Luttrell in Tampa, Florida."

Shade reported to Tampa and had her first match wrestling in a

*"The Hammer" Beverly Shade.* GREG OLIVER COLLECTION

five-women pinfall elimination battle royal in Lakeland, Florida, in 1957.

After the match, Cowboy Luttrell checked up on his new recruit. She was struggling to breathe. Her knees and elbows were skinned and bleeding. "Do you still want to learn to wrestle?" he asked. "I would have done it then or died," Shade said. Her training was under way. She wrestled as an independent, without joining up with Moolah's group of wrestlers, and competed primarily in Florida, Georgia, and Tennessee for promoter Nick Gulas. She married wrestler Billy Blue River (Bill Wenhold) and wrestled in several mixed tag team matches, teaming with her husband and wrestling under the name Beverly Blue River. When her husband began running a non-NWA-affiliated promotion in St. Petersburg, Florida (non-NWA promotions were known as outlaw promotions), she assisted in booking and running the company, in addition to wrestling.

In 1979, she was recruited by Moolah for a tour of Japan, and she worked with Moolah for a four-week tour of the Northeast in 1980. But she had no interest in signing on with Moolah for bookings.

"I told her, 'I couldn't work for you. I ain't giving you all my money,'" she said. "Moolah and I got along pretty well, but I was never obligated to her. She kept her girls so far in debt that they had to stay with her because they couldn't afford to get away."

In 1983, Shade began teaming with one of her trainees, Tracy Richards, as the Arm & Hammer Connection and adopted a move that would become her calling card, a double axe handle off the top rope she called "the hammer." The Hammer would become her nickname as well. She completed two tours of Trinidad, Thailand, Nigeria, and Puerto Rico for promoter Carlos Colon. Over the course of her career, she won the All-Star Wrestling women's title twice (in 1968 and 1985), the NWA women's tag team title, the Florida women's title, and the IWA women's tag team title.

Shade retired from wrestling in 1989 at the age of 52. After retiring, she took a job in customer service with a packaging and canning company. "I used to go out and meet with customers and get jumped on if the cans weren't right," she said. "I did that for about 10 years. It was just like wrestling. You got to know how to bullshit. That's what it all boils down to."

## Donna Lemke

A 1970s crowd favorite known for her hot, hip-shaking comebacks and fighting spirit, Donna Lemke was born Dawn Lemke on March 15, 1953, in Milwaukee, Wisconsin. She made her pro wrestling debut in March 1970.

"When I was a little kid, I would get up at 6 in the morning and watch wrestling," Lemke said. "I just loved it. Never in my mind did I think that I would be able to wrestle. You idolize these people. Then, once you're in the business, it's a whole different thing."

Lemke trained under Cesar Pabon in South Milwaukee and went on to wrestle for Verne Gagne's American Wrestling Association in Minnesota; she also competed in Oklahoma (for Bill Watts), Florida (for Eddie Graham), Texas (for the Funks), and Hawaii (for Sammy Steamboat). She was a popular, petite, and attractive babyface who was an expert at selling and making the hot comeback. In addition to learning how to wrestle, she quickly learned the importance of complying with the state athletic commissions' regulations regarding women's wrestling gear.

*Donna Lemke, during one of her hot, hip-shaking comebacks.* DONNA LEMKE COLLECTION

"We had special rules about tying our suits. We had to weave elastic in and wear rubber in here [at the hem]," she said. "What we used to do was take a safety pin with elastic and a little bitty hem and you'd have to weave it through so you'd have these long elastics and tie it so your butt wouldn't hang out. You couldn't have any butt cheek hanging out. And there were a lot of boxing and wrestling commissions that would check you before you went out."

Unlike so many girls, Lemke didn't work for Moolah's office, instead finding a mentor in Kay Noble. "She asked me if I was independent or if I worked for Moolah. I said no, I don't work for Moolah. And she asked if I would be interested in going on the road with her. She was 33 and I was 18. Kay took such good care of me. She took me under her wing. She smartened me up to a lot of things, both inside the ring and out of the ring."

She also dated Dusty Rhodes for six and a half years and the two became traveling companions. "We had a lot of fun on the road," she told the website Online World of Wrestling. "The car trips to the next match were always amusing."

With such signature moves as the flying dropkick and notable feuds with Vivian Vachon, Betty Nicoli, and Kay Noble, Lemke was exposed to the realm of professional wrestling as much as any women, or man for that matter.

"We took the lumps and the bumps. Unintentionally, we'd get hurt. I hurt my shoulder, I hurt my knee, I hurt my leg. We did the same as the men, but didn't make the money they did. But if they needed to boost the sales, the midgets and the women came in. We were gimmicks."

There often wasn't enough security to adequately protect the wrestlers, especially the female wrestlers who were subject to various forms of harassment from the fans.

"I got a big scar from a riot. We're down in Louisiana and I get word to stay in the ring and kick the crap out of Kay. It was supposed to help calm the crowd down. Finally some more police came. As we're walking out, a guy cuts me in the thigh and rips the back of my swimming suit. My butt was hanging out. They would grab your boobs, they would grab your butt. You really got manhandled."

## APARTMENT WRESTLING AND THE SEXUALIZATION OF WOMEN'S WRESTLING

Sex appeal has been an inherent part of women's wrestling since its earliest days as a novelty attraction on the carnival circuit. The erotic and sensual components were important when women (and men) showed their perfect body outlines. At times, that sex appeal has been subtle, and at times it has been overt.

Although Mildred Burke strove to be in ideal physical condition and worked to be perceived as an athlete first and foremost, she knew the universal truth: sex sells.

"Wrestling has always had strong sex appeal," she wrote. "Fantasies are lived out by fans through the various personages in wrestling. Right and wrong and good and evil meet in a primal struggle under the lights. Human beings are sexual beings — all of them. The wrestling game allows all manner of drives and frustration to be vented."

From Penny Banner's "scandalous" leopard-print bikini to Sable's body-painted bare breasts, the sexual component of women's wrestling has evolved with the times. Today's female wrestlers strive to be sexy but not sexual, to exude a certain sexiness without being crass. There is a greater emphasis on athleticism and workrate than ever before, but breast implants (or push-up bras), hair extensions, makeup, tanner, and a host of other cosmetic supplies are still essential commodities for most female wrestlers.

"We're catering to a male-dominated audience," Angelina Love said. "Of course you want to be a good wrestler. Of course you want to be respected for your talents and your passion. But, let's face it: with a male-dominated business, everybody wants to see how hot you are. Everybody wants to see really good-looking women in not a lot of clothing with their hair and makeup done. That's just the presentation of female wrestlers. That's something that's very important."

So important that the women at NXT now have makeup classes to learn how to do their makeup properly for HDTV. In reality, pro wrestling is no different from other sports in terms of beauty. Alex Morgan in soccer, Danica Patrick in car racing, and Eugenie Bouchard in tennis are all examples of women getting more attention because of their look.

"Looks [are] very important in how they [WWE] judge women, way more important than [they] should be," opined Meltzer on his radio show. But looks don't mean everything, he added. "Looks alone, whether it's a guy or a girl, if you got looks but no personality that gets over with the fans, looks don't mean shit. There are plenty of good-looking guys and good-looking women that got into pro wrestling that never connected with the fans."

*Like it or not, the sales were good with this kind of cover.* PRO WRESTLING ILLUSTRATED

In her book *She's a Knockout*, L.A. Jennings argued that "for many women, their popularity as an athlete is invariably tied to the presentation of their sexuality. Auto racer Danica Patrick received little public attention until famously posing for *Playboy* magazine in 2009. For women who participate in historically male sports, posing in bikinis for men's magazines is a way to reassure viewers that while they are competing in a male arena, they also fulfill the expectations of conventional femininity."

Although maintaining a sexpot look while traveling, training, and competing can be a daunting challenge, veteran wrestler Malia Hosaka says not every woman needs to fit the same cookie-cutter mold.

"There's a fan base for every body type there is. You don't have to be 5 feet tall, 36DD boobs, 24-inch waist, rolling around with no talent. Babyface, heel, giant, powerhouse, whatever your style. Even your big girls can still be sexy."

Professional wrestling distances itself from the catfights, "Foxy Boxing," and fetish wrestling markets, but the lines occasionally get a bit blurry. Sometimes the sex appeal becomes the driving force and the wrestling takes a back seat.

In 1973, magazine publisher Stanley Weston introduced the world to a new sort of women's "wrestling." Weston had founded *Boxing Illustrated/Wrestling News* in 1958 and had developed that brand into several boxing and wrestling magazines, including *The Ring*, *The Wrestler*, and *Inside Wrestling* (*Pro Wrestling Illustrated*, which would become the flagship wrestling magazine in the group, was introduced in 1979). Magazine sales were down, and Weston wanted to try something novel.

"Stanley Weston calls me in, opens up a package from Theo Ehret, our Los Angeles photographer, and says 'Look at this.' It's bikini-clad hot babes wrestling in an apartment," longtime wrestling journalist Bill Apter told Chris Jericho in a 2015 appearance on the *Talk Is Jericho* podcast. "'We're going to call this *apartment wrestling*. We're going to make a fortune out of this, and I don't care what the promoters say.'"

There was little competitive pretense to apartment wrestling. Models in suggestive wrestling poses were photographed in bikinis or lingerie, resulting in little difference between apartment wrestling and a *Playboy* pictorial. Weston ran a special on apartment wrestling in *Sports Review Wrestling*, to Apter's chagrin.

"I didn't express my feelings . . . that these salacious images did not belong in a wrestling magazine," Apter wrote in his book *Is Wrestling Fixed? I Didn't Know It Was Broken!* "Kids who were wrestling fans bought the magazine, so this seemed wrong to me."

Apartment wrestling had plenty of critics within the wrestling industry, including Vince McMahon Sr., who threatened to revoke the magazines' press access if the feature wasn't pulled. Apartment wrestling was essentially soft-core pornography tucked in the pages of a wrestling magazine. Several wrestlers hated having their photos and names in magazines that featured "that smut." But Weston wasn't about to back down, especially since sales of *Sports Review Wrestling* went through the roof.

In the kayfabe style of the era, storylines were invented to provide text to accompany the photos. Writer Dan Shockett took the lead, adopting the alter-identity of "Dave Moll," a millionaire apartment wrestling aficionado who ostensibly ran the underground wrestling league. A blonde model known as Cynara became one of apartment wrestling's most celebrated "competitors."

The apartment wrestling fad eventually ran its course by the early 1980s, disappearing from the pages of *Sports Review Wrestling*. However, back issues remain sought-after commodities among collectors even today. Although the apartment wrestlers were not pro wrestlers, they received more coverage in the magazine than legitimate female wrestlers, and apartment wrestling colored the perception of women in wrestling in the 1970s.

## THE STORY OF TITI PARIS AND THE LEGALIZATION OF WOMEN'S WRESTLING

Only one hundred years ago, women were not allowed to vote in the United States, and in 2016 a woman is a presidential nominee — but equal rights is still a battle fought by women today. It was only in 2007 that female tennis players received equal prize money in all four tennis majors and equal compensation continues to be an issue in sports. Although men's freestyle wrestling has been part of the Olympics since 1904 and is viewed as one of the oldest sports, women's freestyle wrestling was not considered an Olympic sport until 100 years later, in 2004.

In professional wrestling, many women have fought for equal rights, but perhaps none to the extent of Titi Paris. As late as the early 1970s, women were not allowed to wrestle in the state of New York. Several states banned women's wrestling in the first half of the 20th century, including California in 1944, Michigan in 1939, and Pennsylvania a decade later. Numerous reasons were given: it wasn't considered lady-like to wrestle; it wasn't a good thing for children to see; it was too violent for television; it was a disgrace to womanhood, being compared to illegal cockfights; it was dangerous for women, who, in addition to risking direct injury in the ring, may have been exposing themselves to an increased risk of breast cancer or other ailments caused by repetitive blows or falls, according to some medical theories of the time. A lot of times, the authority would just not elaborate on their decision, fearing retaliation. In a match between June Byers and Rose Evans in Verdun, Quebec, a Montreal suburb, the women not only had to wear sweatshirts and slacks to wrestle, but Verdun's mayor at the time was quoted as saying, "Such shows bring no honor to a city."

In 1951, a man sent a letter to his local newspaper's editor in Pittsburgh, explaining why women's wrestling should be banned: "If they don't have sense enough to stay out of the ring, there should be a law passed to make them stay out of the ring. It's bad enough to see two males groaning and grunting away the hours and pounds, let alone the weaker sex. After viewing one of those female set-tos, what man in his right mind will believe the little woman's too weak to tote ladders around or wash the kitchen ceilings?"

In his book *Whatever Happened to Gorgeous George?* Joe Jares talks about how hard it was for women to get recognition and acceptance: "Their toughest opponents have been the do-gooders, lawmakers and bureaucrats, such as the Michigan athletic commissioner who asked in 1963 'Would you like to see your sister wrestling?'"

With the Civil Rights Act of 1964, America was, slowly but surely, opening itself more and more. Bans began to be lifted, and by the end of the 1970s, women's wrestling was allowed in 47 states in the United States and almost everywhere in Canada. After all, the Civil Rights Act was all about eliminating discrimination, and ending the ban on women's wrestling was a clear-cut case. Or so it seemed.

Algerian-born wrestler Fathia Djaileb, better known by the name of Titi Paris, did not want to travel too far from her home in Brooklyn in order to work. From November 1971 to March 1972, she sent letters to pretty much anybody who could actually help her: the chairman of the New York State Athletic Commission, congressmen, congresswomen, the National Organization for Women, and state assemblymen. She knew she had a case when she was told by the athletic commission that, indeed, according to the Civil Rights Act, she should be able to get a New York State wrestling license (needed to perform at the time). Still, a law needed to be passed.

Thanks in part to Emmy Award–winning screenwriter and novelist Rosalyn Drexler, who argued the case in the media, and to baseball legend Jackie Robinson, who was on the commission because a comparison had been made between the state's not allowing women to wrestle and baseball's not allowing blacks in the major leagues, that decision came on March 7, 1972. A bill was introduced granting female wrestlers the right to practice their trade in the state of New York. The bill officially went into effect on June 5, but Paris couldn't wait that long. On March 8, less than 24 hours after the decision was made, Paris wrestled Cora Combs at Gil Clancy's Telstar boxing gym, in what was the first women's match in New York City since the sport was first banned.

Other female wrestlers had also lobbied to have the ban overturned, Betty Nicoli being one of them. She was able to get a hearing in front of the commission and get some newspaper interviews.

"I fought the courts in New York and got women licensed," Nicoli said. "I went up for a three-judge hearing, a couple of Catholic priests that were against it. They looked at me and said, 'You don't look like a wrestler. You look like a very pretty young lady. Why would you want to get into a man's sport? Why would you want to fight men?' When it was all said and done, [one of the judges] said, 'Well, I guess we'll just give you a license.' Then Vince McMahon Sr. said — the reason I fought and spent the money, and went through the trouble of years fighting in the courts, was to be the first woman to walk into Madison Square Garden. And what does that S.O.B. do but say, 'Hey, I don't need to use you. I can use anybody off the street. They want to see women up here.' So he wouldn't let me. I said, 'Listen, asshole, I'll wrestle for nothing. I fought this to be the first one in there.' I never even got a foot in the door. The closest I ever came to Madison Square Garden was Buffalo, New York."

Because of the company she was running, the Fabulous Moolah was obviously an opponent of the ban. When the ban was lifted, both she and New York City wrestling tsar Vincent James McMahon were pleased with the decision.

On July 1, 1972, McMahon pit Moolah against barefoot wrestler Vicki Williams, billing it as the first women's match in the history of New York City. In reality, it was the first ever held at Madison Square Garden. From that point on, both McMahon and Moolah — and, to the chagrin of Paris, most of the media — recognized that match as the first ever in the city. If that wasn't enough, in typical Moolah fashion, she would block Paris from wrestling any venues promoted by McMahon. She would do the same thing to Nicoli. Moolah took all the credit and rewrote the history books to her advantage.

Paris, who wrestled under different names such as Princess Che Che, the Empress of the Black Dagger, and Chi Chi Paris, went

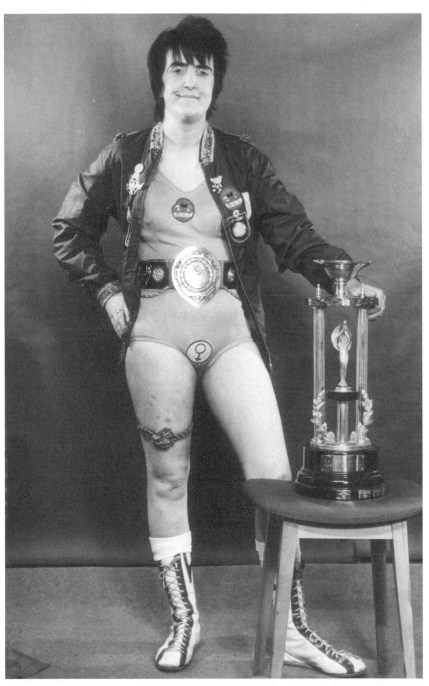

*Much like Titi Paris in the U.S., Sue Brittain fought for women's wrestling to be legalized in England.* WRESTLING REVUE ARCHIVES/WWW.WRESTLINGREVUE.COM

after both McMahon and his champion, trying to get vindication. The great Mildred Burke, also motivated by her hatred for Moolah, tried to help her.

She sent a letter to the *New York Daily News* stating that "Chi Chi's efforts alone got New York to legalize women's wrestling," and that McMahon arranged to have Moolah "move in and reap the rewards." Even the chairman of the New York State Athletic Commission sent a letter to McMahon, but alas, Paris would never work MSG.

As the years went by, women's wrestling was legalized pretty much everywhere. In England, it was the work of Sue Brittain that got women's wrestling legalized. Brittain, who wrestled from the 1960s to 1982, won a two-day court hearing in 1979 to be able to wrestle in London's first women's match since the 1930s. When she passed away in 2013, the BBC even compared her to Emmeline Pankhurst, the leader of the British suffragette movement that helped women get the right to vote in England. Three years after her passing, Pro Wrestling EVE held the first all-women show in the capital. In Ontario, Canada, the work of promoters "The Bearman" Dave McKigney, Phil Watson, and Frank Tunney had the ruling changed in the 1970s. In Montreal, Quebec, the ban was lifted in 1985 for a match between Wendi Richter and the Fabulous Moolah, thanks to Gino Brito and the deputy mayor. Mexico City was probably the last of the big wrestling cities to legalize women's wrestling in 1986.

In 2015, at the brand new Barclays Center in Brooklyn, New York, Bayley and Sasha Banks offered a performance that spectators will remember for a long time. Without the work of Titi Paris, Betty Nicoli, and even the Fabulous Moolah, that match would never have happened. Let's hope nobody forgets about it now.

# The ROCK 'N' WRESTLING CONNECTION and the 1980S

## Girls Just Wanna Have Fun

As a whole, the wrestling business suffered a decline in the 1960s and 1970s after experiencing a golden age during the 1940s and 1950s. The business would go through a dramatic and unprecedented change in the 1980s with the rise of Vincent Kennedy McMahon and his new vision for professional wrestling or, to use the term he coined, sports entertainment. The 1980s marked the start of the Rock 'n' Wrestling Connection and the World Wrestling Federation's rise to the top of the wrestling world, and women's wrestling had a huge role to play.

Vince McMahon Jr. purchased the WWF from a consortium made up of his father, Gorilla Monsoon, Arnold Skaaland, and Phil Zacko in June 1982. With his health failing, the elder McMahon had withdrawn his membership from the NWA, and his son had his eyes on a much larger market than the WWF's traditional stomping ground in the Northeast. The younger McMahon wanted to take his company national, effectively upsetting the apple cart of the NWA.

It would have been insane to start promoting shows in other territories without getting television first, and he realized that cable television would allow him to do that at a faster pace. In 1984, the year in which the first personal computer was introduced and the video game *Tetris* was invented, only 41 percent of the United States, or 84 million homes, were wired for cable. Vince knew he needed that to get to the next level. In late 1983 and early 1984, he secured himself spots on both the USA Network and TBS Superstation, although he would sell the latter about a year later. On May 24, 1984, Vincent James McMahon passed away without seeing the full realization of what his son was about to do.

Vince Sr. knew his son would run things differently from him the moment he chose Hulk Hogan as his champion in January 1984. But neither of them knew how important two managers, a singer, and a female wrestler would become to the success of the WWF.

In 1983, one of the WWF's longtime employees, Captain Lou Albano, appeared in the music video for pop star Cyndi Lauper's song "Girls Just Want to Have Fun," playing Lauper's dad. Lauper had met the rotund wrestling manager on a flight, and she and her manager/boyfriend David Wolff were immediately taken by the colorful and charismatic Captain.

Lauper was planning a music video for her first single with Epic Records. She knew she had just met her MTV-ready father figure.

"At the last minute, Wolff asked Epic to call the World Wrestling Federation and inquire if Albano was available to play Cyndi's father. At first, the grandfatherly grappler said he wasn't interested, but on the evening before filming, his wife convinced him to change his mind," wrote Shaun Assael and Mike Mooneyham in *Sex, Lies, and Headlocks*.

The song and the video became worldwide hits and one of the best-known '80s anthems. It was the 30-year-old Lauper's first hit, and it came right as MTV and music videos were hitting the cultural zeitgeist. By the spring of 1984, Lauper's video was one of the most played videos on MTV. Lauper's album, released on October 14, 1983, went on to sell six million copies in the United States and more than 20 million worldwide. Lauper became a teen idol.

MTV had grown from 2.5 million homes when it launched in August

1981 to more than 20 million homes in the spring of 1984. With two-thirds of its audience under the age of 25, it was exactly the demographic that Vince was aiming for when he decided to replace his vanilla world champion Bob Backlund with the more charismatic Hogan. Wolff, who used to watch wrestling when he was younger, probably did the math as well and pitched an idea to McMahon in the spring of 1984.

"The idea, Wolff explained, was to stage a feud between his girl-friend and Albano," Assael and Mooneyham wrote. "Wolff knew his girlfriend was no wrestler, but, he told Vince, she'd be a perfect manager and therefore a perfect foil to play off against Albano at ringside."

The payoff of that feud would be a match at Madison Square Garden between two wrestlers handpicked to represent both Lauper and Albano, a heel manager.

Wolff was so high on the idea that, according to Assael and Mooneyham, he told Vince it "will make us a fucking fortune, Vince. I mean it. A fucking fortune!" That's all it took for Vince to get on board.

On April 17, at the television tapings in Allentown, Pennsylvania, Albano appeared with Roddy Piper on a pair of *Piper's Pit* segments, taped to air in successive weeks. In these segments, Albano took credit for Lauper's success and turning her from a nobody into a pop star. He also said he could bring Lauper to *Piper's Pit*, as if he were her manager.

Three weeks later, at the next set of tapings in Allentown, Piper read a letter from Wolff threatening Albano and telling him to stop lying about being Lauper's manager. But the heel manager ignored it, saying he would deliver on his promise. Wolff went on to appear on *Piper's Pit* to confront Albano and call him a liar, saying he had nothing to do with Lauper's success and that he would bring the pop star to the show himself to settle things once and for all.

Three weeks later, Lauper appeared and stated the obvious. "I love Lou, but he's not my manager," she told Hot Rod.

Albano disagreed and played the misogynist card to boot. "Tell them how women, Cyndi, belong in the kitchen and pregnant, Cyndi. That no woman has ever accomplished anything without a man behind her."

Lauper asked Albano again to stop fooling around. Albano told her to shut up and countered with another sexist remark. To intensify the whole thing, Piper asked Lauper if she was calling Albano a liar. But when Albano called her "a broad," Lauper lost control, flipped a table, and started to hit both Albano and Piper with her purse, until Wolff broke things up.

The girl who just wanted to have fun was now part of a wrestling angle. Lauper went on to issue a challenge to Albano, daring him to find himself a female wrestler to face one of her own choosing, looking to prove Albano knew as little about wrestling as he did about music. On June 19, in what would be the last regular TV tapings WWF would hold in Allentown, both managers made their choices. Albano made the obvious choice: the women's champion, the Fabulous Moolah. Lauper chose the lesser known Wendi Richter, a 22-year-old who had been trained by Moolah.

Wolff went to MTV director of programming Les Garland and asked if Music TV would be interested in some wrestling. Garland gave it the green light provided the event aired live.

Moolah had controlled the women's title for decades and had cornered the market on women's wrestling. In June 1984, McMahon asked her if she would be willing to sell him the rights to the women's title. As a longtime friend of the McMahons — and having just turned 60 years old and facing the end of her active career — Moolah accepted the offer, giving McMahon control of the women's title and preventing NWA promoters from cashing in on the newfound popularity of women's wrestling. Even though the NWA had stopped regulating the title years before, they were still promoting it whenever a promoter needed it.

On July 23, MTV aired a match live from Madison Square Garden that Garland had billed as "The Brawl to End It All," a bout pitting the chauvinistic Albano's champion against the "Girls Just Want to Have Fun" songstress's challenger.

With Lauper in her corner and Wolff providing guest commentary, Richter overcame the odds and won the match and the title in a little more than 11 minutes, lifting her shoulder at the last second after getting caught in a bridged roll-up, a way to protect the veteran in defeat. Women's wrestling had a new sheriff in town! In the postmatch interviews with "Mean" Gene Okerlund, WWF champion Hulk Hogan came to congratulate Richter. The champion even called Richter the Marilyn Monroe of wrestling.

*Richter and Lauper: two girls who just wanted to have fun.* COURTESY OF WORLD WRESTLING ENTERTAINMENT, INC.

The match was a ratings monster. MTV drew a 9.0, the highest rating in the history of the network. For comparison, that number is higher than the most-watched *Raw* segment ever. For the WWF, it was also a home run, with thousands of teenagers getting to know — and enjoy — professional wrestling. "I don't want to say that this match put them on the map, but it put them on a map they weren't on," said Meltzer.

For the second half of the year, based on the popularity the match had on MTV, McMahon brought the rematch to all the big cities he could, including some new markets. From Atlanta to Minneapolis, from the East Coast to the West Cost, Richter successfully defended her title against Moolah through the rest of the year. But the angle with Lauper didn't stop there. McMahon had bigger plans in mind.

The WWF brought Lauper back for the Christmas show on December 28 at MSG to present her with an achievement award for her contribution to the world of women's wrestling. Radio and television personality Dick Clark presented Lauper with the award, and Lauper presented the WWF with a gold record. Accepting the record on behalf of the WWF were Hogan and Richter, equally sharing the spotlight.

Lauper also buried the hatchet with Albano, presenting him with a gold record in recognition of his efforts in helping her raise more than $4 million for the fight against multiple sclerosis, effectively turning the Captain babyface. That was the cue for Piper and his ally, Cowboy Bob Orton Jr., to come to the ring and raise some hell. Piper smashed the record on Albano's head, kicked Lauper in the face, and body-slammed Wolff until Hogan came back to save the day. The groundwork for WrestleMania had been laid.

On February 18, the WWF presented "The War to Settle the Score" at Madison Square Garden, pitting Hogan (with Lauper and Albano in his corner) against Piper. Once again, the match aired on MTV. However, on the undercard of the show, Richter suffered an upset loss as Leilani Kai capitalized on Moolah's interference and defeated Richter for the women's title.

Kai had a 20-pound weight advantage over Richter and was an effective foil for the pretty Dallas cowgirl, particularly with Moolah in Kai's corner. Richter had gone from champion to challenger, and the fans were clamoring to see her fight her way back to the title.

On March 31, 1985, Richter defeated Kai to regain the title in a featured match at the first WrestleMania extravaganza, an event that would change wrestling completely. Once again, Lauper proved to be Richter's good luck charm, cheering her to victory from ringside.

The first WrestleMania became a great success. It led to the WWF getting a deal with NBC for its *Saturday Night's Main Event* specials and with CBS for *Hulk Hogan Rock 'n' Wrestling* cartoon, and it established WrestleMania as wrestling's signature annual event. "I attribute most of our success to the efforts of Dave Wolff and Cyndi Lauper. The two not only lent their lives to the wrestling world, they were solely responsible for putting the rock in the rock-and-wrestling product of the 1980s," said Piper in his autobiography. The April 1986 cover of *Pro Wrestling Illustrated* featured Richter with a headline reading "Women's Wrestling Comes of Age: Is Wendi Richter More Popular than Hulk Hogan?" It was a valid question at the time . . . but Richter's run on top was destined to be brief.

# WENDI RICHTER

Wendi Richter's career was arguably defined by her 1984–1985 run as a two-time WWF women's champion, when she was featured on MTV and at the first WrestleMania. She was the heir apparent to Moolah. But her fall from the top was just as sudden as her rise and Moolah was heavily involved in both.

Born in Fort Lauderdale, Florida, on September 6, 1961, but raised in Bossier City, Louisiana, Victoria Lynn Richter was only 18 years old when she enrolled at the famed Lillian Ellison School of Professional Wrestling in Columbus, South Carolina.

"Wrestling was my ultimate dream. From the first time I ever watched a match, I knew that was what I wanted to do," she said.

Joyce Grable was Richter's primary trainer. "She helped train me as well as a hundred other ladies. I learned so much from [her]," said Richter during her Pro Wrestling Hall of Fame acceptance speech in Amsterdam, New York.

She made her debut in 1980 as part of Moolah's troupe, booked through Moolah's office. In 1982, she had two tag team championship reigns with Grable, dubbed the Texas Cowgirls. She also went to Japan, working a program with WWWA champion Jaguar Yokota.

She was largely a journeyman without much of a push, working in tag team matches and singles bouts to fill out the card. As late as April 1984, she was in a program teaming with Peggy Lee Leather against women's tag team champions Velvet McIntyre and Princess Victoria. She had a pair of unsuccessful shots at Moolah for the title in May, including a bout at Madison Square Garden where she was disqualified for shoving the referee. Since the women were in a touring division and not usually featured on TV, there were few true storylines for the women. One night, Richter would be facing Donna Christantello in Utica, New York; three days later, they would be teaming in Green Bay. Just days before she was announced as Lauper's pick for the match, she was on the losing end of a tag match in front of more than 21,000 people at the Superdome in New Orleans. A funny note on that show is that Richter, a heel then, helped Jim Cornette escape from Jim Duggan. Cornette's

*Wendi Richter, one of the best known wrestlers of her era.*
AL FRIEND COLLECTION

Midnight Express won their match against the Rock 'n' Roll Express, and on the TV tapings that followed, Cornette made Richter an honorary member of the Midnight Express. Duggan interrupted the ceremony and planted a huge, sloppy kiss on Richter.

McMahon chose Richter as his new female superstar because she looked the part. While not a great interview, she was young, tall, and attractive. She was the right fit for Lauper; no other women in the WWF at the time really fit that description.

"I know Vince liked Wendi a lot, because she was tall and had that big, bright smile," said Leilani Kai.

"The goal was to have a male and a female star. They tried to headline with her and it bombed. Fans weren't ready for that," said Dave Meltzer.

Although her match against Moolah was a ratings hit, it was not a particularly good match. It was voted Worst Match of the Year in the *Wrestling Observer Newsletter* awards. But it was never supposed to be about workrate; it was a chance to make Richter a star, and it worked. Among her peers, Richter had the reputation of being a good worker, while Moolah was near the end of her career. "What an awesome woman. She could put a beanbag over," said Vicki Otis, better known as Princess Victoria, in an interview in 2011.

Richter was announced as the youngest ever women's champion. In reality, she was the second youngest, as she was five months older than Susan Green when Green won the belt in 1976.

Richter and Lauper joined Hogan and Mr. T in the opening segment of the first *Saturday Night's Main Event*, and both Richter and Moolah were included in the WWF's foray into Saturday morning cartoons, appearing as animated characters on *Hulk Hogan's Rock 'n'*

*Moolah and Richter, a rivalry in and out of the ring.*
PAT LAPRADE COLLECTION

*Wrestling.* But by November 1985, Richter was gone from the WWF, the victim of a title screwjob. Although she continued to wrestle for several years, she never wrestled for the WWF again.

Richter eventually resurfaced on the independent circuit before landing in Puerto Rico and becoming the first women's champion of Carlos Colon's World Wrestling Council. She moved on to the AWA and defeated Madusa Miceli for the women's title on November 26, 1988. She vacated the title a year later and went into semi-retirement, wrestling her final match in 2005.

Almost a quarter-century after she left the WWF, McMahon extended an olive branch, inviting Richter to compete in a women's battle royal at WrestleMania 25 in 2009. She declined the offer but did accept an invitation to be inducted into the WWE Hall of Fame in 2010. Her old rival Roddy Piper inducted her.

Richter returned to WWE one more time in 2012, making her *Raw* debut. She rejoined Lauper and Piper in a nostalgic segment that served as a buildup to the 1,000th episode of *Raw*. She continues to make occasional appearances at wrestling conventions and reunions.

"I have to thank Cyndi Lauper, also, for her contributions, because it was her influence that skyrocketed my career, as well as Roddy Piper and the late Lou Albano," said Richter during her acceptance speech at the Cauliflower Alley Club in 2012.

Although Richter was in the right place at the right time, the fact of the matter is that she was a true wrestler through and through.

"I'm so proud to have trained on the mat for hours, day after day, smearing my blood the hard way on the mat, not wearing elbow pads and knee pads to make me tough," she said. "Also, I'm proud of sacrificing my personal life, year after year, to be on the road, driving hundreds of miles a day, and getting paid next to nothing because I loved this sport."

## The Original WWF Screwjob

The match between Bret Hart and Shawn Michaels on November 9, 1997, in Montreal — better known as the Montreal Screwjob — was hardly the first screwjob match in the history of professional wrestling. It wasn't even the first screwjob in WWE's modern era.

On November 25, 1985, almost 12 years to the date before the most famous screwjob match ever, the Fabulous Moolah, dressed as the Spider Lady, defeated Wendi Richter at Madison Square Garden, regaining the women's title. It came as a surprise, considering Moolah's advanced age and Richter's popularity over the previous year. Many of the questions surrounding the match were answered when it came out that the match was, in fact, a screwjob.

Penny Mitchell had begun wrestling as the masked Spider Lady shortly after WrestleMania. Mitchell wrestled on and off as the Spider Lady over the summer, and at the end of August, she faced Richter for the first time with the new gimmick. On October 19, in San Juan, Richter, accompanied by Lauper, wrestled Spider with none other than Moolah in her corner. From there, Richter and Mitchell wrestled each other on a regular basis.

For the fans, it was just another feud for the champion, but internally, a bigger dispute was going on. In 1985, Richter was on top of the world. A two-time women's champion, she had become the face of the women's division. But following

*MSG, New York, November 25, 1985, a sad day for women's wrestling.* PRO WRESTLING ILLUSTRATED

WrestleMania, she felt she was underpaid. According to some sources, the main male stars of the show received huge paydays: Paul Orndorff reportedly received $20,000, Mr. T received $100,000, Roddy Piper received $75,000, and Hulk Hogan got between $75,000 and $100,000. Wendi Richter was paid $5,000. Despite being a household name who had helped a lot with the first MTV shows that led to WrestleMania, her weekly average was about $2,500, before travel expenses. At the "Brawl to End It All" match against Moolah the year before, she had reportedly received $1,500.

Richter felt she was getting screwed by the company and asked for a better contract. Also, since she was showcased in the cartoon show, she wanted royalties for that, at a time when royalties weren't given to everyone. She also refused to sign a merchandise contract. However, it wasn't that she didn't want to sign a new contract, as some have reported in subsequent years. She had a five-year deal in place, but she wanted to renegotiate it, or at the very least get some compensation for what she had brought to the company over the previous 16 months.

"[McMahon] didn't want to pay me," Richter said in an interview. "I was being paid what the people in opening matches were being paid." Richter also said Vince was telling her she had a legitimate complaint over this, but he would never do anything about it.

Putting things into context, even if Richter felt underpaid, she was paid more than all the other female wrestlers, except for Moolah.

"When I dropped the belt at WrestleMania to Wendi Richter, a woman I had trained, she was paid twice as much as the challenger as I was as the defending champion," said Leilani Kai.

When November 25 came around, Richter and McMahon were at an impasse. Richter arrived at the arena and was surprised to see Moolah backstage. Moolah was already semi-retired and was only attending shows when she was booked. Richter knew something was fishy. At that time, heels and babyfaces didn't share the same locker rooms and in most cases didn't talk to each other before the match. A referee or an agent would go to both locker rooms and give the cues to the wrestlers. If one had a message for the other, that same referee or agent would play messenger. Richter was scheduled to win the match and retain the title.

When she got in the ring, Richter's suspicions were confirmed as she recognized Moolah right away beneath the Spider Lady costume. How couldn't she? She had worked with her so many times, and she had worked with Mitchell, too. Even the fans in attendance started chanting "Moolah" at Spider Lady less than a minute into the bout.

The match lasted only 6:38. At the end, Moolah put Richter in a small package and referee Jack Lutz started the count. After the one count, Richter clearly kicked out, but Lutz had been instructed to keep counting, and that's exactly what he did. It wasn't even a close count. After the three count, confusion reigned. Lutz remained in the ring, but by his body language, it was easy to see that it was the last place he wanted to be at that moment. He didn't even go to Moolah right away and raise her arm. Some 10 seconds later, Richter attacked Moolah and went for her mask, which she was able to remove. She was hitting Moolah with some shots that the latter wasn't selling at all. Then Richter went for a back breaker that clearly caught Moolah by surprise and went for the cover. When she realized the referee wasn't counting, she got back up and continued her assault on Moolah. Finally, 90 seconds after the match was over, ring announcer Howard Finkel announced the winner. Richter continued to throw stiff punches at Moolah, who defended herself before heading for the safety of the locker room.

"I was so angry," Richter said. "Vince wronged me. I was humiliated, and embarrassed in front of millions of people. I loved wrestling and that's why it hurt me so much that it ended with the WWF."

Realizing she'd been double-crossed, Richter didn't waste time hanging around and stormed out of the arena and to the airport without changing out of her wrestling gear. She never spoke to Moolah again and has spoken to McMahon only in recent years.

And she was left with a sour taste in her mouth, especially when talking about Moolah. To this day, she rarely has a positive thing to say about Moolah.

"I have to thank the outstanding wrestlers that I worked with, like Judy Martin — I mean that from the bottom of my heart," she said. "Her, Joyce Grable, Leilani Kai, Velvet McIntyre, Princess Victoria. They were excellent wrestlers and I learned so much from them. And from Moolah, I learned what not to do."

# LEILANI KAI

Although she'd already been wrestling for nine years, Leilani Kai had her first moment on the national stage at WrestleMania I, defending the women's title against Wendi Richter. But because of a late flight back from Japan, she almost missed the show.

"They had me go from a helicopter to the arena because I had gotten in so late," she said in an interview. "When I got there, it was so huge, and I could see it was different. I had been at Madison

Square Garden several times, but this was a little different. But even afterwards, I didn't realize just how big it was."

Born on January 23, 1957, Patricia Seymour knew she wanted to be a wrestler after seeing a women's match as a kid in Tampa, Florida. She was 19 when she was referred to Moolah's school by Susan Green. Moolah gave her her ring name because she thought Seymour looked Hawaiian, and the exotic name gave her a marketable appeal. Professor Toru Tanaka and Mr. Fuji, both Hawaiians, had pitched a few names to Moolah, and she went with Leilani (meaning "heavenly flowers") and Kai (meaning "ocean water").

Kai had her first tour of Japan in 1978, the first of more than 40 tours she would make to that island nation throughout her career. She would have an eight-month run as All Pacific women's champion in 1986, feuding with Chigusa Nagayo for that title.

Following her brief run as WWF women's champion, she was put in a tag team with Judy Martin, and the two were awarded the WWF women's tag team title, with a storyline explaining they had won the belts in Egypt in a match that never actually took place.

The WWF women's division was struggling in the post-Richter era. Moolah was 62 years old. The division was in desperate need of some new blood. Kai and Martin suggested they look to Japan, but Moolah was having none of that idea. The champ had no interest in bringing in women who weren't under contract to her, especially the ultra-athletic Japanese women with whom she could no longer compete.

"We wanted to do something different. But she didn't understand that kind of wrestling. And I think she wanted to manage us. But I just knew it wouldn't work like that," Kai said.

Kai and Martin went to McMahon, who rebuffed the idea at first, probably influenced by Moolah's opinion. So Kai and Martin went to see McMahon's right-hand man, Pat Patterson. He thought it was a good idea and that it was different. He came back 20 minutes later with approval from Vince.

Kai and Martin weren't finished making suggestions to creative. Next up was a makeover. Kai said she and Martin wanted to change their look as a team, so they went to Jimmy Hart to ask for advice.

"I told Jimmy that we had this idea to change our image a little bit. We wanted to be a little more colorful as a tag team. He came up with the idea of us dyeing our hair blonde. I thought, 'Blond hair on a Hawaiian?' But it worked out." Hart also came up with the Glamour Girls nickname, adding some glitz to the team, and

*Leilani Kai, with her Hawaiian look.* CHRIS SWISHER COLLECTION

came on board as their manager, which was a major advantage since neither Kai nor Martin was particularly strong in interviews.

The Glamour Girls brought Itsuki Yamazaki and Noriyo Tateno, collectively known as the Jumping Bomb Angels, into the WWF. The Girls faced the Angels almost every night through the summer of 1987, often putting on one of the best matches of the night. The Angels returned to the WWF in November for the Survivor Series pay-per-view which featured Kai, Martin, Sensational Sherri, Donna Christantello, and Dawn Marie (not to be confused with ECW's Dawn Marie) vs. the Angels, Velvet McIntyre, Rockin' Robin, and a babyface Moolah.

"Moolah didn't really like it when we did the Survivor Series," Kai said. "Judy and I had to put our heads together to get everything put in the way they wanted it, along with all the high spots. They wanted the Bomb Angels over, so that was good since I knew they [the WWF] liked them. Moolah just couldn't understand that kind of wrestling."

The Glamour Girls and the Jumping Bomb Angels continued to

*The Glamour Girls vs. The Jumping Bomb Angels in the WWF.* ITSUKI YAMAZAKI COLLECTION

face each other into 1988, including a match at the 1988 Royal Rumble in Hamilton, Ontario.

All Japan Women and the WWF agreed to bring the two Americans to Japan to continue the feud. The plan was for the Bomb Angels to retain the title in Japan, so that the Glamour Girls could win it back at home. But it didn't happen that way.

According to Kai, Moolah, who still owned the tag team belts, called the office in Japan and told them to make the title switch, claiming she was acting on authority of the WWF. In fact, Moolah was acting on her own, but when Kai and Martin returned to the United States with the belts, the heat fell squarely on them.

"Upon returning to the U.S. Judy and I found out that we were no longer employed in the WWF," Kai said. "The promotion phoned Judy when we returned and asked her how we could do something as stupid as winning the belts in Japan after all the hard work put into the angle."

After her stint with the WWF was over, Kai started working for the short-lived Ladies Professional Wrestling Association as well as fighting some matches in WCW. She was brought back by the WWF in 1994 to put over the new champion Alundra Blayze and went back to WCW under the name of Patty Stonegrinder. While working indie promotions for the next decade, she also trained some women from the west coast, including Amber O'Neal-Gallows. She remains involved in the business today, working for the Florida-based women's promotion SHINE, a way for her to give back to the new generation.

"If it weren't for the old-school women who were active in wrestling when I started, I wouldn't have come this far," she said.

## JUDY MARTIN

Judy Martin started training in 1979 after she approached Blackjack Mulligan and Dick Murdoch at a wrestling show and they suggested she should go to Moolah's school. At the time, she didn't even know there were women in wrestling.

"I learned a lot from those guys," Martin said at the CAC Reunion in 2012, when she was honored with a Women's Wrestling Award. "Blackjack Mulligan, he made me make him a promise, along with Dick Murdoch, that I would never embarrass him as a wrestler, and I've tried to keep that promise."

Born Judith Hardee on October 8, 1955, she made her wrestling debut in 1979. She quickly developed a reputation as a tag team expert, forming a championship pairing with Kai and teaming with several other women in the early 1980s. She later emerged as a singles contender for Richter's WWF championship and was widely considered to be one of the best pure workers among Moolah's stable.

Outside of the WWF, she was recognized as the U.S. women's champion, and she also won the All Pacific women's title for All Japan Women, the second-most prestigious singles title in the company at the time. Known to be one of the first wrestlers — male or female — to use the powerbomb in the United States, she also earned a reputation as a solid worker, which helped her fit in with the Japanese girls.

"Judy Martin is one that when she stomps yah, you know you've been stomped. You know that she has hit you," said fellow wrestler Susan Green.

*Judy Martin, one of the Glamour Girls with Leilani Kai.*
WRESTLING REVUE ARCHIVES/WWW.WRESTLINGREVUE.COM

After Kai and Martin were fired from the WWF in June 1988, Martin continued working the different territories before being brought back at the end of the year to start a program with the new women's champion, Rockin' Robin. "When you talk about Judy, you talk about respect, work, and work ethic. What a professional," Rockin' Robin said. "I was fortunate to learn a great deal from her."

The rivalry between the two lasted through June 1989, when the title was deactivated, along with the entire women's division. Martin still believes McMahon made a mistake by eliminating women's wrestling at the time.

"Honestly, I think if [Vince] gave the girls the exposure he did the guys, we would have done very well," she said. "There was a lot of talent there and I think it was a mistake."

After working for the AWA, LPWA, and WCW, Martin finally ended her career in the late 1990s. After a career that spanned two decades and took her all over the world, Martin is happy to offer advice to today's women. "If I could pass on anything to any females that are in this business, it's this: when you go to that ring, you give 110 percent and be proud to be a professional."

# VELVET MCINTYRE

The biggest accomplishment in Velvet McIntyre's career was bitter-sweet: she won the WWF women's title in 1986, but it was a short reign that was never officially recognized by the federation. At that time, many overseas title changes were not recognized if they were not televised; they were simply title changes to excite the local crowd, with the champion regaining the title by the end of the tour. McIntyre won the title on the first day of an Australian tour, beating Moolah on July 3, 1986, in Brisbane. After defending the title a few times, she lost it back to Moolah on July 9, in Sydney.

She earned a title shot against Moolah at WrestleMania 2, but it was easy to see how far the WWF women's title had dropped off over the preceding match. Moolah vs. McIntyre was a forgettable undercard match that went barely a minute long. The most memorable aspect of the bout was the fact that McIntyre wrestled barefoot, something she had just begun doing that would become one of her trademarks.

"I wore boots for about the first four years of my career, but one day somebody took one of my boots as a joke, and I only had one boot in my bag. I was wrestling with Leilani, actually. I said, 'Well, I guess I've got to go barefoot.' Away I went, and I never looked back," she said.

Born on November 24, 1961, in Elliot Lake, Ontario, she had moved to Vancouver at a very young age. That's where she developed an interest in pro wrestling, right after finishing high school. "I heard that Sandy Barr was looking for women's wrestlers in Oregon and I went there to train in 1980," said McIntyre.

By 1982, Barr had contacted Moolah and asked if she wanted to take over the booking for his women. "They had a different style than Moolah's girls and they could wrestle," said Barr, referring to McIntyre and Princess Victoria, frequent tag team partners who had come from his school.

Even if she had a style different from her other girls, the Canadian's skills and work ethic impressed Moolah. "She did her best, she never gave up, she kept going. She was forever training and working out," Moolah said. "She was just a great wrestler. I would say she was the

*Velvet McIntyre got her start with her co-champion, Princess Victoria.* CHRIS SWISHER COLLECTION

best Canadian wrestler." Quite a compliment from Moolah, considering she had also wrestled Vivian Vachon.

Like most of the women at the time, McIntyre ended up working throughout the United States and Canada, as well as tours of Japan that she particularly enjoyed. "I used to go to Japan, steal all the girls' moves and bring them back here. Voila!" she quipped. She began using moves like a swinging hurricanrana, flying headscissors, and single-leg dropkick, moves rarely used by women (or men) in North America at the time.

McIntyre remained in the WWF until 1988, when she had a series of matches against champion Sensational Sherri Martel. After leaving the WWF, she primarily worked the independents, including winning the Extreme Canadian Championship Wrestling women's title on two occasions. Having toured the world, working in every U.S. state, every Canadian province, Japan, Puerto Rico, Singapore, Thailand, France, Germany, Egypt, India, Peru, and Australia, she stopped wrestling in 1998 when she became pregnant with twins. In fact, in her last match, she was already carrying them but didn't know about it yet.

"If I didn't have the kids, I'd probably still be doing it. But your priorities change. Now it matters if I break my neck," she said.

# SHERRI MARTEL

"She was the greatest female performer in North America during the 80s and 90s," Dave Meltzer said, assessing the career of Sherri Martel.

Martel had successful careers as both a wrestler and a manager/valet, and she managed a veritable who's who of superstars, including Randy Savage, Shawn Michaels, Ric Flair, and Harlem Heat.

Born Sherry Russell on February 8, 1958, in New Orleans, she was first exposed to wrestling at the age of 13, when she saw matches with her mother in Hattiesburg, Mississippi. Wrestling didn't immediately appeal to her. Her dream at the time was to join the circus as a clown. But there were more opportunities for wrestlers than for clowns, so at the age of 16, she approached wrestler Grizzly Smith and asked if he would train her. He turned her down and told her to come back when she was 21.

A few years passed, and after a pair of brief marriages, Russell found herself living in Memphis. Becoming a wrestler was still a goal, so she began training at a small wrestling school in town. She ran into Grizzly Smith and told him she had begun training, and he told her if she wanted to make it in wrestling, she needed to call Moolah.

"When I first met her she had legendary status in 1980, 1981," Martel recalled in an online interview. "She was very strict, very demanding . . . She was the most phenomenal woman, but she demanded perfection from you and knew how to get it." Martel enrolled in Moolah's school and continued to train under Moolah and Donna Christantello.

After she made her debut as Sherri Martine in 1980, Moolah — probably influenced by the success Rick Martel had at the time — changed her name to Sherri Martel and sent her to Japan in 1981.

In 1982, Martel was injured in a freak accident when Plowboy Stan Frazier (later known as Uncle Elmer) fell on her leg in a battle royal. Although the leg wasn't broken, it was badly dislocated, and she had to wear a brace on her left leg from the hip down. The injury put her wrestling career on hold for a couple of years, so she turned her attention to managing, taking on Buddy Rose and Doug Somers in the AWA.

*AWA women's champion Sherri Martel.* LINDA BOUCHER

She returned to action in 1985, embarking on a feud with AWA women's champion Candi Devine. On September 28, 1985, at SuperClash at Chicago's Comiskey Park, in front of 21,000 fans, Martel defeated Devine for the belt. Devine and Martel continued their program for the next two years, occasionally swapping the title. Martel started to get a reputation as a very good grappler. She was also known to speak her mind and not let anybody step on her toes. In other words, she was a tough cookie.

By the summer of 1987, Moolah's time on top of the WWF had run its course, and Vince McMahon — who always seemed to enjoy taking a jab at AWA promoter Verne Gagne — decided that Martel would be the new face of his women's division. Gagne had never signed Martel to a contract, so on July 24, 1987, three days after successfully defending the AWA women's title, Martel defeated Moolah for the WWF women's title in Houston without ever dropping the AWA title.

She was dubbed Sensational Sherri shortly after her title win, and she became the new heel champion. Ironically, Grizzly Smith's daughter, Rockin' Robin, defeated her for the title. After having a bunch of rematches throughout 1988 and 1989 — really the only program in the women's division — their last match together was in June, but Sherri had already begun working double duty as Randy Savage's valet.

Her valet role got her back in the ring in 1990, when she teamed with Savage against Dusty Rhodes and his valet, Sweet Sapphire, at

WrestleMania 6 in Toronto, followed by many subsequent rematches and singles bouts between Sherri and Sapphire. She had another in-ring program against Luna Vachon in 1993 but was released by the WWF later that year because of personal issues with drugs and alcohol. The timing was terrible, as she was released before McMahon reactivated the women's title and restocked the women's division.

She wrestled Malia Hosaka in ECW before heading to WCW, where she was mostly used as a valet. She kept working after WCW, winning the NWA world women's title from Debbie Combs, at a time when the title didn't mean much. She did only a handful of indie appearances in the 2000s because of a persistent back injury. She wrestled her last match at WrestleReunion in Tampa, Florida, in January 2005.

Martel was inducted into the WWE Hall of Fame in 2006 by another former protégé of hers, "The Million Dollar Man" Ted DiBiase. A little over a year later, on June 15, 2007, her husband found her dead of an overdose at the age of 49. At the time of her passing, she was considered by WWE to have been its first female agent, showing the women there how to be more credible and expressive in the ring. Sherri Martel could talk, wrestle, be tough, and be mean. She was a pretty woman who could drink like a man and perform like one too, making her the total package for the women's division in that era, respected by her peers and the fans alike.

# ROCKIN' ROBIN

Rockin' Robin's journey in professional wrestling didn't last long, but it had its highlights, including a win over Sherri Martel for the WWF women's title in Paris in October 1988.

Born Robin Smith on October 9, 1964, she was a second-generation wrestler, the daughter of "The Kentuckian" Aurelian "Grizzly" Smith. Her brother, Mike Smith, went on to wrestle under the name Sam Houston, and her half-brother was none other than Aurelian Smith Jr., better known as Jake "The Snake" Roberts.

Growing up in a wrestling family is always unusual, and it was no different for her. "Every Monday, a teacher in grade school asked about the weekend. Most kids would talk about their grandma coming over, or little things, like the preacher coming over," she recalled in her CAC speech in 2011. "They get to me, and I said, 'Well, I watched my mom and dad play poker with a giant, two midgets, and a real nice guy in a mask.' Of course, she would ask, 'What did you learn on the weekend?' 'Well, midgets cheat!'"

But there was also an ugly side to Smith's childhood. She has said she was molested by her father, starting around the age of six or seven. "As a child, you feel a tremendous amount of guilt," she said in a Highspots.com interview with Steve Corino. After a period of time, her mother became suspicious and had a talk with her, empowering Smith to open up about the abuse for the first time. "He ruined enough of my life. He ruined my childhood. I certainly wasn't going to let him ruin the rest of my life."

She made her debut in 1987, after being trained in North Carolina by wrestler Nelson Royal. "I wanted to be trained like one of the guys. I didn't want to be trained like you see some of the women train," she said, explaining why she opted not to go to Moolah's school. She also trained with her sister-in-law, Nickla Roberts — the daughter of Lorraine Johnson, a well-known wrestler in her era — who had a successful career as a valet under the name Baby Doll.

Smith debuted in the WWF in November 1987 and immediately started a program with Sherri. On October 7, 1988, she defeated Martel to become the new WWF women's champion.

"I won it two days before my birthday, so it was a great birthday present," she said. "And being in Paris at that age, and just traveling the world, is something that most people don't get to do, so I appreciated every minute of it."

But the WWF women's division was on its last legs, Smith almost exclusively wrestling Martel. Women were used rarely, and the division was scrapped entirely in 1990, although Smith did make an appearance at WrestleMania 5, not in a match but to sing "America the Beautiful."

In late 1990, through promoters Howard Brody and Hiro Matsuda, Smith went to Japan alongside Luna Vachon, an experience she has said she will never forget.

"We were the only two that spoke English, and everyone else spoke Japanese," she said. "After about eight hours on a bus, you get bored, and think, 'Well, what can we do now?' So we decided to teach the Japanese girls to speak a little English. My guess is that there's still probably 30 girls in Japan still running around saying, 'Kiss my ass, you S.O.B.!'"

After a couple more years in the business

*Rockin' Robin was the last WWF women's champion of the 1980s.* COURTESY OF WORLD WRESTLING ENTERTAINMENT, INC.

working some independent promotions, she retired and became very successful in both telemarketing and real estate.

# DEBBIE COMBS

Another female wrestler who didn't follow Moolah's lead to get a name for herself in the wrestling business, Debbie Combs could count on her own veteran wrestler to train her and provide advice: her mom.

She was born Debbie Szestecki on April 18, 1959, in Fort Campbell, Kentucky, the daughter of Cora Combs. She was introduced to the business as a child and had both Ella Waldek and Mars Bennett, the former circus performer turned wrestler, as frequent babysitters.

As years passed, it was clear she wanted to get involved in her mom's business and begin training. She had her first match in 1975, for

*Cora Combs' daughter, Debbie.* CHRIS SWISHER COLLECTION

Angelo Poffo's ICW in Tennessee, in a seven-woman battle royal. She also began dating one of Poffo's sons, Randy, better known as Randy "Macho Man" Savage, before the latter had ever met Miss Elizabeth.

"She went with me, and one of the girls didn't show up and we put her in the ring. She lasted five minutes and she fell in love with it like I did," remembered Cora Combs.

In her late 40s, Cora mentored her daughter by working with her under a mask as Lady Satan, a very mean wrestler in the ring, an experience she found to be bittersweet. "Yeah, it was hard, because I didn't want to hurt her," she said.

But in 1979, in St. Louis, they had the chance to work together as a rare mother–daughter combo in wrestling's history, the only time they would do so. "We have a relationship that is not very often seen in people," said Cora. "I don't do no harm, no wrong in her eyes and she don't do no wrong in mine. I love her with all my heart."

The flip side of not being part of Moolah's stable was that it was tougher getting bookings in the bigger markets and for the bigger promotions. But with more girls working almost exclusively for the WWF, it opened some spots for other women, and Debbie went to the AWA in 1985. In 1986, she won the NWA women's title, a watered-down version that was created in the wake of Moolah's selling her title to the WWF and that had nothing to do with the old title. That being said, Combs is recognized as the first NWA women's champion of the version of the title still defended today; but any link to Burke, Byers, or Moolah is tenuous at best. And since the title was not properly regulated and barely defended, she claimed the title until 1997, after which it was declared vacant by the NWA. It remained inactive for three years.

In mid-1987, she finally made her WWF debut and was put in a program with Moolah.

After spending the late '80s and early '90s working here and there, Combs was awarded the USWA women's title in April 1994 and got into a rivalry with her mom, the latter having just turned 67 years old. In 1996, using her mother's heel gimmick of Lady Satan, she won the USWA title another time, beating Miss Texas.

In addition to competing on tours in Japan and Africa, she very briefly wrestled for WCW in 1997.

# MISTY BLUE SIMMES

Although her time on the national stage was limited, Misty Blue Simmes became one of the most recognizable female wrestlers of the late 1980s and early 1990s by virtue of gracing the pages (and covers) of magazines such as *Wrestling's Main Event*, *Wrestling Confidential*, and *Wrestling News*.

Born Diane Syms on February 8, 1962, in Glens Falls, New York, Simmes was the quintessential blonde-haired 1980s pinup beauty, wrestling's answer to Farrah Fawcett. Like Farrah, Simmes frequently posed for photos that were a tad more provocative than those of the Wendi Richters and Leilani Kais of the era, with her thin one-piece bathing suits leaving precious little to the imagination.

Simmes enrolled in Killer Kowalski's wrestling school in 1984, where she trained for 18 months until making her pro debut in 1985.

She started her career in the AWA and made a run through Texas's World Class Championship Wrestling before working with the NWA in 1986. After Vince McMahon bought the world title, the NWA dug into its history and raised the U.S. women's title, which hadn't been defended since 1980, from the ashes. Simmes took her role as

*NWA U.S. women's champion Misty Blue Simmes.*
BERTRAND HEBERT COLLECTION

U.S. champion to heart, adopting red, white, and blue ring gear, complete with star-spangled bandanas tied around her boots.

By 1989, the NWA had suspended its women's division, and Simmes set off to the independent circuit.

She landed in the fledgling LPWA in 1990. She formed a tag team with Heidi Lee Morgan, adopting the name Team America, and feuded with former WWF women's tag team champions the Glamour Girls and the Nasty Girls (Kat LeRoux and Linda Dallas) over the LPWA tag team title.

Simmes went on to work for the WCW, but the promotion allocated few resources to its women's division, and Simmes was rarely used on television, appearing sporadically on *WCW Saturday Night* and *WCW Main Event*.

After parting ways with WCW, Simmes returned to the independents and continued to wrestle on and off until she retired in 1997. She was inducted into the National Wrestling Alliance Hall of Fame in 2012.

## CANDI DEVINE

Candi Devine's four reigns as AWA women's champion were a bit odd, considering she beat the champion only once.

The first time Devine was awarded the title was in November

1984, when she won a battle royal. But, without any official explanation (although probably because of the lack of female contenders at the time), the title was declared vacant in 1985 before being reawarded to Devine, technically making her a two-time champion.

When Sherri Martel arrived in the promotion and defeated Devine on September 28, 1985, at SuperClash in Chicago, the title change was recognized only in select AWA markets; Martel had to beat Devine a second time before parts of Canada and other AWA outposts recognized the switch.

On January 16, 1986, Devine started what was considered her third reign, the only one where she would actually defeat the champion with a win over Martel. Martel took her title back in Oakland on June 28, 1986, in a bout showcased on ESPN. When then-champion Richter left the AWA in December 1989, the title was declared vacant, and on December 6 in Toronto, Ontario, Devine won it for the fourth and final time with a win over Judy Martin, who had just left the WWF.

With the AWA closing in January 1991, the title was officially retired although Devine was barely working for the company anymore, her last run having been during the infamous Team Challenge Series in 1990.

Born Candace Rummel on January 1, 1959, in Nashville, Tennessee, she was working as a Gray Line tour employee in the early 1980s when she developed a major crush on Lanny Poffo. At the time, Randy's brother was wrestling for his dad's promotion, International Championship Wrestling, in Kentucky. Rummel created a fan club for Lanny and a newsletter called *The Leap*, and eventually she became a ring girl for the promotion. But when she wanted to start wrestling she was shown the door.

Back home, she trained under Don Fargo and began wrestling, although she struggled to learn the basics. Her career could have ended as early as 1985, when she suffered a fractured jaw in a match against Amy Monroe in Memphis. Instead, the injury reaffirmed her commitment. "When I think of Candi Devine, I think of T and A, for Talent and Athleticism," said former wrestler Lisa "The Adjuster" Haynes.

Like many others at the time, with no serious women's division

One of the AWA staples, Candi Devine.
LINDA BOUCHER

in either of the now-big two promotions, she started working the independents, something she was still doing until fairly recently. Although she had earned national attention from her time in the AWA and on the independents, she had never had a run with the WWF. In March 1995, when she was 36, the WWF finally came calling, and she was brought in to put over Alundra Blayze in a house show. Now residing in Nashville, she also had a 20-year on-and-off relationship with former wrestler the late Tom Burton.

## MADUSA/ALUNDRA BLAYZE

Many great wrestlers came out of the Minnesota territory over the years. From Joe Stecher to Curt Hennig and from Verne Gagne to the Road Warriors, Minnesota — especially after Gagne took over the territory — has built a reputation as a home of wrestling champions. Debrah Miceli was one of those champions.

Born in Milan, Italy, on February 9, 1964, but raised in Minneapolis, Miceli wasn't aiming at a wrestling career until she met Eddie Sharkey. By her 20th birthday, she had worked as a nurse, a dog groomer, and a stuntwoman. It was a Hollywood stuntman who suggested she become a pro wrestler.

Although he was honest about what she'd have to go through in the wrestling business, Sharkey managed to convince her and started to train her in 1984. To his credit, Sharkey had a very good resume, having trained Rick Rude, Hawk and Animal, and former Minnesota governor Jesse "The Body" Ventura.

Soon enough, she started working some small shows for Sharkey, in bars and other similar venues, most of the time for nothing or a $5 payout. But she had the dedication and the passion to overcome all that.

"It was pretty easy with her. She wanted it real bad, and nobody was ever going to stop her or get in her way," said Sharkey. "Boy, she got it too. She went to Japan, she went to Australia, she got it done. She was a hell of a girl."

In 1986, Miceli got a break when Wahoo McDaniel convinced the office to bring her to the AWA to work with Sherri Martel. When Martel quit the AWA to go to the WWF without dropping the title, it opened a spot for a new champion to be named. On December 27, 1987, at the Showboat Sports Pavilion in Las Vegas, Miceli defeated former AWA women's champion Candi Devine to win the vacant title. She remained champion almost a full year, losing the title in November 1988 to former WWF titleholder Wendi Richter. However, a month before that match, Miceli had a match against All Japan Women's icon Chigusa Nagayo in Las Vegas. Nagayo helped put Miceli in touch with Japan, a relationship that would dramatically affect her career.

All Japan Women signed Miceli to a contract, making her the first American to receive a full-time contract with the company. She wrestled exclusively in Japan in 1989 and 1990. She made some appearances on the independents and in WCW, facing the likes of Bambi, Leilani Kai, and Judy Martin, and finished up with All Japan in 1992.

In 1993, Vince McMahon saw the opportunity to revive his women's division, building around Miceli. She was given the name Alundra Blayze and won the women's title, defeating Heidi Lee Morgan in a tournament final on December 13, 1993. She defended her title against Morgan, Luna Vachon, and the returning Leilani Kai, but Blayze

*Alundra Blayze had success in the U.S. and Japan.*
BERTRAND HEBERT COLLECTION/WWE

wanted to face new opponents and pushed to bring in some of the women from Japan. Bull Nakano was the chosen one. The two of them had a good program, although they were used sporadically. In the spring of 1995, Blayze reportedly asked for a medical leave, and on a *Raw* episode where she had beaten Nakano, Rhonda Sing — who was to be known as Bertha Faye — came and attacked Miceli to explain her absence.

"It was generally believed using Bertha Faye, nearly 15 years past her prime when she was a top heel in both Japan and Mexico, would result in killing whatever was left of [the women's division], and when Faye's character was changed from her former Monster Ripper to the love interest of Harvey Wippleman, that was the death of it as the comedy turned into a total failure," wrote Dave Meltzer.

Even though the WWF brought several other Japanese wrestlers throughout 1995, the women's division was doomed, and Blayze's contract, which expired on December 13, wasn't renewed.

## WCW: *"Where the big girls play"*

With Blayze still technically the WWF women's champion but without a contract, and with the Monday Night War between WWF and WCW just starting, Eric Bischoff saw an opportunity to take a shot at his opponent. On December 18, 1995, only five days after she was let go, Miceli showed up on *WCW Monday Nitro* ... and she brought the WWF women's title belt.

She called herself Madusa, adding that she used to be Alundra Blayze in the WWF. In a gesture that would be played over and over again for the next 20 years, she dropped the belt in a trash can, saying that was what she thought of the belt. She concluded her promo by saying: "This is where the big boys play, and now, this is where the big girls play!"

Miceli didn't think this angle would become what it actually did.

"So they got rid of the women's division and I was let go. Not in a bad way. It was just, 'Here you go. Here's a letter. We're doing some changes,'" she recalled in a *Table for Three* interview on the WWE Network. "In a matter of 24 hours, it gets out. That's when I got the phone call. 'Hey, 'Duce, we heard you were let go. Is it true?' 'Yeah, I was let go. What's up?' 'Well, you still got that title?' I said, 'Yeah.' And Bischoff said, 'How would you be interested in bringing that to *Monday Night Nitro* and let's talk about a contract.'

"I was like, wow, it's been less than 24 hours. My contract's good. Back then, they didn't have that whole six-month clause where you couldn't wrestle somewhere else, so I was good to go. I was like, 'Damn, I have to put food on the table.' I was the breadwinner. I had to do what I had to do. I was doing what any male or female would have done in the business at that time when you had to survive. So I went over there. I brought the belt not knowing what was going to happen. And then he came in and said, 'Hey, 'Duce, where's that belt?' I said, 'I got it but I've got to give it back.' 'Well, how about you throwing that title in the trash tonight live on TV?' Just so I get it back. I need to get it to Vince. That was all I was thinking. I wasn't thinking I was going to make this — all the shit that happened. I never thought it would blow up the way it did. And I was kind of hurt that I was one of the first to go because I worked so hard. I loved my job in wrestling. So I said, 'Yeah, I can do that, just so long as I get it back.' It's probably no big deal. I thought, 'God, this is going to be a great angle. People are going to love this. People are going to

*Twenty years after being thrown in the trash, the WWF women's title came back to where it belongs.* COURTESY OF WORLD WRESTLING ENTERTAINMENT, INC.

talk about it.' I swear to God, that's all I thought." Although it didn't by any means start the war, as is so often reported, it's still one of the most talked about segments of that era.

The idea for WCW behind bringing her over was to capitalize on the fact that WWF had given up on the women's division to create its own division. Starting in the summer of 1996, they brought in Nakano, Malia Hosaka, Leilani Kai, Debbie Combs, and Akira Hokuto to work with Madusa. At Starrcade that year, in a surprising move, they held the final of the tournament to crown the first WCW women's champion, and instead of going with Madusa, they put the belt on Hokuto. Six months later, after a handful of matches, Madusa lost a very good match against Hokuto with the stipulation being that she would have to retire. The real reason behind this was that WCW wanted to use her as a valet instead. A short time later, WCW dropped the women's division. Ironically, Madusa would never win the belt she was brought in for.

In 1999, she began wrestling again, with her gimmick being that she would fight men. She was part of the WCW world heavyweight title tournament and had a brief run as the WCW cruiserweight champion. But when Vince McMahon bought the WCW, there was nowhere for her to go.

She retired and became a huge monster truck star. In 2015, against all odds, WWE came calling about inducting her into its Hall of Fame. Of course, they would need to do a skit about what had happened two decades earlier. At the end of her induction speech, she pulled the belt from a trash can and said that after 20 years, the belt was finally "back home where it belongs."

As they were rehearsing the ceremony, Miceli met with Vince McMahon for the first time in more than a decade.

"We both just held each other and I squeezed him so tight," Miceli said in an interview with Daniel Pena. "I started getting emotional and kind of crying."

Miceli apologized to McMahon, and he told her she could keep the belt if she wanted and that she was exactly the kind of female wrestler WWE needed today.

If wrestling had been out of her life for the past 15 years, the Hall of Fame ceremony helped reconcile her with the wrestling world. Miceli appeared on the WWE Network and was named commissioner of the all-female Stardom promotion in Japan.

## GLOW: Gorgeous Ladies of Wrestling

Created in 1985, *Gorgeous Ladies of Wrestling* was a campy, wrestling-based variety show developed by producer David B. McLane to capitalize on the growing popularity of pro wrestling and the success of the WWF and WrestleMania.

McLane wasn't an outsider to the wrestling business as he had previously worked in Indianapolis for Dick the Bruiser as a ring announcer and commentator among other things. In partnership with Jackie Stallone (the mother of Sylvester Stallone), who owned a women's gym, and with Matt Cimber as the head writer, he cast a crew of actresses, models, stuntwomen, and dancers and signed them up for a crash course in wrestling, under the tutelage of Mando

Guerrero. The *GLOW* girls were taught the basics of wrestling and given names such as Americana (the patriotic All-American girl), Susie Spirit (the cheerleader), Little Egypt (the belly dancer), and the punk rock Valley girl tag team of Hollywood and Vine. There were farmer's daughters in Daisy Duke shorts, California girls in bikinis and tube tops, and Southern belles ... essentially, every fetish type was represented. Guerrero was only there at the beginning, though.

"If I would have kept on going, they would have been a lot better, a lot better, because I taught them the way I was taught. I didn't go straight to wrestling. I'd give them drills first, the way they stand," he said.

Episodes were filmed at the Riviera Hotel in Las Vegas, and *Gorgeous Ladies of Wrestling* debuted in syndication in 1986. Short wrestling matches were interspersed with comedy skits and interview segments, and each *GLOW* girl performed her own rap theme song, inspired by the success of the 1985 Chicago Bears' "Super Bowl Shuffle."

Intentionally hokey, *GLOW* was more *Hee-Haw* than pro wrestling, with skits that saw the girls visiting the official *GLOW* physicians "Dr. Fiel" and "Dr. Grope" and other cornball comedy and double entendres. But the show quickly attracted an audience who regularly tuned in to watch the *GLOW* girls in their revealing outfits, featuring plenty of cleavage and low-cut tights. Although *GLOW* recognized a championship (a tiara as opposed to a traditional title belt), the promotion made little attempt to present itself as an athletic competition — it was simply attractive women writhing around together.

Because of the show's popularity, the *GLOW* girls were invited to appear on celebrity editions of *Family Feud*, which was a clear sign of the show's success. Matilda the Hun (who also wrestled as Queen Kong) had a bit part in Aerosmith's "Love in an Elevator" music video in 1987. But the success of *Gorgeous Ladies of Wrestling* didn't sit well with many female wrestlers.

"I had no respect for them," said Malia Hosaka, who was just breaking into wrestling and training under Killer Kowalski as *GLOW* was taking off. "I actually had one *GLOW* girl tell me that they were out there to make fun of women's wrestling. They weren't out there to

*A GLOW reunion in Las Vegas, with then-CAC president Karl Laurer.* SCOTT ROMER

look like women wrestlers, they were out there to make a comedy skit about women's wrestling. So, basically, you're telling me that you're out there to degrade those that have paved the way for you to have this."

*GLOW* survived for four seasons, making 104 episodes and ultimately featuring a cast of more than 60 women. A handful of *GLOW* girls continued wrestling after the show concluded, working for either the AWA or the WWF: Olympia Hartauer, Brandi Mae, Killer Tomato, Princess Jasmine, and most notably Tina Moretti, who performed as Tina Ferrari in *GLOW* and went on to wrestle for the WWF as Ivory for several years.

Subsequent attempts at revivals never quite got off the ground. In 2011, several of the *GLOW* girls reunited for a documentary titled *GLOW: The Story of the Gorgeous Ladies of Wrestling*, which went on to receive glowing reviews on the film festival circuit.

"Little Egypt" Angelina Altishin organized a reunion of the *GLOW* cast at the 2011 Cauliflower Alley Club Reunion, which proved to be a difficult task.

"One of the oddities of the *GLOW* shows is that we were given characters and then we were given fictitious names to go along with those characters," Altishin said in an interview with David Buckler for Diva-Dirt. "So that when we were working in those seasons, we never referred to each other by our real names. We always referred to each other by our character names. Trying to find those characters was almost impossible."

In 2016, it was announced that the creators of the hit series *Orange Is the New Black* were working on a comedy series for Netflix based on *GLOW*, in which actress Alison Brie and comedian Marc Maron will star. Coincidentally, Mando Guerrero's nephew, Chavo Jr., was hired to train the actresses, the same role his uncle had. Although it was a polarizing and nontraditional program, *GLOW* proved to be one of the most prominent and popular female wrestling promotions of all time.

# The ATTITUDE ERA
## The Revival of the WWF's Women's Division

The period between 1996 and 2002 in pro wrestling is referred to as the Attitude Era, a period marked by provocative storylines, scantily clad women, and adult language. The WWF began to introduce edgier content into its storylines, taking a cue from the upstart Extreme Championship Wrestling, a Philadelphia-based promotion that was building a national cult following for its unique brand of hardcore matches, profanity, and catfights.

The Attitude Era was outrageous for the sake of being outrageous, and the effect it had on women's wrestling was to dramatically increase the sexual component of the matches and the company's presentation of women. Valet Sunny (Tamara Sytch), known as one the original Divas, was AOL's most downloaded celebrity in 1996. Although she didn't wrestle, she was used in increasingly sexual situations and appeared nearly nude in photo shoots. Bra and panties matches became commonplace, alongside lingerie and evening gown matches, but even those became passé and were replaced by mud matches, chocolate pudding matches, gravy boat matches, and frequent bikini contests. Expressions like Jerry Lawler's "puppies" or Eric Bischoff's "HLA" (for hot lesbian action) became as much used as body slam or hip toss. "It was not easy being a woman in that period," recalled Stephanie McMahon. Traditional wrestling matches were simply not emboldened. "I remember a line being given to me was: 'That's not how the women fight,'" remembered Trish Stratus. "I was like but we did. We just did. What do you mean 'the women'? What does that mean?'"

Ironically, some of WWE's top female wrestlers emerged in an era where bra and panties matches and gimmick matches were the norm.

## SABLE

"For the men who come to see me, and the women who want to be me."

From her painted-on handprint "bikini" top to her three appearances on the cover of *Playboy*, no female wrestler better encapsulated the WWF's Attitude Era than Sable.

Born August 8, 1967, Rena Greek grew up in Jacksonville, Florida. She was active in horseback riding, gymnastics, and softball before turning her attention to beauty pageants when she was 12. Her success in the pageant field led her to modeling.

She married Wayne Richardson in 1986, but Richardson was killed in an automobile accident not long after the birth of the couple's daughter. In 1993, she met wrestler Marc Mero, who had been competing as the flamboyant Johnny B. Badd in WCW. She and Mero married in 1994, and when Mero signed with the WWF in 1996, Rena was signed on as his valet. That would end up changing Greek's life.

The pair debuted at WrestleMania 12, with Rena accompanying Hunter Hearst Helmsley to the ring for a match against the Ultimate Warrior. Triple H was soundly thrashed by the Warrior and was taking his frustration out on his valet backstage, when the debuting Mero played the white knight and saved the damsel in distress, launching a feud with Triple H.

Unfortunately for Mero, the Wildman was quickly outshone by his beautiful wife. Sable became one of the most popular personalities in the company while Mero languished. Along with Tamara "Sunny" Sytch, Sable injected a massive dose of sex appeal into the WWF, but unlike with Sunny, the decision was made to transition Sable into a wrestler, something she

One of the first Divas in the Attitude Era, Sable.
JEAN-FRANÇOIS LEDUC COLLECTION

had reservations about, because of her lack of training and the fear her breast implants would cause her trouble taking bumps.

Nevertheless, at WrestleMania 14, the team of Sable and Mero defeated Goldust and Luna Vachon in a mixed tag match that saw Sable unveil her "Sable Bomb" powerbomb and a version of Mero's TKO finishing move to pin Vachon.

But Sable's lack of wrestling skills didn't make her a backstage favorite, especially with some of the veterans. In an interview with WWE.com, Luna expressed her thoughts about Sable that night.

"Sable wasn't a wrestler until I made her one. A real wrestler can wrestle a mop and make it look like the mop is kicking their ass, and that's what happened that night. She beat me, and when we got to the back there was champagne and confetti and everyone wanted to celebrate with Sable. I kept walking until Owen Hart came up to me and told me I had just put on the match of my life. It meant a lot to have someone like him say that to me."

In the storyline that followed, Mero became jealous of Sable's popularity and turned against her, taking on Jacqueline as his new manager. Consequently, at the 1998 Survivor Series, Sable pinned Jacqueline to win the WWF women's title.

However, the women's title wouldn't become Sable's biggest claim to fame. In April 1999, she was featured on the cover of *Playboy* magazine for the first time. Her wrestling popularity helped it become one of *Playboy*'s top-selling issues of all time. The success led to a storyline in which Sable adopted a more arrogant attitude and turned heel, borrowing some mannerisms and catchphrases from Rick Rude and debuting her signature taunt, "the grind," where she gyrated over a fallen opponent.

As a heel, Sable's defense of the women's title became virtually an afterthought. Her title reign lasted almost six months but was punctuated by periods of inactivity.

"As for the wrestling part of her career, it is difficult to take her in-ring role 100 per cent serious when she admitted on-air that it's part of her contract not to take bumps," wrote Greg Oliver following Sable's appearance on TSN's *Off the Record* in January 1999.

She lost the title in one of the all-time low points in the history of the women's championship, defeating Debra in an evening gown match where the objective of the match was to strip your opponent down to her bra and panties. Sable won the match, but WWF commissioner Shawn Michaels thought Debra looked so good in her underwear that he decided to name her the new champion instead.

Although Sable was popular and somewhat of a draw, relations between the champion and Vince McMahon and the WWF were already in bad shape, which is why that title switch happened the way it did.

"Mero suggested losing the title, but asked that it not be on television. McMahon disagreed, saying that if she didn't appear at the May 10 live *Raw* in Orlando, Florida to drop the title, it would be a breach of contract. She still refused and brought her lawyers to the taping and wrote her own terms for agreeing to drop the title [which led to the ridiculous scenario they did]," wrote Dave Meltzer.

Sable left the WWF a short time later and filed a $110 million lawsuit against the company, claiming sexual harassment and unsafe working conditions. As part of her suit, she claimed the WWF was pressuring her to participate in a lesbian storyline and to go topless during a match, likely as an "accidental" wardrobe malfunction on pay-per-view.

"Men would routinely walk into the women's dressing room as if by accident; men would cut holes in the walls to watch the women dressing," she claimed in court papers. "Extras were hired as WWF regulars to expose their breasts, big nipple contests were engaged in; men regularly bragged about their sexual encounters without regard to the women present."

The lawsuit was eventually settled out of court. Surprisingly — despite the bad blood from her departure from the company and the lawsuit — Sable returned to WWE in 2003 . . . and took part in a lesbian storyline with Torrie Wilson to promote a *Playboy* pictorial featuring both Divas. She also played the role of Vince McMahon's mistress. She retired from wrestling in 2004, divorced from Mero that same year, and married former UFC champion and current WWE Superstar Brock Lesnar in 2006.

# CHYNA

Before she was "the Ninth Wonder of the World" (in wrestling circles, Andre the Giant has the designation of "Eighth Wonder of the World" all wrapped up), Joanie Laurer was a young girl growing up in — by her own admission — a toxic family environment in Rochester, New York.

She was born two days after Christmas, on December 27, 1969. Her parents divorced when she was four. According to her 2001 autobiography, her mother was verbally and emotionally abusive to Joanie and her siblings (a brother and a sister), her father was a con man, and her mother introduced a string of stepfathers to the children in rapid succession.

She was always tall for her age and would grow to a full height of 5'10". Her height made her stand out. In the seventh grade, a male teacher kissed her and declared he loved her; when she rebuked his advances, she received a C in his class. She developed bulimia and eventually became interested in physical fitness competitions. She began competing in Fitness America pageants after graduating from high school, but at her size, she stood out like a sore thumb and watched as the more petite girls were declared the winners.

She enrolled at the University of Tampa and then bounced around between several jobs including waitressing in a strip club, belly dancing, answering the phone for a 900 party line, and eventually selling pagers, a hot commodity among drug dealers of the era. She was looking for a new direction in her life when she saw pro wrestling on television.

"There it was in all its epic ambition, its winking boorishness, its harmless heroics," she wrote. "'I CAN DO THAT!' I got up, paced, pointed at the set. 'Look! Look at those guys! Look at their faces! They're having fun.' And I wanted in. It was kooky, it was wrongheaded, it was MY CHOICE. And I didn't know the first thing about it. Was there a how-to book I could read?"

She heard about a wrestling school operated by Wladek "Killer" Kowalski in nearby Malden, Massachusetts. She paged through the phone book and found his number, then cold-called to find out how to enroll in the Killer Kowalski Institute of Professional Wrestling.

For a fee of $2,000 Kowalski took her in. He was impressed by her size and strength (according to her memoir, she was able to bench-press 315 pounds at the time). After a brief period of training, Kowalski booked her on independent cards in Massachusetts. She wrestled her first match in 1995; because another woman wasn't available, she faced a male wrestler in drag. "Just make sure not to body-slam him and make his [false] boobies go funny," Kowalski reminded her before the match.

But Laurer had no intention of staying on the indies for long. A friend gave her the name of a WWF agent, and she tracked the agent down at the local Holiday Inn when the WWF came to Springfield, Massachusetts. Armed with her publicity photos and videotapes, she lobbied for a job with the WWF. The agent didn't bite, but she met Triple H

*"The Ninth Wonder of the World" Chyna.*
JOANNE ROUGEAU COLLECTION

and Shawn Michaels as they arrived at the hotel. Laurer bonded over Kowalski stories (Triple H also got his start at the Institute). Impressed with her look, and looking for a new element to add to D-Generation X, Triple H and Michaels went to Vince McMahon and pitched a scenario that saw them bring her on as a sexy female bodyguard.

McMahon wasn't having it. "Vince hated the idea," she wrote, Triple H having filled her in on what was said after the fact. "'She's never really worked anywhere. What if she's a flake? And what's a woman going to do, bust up the guys? No one's gonna go for that. She's gonna hit guys? . . . I personally have no interest in seeing a big woman ass-kicker.'"

In the fall of 1996, Laurer went to a LIWA convention in Las

Vegas with Professional Girl Wrestling Association promoter Randy Powell, and she really got a lot of attention.

"She was like a magnet. Nobody knew who she was," recalled Powell. "I had to basically beg Moolah, and she would not put Joanie on the card."

Whether McMahon heard about that Vegas trip or not, and despite his reservations, the Clique eventually sold him on the idea. She debuted at In Your House 13 as a fan who attacked (and dwarfed) Marlena (Terri Runnels) during Triple H's match against Goldust. She was later introduced as the bodyguard and enforcer of DX and given the name Chyna. A name that connoted fragile finery was being used in reference to the most dominant female ever presented in the WWF.

While the WWF women's title was being contested in ridiculous evening gown matches and bra and panties bouts, Chyna's physicality involved sneak-attack low blows on male wrestlers and wrestling exclusively against male opponents. Everyone from Steve Austin to Mick Foley, the Rock to Eddie Guerrero, sold for her and made her look like gold. In other words, she was protected. However, while fans remember her matches against men, in reality, she only had a handful of matches. By the end of 1999, she had only wrestled in 41 matches, almost all of them on TV or on PPV, since she was said to still be limited in what she could do in the ring. Despite all that, in January 1999, she became the first woman ever to compete in the Royal Rumble pay-per-view. She competed in the 1999 King of the Ring Tournament, beating Val Venis in the opening round before losing to DX stablemate Road Dogg in the quarterfinals.

In October 1999, Chyna defeated Jeff Jarrett to become the first woman to hold the Intercontinental title. The match almost didn't happen, though. Through a huge snafu, Jarrett's WWF contract had been allowed to expire — unnoticed — the day before the No Mercy pay-per-view. Jarrett and Chyna were scheduled to have a Battle of the Sexes "Good Housekeeping" match (where household items could be used as weapons), but Jarrett wouldn't wrestle unless McMahon agreed to an outrageous one-night contract . . . either that or he would be forced to cancel an advertised title match, deal with potential refund claims from PPV buyers, and — worst of all — helplessly watch his Intercontinental champion jump to the rival WCW. McMahon and Jarrett eventually struck a deal — a reported $250,000 — and the match took place. At the end of the night, Chyna was the IC champion.

"My favourite moment in the WWF is probably winning the Intercontinental Championship. I worked very hard for it and felt honoured to hold a title that so many greats before my time had done," she said in an interview with Steve Gerweck.

She then moved into a feud with WWF newcomer Chris Jericho, losing the belt to him, then regaining the title after a double-pin finish that resulted in Jericho and Chyna being billed as cochampions for several weeks. She was then paired with another newcomer, Eddie Guerrero. Several observers thought the pairing was a rib on Guerrero, who stood several inches shorter than Chyna, but Guerrero made it work, declaring Chyna his "Mamacita." Guerrero and Chyna defeated Trish Stratus and Val Venis in a mixed tag at SummerSlam. Chyna scored the pinfall, regaining the IC title in the process. She later lost that belt to Guerrero.

In January 2001, the WWF ran an injury angle where Chyna had her neck damaged by Ivory, who was with the Right to Censor group and was protesting Chyna's pictorial in *Playboy*. The injury was presented as career threatening, but Chyna returned to beat Ivory for the women's title. But Chyna lost something as an attraction when she was competing against women . . . she was no longer something *special*.

On top of that, her real-life boyfriend, Triple H, had moved into a storyline marriage with Stephanie McMahon, which would eventually become a real marriage. A lover's triangle had developed, and Chyna was cut out. She vacated the women's title and officially left WWE in November 2001. Before leaving, she was offered a downside guarantee of $400,000 per year but wanted a base salary of something closer to $1 million. "It was an outrageous demand that wasn't even realistic," said Jim Ross to the Bleacher Report, adding that she would have ended up making more than double what they were offering.

With WCW's sale, she had no real alternative. She made a few

*A tragic end for one of the best known women in WWE history.* PAT LAPRADE COLLECTION/RICH FREEDA WWE

appearances for New Japan Pro Wrestling in 2002 (which used her against opponents like Masa Chono) and had a one-off appearance in TNA in 2011, rekindling her feud against Jarrett as she and Kurt Angle defeated Jarrett and his wife, Karen, in a mixed tag.

Following her departure from wrestling, she tried her hand in acting and eventually in pornography, starring among other films in a homemade sex tape with Sean "X-Pac" Waltman dubbed *One Night in Chyna.* She also appeared on the reality show *Celebrity Rehab with Dr. Drew* in 2008.

Laurer was found dead in her home in Redondo Beach, California, on April 20, 2016. She had lost her long battle with addiction, dying at the age of 46. Her brain was donated to science to study the effects of chronic traumatic encephalopathy. The wrestling community exploded on Twitter, with many of her peers, such as Trish Stratus, Lita, Mick Foley, Tommy Dreamer, Shawn Michaels, Stephanie McMahon, and of course, Triple H, paying their respect. Her death was heavily covered by the media, and on the following *Monday Night Raw*, a very nice video tribute was shown. Waltman said that he would do anything in his power to make sure she gets in the WWE Hall of Fame.

Whether she gets inducted or not, many women in wrestling, such as Mickie James, Beth Phoenix, and even the late great Sherri Martel, looked up to Laurer at one point or another and saw her as a positive for women's wrestling. But it's probably Serena Deeb (Serena in WWE) who expressed it the best.

"When I was 11 years old, I fell in love with pro wrestling and my very first inspiration was Chyna," she said on her website. "She was such an unconventional female and I feel she was a wonderful role model for young women because she made it ok to be 'different.' The company built her as such a strong woman, literally and figuratively. She was the first woman to hook me on wrestling."

## TRISH STRATUS

The youngest wrestler ever inducted into the WWE Hall of Fame, Trish Stratus revitalized women's wrestling in WWE in the 2000s, restoring credibility to the women's title while carrying the division.

Born Patricia Stratigeas in Richmond Hill, Ontario, on December 18, 1975, she played soccer and field hockey.

"Growing up, one of my favorite TV shows was *Wonder Woman*," Stratus said in 2016 as she received the Iron Mike Mazurki Award, the highest award given by the Cauliflower Alley Club. "I loved that she could kick ass while looking good doing it. Even back then, I realized that was a hard balance to achieve. And the other show that I used to watch was wrestling. I grew up in a large Greek family. Including my sister, there were eight of us cousins, all about the same age. We figured we had just about enough of us to start our own wrestling federation. We put on wrestling matches for our parents who would begrudgingly watch. . . . My sister and I had wrestling matches with our Barbie dolls. I don't know how many girls do that."

She went on to university, where she studied biology and kinesiology. A health and fitness nut, she was approached by *MuscleMag International* and asked to pose for a shoot, beginning her career as a fitness model. Her physique and sultry look were noticed by WWF

*From Toronto, Ontario, Canada, Trish Stratus.*
PAT LAPRADE COLLECTION/RICH FREEDA WWE

scouts, who asked her if she was willing to work for the company. Actually, WCW was also interested, and Terry Taylor had told Jim Ross that he would call her if WWF didn't. A longtime wrestling fan, she quickly accepted the offer, signing with the WWF in 1999. She began training with Ron Hutchison at Sully's Gym in Toronto.

"Trish had the guts to enter a boys' world and more than held her own. She was the only female trainee at the time," remembered Hutchison. "She came into the gym, saw that it was populated with just guys [who were taking a pounding] and told me, yes, she was certain she wanted to learn. I tried to scare her off. It wasn't going to work. She came, got down to business and, in reality, put a lot of the boys to shame."

She debuted with the WWF under the name Trish Stratus in March 2000, acting as manager of the tag team Test and Albert, known as T&A. Her first major physical storyline saw her take a vicious powerbomb through a table from Bubba Ray Dudley at Backlash 2000. She began a rivalry with Lita as her team feuded with the Hardy Boyz, defeating Lita in an Indian strap match in July 2000, thanks to an assist from Stephanie McMahon.

In 2001, Stratus was placed in a storyline where she portrayed Vince McMahon's younger mistress while his wife, Linda, had been institutionalized and heavily sedated after demanding a divorce. McMahon and Stratus would have graphic make-out sessions, often right in front of Linda, creating a storyline rift between Trish and Stephanie. The low point of the bizarre angle came in March 2001, when McMahon tried to publicly humiliate his "mistress," forcing her to get down on her knees, bark like a dog, and strip down to her underwear in the middle of the ring. It was an uncomfortable segment that was one of the most controversial moments in WWF history, but it succeeded in making Trish a sympathetic character. At WrestleMania 17, Stratus completed her babyface turn, slapping McMahon in the face.

Stratus won the WWF women's title for the first time at the 2001 Survivor Series, winning a six-pack challenge match to claim the title. It would prove to be her first of a record-setting seven WWF women's title runs.

At WrestleMania 18, Stratus wrestled in her hometown of Toronto, facing Jazz and Lita in a three-way match for the women's title. The match was scheduled in a tough spot, following the massively popular contest between icons the Rock and Hulk Hogan. "It was really a tough act to follow," Stratus told Arda Ocal in a 2012 interview on *The Score*. "The crowd actually surprisingly was with us, which was great because it was a testament to the hard work that the women's division had done. Something interesting had happened. When the guys [the Rock and Hulk Hogan] had their match, the one thing I remember was I was about to go out to perform. It's my first WrestleMania as a wrestler. I got the heads-up from Hulk and the Rock. Rock said to me, 'Good luck, go get 'em kid,' and Hogan said, 'You got this, kid.'"

In May 2002, she won the WWE hardcore title, which was defended under 24/7 rules, meaning the champion could be attacked and pinned at any moment, as long as there was a referee nearby to count the fall. She surprised Crash Holly to win the belt, then lost it to Stevie Richards the same night.

In September 2002, Stratus beat Molly Holly to win the women's title for a third time. She lost the belt to Victoria in a hardcore match at the 2002 Survivor Series, then regained the belt at WrestleMania 19, winning a three-way bout over Victoria and Jazz.

"I found that when Jazz and I were given the opportunity to have — I guess you'd say, 'men's style matches' instead of 'chick fights' — that it took the fans, who were all into screaming 'Puppies' [announcer Jerry Lawler's euphemism for breasts], some time to get used to it," she said in an interview with the British website Sportsvibe. "So we just worked our butts off and agreed that we were going to do something a little better every week and give them something different so that they can get used to seeing this. And then after a while people started getting into it."

She was named Diva of the Decade on January 14, 2003, in honor of *Raw*'s 10-year anniversary.

Soon after, Trish had a heel turn, instigating a feud with Chris Jericho, and won the women's title for a fourth time at Bad Blood. On December 6, 2004, she lost the women's title to Lita in a match that main-evented *Raw*, a first for the flagship show. "You never would have thought I'd be so happy to lose my championship," said Stratus. She regained the title at the 2004 New Year's Revolution PPV, when Lita tore her ACL during the match. Still in 2004, a herniated disc kept her out of action for six months, although she was allowed to keep the women's title during that time.

Upon returning, she embarked on a storyline where she was stalked by Mickie James, portraying an obsessive fan with a crush on Stratus. Stratus lost the belt to James at WrestleMania 22 in a critically acclaimed bout, ending Trish's 448-day title reign.

In August 2006, she announced she would be retiring, with her last match taking place at the Unforgiven pay-per-view in Toronto. Stratus won her retirement match, beating her archrival Lita (who had become her best friend in reality) to win the women's title for a seventh time. She retired as champion.

"I think it really became more special during the end of my career

*Trish Stratus is the youngest WWE Hall of Famer.* MIKE MASTRANDREA

when I had the retirement match with her," she said in an interview. "To me, it meant a lot. Did I handpick her as my opponent? Yes, I did. I proposed that idea to Vince [McMahon], and he loved it. I thought, 'Great, I can't think of a better way to go out than with my best friend, a fellow coworker who I had this rivalry with my entire career.'"

Following her retirement, Stratus went on to open a yoga studio in Toronto and did some acting and stunt work. She came out of retirement to wrestle at WrestleMania 27, teaming with John Morrison and reality TV star Snooki to beat Michelle McCool, Layla El, and Dolph Ziggler. She was inducted into the WWE Hall of Fame in 2013 at the age of 37. In 2015, she had a baby boy; she named Lita as her son's godmother.

She will be remembered as a woman who took wrestling very seriously, who was constantly improving. For her original trainer, that really wasn't a surprise.

"I think the key to her success lies in her motto that 'preparedness meets opportunity.' In short, she prepares for every opportunity that comes her way and she works hard to make sure that she is ready to capitalize on an opportunity should it be offered. Her mind-boggling success in the world of women's professional wrestling is no accident. She's put in the work and I am so proud of her and her successes both in and out of the wrestling world," concluded Hutchison.

# LITA

With her flame-red hair, contagious can-do attitude, and of course, her signature visible thong poking out from beneath her hip-huggers, Lita became one of wrestling's most popular stars in the early 2000s.

Prior to joining WWE, where she was a member of Team Xtreme with Matt and Jeff Hardy, Lita actually began training for a career in wrestling in Mexico, having moved south of the border due, in part, to a fascination with Lucha Libre.

Born Amy Dumas on April 14, 1975, she grew up in Fort Lauderdale, Florida. She dropped out of college and was searching for a career path when she came across wrestling on television. She took a particular interest in Rey Mysterio Jr. and the other Mexican luchadors who were being featured on *WCW Monday Nitro* in the mid-1990s. She was captivated by the look and agility of Mexican wrestling, and she wanted to learn more about it.

"I saved my money and called my travel agent and said, 'I want to go to Mexico.'" She said in a 2000 interview with Alex Marvez. "I took a taxi to the arena and sat in the front row and was all excited to see the lucha and try to figure out how to do it. I knew what I wanted to do but I had no idea how to go about doing it. I was the only white girl in the audience."

She stayed in Mexico for six weeks, regularly attending Consejo Mundial de Lucha Libre cards and taking what she described as a "crash course" in Lucha training with Ricky Santana and Miguel Perez Jr. She learned the basics of bumping, then returned to the United States, where she looked to make contacts on the indies. She went to Chicago and received a bit more training, working primarily as a valet before meeting the Hardy brothers, who offered to train her in the Carolinas.

In 1999, she was brought into ECW, where she worked as a valet for Danny Doring under the name Miss Congeniality, later changing her name to Angelica. While still very green in terms of wrestling abilities, she had presence, a good look, and the willingness and desire to learn. She enrolled in Dory Funk Jr.'s Funkin' Conservatory training school over the summer of 1999 and was offered a WWF developmental contract in November 1999.

*A daredevil of her own, Lita.* PAT LAPRADE COLLECTION/WWE

After several months of training in the Memphis Championship Wrestling developmental system, she was brought to the main roster as Lita, a valet for Essa Rios. She quickly showed she was more than just a pretty face by mimicking Rios's finisher, hitting his opponents with beautifully executed moonsaults after the match.

The pairing with Rios didn't last long, and Lita was partnered with the Hardys; not only were they her trainers, but she was also dating Matt at the time. Now that she was a part of Team Xtreme, Lita began dressing the part, adopting her low-riding pants and thong. It was a fashion choice that left some people perplexed.

"[WWF management] didn't get it at first," Lita told Marvez. "There was a women's battle royal the first time I wore the pants live and had my thong exposed. That was the beginning of the look. They said, 'You had a really good match but you have to do something to get your pants to stay up.' I thought they knew they were where they were supposed to be. They said, 'We could see your underwear the whole time!' And I said, 'Yeah, I know.' . . . It's kind of something where you want to be feminine but it's got a kind of hang-boy type of look."

The Hardys and Lita moved into a feud with T&A (Test and Albert), managed by Trish Stratus, leading to a six-person tag bout at Fully Loaded 2000, where Lita pinned Stratus. This would be the start of a long-running rivalry in the ring and a very close friendship between the two.

On the August 21, 2000, edition of *Raw*, Lita defeated Stephanie McMahon to win the WWF women's title. With The Rock as guest referee, and Triple H and Kurt Angle at ringside, the match was the first time a women's match main-evented an episode of *Raw*, and the show garnered a 6.25, making it the last time an edition of *Raw* achieved at least a 6.0 rating.

"Lita was a rebel in a division of normalcy," said Serena Deeb. "I think she drew a great following because of that."

Lita held the title for nearly four months until losing it to Ivory. Lita and Stratus found themselves on the same side during the WCW/ECW invasion storyline and teamed up to face WCW alumni Torrie Wilson and Stacy Keibler.

In April 2002, Lita suffered a severe neck injury while filming scenes for the TV series *Dark Angel*, suffering three cracked vertebrae and requiring surgery. The injury kept her out of the ring for almost a year and a half, and it also forced her to change her wrestling style, adopting a more conservative style and avoiding any potentially dangerous bumps that could aggravate the injury. She returned to WWE in September 2003, and in November, she wrestled Victoria in the first women's steel cage match in WWE history.

In December 2004, after being part of a bizarre angle with Kane and Gene Snitsky, she won the women's title for a second time, beating Stratus for the belt. Stratus won the belt back the following month, setting the table for a title match at WrestleMania 21, but Lita tore her ACL in a match against Trish at the 2005 New Year's Revolution PPV, putting her back on the disabled list.

In 2005, Lita had begun a romantic relationship with Edge, causing a split between her and Hardy, which was then used as a storyline. Lita became Edge's valet, and Edge quickly became the top heel in WWE. To celebrate Edge's WWE championship win over John Cena in January 2006, Edge and Lita had a "live sex celebration" in the ring, where they stripped down to their underwear and simulated having sex in a bed set up in the ring, until Ric Flair showed up to ruin the fun. The segment earned a 5.2 rating, making it the most-watched segment in more than a year.

Lita won the women's title for a third time in August 2006 with a win over Mickie James. She lost the belt to Stratus in Stratus's retirement match at Unforgiven, then won the belt for a fourth and final time, winning a tournament to crown a new champion. She wrestled her retirement match at the 2006 Survivor Series, where she lost the title back to James.

Lita was inducted into the WWE Hall of Fame in 2014 by her "bestie" Stratus. She worked as a trainer for *Tough Enough* in 2015 and went on to perform for a punk rock band called the Luchagors. She was also part of WWE's creative team, helped to train talent at the Performance Center, and was part of a panel on the *Raw* and *SmackDown* preview shows on the WWE Network, before parting ways with the company in December 2016.

"We debuted only a few weeks apart; we retired only a few weeks apart. My first match was with her, and of course, my last match was with her," Stratus said in Lita's introduction speech at the WWE Hall of Fame. "The second that we got on screen together, we were just there, there was just that chemistry. She was relatable, girls saw something in Amy that they saw in themselves. Amy was doing things we've never seen from a woman. She was cool."

# IVORY

The journey to the top is sometimes an odd ride. For Lisa Moretti, one booking as a "bumping ho" led to a six-year run in WWE and three women's championships.

Moretti was born in Inglewood, California, on November 26, 1961. She studied public relations at the University of Southern California and became a cheerleader for the USFL's Los Angeles Express Franchise in the mid-1980s. When the new *Gorgeous Ladies of Wrestling* promotion announced auditions in Las Vegas, Moretti was persuaded by a friend to give it a try. She was signed to *GLOW*, and she and her fellow signees — mostly models and hopeful actresses — were assigned to six weeks of training under Mando Guerrero.

"He's the man that really got me into wrestling," Moretti told SLAM! Wrestling. "Mando was the guy that made me feel passionate towards the sport because he had such a passion for it himself."

Guerrero further endeared himself to Moretti for his refusal to put up with students who weren't taking their training seriously.

"[One time] he just hopped right up in lickety-split time and grabbed this big, voluptuous blonde by the hair, threw her down to the mat, tied her up into a pretzel. She was crying. I thought to myself, 'Man, I like this guy.' He meant what he was saying. Pay attention."

Moretti debuted in *GLOW* in 1986 as good girl Tina Ferrari. She went on to win both the *GLOW* tag team title (with Ashley Cartier) and the *GLOW* championship tiara. She wrestled a handful of matches for the AWA and other independents under the names Tina Moretti and Nina, including a nine-woman lingerie battle royal at the AWA's SuperClash III event on December 13, 1988, which was headlined by Jerry Lawler vs. Kerry Von Erich. She also had the opportunity to work with Judy Martin, which gave her insight and respect for the female wrestlers who paved the way before *GLOW* came along.

After some money issue with David McLane's other promotion, Powerful Women of Wrestling, Moretti went into semi-retirement for several years until January 1999, when she received a call from Jim Cornette. "Cornette called and said the WWF needed 'a bumping ho' to accompany the Godfather," Moretti said at the 2012 Cauliflower Alley Club Reunion, where she received the organization's Women's Wrestling Award.

Moretti accepted the booking and was eventually offered a WWF contract. She made her in-ring debut soon after.

On June 8, 1999, Ivory defeated Debra to win her first WWF women's championship. Despite her beginnings in *GLOW*, Ivory took the women's title in a different, more athletic direction. Debra had "won" the women's title when acting WWF commissioner Shawn

*Right to Censor's Ivory.* PAT LAPRADE COLLECTION/RICH FREEDA WWE

Michaels had awarded it to her when she was stripped of her evening gown in an evening gown match against Sable; she had shown the most skin and got the belt as a reward.

"I was just on the heels of the Sable era, when the Divas were Divas," she told SLAM! "I was really, really scared that they were going to put me in a pair of high heels and make me prance around in a bikini or something. I was happy that they expected me to lift up my boots and get in there. After 10 years, there was a lot of ring rust to shave off."

Ivory was presented as a more traditional wrestler, a point she proved by instigating a feud with none other than the 76-year-old

Fabulous Moolah, losing the belt to Moolah but winning it back a week later, a positive experience for her.

"If you need their help, they [Moolah and Mae Young] are more than willing to give it to you. I think that anyone that's not asking for their help, they're making a big mistake," Ivory said at the time. "I had a great time working with them when they first came on board. I've been beat up by them, wrestled with them."

After losing the title to "The Kat" Stacy Carter in one of the signature moments of the Attitude Era, when Carter removed her bra and briefly exposed her breasts following the match, Ivory developed into a conservative character who opposed the T&A direction the women's division was moving toward. In 2000, she joined Right to Censor, a heel faction that opposed the risqué storylines of WWE, consisting of Stevie Richards, Bull Buchanan, the "reformed" Val Venis, and the Godfather (now known as the Goodfather). Dressed in a white button-down blouse and an ankle-length black skirt, Ivory feuded with the likes of Lita and Trish Stratus, ushering in an era of athletic, exciting, and technically sound women's wrestling in WWE.

"I loved my time with Right to Censor. It was awesome as it was something you could really sink your teeth into. I loved to have that challenge as a performer, being somewhat the opposite of what you are," she said, adding it was one of her favorite times in the WWF.

Ivory won the women's title for the third and last time on October 31, 2000, winning a fatal four-way bout against champion Lita, Stratus, and Jacqueline in Rochester, New York. She retained the championship in a match against Lita at the 2000 Survivor Series, mostly remembered because Lita bled heavily after suffering a laceration to the head early in the match, and held it until April 1, 2001, when she lost the belt in a featured match against Chyna at WrestleMania 17 in Houston.

It was a match that made Mando Guerrero very proud. "Ivory, God, did you see the bumps she was taking off Chyna?" Mando asked Greg Oliver in an interview. "Chyna would pick her up and pop her on her shoulders and do that slam. Did you see how in control she was? I was always so proud of her because she listened, she was one of the few that listened. She was very determined when I met her. She was awesome. She was always looking at me, asking me questions. . . . She wouldn't argue with me, she would get there, would listen to me."

Ivory remained with WWE until 2005, although her appearances became less frequent. She served as a trainer for the second season of *Tough Enough* and worked as a broadcaster on *WWE Experience*. After leaving WWE, she made some appearances on the independent circuit, including Women Superstars Uncensored, and eventually opened her own animal daycare, boarding, and grooming business.

# JACQUELINE

An underrated performer whose in-ring career lasted more than a quarter of a century, Jacqueline Moore made a career out of doing the unexpected.

In her days as Miss Texas in the early 1990s, she made waves by regularly competing against — and beating — male wrestlers, which earned her a spot in the 1993 PWI 500 ranking, becoming the first female ever to make that list. She debuted in WCW and earned a clean win over Disco Inferno. She not only won the WWF women's title on two occasions (becoming the first African-American WWF women's champion) but also won the WWF cruiserweight title with an upset win over Chavo Guerrero (which would actually make her the first African-American female to hold that title, too).

"Pretty much my whole life I grew up a tomboy," Moore told Alex Marvez in 2007. "I played all kinds of sports like football with my brothers. I did martial arts, basketball, soccer, gymnastics — I did it all. But growing up in Dallas, I loved wrestling. The Von Erichs were so big down here. I used to go to the Sportatorium to see them live. That's when I knew I wanted to be a wrestler. I met Skandar [Akbar] at a gym and he trained me. I was the only student in our group that made it out of there. A lot of them quit, and I was the only female out there."

Born January 6, 1964, she made her wrestling debut in Dallas in 1988 under the name Sweet Georgia Brown. She was fortunate enough to get booked on a tour of Japan with FMW in 1990, while she was

*"Miss Texas" Jacqueline, a real bad ass in the ring.*
PAT LAPRADE COLLECTION/DAVID MCLAIN WWE

still essentially a rookie. That exposure to the stiff Japanese style, coupled with the physical, shoot-fight style of traditional Texas wrestling, instilled in her an appreciation of realism. While other women wrestlers of that era may have looked as if they were working through prechoreographed routines, Moore always looked like she was there to fight.

She began to make headlines in the United States Wrestling Association in 1991. Eric Embry and Tom Prichard were representing the state of Texas in a Texas vs. Tennessee rivalry, and they introduced "Miss Texas" as their personal valet. Embry and Miss Texas began a mixed tag feud with "The Dirty White Boy" Tony Anthony and "The Dirty White Girl," which culminated in a hair vs. hair match. Miss Texas lost the fall and had her head shaved.

In March 1992, Miss Texas defeated Dirty White Girl in the finals of a tournament to crown the first USWA women's champion. She would go on to hold that title 14 times between 1992 and 1996.

After working as Kevin Sullivan's valet, and with no viable women's division in WCW, there was little left for her. She had a brief run managing Harlem Heat and a brief feud with Disco Inferno before leaving WCW. She joined the WWF in 1998, where she was paired with Marc Mero.

That's when the WWF made the decision to reactivate the women's championship that had been dormant ever since Madusa had tossed the belt into the trashcan on *Nitro*. In September 1997, Jacqueline defeated Sable in a match and was named WWF women's champion. Two months later, she lost the belt to Sable at the Survivor Series.

In one of the most infamous moments of the Attitude Era, Jacqueline suffered a preplanned "wardrobe malfunction," long before Janet Jackson ever brought that term to the common vernacular. On December 9, 1998, the WWF presented a United Kingdom–only PPV named Capital Carnage at the London Arena. Sable and Christian defeated Mero and Jacqueline in a mixed tag bout. After the match, Jacqueline attacked referee Tim White. White stood up, "inadvertently" lifting Jacqueline onto his shoulders, as Sable tore off her tee shirt, exposing her bare breasts.

Jacqueline split her time between wrestling and being a valet, forming Pretty Mean Sisters with Terri Runnels. She won the WWF women's title a second time in February 2000, trouncing "Hervina," manager Harvey Wippleman in drag, who had won the belt from Miss Kitty. She helped restore some credibility to the title but ultimately lost it to Stephanie McMahon after copious outside interference by D-Generation X.

She went on to have rivalries with Trish Stratus, Jazz, Ivory, and Lita but rarely contended for the women's title in subsequent years. She had a brief feud with Chavo Guerrero, resulting in a two-week run as cruiserweight champion in 2004 and was one of the trainers of the first season of *Tough Enough*. She left the WWF a short time later. She went on to compete for TNA sporadically through the next few years. In a 2008 "street fight" with Gail Kim, she lost her two front teeth when Kim accidentally connected with a broomstick that caught her in the mouth. True to form, Jacqueline continued the match. In 2016, she was inducted into the WWE Hall of Fame in Dallas, Texas, where everything started for her.

"She is what a Knockout is," Traci Brooks once said of Jacqueline.

"She's one of the toughest bitches I know, she's beautiful, and she's been in the business. She is one of the best."

# JAZZ

When fans look back at the women's scene in WWE from 2002 to 2004, Trish Stratus and Lita tend to get most of the kudos for revitalizing the women's division. But you can't have great heroes without a great villain . . . and Jazz was a spectacular villain.

Born August 27, 1973, Carlene Denise Moore grew up in New Orleans, Louisiana. Her mother died when she was two years old, and she was raised by her father. She ran track and played softball and basketball, earning a college scholarship for the latter until a knee injury put a premature end to her days on the hardwood. She subsequently dropped out of college.

Her interest in pro wrestling kindled when she saw Jacqueline Moore compete, and that interest was stoked when she came across an advertisement for the Junkyard Dog's wrestling school in Lafayette, Louisiana. She packed up her bags and moved to Lafayette, where she trained under the JYD. After the Junkyard Dog (real name Sylvester Ritter) passed away in 1998, she continued training under Rod Price, making her pro debut that same year.

"I've never seen a girl who had it right from the start like Jazz did," said veteran referee James Beard, who refereed some of Jazz's earliest matches. "She looked like she had been working for years right away. She was the best girl I've ever been in the ring with."

In 1999, she began getting bookings in Extreme Championship Wrestling. Although ECW didn't have a women's division and was notorious for its panty-exposing catfights, Moore — who took the ring name Jazzmine — was protected and presented as a serious and capable female wrestler. She had a long-running feud with Jason Knight, regularly beating Knight in inter-gender matches.

After ECW folded due to bankruptcy, the WWF signed her to a

developmental contract, and she reported to Ohio Valley Wrestling for seasoning. She made her main roster debut at the 2001 Survivor Series in a six-pack challenge for the vacant women's title. Stratus won the match, but Jazz was an immediate sensation with her muscular physique and bad-ass aura. Jazz wasn't a model turned wrestler; she was a prizefighter coming for the title.

"Eight weeks after I got to Louisville, I got my big break and was called up for The Survivor Series," she told website wrestlemag. com in a 2005 interview. "Right then and there, I told myself that I would

*Jazz found success in both ECW and WWE.*
YAN O'CAIN COLLECTION

become the best female worker that ever stepped foot into the ring. After the PPV, I started my feud with Trish, and I thought we had some awesome matches. Some people up there [WWE] will never admit it, but we had some of the best matches that had ever been seen by two women in the women's division, which was how I wanted things to be. I had a statement to make up there and I made it."

Less than three months after her WWF debut, Jazz beat Stratus for the women's title on the February 4, 2002, edition of *Raw*. At WrestleMania 18, she successfully defended the title in a three-way bout against crowd favorites Stratus and Lita. She was the self-proclaimed Baddest Bitch in wrestling.

Her title run came to an early end when she suffered a torn ACL and was forced to drop the title back to Stratus in May 2002. She returned to the ring in early 2003 and resumed her feud with Stratus, as well as Victoria. These bouts were considered by many to be the best quality WWF/WWE women's matches since the Alundra Blaze/Bull Nakano series a decade before.

Jazz won the women's title for a second time, beating Stratus at Backlash 2003, but injuries again proved to be her undoing. She relinquished the title to the debuting Gail Kim in June 2003 and again stepped away from the ring to rehabilitate her injury.

In 2004, she briefly served as a valet for her husband Rodney Mack before getting released by WWE. She made a few appearances when the promotion relaunched the ECW brand, but she never regained the promotional push she had previously enjoyed.

She gave birth to twin daughters in 2008 and eventually returned to the independent circuit on a part-time basis. She won the Women's Extreme Wrestling title and the Women Superstars Uncensored tag title (with Marti Belle).

She and her husband opened a gym and a wrestling school in Louisiana named the Dog Pound, in honor of her mentor, the Junkyard Dog.

# MOLLY HOLLY

You can call her Lady Ophelia, Mona, Miss Madness, or Starla Saxton, but it's under the name of Molly Holly that Nora Greenwood made a name for herself in the wrestling business. Born September 7, 1977, in Forest Lake, Minnesota, she had just a few years of experience under her belt when she was signed by the WWE, having been trained by Dean Malenko in Florida in 1997 and working for WCW, mostly as Randy Savage's valet.

"WCW was great! I worked one day a week and made more money than any person with barely a high school diploma should ever make," Greenwood said in an interview with Ryan Murphy.

After being released by WCW, she went to meet with WWE, where she had worked at the end of the 1990s as an enhancement talent under the name of Starla Saxton. "In my meeting with Jim Ross, he said a lot of the women start out with the Godfather. I said to him, 'Oh, sure, whatever works for you guys.' But I was really hoping I would not be one of the Godfather's ladies," remembered Greenwood.

*A former two-time WWE women's champion, Molly Holly.* COURTESY OF WORLD WRESTLING ENTERTAINMENT, INC.

But instead of being part of the Ho Train, she was paired with cousins Hardcore and Crash Holly and billed as their cousin. "I really enjoyed being a Holly cousin," Greenwood said. "Crash went out of his way to build my confidence. If I was nervous about something, he would assure me I could do it."

Caught in a feud between the Hollys and the Dudleys, she started to have an on-camera romance with Spike Dudley. But as a wrestler, she was best known as the creator of the Molly-Go-Round, her finishing manoeuver.

"Well, what actually happened is that I had been working on a full-twisting moonsault ever since I got hired from the WWF and was in developmental, because I'm like when I debut in the WWF I'm going to do a full-twisting moonsault for my finish. Well, the day I have a match with Trish Stratus that I actually am going to do our finishing maneuver, I was practicing on a crash pad and I could not do it. So Dean Malenko said, 'You know, I saw Rey Mysterio do a front flip into a hurricanrana thing, but what if you just did a front flip and land on them.' So, I got to practice it a couple of times just on some indie guys that were willing to take bumps from me in the afternoon, and it worked every time. I think Trish might have been the first one to take the Molly-Go-Round, but it was really Dean Malenko's idea to save me from being fired for not having the move that I had planned originally," she said in a 2013 interview.

After graduating from Molly Holly to Mighty Holly, the Hurricane's sidekick, and winning the hardcore title for an hour along the way, she came back to her well-known moniker and won the WWE women's title twice. During that time, she influenced more than one woman to become a professional wrestler, including Serena Deeb and Gail Kim. "I really just loved watching Molly Holly and really admired her, the way she moved in the ring and her work ethic," said Kim.

But despite winning those championships, Molly's biggest moment happened at WrestleMania 20 at Madison Square Garden in New York. It was a match that wasn't supposed to happen to begin with.

After being told there would be no women's title match at WrestleMania, Greenwood went to Vince McMahon and came up with an idea to make sure she would be put on the show: a title vs. hair match against then-champion Victoria.

"Having my hair shaved was the best haircut," she said, half serious, half joking, about the match she obviously lost.

But in 2005, she decided to part ways with WWE, not liking the person she was becoming backstage and playing a character she didn't like on stage. For the last decade, she has done only a handful of matches on the independent circuit, refusing to go to TNA but agreeing to be part of the 25-Diva Battle Royal at WrestleMania 25.

Classic pose from Mildred Burke, flexing her bicep.

*Cora Combs was frequently called Miss Cora.*
JACK PFEFER COLLECTION/UNIVERSITY OF NOTRE DAME

*Classic Penny Banner pose that got her a date with Elvis!*
CHRIS SWISHER COLLECTION

*Baltimore, September 18, 1956, the night Moolah became champion.* WRESTLING REVUE ARCHIVES/WWW.WRESTLINGREVUE.COM

*The Glamour Girls, before they were glamorous!*
WRESTLING REVUE ARCHIVES/WWW.WRESTLINGREVUE.COM

*Debbie Combs worked for the AWA, NWA, and WWF.*

*Wrestling's answer to Farrah Fawcett in the late 1980s, Misty Blue Simmes.*

*The WWF women's champion "Sensational" Sherri Martel.*

*"The Wrestling Queen" Vivian Vachon.*

*Alundra Blayze, sporting the belt she would throw in the trash.* PAT LAPRADE COLLECTION/TOM BUCHANAN WWE

*Chyna with her DX teammates, Shawn Michaels and Triple H.* GEORGE NAPOLITANO

*Bull Nakano and Luna Vachon ready to fight.*
PRO WRESTLING ILLUSTRATED

*The girl who just wanted to have fun, Wendy Richter.*
LINDA BOUCHER

The always poised Cheerleader Melissa.

Paige, becoming the first NXT women's champion in 2013.

She can sing and she can win titles, Mickie James.

Awesome Kong and Gail Kim put women's
wrestling on TNA's map.

*Total Bellas: Brie and Nikki.*
RICKY HAVLIK

*Emma doing her Emmalution dance!*
BILL OTTEN

*Lita brought high-flying to the women's division in the early 2000s.* COURTESY OF WORLD WRESTLING ENTERTAINMENT, INC.

Melina was on top of the WWE women's division a decade ago.
PAT LAPRADE COLLECTION/WWE

A seven-time women's champion, Trish Stratus.
PAT LAPRADE COLLECTION/WWE

Wrong or right, this is the Sable fans paid to see.
GEORGE NAPOLITANO

Crazy, Geek, Champion: A.J. Lee.
BILL OTTEN

*The Four Horsewomen: Becky Lynch, Bayley, Charlotte, and Sasha Banks.*

*What a face-off: Ronda Rousey vs. Stephanie McMahon at WrestleMania 32.*

*The Divas of Doom: Natalya and Beth Phoenix.*

*NXT women's champion Asuka.*

*A new look for Naomi in 2016.*

*What a trifecta: Madison Eagles, LuFisto,
and Mercedes Martinez.* YAN O'CAIN COLLECTION

*The Knight Dynasty: Paige, Becky Lynch,
and Saraya Knight.* DAVE PRAZAK/SHIMMER

*Two-time SHIMMER tag champs, Nicole Matthews
and Portia Perez.* DAVE PRAZAK/SHIMMER

*From Japan to Chicago: Ayumi and Ayako Hamada.*
DAVE PRAZAK/SHIMMER

*The Irish steampunk Becky Lynch.*
RICKY HAVLIK

*Fabulous Moolah, Vince McMahon Jr., and Mae Young.*
PRO WRESTLING HOF COLLECTION

*Gin and Juice: Sasha Banks and her cousin Snoop Dogg.*
RICKY HAVLIK

*She's a hugger.*
GEORGE TAHINOS

*SHIMMER group picture from 2011.*
*Look closely: you might see many familiar faces!* ERIC SALOTTOLO

*The rebirth of the women's division, at Raw after WrestleMania.*
RICKY HAVLIK

*The Future of WWE: Nikki Storm, aka Nikki Cross.*
DAVE PRAZAK/SHIMMER

*The Future of WWE: Athena, aka Ember Moon.*
DAVE PRAZAK/SHIMMER

*The Future of TNA: Cherry Bomb, aka Allie.*
YAN O'CAIN COLLECTION

*The Future of WWE: Jessie McKay, aka Bille Kay.*
DAVE PRAZAK/SHIMMER

*One of the best current joshis, Io Shirai.*
KURT SCHIMMEL

*Lucha Underground's former champion Sexy Star.*
PAT LAPRADE

*Multiple-time Knockout champion Tara.*
LEE SOUTH/TNA WRESTLING

*Manami Toyota winning the WWWA
title on January 4, 2000.* KURT SCHIMMEL

The queen of WWE's women's division, Charlotte.

"It's really fun when they ask me back. I'm always flattered when they remember me."

# LUNA VACHON

Luna Vachon was a wrestler, a performer, and a person like few others. She influenced the careers of many female wrestlers, including the likes of Natalya, Lita, and Daffney, and was known to be a first-class ass-kicker. But despite that reputation — or, perhaps, *because of* that reputation, she never achieved what she considered to be the ultimate prize: the WWF women's title.

"I was scheduled to win the title three times. Once I was caught smoking a cigarette in front of the fans, and the other two occasions Sable forgot the belt in her hotel room. She did it on purpose, I'm positive about that," Luna recalled with conviction.

One of her toughest opponents in and out of the ring, Madusa, did as much as she could to put the belt on Vachon, but she didn't succeed.

"I was the champion at that time and wanted her to win it," Madusa said. "People in the back said, 'No, Alundra. You're keeping the title.' I said, 'Well, we are in Luna's hometown, and she deserves it. Can't we just do her a favor?' They wouldn't go for it. So I told Luna in the dressing room that I wasn't going to kick out or anything. I told her she should just take the belt. She sat there and cried. She told me nobody has ever suggested or done anything like that for her. We went to wrestle. I knew the repercussions I would get later; still, I laid there, but the referee wouldn't count. It was deplorable. The poor kid never got a solid break. The night ended, and I left with the title. I felt really bad for her."

Born Gertrude Wilkerson on January 12, 1962, in Atlanta, Georgia, she was adopted when she was three and a half years old by her mother's new husband, wrestler Paul "The Butcher" Vachon. From that moment, even though Paul and her mom, Rebecca, divorced, she would always be considered a Vachon.

"I'm the only father she has ever known," Paul said. "My father

*Luna Vachon had the voice and the in-ring antics of her uncle Mad Dog.* PAT LAPRADE COLLECTION

means so much to me," Luna said after receiving an award at the Cauliflower Alley Club in 2009. "I was crying when I received the award, just because my father and uncle were present."

Her uncle, of course, would be Maurice "Mad Dog" Vachon. But Paul's sister, Vivian, also greatly influenced her and became her idol.

"Vivian and her husband Buddy Wolf started coaching me on a mattress in Minnesota. I was only 16 years old," she said. "Then my father sent me to Moolah in Columbia, South Carolina." She weighed only 110 pounds at the time. "I was told that I was too skinny to be a heel. But I wanted my aunt to be proud of me, so I persevered. It's funny because today all the Divas are very skinny." Her first match was for Moolah at the age of 21. She won a match against Peggy Lee Leather and lost on the same card against Donna Christantello.

"As a student, she was very interested, and very involved in really, really wanting to do the thing. She had good hopes," Moolah said.

She didn't like it there, though. She didn't like the fact that Moolah was making the girls take sexy pictures and that she was taking 25 percent of her pay. Subsequently, she left Moolah and settled down in Florida. It was there that everything really started for her.

Her ruthless actions and her rasping voice were a homage to her uncle, which is why many people over the years thought she was Mad Dog's daughter, even the boys in the back.

"Once, Jake Roberts started yelling, 'You're a Vachon. You're Mad Dog's daughter!'" she remembered of her debut in the Sunshine State. That was also where she got the nickname Luna for the first time.

"At the beginning they wanted to call me Moaning Mona, but Nancy Sullivan, Kevin's wife at the time, said that I didn't look like the moaning type. So she proposed Luna, short for lunatic. It was actually Nancy who shaved my hair. She was one of the rare female friends that I've ever had," she said. Luna had previously wrestled under the name Angelle Vachon, a name Moolah had given her.

Luna would travel a lot, going to Japan 17 times, but also to Australia, Singapore, Europe, Puerto Rico, and Dubai. She also worked for the AWA and some indie promotions at the turn of the decade before getting signed by the WWF in 1992.

Luna made her debut at WrestleMania 9, aligning herself with Shawn Michaels in what was the debut angle of her rivalry with Sensational Sherri. "Many people credit Sunshine and Precious with pioneering the catfights. I say Sherri and Luna perfected it in 1993," Missy Hyatt said. Unfortunately Sherri left the company in August 1993, which put an end to a feud that worked very well. After leaving the company, Luna came back a few years later, but she had a hard time getting along with some of the WWF Divas, especially Sable.

"I wanted to help her at the beginning, but she told me that she didn't need to learn how to fall, as she was going to become a champion anyways. She started to believe that she could wrestle anybody! She had not paid her dues, she had not been trained. I grew up protecting the wrestling industry. I was used to the old-school mentality, not the entertainment one," Luna said.

Besides WWE, she also wrestled for WCW and ECW, where she wrestled against a man, Stevie Richards, for the very first time. By the time the new millennium arrived, she was wrestling mainly for independent federations throughout the United States. She retired in December 2007. "I have so many problems with my neck and back that surgery would be useless," said Luna.

On August 27, 2010, Luna was found dead in her house by her mother, after an overdose of painkillers. She was buried in North Carolina where Andre the Giant — a man she considered an unofficial godfather — used to have his ranch. The wrestler who was famous for her sturdiness, her in-ring abilities, and her particular look was also an incredibly nice girl who helped all those she loved and would go to battle for them. "She was willing to beat up a drunken New Jack for disrespecting me. I would like to think that Luna is in heaven, since the devil was afraid that she would take his spot," Hyatt said.

"Luna was a definite inspiration for me — she had a wild look and was a genuinely tough female wrestler," Lita wrote in her autobiography. "Luna had a reputation for being kind of crazy, but I found her to be as sweet as could be. We chatted a bit and actually corresponded for a while, writing letters back and forth. She was always very encouraging, telling me to stay true to myself as far as refining my wrestling persona."

In her last interview with WWE.com, Luna thanked the fans, as if she knew it would be her last chance to do so. "Thank you for all the years. Thank you to those that knew me back then and those that still remember me today. Thanks to everyone that ever screamed at me, cheered for me, spit at me or threw beer on me. I want to thank them for everything."

# TORRIE WILSON

Torrie Wilson walked into a wrestling arena as a fan, was asked to become part of the show, and wound up becoming one of the most famous wrestling women of the Attitude Era.

Born July 24, 1975, Wilson grew up in Boise, Idaho. She was active in cheerleading and dance before going into modeling in high school. The pressure of attaining the perfect model look as an adolescent caused her to develop eating disorders anorexia nervosa and bulimia. After struggling with those disorders and body dysmorphia issues,

Wilson discovered the importance of proper nutrition and took up fitness training.

In 1998, Wilson won the Miss Galaxy fitness competition and took first place in the Grace and Physique round of the Women's Tri-Fitness championships. She then moved to Los Angeles to pursue her dream of becoming an actress.

That's when fate intervened.

Wilson attended a World Championship Wrestling event in 1999 and was introduced to Kevin Nash. Nash had seen her work in fitness magazines and was

*Torrie Wilson.* PAT LAPRADE COLLECTION/RICH FREEDA WWE

struck by her beauty and presence. He pitched the idea of having her work an angle with the New World Order to WCW management. The following night, she accompanied Scott Steiner to the ring as a valet, and WCW offered her a spot. She was paired with David Flair in a storyline where she worked with the nWo and tried to turn David against his father, Ric Flair.

Wilson continued working as a valet with WCW for the next two years, working with Billy Kidman (whom she married in 2003 and divorced in 2008), Shane Douglas, and the Filthy Animals. When Vince McMahon purchased WCW in 2001, Wilson joined the WWF in a storyline as McMahon's newest love interest. At the 2001 Invasion pay-per-view, Wilson teamed with fellow WCW alumnus Stacy Keibler to face Trish Stratus and Lita in a bra and panties match that saw Wilson and Keibler get stripped down to their lacy undergarments.

Wilson specialized in the gimmicky bra and panties and catfight matches that were popular in WWE in the early 2000s. Although Wilson was never an elite wrestler, she had the look and the ring presence to shine in these shorter, heavily sexualized matches.

"The women's locker room was tricky at times," Wilson said in a 2010 interview on the *Monday Night Mayhem* radio show. "I can't say that I got along just peachy with some of the people, but for the most part I had a great relationship with everyone that was in the locker room. Being someone that came from the fitness industry and wasn't a wrestler — and I didn't work the independent scene for years — I think that there are certain people that don't respect that, and think you should have 'paved your way,' and I personally think that's pretty lame. There are a lot of industries where people all go in in all different ways. Some people fall into it, some people have a lucky break right away, some people work for years on the independent scene or whatever it is. That was frustrating at times."

In 2003, she feuded with Dawn Marie in a bizarre storyline that saw Dawn Marie seduce (and eventually "marry") Wilson's father in an attempt to blackmail Wilson into a lesbian affair. Wilson defeated Dawn Marie in a stepmother vs. stepdaughter match at the 2003 Royal Rumble.

Wilson twice posed for *Playboy* magazine, making the cover both times. She had in-ring rivalries with Candice Michelle, Ashley Massaro, and Sable, and she teamed with Sable to win a heavily promoted *Playboy* evening gown match against Keibler and Jacqueline at WrestleMania 20. Although she split her time between being a wrestler, a spokesperson, and a valet, she wrestled about 300 matches in her career and appeared in some of WWE's most over-the-top storylines.

In a 2011 interview with the *Miami Herald*, Wilson indicated she had some mixed feelings about the style that was in fashion while she was in WWE.

"I often wish it was more PG when I was there because I was always doing some bra and panties matches or something," she told reporter Scott Fishman. "I always wanted to keep showcasing my athleticism and getting better. I think it's great that they get to showcase that more [today]. I still think they don't get the time they probably should in TV to have longer matches and storylines. Sometimes it can go a little too far PG. I mean, it *is* pro wrestling after all."

Wilson retired from wrestling in 2008 and underwent back surgery to address cumulative injuries from her wrestling career. She made a one-off return at WrestleMania 25 in 2009, competing in the Miss WrestleMania battle royal. Even after leaving wrestling, she still made the gossip columns as she dated New York Yankee Alex Rodriguez from 2011 to 2015.

## STACY KEIBLER

Although today she's best known as an actress, television personality, George Clooney's ex-girlfriend, and former *Dancing With the Stars* contestant, Stacy Keibler got her big break in wrestling, debuting as Miss Hancock in WCW in 1999.

Born October 14, 1979, she grew up in Rosedale, Maryland. She took dance classes as a youngster and became a cheerleader for the Baltimore Ravens after graduating high school. She became a huge wrestling fan during the Monday Night Wars era, watching the PPVs, wearing wrestling T-shirts, and even holding signs at live events.

In 1999, she entered a contest to win a spot on the Nitro Girls, WCW's dance troupe. She won the contest and a $10,000 prize and joined the Nitro Girls using the name Skye.

However, with her girl-next-door looks, charisma, and shapely 42-inch-long legs, it didn't take long for WCW management to decide to give her an expanded role. She was pulled from the Nitro Girls, dressed in a business jacket with a tiny miniskirt, and named Miss Hancock, sometimes spelled Handcock to spell things out for even the most obtuse viewer.

*Stacy Keibler.* PAT LAPRADE COLLECTION/CRAIG AMBROSIO WWE

She became a crowd favorite for dancing on top of the announcer's table while TV cameras typically shot directly up her skirt. She was introduced as the manager for the tag team of Lenny and Lodi before being the valet of David Flair, whom she was dating at the time. She had her first match at the 2000 Bash at the Beach, losing to Daffney in a wedding gown match, where the first woman to strip the other of her dress would be declared the winner. She competed exclusively in similar gimmick matches, including mud-wrestling matches, for the duration of her stay in WCW. To use Lou Thesz's description, Keibler was "an attraction," not a wrestler.

However, when WCW closed in 2001, Vince McMahon saw value in her and bought her contract. She started with the WWF in the summer of 2001 and soon was managing the Dudley Boyz. It was during that time that she was part of the first-ever WWE lingerie match against former tag team partner and WCW alumni Torrie Wilson, although she is most remembered during that period for taking a nasty powerbomb into a table, thanks to her former protégés Bubba and D-Von.

She then challenged Stratus for the women's title several times before settling back into a mostly out-of-ring role. At WrestleMania 20, she and Miss Jackie lost a tag team evening gown match to Wilson and Sable, which was purely to promote Wilson's and Sable's appearance in *Playboy*. Keibler herself turned down offers to pose for the magazine. She remained with WWE until 2006, when she left to pursue acting and modeling opportunities.

In an interview with Sam Roberts in 2013, Keibler was very candid about her pro wrestling abilities.

"I had to kind of learn as I was going and I think that's why I was so terrible at wrestling. And I was not very tough at all, but the choreography came naturally because of my dance background. It's all an act and it's a character that I was playing the whole time, and I loved that part of it and I loved the fans and the energy, but the actual physical wrestling scared the shit out of me every single time. Because I didn't want to hurt anyone and I didn't want to get hurt." Although she was rarely promoted as a serious wrestler, she was one of the most recognizable stars in both WCW and WWE during the height of their popularity. She enjoyed mainstream success after leaving the ring and remained very popular among wrestling fans.

## VICTORIA/TARA

Whether she's known as a Diva or a Knockout, no one can deny that Lisa Marie Varon was among the most accomplished women wrestlers of her era.

Born Lisa Sole in San Bernardino, California, on February 10, 1971, she was the only girl in a family with three older brothers, all of whom wrestled in high school. She went the more traditional route, becoming involved in cheerleading and track and field. After studying biology, she took a job as an organ harvester. In addition, she started working as a physical trainer and taught aerobics, which introduced her to the world of bodybuilding and fitness competitions.

She competed in ESPN2's Fitness America Series in 1997 and in the 1998 Miss Galaxy competition, where she met and befriended Torrie Wilson. When Wilson was hired by WCW, she invited Sole to a WCW event, which piqued her interest in wrestling.

She moved to Los Angeles and continued competing in fitness competitions. In 2000, she put together a portfolio and sent it to the WWF. Apparently the WWF liked what they saw, as they scheduled an interview. She enrolled in the Ultimate Pro Wrestling training school and began to learn the basics and fundamentals. She was brought into the WWF as one of the Godfather's "hos" in 2000 and ended up being powerbombed through a table as the Godfather renounced his pimping ways.

She was sent down to the developmental territory in Memphis, serving briefly as commissioner of Memphis Championship Wrestling before moving down to Ohio Valley Wrestling in 2001. She was christened Queen Victoria and served as the manager of "The Machine" Doug Basham.

She debuted in WWE in July 2002, cast as a psychotic former fitness model associate of Trish Stratus's who carried a grudge against Stratus. She was portrayed as insane and schizophrenic, and she often pulled at her own hair and seemed to be listening to voices in her head. Her name now shortened to Victoria, she defeated Stratus to win the WWE women's title in a hardcore match at the 2002 Survivor Series. She lost the title back to Stratus at WrestleMania 19 in a three-way match that also included Jazz.

Victoria won the title a second time in February 2004. At WrestleMania 20, she defended the title against Molly Holly in a hair vs. hair match. She defeated Holly in a five-minute match and then proceeded to shave Holly's head in one of the most memorable moments of that year's WrestleMania. She lost the belt back to Stratus two months later. Her two title reigns lasted a combined total of 244 days.

In 2009, she made the difficult decision to leave WWE. "Choosing to leave was a very difficult decision," she wrote on MySpace. "I think many of my colleagues considered me a lifer. That is, they thought I'd be with WWE until I was old and grey. But I was not happy with the opportunities that were available to me within WWE. And at the end of the day, there are thousands and thousands of women who would kill or die for the chance to be a WWE Diva. It isn't right for me to fill that spot if my heart wasn't in it."

She began training for competition in MMA and studied jiu jitsu, but she decided to sign with TNA when she was contacted by Dixie Carter. She debuted in TNA in May 2009, using the ring name Tara and carrying a pet tarantula with her to the ring. She defeated Angelina Love for the TNA Knockouts title in July 2009 but dropped it back to Love two months later at the Victory Road PPV.

*Victoria in WWE or, if you prefer, Tara in TNA.*
LEE SOUTH/TNA WRESTLING

Tara remained with TNA for four years, winning the Knockouts title five times and winning the Knockouts tag team title with Brooke. During her run with TNA, Tara had memorable rivalries with Mickie James (including a steel cage match where she hyperextended her arm and tore a ligament in her elbow), Gail Kim, ODB, and the Beautiful People. She ended up leaving TNA when the two sides couldn't come to terms on a new contract. The situation turned ugly, and she later commented that she would never work for TNA again.

"I came to TNA because I still had a lot of wrestling left in me," she told the *Observer*. "I was paid a fraction of what I thought I deserved. I want a modest pay increase. They don't want to pay me what I think is fair. . . . Unnamed sources claim that I am hard to work with and that I didn't give my best effort. My only response is that TNA made an aggressive effort to re-sign me, among other things saying that they want to build the women's division around me. And I think wrestling fans see, both on TV and at live events, that I always give 100%. I take pride in that. Smearing me on the way out the door is an act of second rate character."

A true entrepreneur, in 2013 she opened a wrestling-themed restaurant in Chicago named the Squared Circle. She previously owned a pizzeria and a custom car shop in Louisville, Kentucky.

"I always have my best matches with Victoria. She's such a good wrestler and a good teacher. Most importantly, she's not afraid to make me look good. A lot of people don't like to do that, because in return it makes them look a little less. But she's so confident in her abilities that she's not afraid to look bad," said Torrie Wilson about her friend.

# TOTAL NONSTOP ACTION
## *A New Frontier*

The end of the Attitude Era coincided with the start of a brand new promotion. With both WCW and ECW out of business, Total Nonstop Action became the only other place for female wrestlers to find work on a national stage. With a mix of veterans and new faces, TNA would establish what was at one point the strongest female division in all of wrestling.

TNA held its first event on June 19, 2002. Women's wrestling, however, wasn't a high priority. In its second event, NWA-TNA held a lingerie battle royal to crown Miss TNA. That match was won by Taylor Vaughan, who had previously had a brief run as B.B. in the WWF. Over the next few months, Vaughan would feud with Bruce (former WCW wrestler Allan "Kwee Wee" Funk) over the Miss TNA title in a series of inter-gender comedy matches.

In March 2003, TNA broadcast a catfight between Lollipop (a Nitro Girl–style cage dancer known for sucking on a lollipop) and

Holly Wood that saw Lollipop's breasts exposed in an intentional wardrobe malfunction.

Things got even worse when Leilani Kai, the NWA women's champion, complained about the presentation of women in TNA and objected to defending her championship in TNA. She was subsequently stripped of the NWA women's title.

But in 2007, there was an attitude change in the presentation of women's wrestling. TNA had amassed an impressive array of female talent from the independent circuit, as well as former WWF women's champions Gail Kim and Jacqueline. With WWE choosing to present its women as Divas, TNA branded its women under a name that connoted action and excitement as well as beauty. The Knockouts Division was born.

On October 14, 2007, Kim won a 10-woman gauntlet match to become the first Knockouts champion. The match also included Traci Brooks, Jacqueline, Shelly Martinez, Awesome Kong, Christy Hemme, ODB, Angelina Love, Velvet Sky, and Roxxi Laveaux.

A subsequent feud between Kim and Awesome Kong helped put the Knockouts division on the map. Kong defeated Kim for the Knockouts title in a match that was presented as the main event of the company's weekly television show, *TNA Impact*, which aired on Spike TV. It was a very rare instance of the women being given the opportunity to main-event, standing in stark contrast to WWE, which usually positioned women's matches as three-minute "bathroom breaks" as opposed to competitive matches.

The Knockouts Division quickly became one of TNA's signature attractions, along with the innovative X Division of cruiserweight wrestlers. The Knockouts consistently drew the highest television ratings on Impact, frequently topping the 1.0 mark and reaching as high as 1.23.

Dutch Mantell (Zeb Colter in WWE) and Scott D'Amore worked behind the scenes as agents for the Knockouts Division, helping reinvigorate interest in women's wrestling and making TNA a flagship for women's wrestling worldwide.

"What was different for us in TNA was that all of us were indie wrestlers and all of us were different," said five-time Knockouts champion Angelina Love. "It wasn't 12 or 15 girls all cut from the same mold. We all had very different looks, some very unconventional from the typical WWE Diva look. There was a lot of talent. You had Kong, you had Roxxi, you had Traci Brooks, you had the Beautiful People. Each one of us was different in our own way. We had our own sex appeal and catered to different people's tastes. All of us had a strong wrestling background because they used all indie girls and not models.

"Jeff Jarrett gave us the chance and supported women's wrestling," Love continued. "Dutch Mantell has got great ideas. He understands how the business works and how the fans work — what they want, how they react, and what they want to see. He helped all of us out with characters and things we needed to do and get across in matches."

But it wasn't love at first sight for Mantell.

"Dutch is definitely old school, and it took a while for him to warm up to the girls," said Velvet Sky in an interview with Mike Mooneyham. "At the time he was so 'not women's wrestling.' He was so against it. But that was fine. The harder we worked, and the better we all did, Dutch started to warm up to all of us. He actually started to look at us in a new light where he would be pleasant instead of ignore us."

Melissa Anderson also praised Mantell's work. "Dutch Mantell has a very good eye for talent," she said. "He's very creative. He saw something special with the Knockouts at the time and he was putting the matches together. It was a big success and we owe that to Dutch."

Unfortunately, Mantell was let go by TNA in 2009, and with the arrival of Hulk Hogan and Eric Bischoff just a few months later, the women's division never got back to where it was. In recent years, the company put their faith in indie wrestlers such as Jessicka Havok, Jade, Sienna, Rosemary, and Allie, who all won the Knockouts title at one point. According to three-time Knockouts champion ODB, the main thing that differentiated TNA's Knockouts division from other promotions was that TNA was willing to give its women a visible platform.

"They gave us TV time. They invested in our characters. We got two segments on the show — the highest rated segments for a few years. They invested in the Knockouts division, and I'm so happy that they did that. And it took off."

## GAIL KIM

One quiet morning in a suburb of Toronto, Ontario, Ron Hutchison was enjoying a cup of coffee and opening up the *Toronto Sun* when he saw a sight that almost made him do a spit-take. Like its tabloid counterparts in the United Kingdom, the *Sun* was known for featuring models posed in various states of undress on page 2. These were known as Sunshine Girls . . . and they were one of Ron's favorite parts of the *Sun*. This particular Sunshine Girl stood out for a few reasons. A petite girl of Korean descent, she had a smoldering look posed in her bikini. And under her future goals, the profile said she was interested in becoming a professional wrestler.

Having already trained several wrestlers, including Edge, Christian, and Trish Stratus, Hutchison knew right away that he needed to meet Gail Kim.

That Sunshine Girl went on to become one of the most successful female wrestlers ever to lace up a pair of boots. The accolades are amazing: the WWE women's title, six TNA Knockouts titles, the TNA Knockouts tag team title, and the number one spot in the 2012 PWI Female 50.

Born February 20, 1977, Kim grew up in Toronto. She studied kinesiology and nutrition and graduated from Ryerson University. She did a bit of modeling, which led to the Sunshine Girl opportunity and ultimately her meeting with Hutchison. She began to train at his school in 2000.

"Gail took to training like a duck to water. She really was a natural and, to this day, holds the record for being the fastest trainee that I had deemed ready for the ring, either male or female," Hutchison said. "She never missed a training session, never complained, was always pleasant, and really just a joy to be around."

She wrestled her first match in December 2000, competing under a mask as La Felina. Wrestling under a mask gave her a degree of anonymity as she continued to learn, so she could potentially be reintroduced under a new persona once she was a bit more advanced, and any rookie mistakes wouldn't tarnish fans' first impressions.

Kim said the La Felina name was perplexing at the time.

"I'm not a catty girl," she told *PWI* in a 2006. "Everyone said I

*TNA Hall of Famer Gail Kim.* LEE SOUTH/TNA WRESTLING

was cat-like, and I never really understood why. I guess it's because I'm athletic, like I move like a cat."

She bid the feline gimmick farewell when she was unmasked by Traci Brooks in a hair vs. mask match in Hutchison's Apocalypse Wrestling Federation and started competing under her real name. She worked throughout Canada, including a stint with Scott D'Amore's Border City Wrestling in Windsor, and received further training at Rob "El Fuego" Etcheverria's Squared Circle Pro Wrestling school.

Introduced to Molly Holly by fellow Torontonian Jason Sensation, Kim was encouraged by Holly to send her tapes and pictures to WWE. In 2002, less than two years after her debut, she signed a contract with

WWE and relocated to Louisville to work at Ohio Valley Wrestling. An injury to women's champion Jazz proved fortuitous to Kim, as she won the women's championship in her WWE television debut, in a battle royal for the belt on June 30, 2003, in Buffalo.

"Traci Brooks, Gail Kim, myself, we had gone to our first WWE tryout, all three of us together. Gail Kim was signed that day and became women's champion just a couple of months later," remembered Beth Phoenix. "What Ron taught us was that if you want this, then you can go get it. I think his group of wrestlers really lived by that."

Kim's title reign proved to be short, as she lost the belt four weeks later to Molly Holly. She had a brief feud with Trish Stratus before breaking her collarbone in November, putting her out of action for six months. She returned to the ring in April 2004, but she was released by WWE in November of that year, being told they were looking to take the women's division in a new direction.

She reestablished herself on the independents and competed internationally, including tours of Mexico, South Korea, and Australia, before signing with TNA in September 2005. The company did not have a viable women's division yet, so she was paired with America's Most Wanted (James Storm and Chris Harris) and Jeff Jarrett as a manager, frequently interfering in their bouts with cross-body blocks, dropkicks, and ranas off the top rope.

"I've been very fortunate to be in this business for as long as I have been, and I've been very fortunate to be part of three very strong eras of women's wrestling," Kim told the *Miami Herald* in 2013. "The WWE era with Trish [Stratus], Victoria, Jazz, Molly Holly was a great experience. It was what I always dreamed of, but looking back now I was very green and inexperienced. So for me it was a great learning experience, and it was an honor to be a part of that. The other great era I was a part of was when the Knockouts division was actually born. That came about a year and a half after I came to TNA. We had no women's division when I initially came there the first time. I begged and begged, after a year of managing. I couldn't stand to watch the guys doing what I loved. I liked managing, but my talents were in the ring."

On October 14, 2007, Kim won a 10-woman gauntlet match to become the first TNA Knockouts champion. Her subsequent feud with Awesome Kong became the cornerstone of the fledgling Knockouts division. She and Kong main-evented the January 10, 2008, edition of TNA Impact, which saw Kong beat Kim for the title.

She remained with TNA until 2008, when she returned to WWE. However, her second WWE run proved disappointing. The Divas division was not prominently featured, and Kim received little television time. She was paired with Daniel Bryan as his on-screen girlfriend and used primarily as a valet. She left WWE when her contract expired in 2011 and returned to TNA.

"I heard many times that [WWE wants] the Divas to be girly. They didn't care about the heel girls getting any heat," she told the U.K. *Sun* upon leaving WWE. "We just didn't understand. They did everything in their power, it seemed, to take everything to give us a good match, for the heels to get any heat. It was no kicking one week, or no punching the next. No this, no that. It was at the point where I was asking if we could do anything at all."

This WWE run wasn't all that bad, since she met her husband, celebrity chef Robert Irvine, through a company event. They tied the knot in May 2012.

Upon coming back to TNA, Kim picked up where she had left off, becoming the cornerstone of the Knockouts division once again and winning the Knockouts championship multiple times. This second run with TNA proved to be as good, if not better, than her first — since being voted the best woman wrestler in 2012, Kim is the only one to have finished in the top 10 of the PWI Female 50 every year. In June 2016, she became the first female inductee into the TNA Hall of Fame.

"I believe that the key to her success and longevity is the fact that she really was — and is — a wrestling fan first," Hutchison said. "She wasn't looking for a television career to use the business as a springboard into something else. She really wanted to wrestle and to be the best she could at it. She worked and continues to work hard and learned her lessons well. Gail will be around the business as long as she chooses to be. There are a lot of girls who would benefit by not only tapping into her knowledge of wrestling and fitness but also — if it's possible — tapping into her enthusiasm and love of the sport."

## AWESOME KONG

Men's wrestling has always had its behemoths and juggernauts, powerhouses who would use raw power to steamroll their opponents. From George Hackenschmidt in the early 1900s to Brock Lesnar, strongmen have been prominent figures in wrestling.

Awesome Kong proved that men don't have a monopoly on the power game. There had been strong women wrestlers prior to Kong; Mildred Burke was lean and muscular, Chyna had the powerbuilder's physique, Monster Ripper and Bull Nakano were big and intimidating. But Kong was unique. At a billed height of 5'11" and weight of 272 pounds, she shattered the mold when it came to women's wrestling in the United States. Unlike Monster Ripper and Bull Nakano when they appeared in the WWF, she was not ridiculed for her size. She was presented — and came across — as a legitimate brawler who could hold her own with any man or woman in the company. She was no novelty act . . . Kong was the real deal.

Kia Stevens was born on September 4, 1977, and grew up in Carson, California. She saw Lita and Chyna wrestling in the WWF and was inspired to try the sport herself. She appeared on the television show *Discovery Health Body Challenge* on the Discovery Health Channel, looking to lose weight and get in shape to pursue her dream of becoming a wrestler, leaving behind her career as a social worker. The producers of the show arranged a surprise visit from Chyna, who stopped in and encouraged Stevens in her pursuits.

She began her training at the School of Hard Knocks in San Bernardino and wrestled her first match in October 2002. Her size made her stand out, and her stature caught the eye of Japanese scouts who envisioned the sight of a large black woman selling out arenas in Japan — as a cultural curiosity, if nothing else.

She moved to Japan and began training at the All Japan Women's dojo. As a nod to veteran Japanese wrestler Aja Kong, she was given the name Amazing Kong. In January 2004 — barely 15 months into her career — she won the prestigious WWWA championship. She also captured several tag titles with Aja Kong, including the WWWA, GAEA, Ladies Legend Pro Wrestling, and HUSTLE tag titles.

*The Amazing, Awesome Kong.* YAN O'CAIN COLLECTION

"On my very first trip to Japan she was probably the most inspiring person I worked with," said Natalya to Greg Oliver. "She just made me take everything I've ever learned in professional wrestling, from every different angle, from everyone I've ever worked with, men, women my coaches, my trainers."

In 2006, Kong returned from Japan and became a featured star in SHIMMER. She contended for both the SHIMMER title and the tag title. She also made an appearance in Ring of Honor in late 2007.

In October 2007, she debuted as Awesome Kong in TNA. She quickly emerged as the top contender to Gail Kim's Knockouts title, eventually winning the belt from Kim in January 2008. After running roughshod over the Knockouts division for several months, Kong and manager Raisha Saeed (Melissa Anderson) announced an open challenge, offering $25,000 to any fan who could beat her. Ultimately, that challenge was fulfilled by the debuting Taylor Wilde, beginning a feud between the two.

But what really stood out from 2008 was her series of matches with Kim, something her opponent also remembers quite frankly.

"It was very physical. Like I've gotten hit by a truck after a match!" Kim said to Oliver. "This is the one angle or feud that I've been involved in that I'm very, very proud of, and I'm pretty hard on myself when it comes to my work. It's the perfect David and Goliath feud, I guess you could say. She's an amazing heel; she is a monster. I love the physicality. She came from working in Japan all those years, and I love it."

Subsequently, Kong was named number one in the inaugural PWI Female 50 awards. She won the Knockouts title twice and the Knockouts tag title (with Ayako Hamada). In 2010, the landscape in TNA changed dramatically as Hulk Hogan and Eric Bischoff joined the company and took control of the creative department. Kong got involved in a physical altercation with radio personality Bubba the Love Sponge (Todd Clem, a longtime friend of Hogan who had come aboard as a backstage interviewer) after Clem allegedly made inflammatory remarks about the victims of an earthquake in Haiti, a cause close to Stevens's heart. She was subsequently suspended from TNA and refused to take part in a tour of the United Kingdom, ultimately leading to her release from the company.

In April 2011, vignettes began appearing on WWE television, showing a shadowy figure tearing apart Barbie dolls. On May 1, Stevens made her WWE debut with a surprise attack on Michelle McCool, using the name Kharma because, you know, "Kharma is a bitch!" For the next several weeks, Kharma would appear and attack the "Barbie dolls" of WWE, but the storyline took a bizarre turn. One week, Kharma interrupted a women's tag team match and — instead of attacking her opponents — she began crying. She later announced she was pregnant and would be taking a leave of absence from WWE.

She made a surprise return at the 2012 Royal Rumble, intimidating Michael Cole into eliminating himself and tossing Hunico out of the ring. Even more surprising, TMZ reported that Stevens had given birth to a healthy baby boy, then retracted the story. The baby had not survived. She was released by WWE in July 2012 and has declined to publicly discuss that emotional period in her life.

Kong returned to the independents and then made a surprise return to TNA for a series against Jessicka Havok. She completed a tour of Japan in late 2015 and announced she had wrestled her final match in Japan, which sparked false retirement rumors.

In January 2016, she announced she had become the unlikely new leader of the Doll House, replacing Taryn Terrell, but a few weeks later, she got in a backstage altercation with Matt Hardy's wife, Rebecca. If the Bubba the Love Sponge incident got her the sympathies of many because it looked as if she stood up for herself, allegedly choking Rebecca in front of her child did not do Stevens any favors. She was released by TNA once again in February 2016. Later that year, it was announced that she'd be a part of the cast of Netflix's version of GLOW.

Despite everything, her series of matches with Gail Kim will probably be remembered for a very long time as the program that put U.S. women's wrestling on the map at a moment it really needed it.

"Kong had a really good program with Gail Kim, and in pure terms of drawing ratings, they did excellent. It was the best women's program in years, and TNA got lots of mileage out of it. They had well-worked wrestling matches at a standard well ahead of what WWE women were doing at the time," concluded Meltzer.

## The Beautiful People: ANGELINA LOVE AND VELVET SKY

Six-time TNA Knockouts champion Angelina Love still remembers the moment she discovered professional wrestling.

"I was about seven years old," she recalls. "I had always been kind of a tomboy and athletic and into sports. I was just flipping the channels one day and came across 'Macho Man' dropping an elbow off the top rope. It was so flashy and amazing; the crowd went crazy and all the camera flashes, and I just thought 'Oh my God, what is this? This is awesome!' And I became totally mesmerized by it."

Inspired by Randy Savage and Shawn Michaels, the Toronto native reached out to well-known Ontario trainer Rob Fuego in 2000, starting as a valet on the Canadian independent circuit before finishing her training and beginning to wrestle on her own. Born Lauren Williams on September 13, 1981, she adopted the ring name Angel Williams.

In 2004, she received a few bookings with the fledgling Total Nonstop Action promotion in Nashville, before signing a WWE developmental contract later that year. She trained briefly at Ohio Valley Wrestling in Louisville before being reassigned to Deep South Wrestling in Atlanta, where she worked as both a manager and a wrestler. She suffered a torn ACL in early 2006 and was sidelined for seven months following surgery.

In April 2007, after she had returned to the ring, the Deep South promotion closed down, and Williams was shuffled back to OVW. She debuted on OVW TV in May 2007, but just days after that debut, she was inexplicably released from her WWE developmental contract.

"Creative had nothing for me, even though I was supposed to go to [WWE] TV the next week," she said.

Instead, after a brief tour of Mexico's AAA promotion, she once again turned her attention to TNA, which was in the process of assembling its new Knockouts division. That's where she connected with a girl from Connecticut who had been wrestling under the name Talia Madison.

Born Jamie Lynn Szantyr on June 2, 1981, and trained by Jason Knight, Talia had debuted in 2003 and had earned some notoriety for a tag team she had formed with April Hunter known as T&A. She had competed in World Xtreme Wrestling and Women's Extreme Wrestling and had had some tryouts and guest spots in WWE. She and Angel had natural chemistry.

"No one forced us to be together, no one gave us the gimmick. That was our idea," Love said. "We knew each other previously. [Velvet] had a try-out in developmental when I was there under contract. We had done a couple indies together before either of us had signed with TNA. When we started in 2007, Velvet and I started hanging out with each other immediately. We have a lot of similarities with our sense of humor and all kinds of things, and we got along together very well.

"When they were starting up the Knockouts division, we wanted to do something different and that stuck out," she continued. "Everyone else was doing their own singular character, so we thought 'why not do something together and do a tag team thing?' Vince Russo came up with the name the Beautiful People. We wanted to be 'Velvet Love Entertainment' because both of our names are porn star names, so we thought let's roll with it and have our tag team name be something that sounds like a porn company. They liked the Beautiful People so that's what we went with. Vince totally supported it and handed us the ball and we ran with it."

*The Beautiful People: Velvet Sky and Angelina Love.*
LEE SOUTH/TNA WRESTLING

The Beautiful People became the mean girls clique that ran TNA. They began taunting "less attractive" opponents and putting paper bags over defeated opponents' heads as a "makeover." Their vow was to "cleanse" the TNA roster, "one ugly person at a time."

Although they were often portrayed as ditzy, the Beautiful People became one of TNA's top acts. Love was the ring general, and both could deliver on promos. And their provocative ring entrance (which saw both women straddle the middle rope and gyrate on their way into the ring) was always a focal point of TNA television broadcasts.

"We were the ones who would steal your boyfriend, or the ones your boyfriend would do a double-take to look at as we walked by. We were the princess bitches," Love said. "As much as I shook my ass in front of the camera, when I got into the ring, it was go-time. I was extremely talented at what I did and I was as sexy as possible while doing it."

Over the next eight years, the Beautiful People captured more than their share of title gold. Love won the Knockouts title six times, while Sky won it twice.

In 2009, Love and Sky welcomed Madison Rayne to the Beautiful People, refashioning the group as a sexy sorority called Mi Pi Sexy. That fall, Love left TNA and was replaced by Lacey Von Erich. Love returned to TNA in 2010 and stepped into a feud with her former running buddies. Love and Sky eventually resumed their partnership as both Rayne and Von Erich left the group.

Love again left TNA in 2012. In her absence, Sky flourished as a singles competitor, holding the Knockouts title for four months in 2013. Love returned to TNA in 2014, and she got the band back together. She and Sky reformed the Beautiful People and reunited with Rayne for a three-on-three match against Taryn Terrell, Jade, and Marti Belle in the summer of 2015. During that run, Love also won the Knockouts title a record six times, tied with Gail Kim

In 2015, Love married wrestler Davey Richards. She stepped away from wrestling in order to focus on building a family, effectively ending the Beautiful People. During her pregnancy, her contract with TNA officially expired, and she has done very few indie matches since. In April 2016, Sky also left TNA. However, the group has had plenty of comebacks and lineup changes over the years ... and so another comeback is never entirely out of the question.

# ODB

She was christened Jessica Nora Kresa, but to wrestling fans she'll always be One Dirty Bitch.

Kresa was born on June 6, 1978, in Minneapolis, Minnesota, the heart of the American Wrestling Association. As a girl, she watched AWA favorites like the Crusher and the Bruiser, and then stars from the WWF like Randy Savage, Jake Roberts, Roddy Piper, and the Honky Tonk Man — larger-than-life characters who knew how to talk.

"Back then I never thought about being a wrestler because I never thought you could actually be one. These weren't normal people. I wondered 'Where do these guys come from?' Little did I know that a bunch of them — Rick Rude, Mr. Perfect, the Road Warriors — they all came from my hometown, practically in my own backyard," she said.

*ODB, short for One Dirty Bitch!* LEE SOUTH/TNA WRESTLING

She played ice hockey, captaining her high school hockey team and going on to play collegiately at St. Cloud State University. "I always wanted to be big and buff. And one day I said I'm going to be a wrestler," Kresa said. "I went to college and all that fun stuff, I came home, and that's when it all started."

An avid weightlifter, Kresa began training under renowned Minneapolis trainer Eddie Sharkey, debuting in 1998. She auditioned and was selected to compete in the first season of *Tough Enough* in 2001, but she failed to make the final cut of 25. She went back to wrestling on the independent circuit and was able to wrestle at the South St. Paul Armory, the same venue where she had attended wrestling shows with her parents as a child.

She made some appearances with the fledgling Total Nonstop Action promotion in 2003 and 2004. In 2006, she got a big break, signing with Ohio Valley Wrestling, WWE's developmental system. Her time in OVW helped her flesh out the ODB persona.

"I came up with the name the first time I stepped into a ring. I always had the ODB name. The character took me a while. I was quiet and shy growing up," she said. "When I went to OVW, Al Snow and Danny Davis both told me they wanted to see ODB. 'Why are you ODB? Who is this Dirty Bitch? We want to see it.' They really let me just go. 'We'll tell you if you go too far.' Actually, Dean Malenko told me I went too far once. I was doing the whole 'Bam!' very in your face, grabbing my boobs and everything. He's like, 'Whoa! All right. Well, I've never had to tell anyone to take it back a little bit before.' It obviously wasn't really WWE's style."

In July 2006, ODB declared herself the OVW women's champion, facetiously claiming she'd won the title in a tournament in, of all places, Rio de Janeiro (spoofing a fictitious tournament Pat Patterson was said to have won to become the first WWF Intercontinental champion in 1979; in actuality, Patterson had simply been named champion). She was subsequently awarded the title, making her the first OVW women's champion. She held the OVW women's title on two occasions and had notable rivalries with Serena Deeb, Katie Lea, and Milena Roucka.

But while other OVW women got called up to WWE, ODB never heard the words.

"When I was in developmental they had girls like Kelly Kelly, Alicia Fox, Maryse, and those girls. And they're all gorgeous women, size 2. And then there's me. Size 8. Normal size. Got a few tattoos. I was just bigger. But I thought, there *is* room for me somewhere, somehow," she said. "I knew that someday it would happen, but it took me a little longer. I must have heard 'no' about a thousand times.

"I didn't want to be cookie-cutter. I'm never going to be a size 2, nor do I want to be. I wanted to be me. I was glad I stood out. I never tried to lose weight or anything. I got told to lose weight, but I said fuck it. I'm eating a pizza and I like to drink beer, so that isn't going to work. As long as nothing jiggles, I'm good."

ODB was released by WWE in 2007, and TNA wasted little time in scooping her up, signing her to compete in a 10-woman gauntlet match to crown the first Knockouts champion at Bound for Glory on October 14, 2007. It proved to be the start of a seven-year run in TNA, where she won the Knockouts title four times and the tag team title, with Eric Young, once. "When I got to TNA, they said they wanted to see what I did in OVW. WWE wanted to go PG, but TNA wanted to take me as I was."

Known for her outrageous behavior (including drinking from a flask, grabbing her breasts, and doing rowdy promos), ODB was one of TNA's most colorful characters during a high point for the company. "I came out with the flask. I didn't even ask, because you never ask permission in wrestling," she said. "I walked out with the flask, started grabbing my boobs. When I got to the back, they were like, 'What's up with the boob-grabbing?' I was like, 'I don't know. It's just something I did.' And they said, 'Well, keep doing it.' It worked."

Although she excelled at comedy, she was also a versatile powerhouse who could compete with anyone on the roster. She was the sole female member of the Front Line, a babyface faction formed to fight the heel Main Event Mafia in 2009, and she went on to win a New Year's Knockout Eve tournament for a title shot that same year. Her signature moves included the "Bam" fireman's carry cutter, the running powerslam, and the ever-popular bronco buster.

"She's such a talented girl. She's so charismatic, she can work in the ring, and she's got personality," fellow wrestler Gail Kim once said to *Live Audio Wrestling*.

ODB left TNA in 2015, expressing dissatisfaction with the direction the Knockouts division was taking. She made several appearances in Ring of Honor in 2015, where she aligned with kindred spirits the Briscoe Brothers. When not wrestling, she works as a bartender, and she has begun marketing her own line of One Dirty Bitch hot sauces.

"Every match I did, I went out there and thought what can I do to really make an impact on this show and make people say, 'Who the hell is this girl?' That was my goal in every match," she said. "I wanted to do something to stand out. When people left that arena, they were going to remember the Dirty Bitch."

## DAFFNEY

Initially hired in a supporting role as David Flair's demented Goth-chick girlfriend in World Championship Wrestling, Shannon Spruill got her foot in the door and kicked it wide open, becoming a cult favorite as "The Scream Queen" Daffney Unger.

The daughter of a U.S Air Force serviceman, she was born on July 17, 1975, in West Germany. She moved several times growing up, residing on both sides of the Atlantic and eventually settling in Georgia, where she attended Georgia State University. After earning a bachelor's degree in film and video production, she heard about a casting call at WCW.

"WCW used a lot of extras. They brought me in for an audition. I told them I loved wrestling. I said I wanted to train and asked if I could go to the Power Plant."

She started training there, working hard with Nora Greenwood. Many agents, Terry Taylor in particular, noticed how hard she was working. Next thing she knew, she was signed for a year. So in late 1999, Spruill debuted under the name Daffney Unger. She was cast primarily as a valet, known for dressing in black and for the shrill screams she would emit from ringside.

In an example of booker Vince Russo's anything-can-happen approach at the time, Daffney won the WCW cruiserweight title with an upset win over Crowbar on May 22, 2000, although Daffney had barely any wrestling experience.

"I almost compare it to David Arquette, someone who is just not worthy and who shouldn't be holding a championship belt in a major federation like that," said Daffney herself in an interview with the Diva Dirt website.

Although there were several women on the WCW payroll, the women's division was nonexistent. Women such as Madusa, Major Gunns, Paisley, and others were used as valets. "It was just 'fight alongside your man,'" Daffney said. "The women's roles were changing, but there were no steps toward having a women's belt."

Daffney was released by WCW in February 2001 and went to train at Dusty Rhodes's TCW in Georgia. "I really wanted to be able to do singles matches," she remembered. She eventually landed a WWE developmental contract and was assigned to Ohio Valley Wrestling in the summer of 2003.

*"The Scream Queen" Daffney.* YAN O'CAIN COLLECTION

Although her professional career was looking bright, her personal life was falling apart. "I was going through a divorce, and right around the same time, I found out that I was bi-polar," she said. "I was on no medication." She was released by WWE in December 2003 and fell back into depression. "I took about a year off. I had to find the right medications and get myself right in the head. The ironic thing is I was playing this crazy bi-polar girl, and that's really what I was in real life."

She returned to the independents in 2006, working, among others, for SHIMMER. From 2008 to 2010, she mainly worked for TNA, the company she actually wrestled the most for, grappling with the likes of Angelina Love, Velvet Sky, Madison Rayne, and Taylor Wilde. But at Bound for Glory 2009, she suffered a concussion after being chokeslammed through a board wrapped in barbed wire by Abyss. Six months later, she suffered another concussion when she was injured by Miss Betsy, an inexperienced 300-pounder, in her TNA tryout match.

The concussions would spell the end of Daffney's wrestling career. "My career was ended early due to concussions," she said. "My last match was in December 2010. I had major Grade 2 concussions within a six month span. The first one was a brain bleed. I have made arrangements to donate my brain to science. Chris Nowinski's Sports Legacy Institute has first dibs after I expire."

Spruill sued TNA for injuries sustained during her time there. The suit was settled out of court. She says she has become more aware of the dangers of concussions because of her experiences.

"Any time I hear some girl hit her head, I say, 'Cancel your next freaking booking. You rest. No working out, just light walking and stretching, but no physical exertion where the blood is going to rush to your brain. Because it's dangerous.' I definitely did things in my career that I wish I would have had the balls to say 'no' to," she said. "I went through barbed wire and thumbtacks and tables. You can say that takes balls. But it takes more balls to say no. Your health is too important."

## MICKIE JAMES

Whether she was portraying a psychopathic lesbian stalker, a plucky underdog, or the victim of fat-shaming bullies, Mickie James proved to be one of the most versatile and successful female wrestlers of the early 2000s.

Born August 31, 1979, James grew up in Montpellier, Virginia. Her parents divorced while she was young. A self-professed nerd growing up, she enjoyed music (she played the violin) and horseback riding, as her family had 27 horses. She also took an interest in pro wrestling.

"Wrestling was me and my dad's thing," she said in a 2010

interview with *Pro Wrestling Illustrated.* "[I remember] watching wrestling as a kid and coming off the couch with an elbow on my dad or my brother, and wanting to be a wrestler."

Once the wrestling bug took hold, James enrolled in a wrestling school outside of Washington, D.C., and eventually debuted in 1999 as a valet, adopting the name Alexis Laree. She supplemented her wrestling income by waitressing and modeling.

After working in several Mid-Atlantic independent promotions and attending several wrestling seminars, she landed bookings in the fledgling new promotions Ring of Honor and NWA-TNA in 2002.

In 2003, after years of making contacts and sending tapes to the office, she was signed to a WWE developmental contract and assigned to Ohio Valley Wrestling in Louisville. Laree spent two years in OVW, where she feuded with Beth Phoenix, Jillian Hall, and Shelley Martinez.

In October 2005, James finally got her call-up to the main roster, where she appeared under her own name as a superfan of Trish Stratus. In the storyline, Stratus took James under her wing, and James developed an obsession with her mentor, dressing like Stratus on Halloween, mimicking her signature moves, and finally kissing her under the mistletoe on a Christmas-themed edition of *Raw*, starting a storyline that also included Ashley Massaro. Doing this kind of angle was okay with James, since she was the one who pitched it. But when the creative team was going to give the role to another woman, James went straight up to Vince McMahon himself.

"I walked right into Vince's office and I said, 'Mr. McMahon, I heard you read my storyline, and I wanted you to know there's nobody who can do that character better than me,'" she said. Her gutsy move paid off.

The Trish/Mickie feud culminated at WrestleMania 22 in Rosemont, Illinois, in one of the most memorable women's matches in WrestleMania history. James ratcheted up the lesbian antics during the match, grabbing Trish's crotch at one point and then seductively licking her fingers, a gesture that was subsequently edited out of future broadcasts by WWE and for which she was yelled at by McMahon.

*A huge fan favorite, Mickie James.* LEE SOUTH/TNA WRESTLING

James won the match and became the women's champion, but she was surprised that both she and Trish were hearing cheers from the capacity crowd.

"That totally threw Trish and me for a loop," James told *PWI.* "I expected them to boo me out of the building. But halfway through the match, the crowd was so split and so vocal, with the 'Let's go Mickie,' 'Let's go Trish' chants. It was my first WrestleMania and my mom is sitting there in the front row and I'm winning the title, but to have that kind of reaction was amazing. I get goosebumps thinking about it to this day."

For Trish Stratus, this feud also legitimized the women's division at the time. "The Mickie James feud was probably the pinnacle of women's wrestling. I think people at that point saw us as a legitimate part of the roster; the women's division was the same as any other division in the company," she said in an interview with SLAM! Wrestling.

James had a five-year run in WWE, during which time she won the women's title five times and the Divas title once. James became the cornerstone of the WWE women's/Divas division, serving as bridge from the Stratus/Lita era into the *Diva Search* era. She was named number one in the 2009 PWI Female 50 and was voted Woman of the Year by *PWI* readers in 2009 and 2011.

As successful as she was as the heel antagonist for Stratus, James was equally successful as a fan favorite and developed into one of the most popular women in WWE history.

"In my opinion, the best pure babyfaces of all time are Brad Armstrong, Ricky Steamboat, and Mickie James," Tommy Dreamer said. "Mickie is always moving forward, up on the balls of her feet, going at her opponent. She always has that energy and passion, and it's infectious. Her smile is genuine. When she is winning, we celebrate with her. And when she is getting beat down, we want to fight for her."

While the overt lesbian overtones of the Stratus feud generated controversy, her feud with Michelle McCool and Layla El proved to be even more controversial. McCool and Layla (collectively known as Lay-Cool) made fun of James's weight and began calling her "Piggy James." Both James and McCool later said they had trepidations about a storyline that was designed to humiliate someone over their body type.

"That was one of the toughest things that we ever had to do," McCool told *Pro Wrestling Illustrated* in 2011. "We were on an overseas tour . . . when they had me sing that 'Old Macdonald Had a Farm' song at her, which is where the whole 'Piggy James' storyline evolved. I cannot tell how sick I was that day. When they told me we would be doing that, I thought they were joking. Layla and I both respected her so much. But it connected with the fans. People ate it up. So we did our job, but it was a very tough situation."

It wasn't any easier for James. "I was never part of the cool clique [as a child]," James said. "You reach back to that time. [The storyline] did kind of touch my heart, because you don't really know where that comes from. It could have been just a storyline, or maybe someone pitched that storyline for a reason."

In March 2010, James was diagnosed with a serious staph infection in her knee. If it hadn't been caught in time, she would have risked amputation. She returned to the ring a few weeks later but was stunned to be released by WWE in April. "A lot of times you can see that stuff coming, you can see the handwriting on the wall, but I had just come back from injury and the feud with Lay-Cool. It was shocking. It was heartbreaking," she said. With that said, she doesn't have any bitterness toward the company. "I won't ever say, 'Oh, I'm upset with the way I left the company.' The name Mickie James would not be recognizable without WWE. I'm very grateful for that."

In May 2010, she released her first country music album, and in September 2010, she signed with TNA and debuted as the special guest referee for the Knockouts title match at Bound for Glory. She would end up winning the TNA Knockouts title three times, making her the only woman to hold all three titles (WWE Women, WWE Divas, and TNA Knockouts) and one of the most decorated female wrestlers of the 2000s. During her time there, she began dating fellow TNA wrestler Nick "Magnus" Aldis, and the couple welcomed a baby boy in September 2014. And who did she talk to for advice on being a mom in the wrestling world? Trish, of course!

James made a brief return to TNA in 2015, where she came to Magnus's aid in a feud with James Storm in a storyline that saw Storm push her onto the tracks of an "oncoming train." But even that train couldn't keep her down! She continues competing on the independents and performing concerts, and she has been active in Jeff Jarrett's Global Force Wrestling, which launched in 2015. She made her SHIMMER and NXT debuts in November 2016. Her match against NXT women's champion Asuka received much praise and got her a new contract with WWE, six years after leaving the company.

# JADE

As a member of the Dollhouse in TNA, it's hard to imagine Jade being anything other than the beautiful and confident persona she portrays on *Impact Wrestling*. In reality, she was a very different person until she started wrestling.

"Growing up, I was picked on for being multiracial [she is half-Korean], and was called ugly, fat, and stupid," she said. "I was put in a Learning Disability class in elementary school because people thought I was slow. Wrestling gave me an opportunity to express myself that I had never had before. Once I stepped foot inside the ring, all of my worries and stresses disappeared."

Born April 16, 1989, Stephanie Bell became a wrestling fan as a child. She earned a volleyball scholarship to Marymount University and enrolled in a wrestling school in nearby Manassas, Virginia, at the age of 18.

*Mia Yim or, as she's better known now, Jade.* BOB MULRENIN

She wrestled her first match in August 2009 under the name Mia Yim, wrestling throughout the Virginia area before getting bookings for prominent independent promotion Jersey All-Pro Wrestling. Yim met Daizee Haze, who introduced her to Ring of Honor, where she continued training at the ROH Academy and became the valet for Prince Nana and the Embassy in 2011, barely a year and a half into her wrestling career. She accepted an invitation to train in Japan for REINA that same year.

She served as Adam Cole's valet in Combat Zone Wrestling and was drawn into an inter-gender feud with Cole's adversary, Greg Excellent. Excellent and Yim had a series of surprisingly intense bouts, culminating with Yim winning a tables, ladders, and chairs match over Excellent in March 2012.

Yim quickly developed into a rising star on the independents, emerging as a title contender in both SHIMMER and SHINE. In addition to her arsenal of kicks and attacks based on her tae kwon do training, Yim was known for her package piledriver and her stunning "Sky-Yim" corkscrew moonsault. Her dedication to physical fitness was also apparent as she developed a toned and powerful physique.

In February 2014, Yim teamed with Leva Bates as the Lucha Sisters to win a tournament to crown the first SHINE tag team champions. Interestingly, as Bates and Yim were teaming in SHINE, Bates began wrestling for WWE's NXT brand as Blue Pants, and Yim began wrestling for the rival TNA organization, a rarity in wrestling even today.

On November 16, 2014, Yim defeated Ivelisse Velez to win the SHINE title in Beijing, China, one of the highlights of the World Wrestling Network's ambitious tour of that country. Six months later, she lost that title to NWA women's champion Santana Garrett in a title vs. title match.

Living in Orlando, Yim had made occasional appearances for TNA, but in April 2015, she was signed to a full-time contract and became one of the cornerstones of the Knockouts division, part of the Dollhouse with Marti Belle. However, she had to make some changes. "I signed a deal with TNA and was given the role of crazy, cute doll girl, everything I wasn't in real life," she said. "I never really had a character because I felt that my wrestling style was enough. After a while with the Dollhouse, I was able to drop the skirt and ribbons and put on my shorts and kick pads. I don't want to be a sex symbol. I want to be taken as an athlete."

On March 17, 2016, Jade defeated Gail Kim and Madison Rayne in a three-way match to win the Knockouts title. But on June 12, she lost the title to Sienna, also in a three-way dance that included Gail Kim. "My long-term goal is to make a difference," she said. "I want to be an example that hard work and dedication can bring success."

# The RISE of the DIVAS

Reality television was all the rage in the early 2000s with *Survivor* and *Big Brother* captivating viewers worldwide. WWE dipped its toes into the reality TV game with *Tough Enough* in 2001 and *WWE Diva Search* in 2003.

*Tough Enough* featured a cast of aspiring wrestlers (male and female) competing for a WWE contract. More than 4,000 individuals submitted videotape entries, and a group of 13 contestants were selected to vie for a contract. Maven Huffman and Nidia Guenard were named the winners of the inaugural season of *Tough Enough*, and both went on to short stints in WWE.

*Diva Search* focused entirely on female personalities, with a greater emphasis on appearance than athleticism. The competition was structured much like a beauty pageant and recruited models, fitness competitors, and aspiring actresses, very often at the expense of established female wrestlers. WWE made it clear that it wasn't looking for experienced wrestlers; in fact, it often seemed as if wrestling experience was a liability instead of an advantage. The focus was purely on hiring marketable, attractive women. If they could wrestle, that was an added bonus. In a telling, if accidental, indication of WWE's attitude toward the contest, the theme music chosen for the contest was a song titled "Walk, Idiot, Walk."

The dawn of *Diva Search* resulted in an influx of models in WWE, resulting in a backlash on the independent level and in TNA, whose wrestling-heavy Knockouts division stood in stark contrast to WWE's new direction and helped strengthen an anti-Diva movement on the independents.

The first *Diva Search* took place in 2003 and was won by Jaime Koeppe, who received a photoshoot in *WWE Magazine* as her prize. The following year, the prize was upped to $250,000 and a WWE contract. Christy Hemme won the 2004 *Diva Search*; contestants Amy Weber, Candice Michelle (who received national notoriety for a provocative Go! Daddy commercial during Super Bowl 39), Joy Giovanni, Michelle McCool, and Maria Kanellis were signed to WWE contracts. The contestants competed in a variety of contests, including attempting to seduce Kamala and dissing their competition.

*Diva Search* returned in 2005 and was won by Ashley Massaro. A highlight of the competition saw contestant Leyla Milani disqualified when she accidentally exposed her breast while running an obstacle course. Massaro received a $250,000 prize and a WWE contract, and she went on to be featured in *Playboy*.

Layla El of London, England, won the 2006 *Diva Search*. Unlike some of her predecessors, Layla proved to have a lengthy run in WWE, remaining with the company until retiring in 2015. WWE also signed contestants Maryse Ouellet, the Garcia Twins (better known as the Bella Twins), Brooke Adams (who became Brooke Tessmacher in TNA), Amy Zidian, and Milena Roucka (who took the name Rosa Mendes).

*Diva Search* was held again in 2007, this time won by Eve Torres. Contestants Taryn Terrell, Angela Fong, Lucha Underground's Black Lotus, and Lena Yada also received contracts. Torres was the only one with staying power, remaining with WWE until 2012 and winning the Divas title three times.

WWE is known for having its own vernacular: wrestling is "sports entertainment," wrestlers are "Superstars," fans are "the WWE Universe." Around 2008, WWE designated its female wrestlers (err, Superstars) as Divas. To highlight the moniker, WWE established its Divas title in June 2008. Originally a title defended exclusively on the *Smack-Down* brand, the Divas title featured a big pink butterfly on its faceplate.

The branding of "the Divas" had pros and

*Maryse was one of the Divas champions in the mid-2000s.*
MIKE MASTRANDREA

cons. On one hand, more women were featured in prominent roles on WWE programming. On the other, models and reality-show contestants were earning spots in WWE without "paying their dues," rankling some veterans. It created a combustible environment, one that put more women on WWE TV while simultaneously building a backlash elsewhere. Also, a lot of the matches were multi-woman matches and kept somewhat short. "I'm not a model and I don't want to dance," remembered Natalya. "I dance like my dad in high heels. It wasn't what I came to do in WWE. The average match sometimes for Divas was like three or four minutes."

However, the reality Divas had a golden opportunity by the name of Dave "Fit" Finlay. From the early 2000s until he was fired in 2011 (he was hired back a little over a year later), the Belfast native was put in charge of the women's division and was a huge part of the success when the division transitioned from the bras and panties era to an era of competitive matches.

"He was very good. He was the only one who truly understood women's wrestling and how to work with us," said Maryse Ouellet. It's so different than training guys. All the girls were so disappointed when he was fired."

Maryse wasn't the only one with such a high regard of her trainer. For the man himself, it was all a question of trust.

"They really did some great work for me, and it was a privilege to work with them," he said. "I spent time with them. I got to know them and learn all their habits and their quirky little things. We got along good together. They could come and confide in me. It was a trust-based thing. That is the same you would do with anybody, but the girls were under such a big microscope. They're in a man's world and they're trying their best, and you can sit back and pull them apart, but they are giving their best. None of the guys are perfect. I don't know anybody who's had a perfect match, ever."

## The Bella Twins: NIKKI AND BRIE

Born 16 minutes apart, Stephanie Nicole Garcia-Colace and Brianna Monique Garcia-Colace, the originators of Twin Magic, are best known as the Bella Twins.

Born on November 21, 1983, in San Diego, California, the Bellas grew up in Scottsdale, Arizona. Both played soccer in high school, with a knee injury ending Nikki's dream of playing collegiately. After high school, they relocated to Los Angeles, where they took some acting and modeling gigs, including a stint as the World Cup Twins to promote the 1996 FIFA World Cup tournament. They registered for the 2006 *WWE Diva Search*, and although they didn't win, they impressed

WWE scouts enough to be offered a developmental contract in June 2007. The sisters were assigned to the WWE training program, first to Deep South Wrestling in Atlanta and then to Florida Championship Wrestling in Tampa. With the novelty of being attractive twins, the Bellas were fast-tracked in FCW, a move that garnered them a bit of resentment as they were seen by many as models who hadn't paid their dues.

"I didn't come from the independents, and believe me, I wish I did," Nikki said in a 2015 interview with *Pro*

*The originators of the Twin Magic: Brie and Nikki Bella.*
RICKY HAVLIK

*Wrestling Illustrated*. "I was fortunate in that when I wanted to become a wrestler and I went down to Atlanta, Georgia, to get in that ring, WWE was like 'let's give them a try.' Brie and I weren't just models hired. . . . Brie and I had a big struggle. We legit packed up our cars, went down to that ring in Atlanta, and said, 'Hey, you're going to hire us. We want to be here.' I don't ever want people to think it was really easy for us, because it wasn't. Being a twin was actually difficult. Everything had to be alike. We had to dress alike. They thought they couldn't do storylines with us because we always had to be together. It's like, 'Uhm, no we don't.'"

The Bellas trained under the guidance of Tom Prichard and

debuted in September 2007, working a program with Nattie Neidhart and Krissy Vaine in FCW. It was during their early days in FCW that the Bellas perfected the strategy that would become their trademark in WWE — trading places in midmatch, ostensibly allowing the fatigued or injured sister to substitute out for the fresh sister. This switcheroo would become known as Twin Magic.

The Bellas debuted on the main roster on the August 29, 2008, edition of *SmackDown*, with Brie scoring an upset win over Victoria thanks to that little "twin magic."

The Bellas were primarily utilized as valets — first with Carlito and Primo Colon, then with the Miz and John Morrison — while competing in occasional tag team bouts. Nikki and Brie rarely spoke and were presented as interchangeable twins without distinct personalities. They always dressed alike and almost always appeared on screen side by side. Sharp-eyed fans, however, could spot one difference between the two: Brie had a tattoo below her navel, which occasionally peeked out from the top of her tights. The Bellas also served as hostesses for the weekly celebrity guest hosts appearing on *Raw*. It was a role that kept the sisters on television, but they were rarely treated as serious wrestlers.

"When I came into this industry over eight years ago, I was simply looked at as 'arm candy,'" Nikki told *PWI*. "I was told 'Oh, don't worry, you don't have to learn to wrestle that good.' But that was *the* reason I was here. I want to be a wrestler. I don't want to be just a Diva that's on some guy's arm as they go down to the ring or on the arm of the celebrity guest host on *Raw*. I wanted to be a professional wrestler."

The twins ended up wrestling on a more regular basis, but not until 2010, as they were either used in tag team or in multiperson tag matches. Then, a year apart from each other, they both held the WWE Divas title. On April 11, 2011, Brie defeated Eve Torres and held the championship for three months before dropping it to Kelly Kelly. On April 23, 2012, Nikki upset Beth Phoenix in a lumberjill match. Her first reign was short though, as she dropped the belt to Layla El the following week. The reason was simple: the Bellas were leaving WWE. Their contracts were up, and they wanted to take some time off of wrestling.

"With any career you're in, there's always a life outside of your career and that's one thing when you're on the road 300 days of the year, you start missing your family, you miss your friends, you miss all the things you enjoy in life," said Brie in an interview shortly after their departure.

Like many others, they returned to WWE less than a year later, but Nikki suffered a broken leg in June 2013, which provided Brie with an opportunity to start to establish herself as a singles wrestler. Around that time, the Bellas were also cast on the E! Network reality show *Total Divas*, which allowed both sisters to show their individual personalities. It turns out that Brie and Nikki weren't just interchangeable models after all — they had their own unique personalities, and they quickly became stars of *Total Divas*. Brie began dating and eventually married Daniel Bryan, which was featured on *Total Divas*, while Nikki began dating John Cena. WWE had a pair of new power couples and a show to promote it.

Brie's real-life romance with Bryan was used as a WWE storyline in the summer of 2014. After Stephanie McMahon threatened to fire her if Bryan did not voluntarily forfeit the WWE championship to the Authority, Brie resigned from WWE and slapped McMahon in the face. McMahon reinstated Brie and faced her in a featured match at SummerSlam 2014, one of the highest-profile women's matches in WWE history. McMahon won the match when Nikki shocked the fans and turned against her sister, igniting a feud between the twins.

The rivalry was only short term, and after reconciling, Nikki capitalized on an assist from Brie to win the Divas title from A.J. Lee at the 2014 Survivor Series, something that couldn't have happened some months before.

"Vince McMahon didn't want the title on any *Total Divas* member because he didn't know how it would transition on Sunday night and Monday in case there was a title change and the show was airing," said Nikki.

2015 was a huge year for Nikki as she went on to hold that championship for 301 days until losing the belt to Charlotte at the 2015 Night of Champions PPV, setting a record for longest Divas title reign. By virtue of her reign, she was named number one in the 2015 PWI Female 50.

"I just think of all years and all the 'no's' I heard — where I'd try to pitch Vince or get here, and be told no. It's crazy. Whoever would have thought that Nikki Bella would be number one in PWI's Top 50 Females?" Nikki said in an interview with the magazine. "To finally be where I always dreamed is such an amazing feeling. It feels like I've been training for the Olympics and have finally reached that gold medal."

Each year being different, 2016 had a lot of ups and downs for the twins. Nikki, who had neck surgery at the end of 2015, spent most of 2016 on the shelf, only coming back in the ring at Summer Slam. After wrestling at WrestleMania in Dallas, Brie took a break from in-ring competition to start a family. Also, after being runners-up in 2015, the Bellas won the Choice Female Athlete award at the *Teen Choice Awards*, over the likes of Serena Williams and Ronda Rousey. They are also part of a new series on E! Network, a spin-off of *Total Divas* called *Total Bellas*, proving that in or out of the ring, Nikki and Brie are still very popular.

# MICHELLE MCCOOL

With two women's championships and two Divas championships to her credit, Michelle McCool was one of the most successful WWE Divas of the post–Trish Stratus era. However, as one of the first Divas to enter WWE through a reality television show, not to mention dating and eventually marrying one of the company's biggest stars, McCool also suffered through a backlash that overshadowed some of her greatest accomplishments.

Born in 1980 and raised in tiny Palatka, Florida, McCool was introduced to pro wrestling at a young age.

"Watching wrestling was a bonding experience between me, my dad, and my grandfather," she said. "Mondays were the only night of the week I was allowed to stay up late so I could watch *Monday Night Raw*."

An athlete in high school, she played softball, basketball, and volleyball, and she went on to play softball at the collegiate level at Pasco-Hernando State College.

In 2004, she auditioned for *WWE Diva Search* and made the cut. She finished in seventh place; and although she didn't win

*The cool part in Lay-Cool, Michelle McCool.*
PAT LAPRADE COLLECTION/RICH FREEDA WWE

the competition, she impressed management enough to be offered a WWE contract. McCool debuted as a fitness trainer character in November 2004. She was used mostly in bikini contests and brief catfights before being sent to Deep South Wrestling for additional in-ring training.

On one hand, the contract was a golden ticket into a dream job. On the other, it came along with a lot of resentment from wrestlers, and fans, who felt McCool and other *Diva Search* contenders hadn't paid their dues.

"I paid my dues down in Deep South Wrestling," McCool answered back. "There was no air-conditioning, no frills down there.

I wanted to learn so badly. I would get to shows hours early. I would stay late. I would ask questions. I was really hungry for it. I had such a respect for the business and the people who came before me that I wanted to learn everything I could."

In March 2006, she was moved to Ohio Valley Wrestling in Louisville, where she was used as a valet. She returned to WWE in the summer of 2006, playing a snooty teacher character, based on her former real-life occupation.

In spring 2007, after an injury, McCool was reintroduced as a fan favorite, a happy-go-lucky all-American girl. She had a brief feud with Victoria and earned the right to face Natalya in a match to crown the inaugural Divas champion at the 2008 Great American Bash PPV. McCool won that bout by submission, making Natalya submit to a heel hook.

The fans still weren't quite sold on her, however. The decision was made to turn McCool heel. After losing the Divas title to Maryse on December 22, 2008, McCool viciously attacked special guest referee Maria Kanellis, firmly establishing herself as a villain.

At around this time, McCool had begun dating the Undertaker. Although it was not acknowledged on WWE television at the time, it was widely reported online. With the dynamic of a heel woman dating a beloved fan favorite, McCool received unprovoked scorn from some corners of the internet. The couple married in June 2010.

"People knew I was married to Mark [Callaway, the Undertaker] and I got a lot of heat — not good heat — with people saying I only had my spot because of my husband. That was hard," McCool said.

McCool became the first woman to win both the Divas and WWE women's championships on June 28, 2009, when she defeated Melina at The Bash pay-per-view. She then went on to form a team with fellow former *Diva Search* competitor Layla El. The pairing became known as Lay-Cool. They were two condescending BFFs who ran roughshod over the Divas division, somewhat based on the success that the Beautiful People were having in TNA.

"I was constantly pitching storylines, not just for myself but for the whole women's division. . . . I was there when WWE really started entering the PG era of big corporate sponsorships. You really had to watch everything you said and did. It was difficult for me because I wanted to go out and have some fun and shake things up. I wish I could have gone out there and done some of the things that Trish and Lita were able to do. Molly Holly had her head shaved. I would love to have had my head shaved! It wasn't until the tail-end of my career, during the Lay-Cool period, where Vince loosened the reins and let us just go out and do our thing."

Mickie James defeated McCool for the women's title at the 2010 Royal Rumble, but McCool regained the belt one month later. She lost the women's title to Beth Phoenix at Extreme Rules on April 25, 2010, in an Extreme Makeover hardcore match. However, on May 11, 2010, Lay-Cool faced Phoenix in a handicap match for the women's title. Layla scored a surprise pinfall over Phoenix (who was injured headed into the match). Layla and McCool declared themselves cochampions, with either of them defending the championship.

"That created a ton of controversy," McCool said. "You see, we never knew what was going to happen the next week. We might not be on TV for a month. Every time I was out there, I was looking to see what I could do to try to get attention; what little thing can we do to get people talking and make sure we're on TV again next week? When we won the title from Beth Phoenix, it was Lay-Cool that won the match. I went to the office and wanted to defend the belt Freebirds-style where either of us could defend it. Dave [Bautista] heard us talking about it. He said, 'You know what would really get you heat? You ought to cut that belt in half and share it.' Vince loved the idea. So we went out and had it cut in half and magnetized."

At Night of Champions on September 19, 2010, McCool defended the women's title against Divas champion Melina in a title unification bout. McCool won that match, unifying the championships and ending the lineage of the prestigious women's title in WWE record books.

Fittingly, Lay-Cool lost the Divas belt in another handicap match, falling to Natalya at the 2010 Survivor Series. Lay-Cool also made history at the 2010 TLC PPV, losing to Natalya and Phoenix in the first women's tag team tables match in WWE history.

Despite the heat she took from fans McCool was named number one in the 2010 PWI Female 50. "I honestly thought, 'Those poor guys. They're going to get so much grief over naming me number one,'" McCool said at the time.

At WrestleMania 27, McCool finally got a chance to climb into the ring against Trish Stratus, in a six-person inter-gender match in which Layla, Dolph Ziggler, and McCool suffered a loss to Stratus, John Morrison, and *Jersey Shore* TV star Snooki; Snooki ended up pinning McCool.

Because she had made the decision to retire and to raise a family, McCool wrestled her final match at Extreme Rules 2011, losing a loser leaves town match to Layla. That was not her last battle though; she announced in August 2016 that she had had skin cancer removed.

Looking back, she said she hoped people appreciated her WWE run, even if she was underappreciated by critics at the time.

"Hopefully, the Lay-Cool legacy will live on," she said. "Hopefully, people will look back on my career and see that I could actually work and put my time in. At the end of the day, wrestling took up almost eight years of my life. I achieved something I dreamed of doing as a little girl. Nobody can take that away from me."

# MELINA

Remembered by many for her signature split-legged ring entrance beneath the bottom rope, the former beauty pageant contestant got her foot in the door of WWE through *Tough Enough* and went on to win three WWE women's titles and two Divas titles during a six-year run with the company.

Born March 9, 1979, Melina Perez grew up in Los Angeles. After doing some modeling, she began training at Jesse Hernandez's School of Hard Knocks wrestling school in San Bernardino in 2001.

She wrestled her first match in 2002.

A few months later, she auditioned for WWE's *Tough Enough* and was accepted into the cast for Season Three. She advanced to the final field of 25 contestants before being eliminated from the contest. However, during her time at *Tough Enough*, she met that season's cowinner, John Hennigan (with Matt Cappotelli). She and Hennigan began dating and started a tumultuous relationship that would go on for more than a decade.

Although she wasn't

*Both a women's and Divas champion, Melina.*
PAT LAPRADE COLLECTION WWE

selected on *Tough Enough*, she moved down to Louisville, Kentucky, and joined Ohio Valley Wrestling with Hennigan. The latter adopted the name Johnny Nitro and formed a team with Joey Mercury that would be known as MNM (for Mercury, Nitro, and Melina).

The act was an immediate hit in OVW, winning the OVW Southern tag team belts the day WWE sent members of its creative team (including Stephanie McMahon and Paul Heyman) down for a surprise inspection of OVW in November 2004.

In April 2005, MNM got the call-up to the main roster, debuting on *SmackDown* and interrupting an interview segment featuring tag team champion Rey Mysterio. MNM attacked Mysterio, leading to a title match between MNM and Mysterio and Eddie Guerrero the following week. MNM won the tag belts in their first match, beating two of the most highly regarded wrestlers in the company in the process. It was a true superstar debut.

Melina eased into wrestling herself, beating Torrie Wilson in a bra and panties match at the 2005 Great American Bash PPV and emerging as the top contender for the women's title by eliminating champion Trish Stratus in a battle royal.

WWE split the team in 2006, sending Nitro and Melina to the *Raw* brand as part of an attempt to maintain separate brand rosters. She continued to manage Nitro and again worked her way up into contention for the women's title in early 2007. Her coronation came in February 2007 when she defeated Mickie James to win the women's title. She and James subsequently faced off in the first women's Falls Count Anywhere match in WWE history, which Melina also won.

After exchanging the title with James and losing it to Candice Michelle, she became a fan favorite for the first time in her career after a falling out with Beth Phoenix in the spring of 2008. That led to the first women's I Quit match in WWE history at the One Night Stand PPV. Melina's flexibility was put on full display when Phoenix bent her in half to earn the submission.

Bret Hart has gone on record calling Melina one of his favorite wrestlers to watch, which is heavy praise from a man not known for handing out compliments lightly. "I think Melina is creative and imaginative, and she's an innovator and comes up with some great matches," Hart said on the *Ministry of Slam* show. "In a lot of ways, I think she's the best wrestler in the world right now."

With the creation of the WWE Divas title in 2008, women's wrestling had two main titles, but that would all change in September 2010. Michelle McCool, the women's champion, defeated the Divas champion Melina to unify both titles at the Night of the Champions PPV. Melina left WWE in January 2011.

Since then, she has worked some independent promotions such as WWC in Puerto Rico, *Lucha Underground*, and Stardom in Japan.

In an era where posing for *Playboy* was as important as winning a title, if not more so, Perez made it clear that it wasn't one of her priorities. "I'm sensual but I'm not going to do things that are blatant sex," she said in a 2008 interview with AskMen.com. "I'll never say never, but at this point I wouldn't pose nude. I want people to see me for my abilities and talents."

# BETH PHOENIX

The Glamazon — a combination of glamor and physicality, beauty and power, grace and intensity — was the name adopted by Beth Phoenix, and one that neatly encapsulates her wrestling persona and her overall approach to wrestling.

Elizabeth Kocianski was born on November 24, 1980, and grew up in Elmira, New York. At the age of 11, she won a coloring contest and received tickets to a WWF event as her prize. She was instantly attracted to the larger-than-life spectacle of the WWF. After being the first female varsity wrestler in her high school's history, moving to Buffalo, attending Canisius College, and majoring in criminal justice and public relations, she began training with the All-Knighters, brothers Joey Knight and Robin Knightwing, who introduced her to Ron Hutchison.

"Ron always made sure to give us a hot meal and make sure we got paid and we were taken care of, and we had an opportunity to work and learn. He also worked hard to get us connections and opportunities to get seen by WWE. He was all about his talent, and all about putting on a quality show. He just really, really taught me that, if you love this, that you can be successful," said Phoenix.

She wanted to continue her training at Hutchison's school, but money was tight for a college student living in a new city. That's when she received a gift from an unexpected benefactor. Knight had passed along a video of Beth to Nora "Molly Holly" Greenwald. Impressed with her drive and determination, Greenwald offered to pay for Beth's training, a fact Beth would only discover after the fact.

She continued training with Hutchison and the All-Knighters, accompanying Knight as his valet. She made her pro debut in May

2001, adopting the name Phoenix. She married Knight (Joey Carolan) that same year.

With her amateur credentials and guidance from Hutchison — who had helped launch the careers of Trish Stratus, Tracy Brooks, and Gail Kim — Phoenix began to receive bookings throughout the Northeast United States and Ontario. In 2003, she won the Far North Wrestling cruiserweight title (a men's championship), beating Knight and Kevin Grace (a friend since college) in a three-way match. A photo from that match of Phoenix carrying both Knight and Grace on her shoulders simultaneously in a show of strength ran in *Pro Wrestling Illustrated*, giving her national exposure.

In May 2004, she was invited to a tryout at Ohio Valley Wrestling. She relocated to Louisville and trained at the OVW school, looking to secure a WWE contract, working as a waitress to help make ends meet.

After a tumultuous two years in OVW, she was called up to WWE and debuted on *Raw* in May 2006, preventing Mickie James from attacking Trish Stratus. Positioned as a babyface and immediately thrust into a program with two of WWE's top female stars, Phoenix was poised for a major push when injury struck. As she was starting a match with Victoria, Victoria connected with a hard open-hand slap to the mouth. The two had been arguing and Phoenix' mouth was slightly open. The force of the blow (intended to be a harmless slap to get the match started) cracked her mandible. She finished the match with a broken jaw but needed surgery, requiring a titanium plate and nine screws to fix the damage.

Her WWE push came to an abrupt stop, and Phoenix was sent back down to OVW. She won the OVW women's title in October 2006 and remained in Louisville until July 2007, when she was brought back up to WWE.

Phoenix returned as a heel, referring to herself as the Glamazon. She was presented as a powerhouse and ran roughshod over the women's division, quickly establishing herself as the top contender for the women's title. At No Mercy 2007, she defeated Candice Michelle to win the women's title for the first time.

From that point on, Phoenix became one of the cornerstones of the women's and Divas divisions until 2012. She won the women's title three times and the Divas title once, and she was ranked number two in the PWI Female 50 rankings in 2008 and 2012. During that time, she had notable rivalries with Melina, LayCool, Kelly Kelly, and Eve Torres, as well as a comedic partnership with Santino Marella as WWE's resident power couple, Glamarella. In 2010, she became the second female to compete in the annual Royal Rumble battle royal (after Chyna),

*The Glamazon, Beth Phoenix.* MIKE MASTRANDREA

eliminating a bewildered Great Khali after suckering him with a kiss.

"Being only one of two females that have done that before, it's probably the most intimidating and invigorating experience of my life. It was a very intimidating experience, but it's one of those things where I really admired what Chyna had done in the past. I was thrilled and excited and ready to take on that challenge myself. I can't tell you how awesome it was to be able to do that in 2010."

She then went on to form a tag team with her longtime friend Natalya, known as the Divas of Doom, declaring war on the "pretty bimbos" in WWE.

But in October 2012, Phoenix quietly retired from wrestling. She and her husband had parted ways, and she had begun dating Adam "Edge" Copeland, who had already retired and with whom she had two children. In 2015, she was recognized by both the Cauliflower Alley Club and the Tragos/Thesz Professional Wrestling Hall of Fame.

"I spent my entire adult life on the road chasing this dream, and I loved it. I absolutely loved everything I did with WWE, and I had a wonderful career with them," she said in a 2013 interview with *Monday Night Mayhem*. "It's time to check other things and experience other parts of life that you can't when you're 'married to the business,' and that's literally what you have to do to be successful. To chase other dreams, I kind of had to make that really tough decision to move on to the next phase of my life."

# NAOMI

Trinity McCray signed with WWE in the summer of 2009, during a period where the company was fixated on signing models and dancers and turning them into wrestlers, rather than signing established wrestlers and turning them into WWE Superstars.

That hiring strategy failed more often than it worked, but WWE struck gold when they discovered McCray, a former cheerleader and music video backup dancer and an aspiring singer.

Born in Sanford, Florida, on November 20, 1987, McCray took up dancing at the age of eight and went on to dance for Studio 5D in Oviedo, Florida. After graduating from high school, she became a professional dancer, working for the NBA's Orlando Magic.

Her athleticism, exuberance, and unique look caught the eye of WWE talent scouts, and she was offered a developmental contract in 2009. She reported to Florida Championship Wrestling in Tampa and wrestled her first match in October 2009, teaming with Alex Riley against A.J. Lee and Brett DiBiase, wrestling as Naomi Night.

Although she became the first FCW Divas champion in June 2010, beating Serena Deeb in the final of an eight-woman tournament, she wasn't brought to the main roster as a wrestler at first.

"It definitely takes time getting used to the ring because at first your body is so sore. It's tight and tender and it really hurts. But over time you get used to it and it becomes second nature," she told Jonathan Snowden of the *Bleacher Report*.

After showing presence and charisma and finishing second overall in the third season of the NXT contest, she was brought to the main roster in January 2012. She was paired with Ariane "Cameron" Andrew as the Funkadactyls, a pair of dancing valets/cheerleaders working with "The Funkasaurus" Brodus Clay, who was one of WWE's hottest midcard acts for several

*The Funkadactyl, Naomi.* MIKE MASTRANDREA

months. Although the Funkadactyls were primarily valets, they did work occasional matches, but in February 2014, Naomi suffered her first major wrestling injury when her orbital bone was cracked by an errant knee from Aksana. Surgery was required, but in true Diva style, she began wearing a diamond-blinged eyepatch to cover the injury.

"It's difficult, but I think things happen for a reason. And when things are supposed to happen for me, they will," she said in a 2015 interview. "I think during the injury it would have been a great time. I really thought I was on the path of getting the title and I had a lot of steam behind me. During the meantime, I just had so much time to get better, in the ring, out of the ring, psychology wise. So when my time comes around again, it's gonna be even better than if it were to happen before."

Her wrestling did improve dramatically as she added aerial attacks from the top rope and a variety of kicks to her offensive repertoire. "She's like a little Rey Mysterio to me," said A.J. Lee, certifying her acrobatic side.

And one would probably be surprised to hear about her favorite wrestler to watch.

"My favorite Japanese wrestler was Manami Toyota. I watch her matches and I'm in awe," Naomi revealed to Jonathan Snowden. "I consider myself a high-flyer and I like doing things to make the crowd pop and to stand out from the other girls, but when I watch her I'm really amazed by what she does. There are things she can do that to this day I'm still trying to learn how to do."

Naomi became a featured cast member of *Total Divas* on E! and married Jonathan Fatu (wrestler Jimmy Uso) in January 2014. In May, she released the song "Dance All Night," showcasing her vocal prowess, perhaps trying to reach the level of success her uncle, George McCrae, had with his song "Rock Your Body," a number one Billboard hit in 1974.

In early 2015, the hashtag #GiveDivasaChance began trending on Twitter as fans clamored to see the current crop of athletic wrestling women in more visible roles. For Naomi, that was a huge vote of confidence.

"It was very exciting. As Divas, we felt like, 'Wow, fans really do care about us. We really do matter,'" she said in a 2015 interview with the website This Is Infamous. "We're all competitive and we're all in our own lane and fighting for that top spot, but at the end of the day we really are a sisterhood. We have to get in there and work together. The 'Give Divas a Chance' movement really brought us all together."

After several unsuccessful shots at Divas champion Paige, Naomi turned heel in early 2015. In the summer of 2015, she was paired with Sasha Banks and Tamina Snuka as Team BAD (Beautiful and Dangerous). Along with Team Bella (the Bella Twins and Alicia Fox) and Team PCB (Paige, Charlotte, and Becky Lynch), Team BAD was a featured part of the so-called Divas Revolution of 2015. After WrestleMania 32, Naomi took a little hiatus from WWE, healing an injury and filming the latest Marine movie. She came back a few weeks before Summer Slam, with a new style, entrance and theme.

Unlike many others, Naomi has proven to be one of the most versatile performers on the WWE roster, successfully making the transition from valet to respected wrestler, a spot she clearly wishes to keep in the future.

# A.J. LEE

The ultimate girl next door, A.J. Lee became one of the most beloved female wrestlers in the world during her WWE run from 2011 to 2015.

Born April Jeanette Mendez on March 19, 1987, she grew up in Union City, New Jersey. Money was tight for her family (which included an older brother and older sister); her family lived with friends, in motels, or in the family car at various times. She became deeply interested in wrestling at the age of 12, inspired primarily by Lita. Years later, footage of a 14-year-old A.J. meeting Lita at a 2001 autograph signing shows an emotionally overwhelmed A.J. crying over seeing her heroine.

After leaving an art school in New York, she enrolled in a wrestling school and began training under Jay Lethal. She wrestled her first match in September 2007 using the name Miss April. She went on to Women Superstars Uncensored and teamed with Brooke Carter to win the WSU tag team title in 2009.

A.J. saved her money and invested $1,500 in a WWE tryout camp in May 2009. Although she had been wrestling for less than 18 months, WWE scouts saw something in the 5'2", 115-pound brown-eyed girl. She was signed to a WWE developmental contract and relocated to Tampa to train at Florida Championship Wrestling. She debuted in August 2009 as April Lee, but her name was quickly tweaked to A.J. Lee.

She started winning over WWE fans in the summer of 2010 when she was cast in the third season of *WWE NXT*, a reality show–style competition where developmental rookies were paired with seasoned WWE pros and competed for a spot on the main roster. Lee was paired with Primo Colon. During the competition, Lee began to reveal more of her true personality, which included her passion for video games and her love of comic books. All of a sudden, Lee was the subject of fanboy crushes throughout the WWE Universe. She wasn't the unobtainable supermodel; she was a cute chick who seemed down for an evening staying in and playing *Final Fantasy*, which led to her being nicknamed the Geek Goddess.

"I was the least coordinated person. I really had to force myself to become athletic, and wrestling was the only thing I wanted to do and I had to work really hard to get good at it," explained A.J. "So instead of sports, I turned my attention to other interests. The very first video game I played was on Nintendo and it was *Excitebike*. I was really bad at it."

She formed a tag team with Kaitlyn, adopting the name the Chickbusters. They became a popular team in NXT, feuding with the Divas of Doom (Beth Phoenix and Natalya).

She was brought up to the main roster and paired with Daniel Bryan as Bryan's love interest, a role that would define her throughout her WWE run. She would go on to be cast as the doe-eyed love interest for Dolph Ziggler, C.M. Punk (whom she eventually married in real life), Kane, and John Cena.

When Bryan "dumped" Lee following his 18-second loss to Sheamus at Wrestlemania 28 (he claimed Lee cost him the match by distracting him with a prematch kiss), Lee's character snapped and began to act erratically, eventually leading to one of her nicknames, the Crazy Chick. Looking to use the increasingly psychotic Lee as a pawn in his feud with Punk, Bryan proposed to Lee in the storyline. An elaborate wedding ceremony was scheduled as a highlight for the 1,000th episode of *WWE Raw* on July 23, 2012 (ironically enough, Lee's childhood inspiration Lita returned for a guest appearance on the show). Lee jilted Bryan at the altar and announced she had been named the new general manager of *Raw*, a position that fit her well as she was arguably considered the best woman on promos of her era. Becoming the storyline authority figure of the company was an impressive feat for a 25-year-old just five years out of wrestling school.

After stepping down from her GM position in October 2012, she set her sights on the Divas title, held by her former "bestie" Kaitlyn. At Payback 2013, Lee defeated Kaitlyn to win the title and later took Tamina as her personal bodyguard. In August 2013, she cut a controversial live promo on the rest of the WWE Divas, including the cast of the *Total Divas* reality show.

"Do you want to know what I see when I look in that ring, honestly?" Lee said, directing her comments

*The Geek Goddess, A.J. Lee.* BILL OTTEN

to the Bellas and other WWE Divas. "A bunch of cheap, interchangeable, expendable, useless women. Women who have turned to reality television because they just weren't gifted enough to be actresses. And they just weren't talented enough to be champion. I have done more in one year than all of you have done in your collective entire careers. I have saved your Divas division. I have shattered glass ceilings. I have broken down doors. Why? So a bunch of ungrateful, stiff, plastic mannequins can waltz on through without getting as much as a thank you? . . . I didn't get here because I was cute. Or because I came from some famous wrestling family. Or because I sucked up to the ring people. I got here because I am good. . . . And that is reality."

The "worked shoot" promo was scripted, but it had enough of a foundation in reality that it resonated with fans and generated

*A.J. going crazy on Paige.* BILL OTTEN

additional buzz around the women's division.

The fact of the matter was that Lee really stepped up to the plate as far as quality matches. Her match with Kaitlyn at Payback as well as some matches with Natalya were the best women's matches in WWE in several years.

"For a long time, since I was in NXT, I've kind of wanted to redefine the word Diva and find a way to get people connected and make them want to watch. So we're not just some filler match. I think we have people that are capable of doing that," she further explained to Jonathan Snowden. "It may take some rubbing people the wrong way sometimes, but I think we're getting there. For me it's about leaving things so that when I'm not here one day, or when I'm not in the story, I don't have to be involved for it to be cool and interesting."

Despite alienating the entire women's division in the storyline, Lee held the Divas title for a then record-setting 295 days, including an against-all-odds win at WrestleMania 30, where she defended her title in a 14-woman scramble match. The night after that bout, on April 6, she lost the title to the debuting Paige in an impromptu match.

After a two-month sabbatical, Lee returned to WWE and regained the Divas title for the third time with a win over Paige. The two feuded throughout the summer and fall of 2014. Lee lost the Divas title for the last time to Nikki Bella at the 2014 Survivor Series.

But Lee wasn't done making waves yet. In December 2014, in another controversial speech, this one unscripted, she accepted the Diva of the Year award in a surprising fashion: "Three years ago, I promised all of you that I would redefine the term *Diva*, and I'm very proud to say that I sure have done that. You can be a nerd, you can be a tomboy, and you can still be the longest-reigning Divas champion of all-time. So I hope that means that next year this award is won by Bayley, or Sasha, or Charlotte, or Emma, or Paige," she said, forgetting in the process the women best known as Divas and naming girls that were not even on the main roster up to that point. Whether it was related to Lee's speech or not, Nikki Bella not only broke Lee's record as longest Divas champion of all time the following year, she also won the Diva of the Year award.

After neck surgery and just one week before returning, in February 2015, Lee spoke her mind once more. After Stephanie McMahon praised actress Patricia Arquette's speech about how women should receive equal pay and opportunities, Lee took to Twitter to call her out on WWE's use of its female wrestlers. "@StephMcMahon Your female wrestlers have record selling merchandise & have starred in the highest rated segment of the show several times," she tweeted. "And yet they receive a fraction of the wages & screen time of the majority of the male roster #UseYourVoice."

By calling out the boss, Lee made it clear that she wasn't planning on remaining with WWE for long, especially after C.M. Punk departed the company and was subsequently sued by WWE's doctor. She returned to WWE and teamed with Paige to defeat the Bellas at WrestleMania 31. It proved to be her final match; she announced her retirement less than a week later.

# NATALYA

The journey to become a WWE Diva was difficult for Natalie "Nattie" Neidhart.

It wasn't the wrestling that presented a challenge. In fact, that was the easy part. She grew up in a home that had a wrestling ring erected on the front lawn, and she learned to take bumps almost as soon as she was able to walk.

The biggest challenge was the cosmetic standard for a WWE Diva. "[Then head of WWE talent relations] Johnny Laurinaitis never came out and said 'you're fat,'" Natalya told Heath McCoy for his book, *Pain & Passion: The History of Stampede Wrestling*. "This is showbiz and if you're a representative of the WWE, how you look is important. . . . You've got to look sexy."

Neidhart weighed about 175 pounds on a 5'5" frame at the time of that meeting. She was recovering from a torn ACL from a training session in Japan, an injury that kept her out of the ring for nine months and sent her into a deep depression.

"I felt so sorry for myself. I was in a horrible state. I'm usually a happy person and I had never been depressed like that before," she said. "Bret [Hart, her uncle] and I went for dinner and I told him I was going to quit wrestling. I had already applied to go back to school to be an English teacher."

Instead, she refocused her energies on rebuilding her body. She began working with a personal trainer and developed a new diet. The daughter of wrestler Jim "The Anvil" Neidhart and granddaughter of Stu Hart, Nattie had wrestling in her genes, but she also inherited a sturdy build. She would never be a waif. But, through hard work, she slimmed down to 135 pounds and was rewarded with a WWE developmental contract in 2007.

It was a dream come true for the little girl born May 27, 1982, in Calgary. As a child, she was active in ballet, gymnastics, and tap dancing. She was surrounded by wrestling, with her father and uncles all active in the business. "I didn't really want to be a wrestler at first. I wasn't that interested," she said. "I was more focused on my acting and modeling, and then my cousins and I were fooling around in the ring after one of the shows and we were practicing some stuff and I started to like it, I started to dabble in it. . . . The more I did it, the more I liked it. . . . Now I can't see myself doing anything else."

She became the first female to train at the famed Hart Family

Dungeon in 2000, wrestling her first match later that year. She scored a gig as the host of Eric Bischoff's MatRats promotion, which was featuring teenaged wrestlers in action. After cutting her teeth in Stu's Stampede promotion, she embarked on a tour of the United Kingdom and Japan, which is where she suffered the torn ACL.

Upon signing with WWE, she was sent to Deep South Wrestling

*From the Hart Dungeon, Natalya.* BILL OTTEN

for six months, Florida Championship Wrestling for a month, and then on to Ohio Valley Wrestling. She made her WWE debut in April 2008 as Natalya, wrestling as a heel.

In 2009, she joined her real-life boyfriend, Tyson Kidd, and her cousin David Hart Smith, acting as the manager of the Hart Dynasty. At WrestleMania 26, she and her family were at ringside as Bret Hart faced Vince McMahon in a no-holds-barred match; Natalya even got in a few licks on the WWE Chairman during the course of the match.

At the 2010 Survivor Series, Natalya defeated Lay-Cool in a two-on-one handicap match to win the Divas title. She lost the belt to Eve Torres three months later. In 2011, she began teaming with her close friend Beth Phoenix as the Divas of Doom.

"It's funny, because Beth had idolized my family, before I ever met her, since she was a little girl," she told SLAM! Wrestling. "She loved Bret and Owen, and they were her favorites."

In 2013, Natalya was cast in the E! reality show *Total Divas*, which underscored her metamorphosis into the WWE ideal. She married Kidd in June 2013 in a ceremony that was featured on the show. She also filled a valuable role, splitting her time between WWE and the developmental system in NXT, where she competed with Charlotte and other developmental women. In July 2016, she was drafted on *SmackDown* and was part of the match crowing the first *SmackDown* women's champion.

"Obviously, she's a great worker. That's beyond words," wrote Michelle McCool on her website. As an in-ring talent, a mentor, and a member of wrestling's royal families, Natalya has a unique position among the women of WWE. As fellow wrestler Naomi once said, "Nattie is a wrestling guru!"

# INTERNATIONAL REPORT

Besides the United States and Canada, wrestling is popular in many countries in the world, and women's wrestling is no exception. Whether they are called joshis, luchadoras, or lady grapplers, one can find female wrestlers in every part of the world. Katie Lea Burchill and Alpha Female were born in Germany, Wesna Busic in Crotia, Aksana in Lithuania, Desiree Petersen in Denmark, and Evie in New Zealand, just to name a few. More precisely, four regions are known to have produced some of the best female wrestlers ever: Japan, Mexico, the United Kingdom, and Australia.

# MILDRED BURKE *and the Introduction of Women's Wrestling to Japan*

Following her split from Billy Wolfe, Mildred Burke set out on an ambitious overseas tour — a trip free of Wolfe's interference and meddling. She coordinated a tour of Japan in November 1954, arranging the event through promoters in Hawaii, who procured financial backing from the Sankei Shinbun newspaper group. The newspapers had a vested interest; they were expecting the newspapers featuring the exotic American women wrestlers to be big sellers.

Burke gathered a troupe of girls, including Johnnie Mae Young, Ruth Boatcallie, and Gloria Barattini, women who had remained loyal to Burke after she broke off from Wolfe. The flight touched down in Tokyo on November 10, 1954. If the American girls were unsure of the reaction they would receive from the Japanese, they had to be excited at the sight outside the airplane windows.

"Thousands of Japanese greeters thronged the airport and its approaches, climbing fences, standing on top of cars and trucks, smiling and waving little American flags," Burke later wrote. "When the stewardess opened the airliner door and I stepped out on the little platform, there was a roar of welcome from thousands of fans."

The wrestlers were presented with bouquets of flowers from Japanese women wearing traditional kimonos. Posters announcing their arrival were plastered on almost every flat surface in Tokyo. Before the opening bell sounded, the trip was already a rousing success.

Burke's crew wrestled 26 events, mostly held at U.S. military bases throughout Japan. Many of these events were televised by Japan's Nippon TV. But Burke had a difficult time adjusting to competing in front of Japanese fans compared to U.S. servicemen stationed there; the Japanese fans were stone quiet, a very different fan reaction than she was used to. The silence was a cultural difference. The fans were being respectful and polite, but it was easy to mistake their silence for disinterest. "I became a little unnerved," Burke recalled about her match at the 13,000-seat Kuramae Kokugikan sumo hall. When a Japanese boy presented both Burke and her opponent, Boatcallie, with flowers before the match, she spontaneously gave the boy a kiss, which elicited the reaction from the audience she sought.

"I had really woken them up," she said. "I was told that kissing in public was forbidden in Japan. Within 15 seconds of my first appearance in public in Japan, I had cut down one of their most cherished customs."

Women's wrestling took on a sudden burst of popularity in Japan. In 1955, the All Japan Women's Pro-Wrestling organization was established to regulate the wrestling events that began to spring up throughout the country following that first tour. However, the association was not strong enough to pull the disparate promotions together. It was restructured in 1967 but still struggled.

It was Takashi Matsunaga who truly established women's wrestling in Japan. Along with his three brothers (Toshikuni, Kunimatsu, and Kenji), Takashi established the All Japan Women's Pro-Wrestling Corporation. The brothers had all been wrestlers themselves before deciding to invest in women's wrestling. It was Takashi's passion.

Matsunaga reached out to Vince McMahon Sr. and arranged a tour from champion the Fabulous Moolah. Moolah dropped the women's title to Yukiko Tomoe at the start of her tour in 1968 before regaining the title on the way home, establishing Tomoe as a home-grown star in the process. Moolah's tour was not the financial success Burke's had been, however.

The Matsunaga brothers ran their first All Japan Women's show on June 4, 1968. They also established a wrestling training school for women headed by Kunimatsu and formed an alliance with promoter Jack Britton (who had started midget wrestling 20 years earlier) to have a U.S. base. The tag team of Mary Jane Mull and Lucille Dupree were the headliners for the AJW's first tour, along with Tomoe, Miyuki Yanagi, Kyoko Okada, and Aiko Kyo, which generated enough interest that the Fuji Network began airing it on television.

Matsunaga contacted Burke and coordinated a new tour. "The group made a deal with Burke, who at the time was training women wrestlers in Reseda, Ca., but having difficulty getting them work since all the major promoters were working with Moolah," Dave

Meltzer wrote. "Her very limited operation was kept alive by selling film footage of her women's matches [i.e., custom matches] through the back pages of low-rent magazines."

On October 17, 1970, Aiko Kyo defeated Marie Vagnone to win the WWWA title Burke had toured Japan with 16 years earlier. That physical championship, commonly known as the red belt, remained in Japan and became the centerpiece of All Japan Women, treated as the one true women's championship. The term *joshi* was eventually coined to describe Japanese female wrestlers.

All Japan Women established a successful formula. It recruited attractive young women to wrestle as babyfaces and slightly older, larger women to wrestle as heels. A mandatory retirement age of 26 was established to create room for new, younger wrestlers on their way up. If accepted to the All Japan dojo, the women were expected to abide by a rigorous series of rules and regulations.

"There were the famed 'three no's.' No alcohol, no smoking, and no men," Meltzer wrote. "Every year, several hundred women would send in applications for the annual screening process. The ones with the best athletic credentials, or in some cases the best head shots, would be brought in for the tryout. The established stars would test them in a series of physical activities, lifting weights and different calisthenics, until they dropped. The training, by our standards, was beyond brutal. But they produced the best wrestlers, many of whom on their first day were better than all but the best of the American wrestlers."

The other tactic they used was to promote some of their wrestlers as both wrestlers and pop singers, creating the biggest stars they'd ever have. Because of that, the boom periods for the promotion were in the '70s with the Beauty Pair and then in the 1980s with the Crush Gals.

"During the peak of the Beauty Pair, about 15 million viewers watched the weekly wrestling show, more than *Nitro* and *Raw* combined at the peak of U.S. popularity, and the equivalent to what the NFL was doing in the United States at the same time," said Meltzer. "During their '80s merchandising heyday, they ran more than 300 shows all over Japan per year, drawing between 1,500 and 4,000 fans for regular shows, and larger crowds a few times a year for big arena spectaculars."

The workrate was one of the big differences between eras; the Beauty Pair couldn't match the Crush Gals in the ring, and the 1990s, with Manami Toyota, Bull Nakano, Toshiyo Yamada, Mima Shimoda, Etsuko Mita (the inventor of the Death Valley bomb), Hokuto, Kyoko Inoue, and Takako Inoue, was more than excellent.

"We got up at 5 a.m. Running and skipping rope were a big part of our conditioning program. We would take the same bumps over and over. Each day we gave and took a hundred body slams. Our trainers also taught us kick boxing and the use of martial arts weapons," explained Leilani Kai, who trained and wrestled in Japan. "Before going to Japan I thought I had good wrestling skills. The skills that were learned in Japan were extreme to me. Moolah's school was the best school in the U.S. The skills learned in Japan started where Moolah's school left off."

The other difference is that the 1990s didn't have that pop star–wrestler combination and therefore didn't draw as well, since the audience was no longer mostly teenage girls but a lot of regular wrestling fans. That allowed the group to sell out bigger venues, but the ratings took a fall. The days when thousands of young girls applied to be wrestlers were gone, and so the retirement rule was axed in the 1990s. They needed to keep a good product without having a new crop of young girls coming up.

At the start of the new millennium, a variety of factors combined to spell the end for AJW. New promotions opened. The Fuji Network began airing the show after midnight and then dropped it entirely. All Japan Women ran its last show on April 17, 2005.

The legacy of All Japan Women surpassed the realm of professional wrestling. In fact, it has influenced the success of Japanese amateur women's wrestling in general as well. Japan has become the world leader in women's amateur wrestling with the likes of Kaori Icho, the only wrestler, male or female, in Olympic history to win four gold medals, and Saori Yoshida, arguably considered the best woman wrestler ever with 13 world titles and three Olympic gold medals.

The last WWWA champion, Nanae Takahashi, continued to wrestle on the indie scene. In 2010, with Rossy Ogawa and fellow wrestler Fuka, she tried to continue the heritage of All Japan Women by founding World Wonder Ring Stardom, considered the leading women's indie promotion in Japan, a list that also includes Joshi 4 Hope, Ice Ribbon, Sendai Girls Oz Academy, Pro Wrestling Wave, REINA, and JWP Joshi Puroresu, the oldest women's promotion in Japan. True to All Japan Women's reputation, and influenced by it, the Japanese independent scene has produced what some experts consider some of the best female wrestlers of the last decade, such as Meiko Satomura, Io Shirai, Mayu Iwatani and Kairi Hojo. Also, of the 12 inductees related to women's wrestling in the Wrestling Observer Hall of Fame, 11 come from All Japan Women: Devil Masami, Dump Matsumoto, Jackie Sato, Jaguar Yokota, Chigusa Nagayo, Lioness Asuka, Akira Hokuto, Bull Nakano, Manami Toyota, Aji Kong, and promoter Takashi Matsunaga.

Just as the Beatles, the Rolling Stones, and the rest of the British Invasion took American rock and roll music and reinvented it, All Japan Women had taken women's pro wrestling and turned it into something completely new.

## THE BEAUTY PAIR:
### Jackie Sato and Maki Ueda

Jackie Sato and Maki Ueda attracted a legion of new fans to wrestling arenas throughout Japan. Known as the Beauty Pair, Sato and Ueda became joshi's top drawing tag team of the late 1970s, attracting a passionate audience made up primarily of young girls looking to emulate their larger-than-life heroines.

Naoko Sato (born October 30, 1957) and Makiko Ueda (born March 8, 1958) graduated from the All Japan Women's dojo and began teaming in February 1976. They won the World Women's Wrestling Association tag team title in their first night as a tandem, beating Mariko Akagi and Mach Fumiake for the belts in Tokyo.

Sato and Ueda were young and attractive, unlike some of the

*The Beauty Pair were not just wrestlers, but also pop culture icons, as shown by this album cover.*

burlier, older women who had dominated the sport in Japan up to that point. They introduced youth and sex appeal to joshi wrestling and quickly became a pop culture sensation. To capitalize on their popularity, the duo recorded a pop single that was used as their entrance music, long before entrance music was commonplace.

Sato and Ueda were role models for young Japanese girls. They were strong, independent, graceful, athletic, and successful. They represented upward mobility in a culture where many opportunities were closed to females. The stage was set for the Beauty Pair by Mach Fumiake, the first national star, the first pop star idol for All Japan Women's Pro Wrestling. Fumiake was a singer who advanced to the finals of a nationally televised Japanese talent show. After the contest, the attractive 15-year-old enrolled in the All Japan dojo. When she made her wrestling debut, All Japan recorded a special song for her to perform in the ring. She surprisingly retired the following year. To protect themselves from a hot attraction retiring early, the promotion decided to feature a tag team; that way if one retired, the other original wrestler could carry on the name with someone else. The duo would end up having several top 10 hits on their hands.

"Ueda was the one with girlish long hair and Sato was the one with short boyish hair. They were actually better workers than Fumiake was," said wrestling journalist and author Fumi Saito. "Fuji Television wanted to do what they did with Mach Fumiake with them, singing and dancing in the ring before the match, with even better costumes and a better overall setting than Fumiake's. They were in movies. They were on pop-music TV shows. They had their concerts aside from regular wrestling house shows. They were doing TV commercials. Boy, they were popular. People who grew up in '70s, like myself, have very fond memories of Mach Fumiake and Beauty Pair. The same way American audiences might remember *Roller Games*, *The Monkees*, *Happy Days*, *Brady Bunch*, and *Charlie's Angels*."

The Beauty Pair lost the WWWA tag title to Jackie West and Yukari Lynch in May 1976, then regained the belts in July. They held the belts for another nine months until dropping them to the Black Pair of Yumi Ikeshita and Shinobu Aso in April 1977. During that period, they were so popular that Fuji Network moved the show to a weekly prime-time slot.

Ueda had won the WWA singles championship in June 1976 and again in July 1977. On November 1, 1977, the Beauty Pair faced off in a singles match for the WWWA title. The match was billed as the greatest women's match of all time, the equivalent of an Antonio Inoki vs. Giant Baba match. Sato scored the win over Ueda to take the title in front of 13,000 fans in a sold-out Budokan Hall, only the third time in five years that wrestling sold out the building. They wrestled to a 60-minute draw, with Mildred Burke as the lone judge, and she awarded the match and the title to Sato. In 1979, Sato defeated Ueda in Ueda's retirement match and went on to win the WWWA title three times before retiring in 1981. She died of stomach cancer in August 1999, her passing making the front page of every sports section in Japan

## THE CRUSH GALS:
### Chigusa Nagayo and Lioness Asuka

Chigusa Nagayo and Lioness Asuka — known collectively as the Crush Gals — were not just Japan's most popular tag team, they were the most popular women's tag team of all time. Their fame transcended the wrestling ring and seeped into popular culture as they had several high-charting pop music singles and performed concerts in front of thousands of adoring fans, mostly teenage girls.

Asuka, whose real name is Tomoko Kitamura, was born July 28, 1963, and Nagayo on December 8, 1964. Both were trained in the All Japan Women's dojo, making their wrestling debut when Asuka was only 16 and Nagayo 15.

Before starting to team together, they both had some success. Asuka captured the All Japan Women's junior championship in 1981 before vacating that title when she won the All Japan Women's title in 1982. Nagayo went on to win the vacant junior championship, beating Itsuki Yamazaki for the title on May 15, 1982.

But the year 1983 would change the two young women forever. That's when Nagayo and Asuka joined forces as the Crush Gals. Young and attractive, they were a shot of adrenaline in the AJW tag division. The Crush Gals mixed precision double-team moves with dropkicks, piledrivers, and moves off the top rope, all of which were still quite rare in women's wrestling.

"The pair took women's wrestling to a new level of popularity in the mid-1980s and became heroines for schoolgirls in Japan, who were actually just a few years younger than them," said Dave Meltzer. "They took the popularity of women's wrestling to a mainstream level that it never achieved before and has never achieved since."

The Crush Gals captured the World Women's Wrestling Association tag team title (the championship recognized by All Japan Women) four times in the 1980s, defeating the likes of Dump Matsumoto and Bull

*After her first retirement, Aja Kong became one of Nagayo's most frequent opponents.* KURT SCHIMMEL

Nakano as well as the Jumping Bomb Angels. During their 1980s run, the Crush Gals proved to be one of the most influential acts in wrestling, inspiring scores of young women (and men) to try their hand at professional wrestling. Their rivalries with the Jumping Bomb Angels and Matsumoto and Nakano drew spectacular television ratings, consistently drawing 12 ratings on FUJI TV. Asuka and Nagayo became media darlings, appearing on the covers of teen magazines, music magazines, and of course, wrestling magazines.

"During their short heyday, the Crush Gals were a merchandising phenomenon to the point they achieved mainstream recognition in the *Wall Street Journal* at a time when the American press never covered pro wrestling, with top ten records, and drawing television ratings that would make the NFL, let alone the WWF or WCW, envious," added Meltzer.

The summer of 1985 was especially good for the two of them. On August 25, 1985, a singles match between Asuka and Jaguar Yokota drew more than 13,000 fans to Tokyo's Denen Coliseum, drawing a

gate of $258,000. Three
nights later, Nagayo
was defeated by Dump
Matsumoto in a bloody
hair vs. hair match
in Osaka in front of
a sold-out crowd of
11,000 fans.

The Crush Gals
parted in 1989 and
began feuding over the
WWWA heavyweight
title. Nagayo had de-
feated Yukari for that
title in October 1987.
Asuka was awarded
the championship on
August 25, 1988, when
Nagayo was forced to
vacate the title because
of injury — but Asuka
refused to accept the
championship without

*Lioness Asuka is not only one of the best woman wrestlers
of all time, but one of the best wrestlers period.* KURT SCHIMMEL

a victory. The title was declared vacant until the injured former champion (Nagayo) and the top contender (Asuka) could clash. On January
29, 1989, Asuka defeated her former partner to claim the title. Their last
rematch, on May 6, 1989, when Nagayo first retired, was the first wom-
en's wrestling show to draw a $500,000 house. Six months later, Asuka
retired as champion, having reached the mandatory age of 26 years old.

"Producing several match-of-the-decade candidates, the Nagayo
vs. Asuka feud set a new standard of quality in women's wrestling
and laid the foundation for Manami Toyota, who would lead the next
boom in women's wrestling in the early '90s," wrote John Molinaro
in his book *The Top 100 Pro Wrestlers of All Time* (Molinaro ranked
Nagayo at 45 and Asuka at 70).

The Crush Gals went in different directions as the 1980s came to a close. Nagayo retired for seven years, then formed the women's wrestling promotion GAEA Japan in 1995. She competed in WCW's women's title tournament in 1996, wrestling as Zero and losing to Madusa. Nagayo remained a top star in GAEA until another retirement in 2005, when she lost to her protégé Meiko Satomura, one of the best active female wrestlers in Japan, in GAEA's farewell show. She would eventually come back, working a few times a year in Japan and even wrestling for Combat Zone Wrestling in the United States. Nagayo was also featured in the documentary *GAEA Girls*, which featured her promotion and profiled her as a trainer.

"She's the single most popular, and arguably (with the possible exception of Mildred Burke due to her longevity and being a pioneer in creating the popularity of American women's wrestling) the most historically important female wrestler who ever lived. To this day, in pro wrestling or MMA, not Hulk Hogan, Steve Austin, Kerry Von Erich, Dusty Rhodes or Chuck Liddell could match the reaction I saw that woman receive live in her heyday," concluded Meltzer.

Asuka also returned to the ring in the mid-1990s. She wrestled a tag match on November 20, 1994, at the biggest show in women's wrestling history in front of 32,500 fans (announced as 42,500) in Tokyo. She continued competing on the independent circuit and then debuted as a heel in GAEA, where she feuded with Nagayo for storyline control of the promotion. In 2000, Nagayo and Asuka reformed their team against their mutual rival Mayumi Ozaki, reuniting the Crush Gals as CRUSH 2000. Asuka and Nagayo teamed for a final time on April 3, 2005, beating Chikayo Nagashima and Sugar Sato at GAEA's 10th anniversary event, also marking the end of Asuka's career.

## Jaguar Yokota

The success and popularity of the Beauty Pair inspired 600 teenage girls to apply for an open audition for All Japan Women in 1977. Rimi Yokota was one of those girls.

Born Rimi Yokota on July 25, 1961, in Tokyo, she was not an

athlete in high school but was inspired to try wrestling because she adored the Beauty Pair. After passing her audition, she was given the name Jaguar, a nod to pop culture hero Jet Jaguar, who fought alongside Godzilla in the movie *Godzilla vs. Megalon*.

She wrestled her first match in June 1977 and won her first championship, the AJW junior title, less than seven months later by defeating Chino Sato in January 1978. In December 1980, she became the first All Japan

*Two-time WWWA champion Jaguar Yokota.* KURT SCHIMMEL

singles champion, beating Nancy Kumi to win that title. The newly created title was intended to be a stepping stone to the WWWA championship, and Jaguar used it accordingly. In February 1981, the 19-year-old Yokota upset her inspiration Jackie Sato to capture the WWWA title. Her win marked the start of a youth movement in All Japan Women as stars like the Beauty Pair began to pass the torch to the next generation of joshi stars. Yokota was known to use multiple wrestling styles, from mat wrestling to Lucha Libre.

"Until this, women's wrestling had been a paced imitation of the men's game, which itself was beginning to change in Japan with the debut of Tiger Mask. But now the men's game would begin to imitate the women," according to a 2008 article published on Online World of Wrestling. "The high flying game featured spectacular moves as well as unbelievable bumps. The down side of this was the injuries suffered by the women; many would have to retire early because of their injuries, including Yokota."

Yokota defended the title against *gaijin* (foreign) invaders like Wendi Richter and Monster Ripper until losing the belt to masked wrestler La Galactica in May 1983 in a hair vs. hair match. Yokota's long hair was cut short, but she came back with renewed focus, recapturing the WWWA title with a win over La Galactica one month later. Yokota went on to beat La Galactica for the Universal Wrestling Association (Mexico) women's title, simultaneously holding championships in both Japan and Mexico. Her match with Pantera Surena in 1985 for the WWWA title was voted UWA's match of the year, placing ahead of men's matches.

Her second WWWA title reign came to an end when she suffered a serious shoulder injury during a title defense against Lioness Asuka. The injury appeared to be career ending, and she forfeited the championship and announced her retirement at the age of 24, settling into a role as a trainer at the All Japan Women's dojo.

She returned to active wrestling in 1995, forming the JDStar promotion. JD was built around Yokota, featuring her as its main attraction. She retired once again after losing a retirement match to Devil Masami in 1998. In 2002, she opened a women's wrestling–themed nightclub in the popular Roppongi entertainment district in Japan.

She came out of retirement for appearances in DDT and HUSTLE.

Whether at the AJP dojo or for JDStar, Yokota trained many other women, including the likes of Manami Toyota, Megumi Kudo, Pro Wrestling Wave, Yumi Ohka, and Mariko Yoshida, who herself trained Hiroyo Matsumoto and Tomoka Nakagawa, keeping Yokota's legacy well alive today.

## Devil Masami

She was born Masami Yoshida on January 7, 1962, but to the fans who watched her compete in All Japan Women, GAEA, and JWP Joshi Puroresu, she will always be known as Devil. Masami made her wrestling debut in August 1978. At 5'6" and a sturdy 150 pounds, she had a frame that provided both power and speed. She was a versatile wrestler who could portray a juggernaut against a smaller opponent or use her quickness and stamina to defeat monster heels like Dump Matsumoto.

On May 9, 1981, she beat Tomoko Kitamura to win the vacant AJW title, a championship she held for more than a year. On April 1, 1984, she defeated Judy Martin to win the All Pacific women's cham-

*Wrestling Observer HOFamer Devil Masami.* KURT SCHIMMEL

pionship, a title she later vacated after taking the big prize — the vacant WWWA championship, which she claimed on December 12, 1985, with a win over Matsumoto in Tokyo.

In the summer of 1987, she wrestled outside of Japan for the first and only time, working Stampede Wrestling in Calgary, Alberta, Canada. She mostly teamed with Mika Komatsu against local wrestlers K.C. Houston and Rhonda Singh during those two months.

"I had seen a clip of Devil before and wondered what I was getting into because she could fight guys, kick most guys' butts," said Houston to SLAM! "She's a tough, tough woman."

Back in Japan, Masami left AJW in the early 1990s to work for the newly created Japanese Women Pro-Wrestling Project. In 1995, she also began wrestling for the GAEA promotion. In November

1996, she traveled to Singapore to face Chigusa Nagayo for the first All Asia Athlete Women's title. Masami and the former Crush Gal exchanged the title a few times during the course of 1997 and 1998. She also held the AAAW tag team title with Aja Kong in 2003.

Masami also has the distinction of being the final holder of the WCW women's championship. She won the vacant title in a tournament in September 1997 in Japan, but the title was retired shortly afterward as WCW ended its working agreement with GAEA. Unfortunately, that deprived American TV audiences of an opportunity to see Masami.

She retired in December 2008, one week before her 47th birthday. She wrestled a pair of matches during her retirement show, teaming with Dump Matsumoto and Kaoru to defeat her old rival Chigusa Nagayo (who came out of retirement for the match), Meiko Satomura, and Yumiko Hotta, and then teamed later in the evening with Dynamite Kansai and Carlos Amano in a loss to Aja Kong, Toshie Uematsu, and Ran Yu-Yu.

## Dump Matsumoto

With her black leather jackets, face paint, and ever-present kendo stick, Dump Matsumoto proved to be one of the most influential wrestlers — male or female — of her era.

Born Kaoru Matsumoto on November 11, 1960, she helped change the face of women's wrestling in Japan. She graduated from the All Japan Women's dojo and made her wrestling debut in 1980. Only three years later, she defeated Lioness Asuka to win the All Japan Women's title.

Her rivalry with Asuka would rage throughout the 1980s as she and partners like Crane Yu and Bull Nakano would battle with Asuka and Chigusa Nagayo (the Crush Gals) over the WWWA tag team title throughout 1985 and 1986. In 1985, Matsumoto defeated Nagayo in a hair vs. hair match, forcing Nagayo to have her head shaved. The following year, Nagayo returned the favor, beating Matsumoto in a hair match. Standing at 5'4" and weighing anywhere between 190 and 240 pounds, she would become Nagayo's biggest rival.

"Matsumoto actually pioneered the gimmick that the Road Warriors would later use to great fame in the United States, of being face-painted bikers with bizarre haircuts and monster heels who sold very little, if at all, for the smaller, under matched baby faces," Dave Meltzer wrote in the *Wrestling*

*Dump Matsumoto.* KURT SCHIMMEL

*Observer 1988 Yearbook.* "Matsumoto's impact was so great that she often brought crowds literally to tears with her villainous tactics, and when she would merely walk down the street in any major city, people would scatter in fear."

Matsumoto would menace ringside fans with her kendo stick, swinging wildly at anyone who ventured too close, eliciting shrieks and screams from the predominantly female audience. Like Bruiser Brody, the Sheik, and Tiger Jeet Singh before her, she literally terrified the fans with her unpredictable, violent behavior.

She also brutalized opponents in the ring. Like a shark, she remained constantly on the offensive, unceasingly attacking opponents until putting them away with a lariat.

She was such a sensation in Japan that the WWF brought her in for a few shows in 1986, where she teamed with Nakano as the Devils of Japan. She was also the inspiration for the Sega wrestling video game *Gokuaku Doumei Dump Matsumoto*, named after the heel stable she founded. She was removed from the game and the cast of wrestlers were changed from female to male when the game was eventually released in the United States as the generically named *Pro Wrestling*.

In a show of respect, All Japan Women waived its mandatory retirement rule for Matsumoto, although she did wrestle an announced "retirement match" in February 1989. She continued wrestling part time as a freelancer and remains active today, marking her 36th year in wrestling. She also became a well-known talk and game show television personality in Japan.

"She was more well-known than Steve Austin was at any point in his career, and I'd frame her name recognition as equivalent to Ric Flair in the Carolinas today," concluded Meltzer.

## THE JUMPING BOMB ANGELS:
### *Noriyo Tateno and Itsuki Yamazaki*

*And Now for Something Completely Different* was the title of a sketch anthology film by Monty Python's Flying Circus, but the phrase also aptly describes the impact Noriyo Tateno and Itsuki Yamazaki made when they arrived in the WWF in 1987.

Known collectively as the Jumping Bomb Angels, Tateno and Yamazaki introduced North American wrestling fans to the fast-paced, athletic joshi style. In a promotion dominated by plodding superheavyweights, the Angels were a blur of double-team moves and rapid-fire tags. They ran circles around their primary opponents, the Glamour Girls, who utilized a slower, more conventional style, creating a fresh dynamic between the established veterans and the exciting young newcomers from the Land of the Rising Sun.

Tateno was born on December 1, 1965; Yamazaki was born one month later, on January 3, 1966. Both trained in the All Japan Women's Pro Wrestling dojo and made their pro debut in 1981.

Tateno was the first to win championship gold, defeating Chigusa Nagayo for the All Japan Women's junior championship on August

*The Jumping Bomb Angels once won the WWF women's tag team titles.* PRO WRESTLING ILLUSTRATED

10, 1982. She held that title until January 1984, when she lost the belt back to Nagayo.

On February 28, 1984, Tateno and Yamazaki squared off in Sagamihara, Japan, for the All Japan Women's championship that had been vacated by Lioness Asuka. Yamazaki won that bout and captured the title, which she held until she vacated it herself in February 1985.

With Asuka and Nagayo riding a wave of success in the tag team division as the Crush Gals, Tateno and Yamazaki formed a team known as the Jumping Bomb Angels. When Nagayo was sidelined by injury in December 1985, the Angels stepped in to replace the popular tandem, beating Dump Matsumoto and Bull Nakano to claim the World Women's Wrestling Association tag team title, the top tag championship recognized by All Japan Women.

The Jumping Bomb Angels lost the belts to the Crush Gals on March 20, 1986, in a dream match between two popular teams who had captured the fans' imagination.

The Angels signed with the WWF in 1987. It was an odd pairing. Neither Tateno nor Yamazaki could speak English, and promo skills were a prerequisite in the WWF at the time, but apparently the WWF braintrust was willing to take a gamble and see if the Angels' popularity in Japan could be exported to the United States.

The Angels arrived in the WWF in the summer of 1987, regularly challenging the Glamour Girls for the WWF women's tag team title. They participated in the 1987 Survivor Series as well as the first Royal Rumble in 1988, where Tateno and Yamazaki connected with a double dropkick on Judy Martin in the last of a best of three falls and captured the tag belts.

The Angels held the WWF women's tag title for five months, defending the belts exclusively against the Glamour Girls. On June 8, 1988, the Angels relinquished the title back to the Glamour Girls, losing by count-out in a bout in Omiya, Japan.

"The tour made by the Jumping Bomb Angels nearly changed things. The American audiences wanted more of the Japanese style. We were going to have to change if we were to continue to please the fans. We had the people standing on their chairs. The crowds accepted those matches with the Jumping Bomb Angels and the Glamour Girls. The problem was that the American girls could not work at that level. With few exceptions like Peggy Lee and Velvet McIntyre no one wanted to train at that level," said Leilani Kai in the *LadySports* magazine.

The Angels parted ways shortly after their run in the WWF came to an end. Yamazaki retired in 1991 and eventually relocated to the United States. Tateno continued competing in All Japan Women and defeated Bull Nakano to win the All Pacific women's title on November 13, 1989. In 1992, she jumped to the Ladies Legend Pro Wrestling promotion. There, she captured the LLPW women's title, the six-woman tag title (twice), and the tag team title (with Eagle Sawai). She retired from wrestling in 2010.

## Bull Nakano

Bull Nakano, perhaps the best-known female Japanese wrestler in North America, collected championship belts wherever she traveled, be it her native Japan, Mexico, or even the United States, where she had a memorable run as WWF women's champion in 1994.

Born Keiko Nakano on January 8, 1968, she began training with All Japan Women at the age of 15, wrestling her first match in 1983. She won the AJW junior championship in 1984 and adopted the name Bull, to represent her size and physical ring style. She stood 5'7" (although she often wore her hair straight up, giving the impression of being even taller than that; Andre the Giant wore his hair in an Afro style for

*Bull Nakano, one of the best to come from Japan.* MIKE LANO

similar effect), and her weight topped out at around 220 pounds at her heaviest.

In July 1985, she defeated Itsuki Yamazaki to win the AJW title, a championship she would hold until January 1988. She also formed a tag team with her mentor, Dump Matsumoto. She was one of the most feared heels in All Japan Women in the late 1980s.

In January 1990, she won a tournament to win the vacant WWWA world title, which Lioness Asuka had abdicated when she retired. She held that title for almost three years, finally losing it to Aja Kong in November 1992.

"A teenage Nakano was a pro wrestling prodigy, a name at 16, the Japanese women's champion at 17, and held the WWWA world title, at the time the biggest and most important championship in women's wrestling, for just shy of three years, the longest [reign] in the history of that championship," wrote Dave Meltzer.

In 1992, Nakano left Japan for a stint in Mexico's CMLL promotion, where she became the first CMLL women's champion.

In 1994, she signed with the WWF, quickly becoming a top contender to Alundra Blayze's women's title. She suffered a loss to Blayze at SummerSlam 1994 in Chicago, with Luna Vachon serving as her manager, but defeated Blayze to win the WWF women's title at the mammoth Super Woman Great War extravaganza AJW on November 20, 1994, in front of more than 32,000 fans. The Chicago match represented a high point in the women's division that wouldn't be matched for more than 10 years.

Nakano held the WWF women's title for four months, dropping the belt back to Blayze in Poughkeepsie, New York. She was subsequently released from the WWF, allegedly for cocaine possession.

In 1995, she competed on the record-setting New Japan Pro Wrestling event in Pyongyang in front of an announced crowd of 150,000 people, teaming with Akira Hokuto to beat Manami Toyota and Mariko Yoshida. The following year, she resurfaced in WCW, where she renewed her rivalry with Blayze (now competing as Madusa). Nakano and Madusa faced off in a featured match at Hog Wild 1996, a match Madusa won, thereby earning the rights to destroy Nakano's motorcycle, per the stipulation of the match.

Nakano stopped wrestling in 1997 and went on to become a professional golfer. She qualified for the Ladies Professional Golf Association tour in 2006. She returned to the ring for a tag match with Dump Matsumoto in 2001, promoting her own wrestling event on her 44th birthday in January 2012 when she "officially" retired . . . and got married. The wedding was a surprise attraction. In the final segment of a loaded wrestling card, her boyfriend Daisuke Aoki was introduced. A wedding march then played and Keiko Nakano was introduced, coming to the ring in a white bridal gown.

"Bull Nakano is probably one of the six or seven greatest woman pro wrestlers who ever lived. She's in many ways considered the female equivalent of Jumbo Tsuruta, a legendary Japanese wrestler,

*Top row: Donna Christantello, Brittney Brown, unknown, Bull Nakano, Mae Weston, Fabulous Moolah, Mae Young, Joanie Laurer; Bottom row: Cookie Crumbles, Akira Hokuto, Candi Devine.* MIKE LANO

both because she was big and an excellent worker, and also because she was the main bridge between the two glory eras of women's pro wrestling in Japan," said Meltzer.

### *Akira Hokuto*

Plenty of wrestlers have a reputation for being tough. Akira Hokuto redefines the word.

How's this for tough: In 1987, barely two years after breaking into wrestling, she suffered a broken neck while receiving a tombstone piledriver off the second rope during the second of a best of three falls tag team match. She finished the match, physically holding her head in place in her hands through the rest of the bout. "It was one of those scenes that everyone watching will take to their grave," Dave Meltzer wrote of the injury, which nearly ended her career before it began.

Born Hisako Uno on July 13, 1967, she became a fan of the Crush

Gals and quit high school to enrol in the All Japan Women's dojo at the age of 17. She made her pro debut in May 1985 and was named AJW Rookie of the Year for 1985. She won the AJW title in March 1986, eight months after her first match.

The broken neck kept her out of the ring for a year and a half, and she was told she would never wrestle again. According to Meltzer, she fell into a deep depression and even considered suicide while in the hospital. When she was healthy enough to return, she pleaded with AJW officials to be allowed to come back. She adopted the name Akira Hokuto as a tribute to wrestler Akira Maeda. Essentially, she was symbolically starting a new life. She and partner Suzuka Minami won the WWWA tag titles twice, adopting the team name Marine Wolves. She also won the All Pacific championship on two occasions, vacating the belt in 1993 because of injury.

"Her spirit became well-known throughout wrestling, even though it was nothing new, for working every night with severe injuries, although even a year or two earlier she was nicknamed the Mummy because she was always taped up because of constant elbow and shoulder injuries," Meltzer added.

On April 2, 1993, Hokuto defeated Shinobu Kandori in one of the main events of a show that drew 16,500 at Yokohama Arena and did $1,200,000 at the gate, the first million-dollar gate in the history of women's wrestling. Both the crowd and the gate numbers were more than WrestleMania pulled two days later in Las Vegas. The match itself received a five-star ranking by Meltzer's *Wrestling Observer*. Hokuto married Mexican wrestler Mascara Magica and split her time between Japan and Mexico, winning the CMLL women's title in July 1994 under the name Reina Jubuki. One year after the record gate, she sold out Yokohama Arena again, this time teaming with Kandori against Bull Nakano and Aja Kong, breaking the record with $1,500,000 at the gate.

On November 20, 1994, Hokuto was one of eight women competing in the Five-Star Top Woman Tournament, a featured attraction at the massive Super Woman Great War supercard at the Tokyo Dome. The event was billed as Hokuto's retirement card. In reality, she had planned to retire in Japan and continue to compete in Mexico. Hokuto won the tournament, beating Aja Kong in a gruelling 20-minute war. Her marriage didn't last long, however, changing her plans of permanently relocating to Mexico.

"She had become one of the most popular wrestlers in the country because of her gutsy history of working with severe injuries and her ability to make matches dramatic that greatly exceeded almost any woman wrestler in history," wrote Meltzer.

In November 1995, Hokuto signed with WCW, which was looking to build a women's division centered on Madusa Miceli. She

*Akira Hokuto in her WCW days.* PRO WRESTLING ILLUSTRATED

debuted in WCW, managed by Sonny Onoo, and competed in a tournament to determine the first WCW women's champion. Hokuto had a bit of an unfair advantage in the tournament; she was entered twice, once as Hokuto and once under her CMLL alias Reina Jubuki. She (as Jubuki) lost to Madusa in the opening round, causing CMLL to strip her of that championship. She still managed to win the tournament (as Hokuto), beating Madusa in the finals in Nashville at Starrcade 1995.

She successfully defended the title against Madusa throughout WCW until WCW decided to drop the women's division altogether, deactivating the title. She married legendary wrestler Kensuke Sasaki on October 1, 1995; Sasaki was so smitten with her that he proposed to her on their first date. She returned to Japan and began wrestling for GAEA, winning the AAAW tag team title with Mayumi Ozaki.

But after years of injuries, Hokuto was looking for a more stable life at home with her husband, officially retiring on April 7, 2002. In her retirement bout, she and Meiko Satomura defeated Chigusa Nagayo and Ayako Hamada. Hokuto wrestled the match with a broken rib and still managed to score the winning pinfall in a bout that drew 5,000 fans.

Although she originally intended to keep a low public profile following her retirement, she has embraced her role as a celebrity in Japan. She and Sasaki are active in charities, and she has appeared in TV commercials and magazine advertisements. In September 2015, she underwent successful surgery after being diagnosed with breast cancer, showing that much like when she first started, she continues to simply be tough.

## Manami Toyota

In his 2002 book *Top 100 Pro Wrestlers of All Time*, John F. Molinaro refers to Manami Toyota as "the Ric Flair of women's wrestling, arguably the greatest female pro wrestler of all time."

It's heavy praise, but it may just be warranted. Toyota raised the bar for women's wrestling to even greater heights in All Japan Women during the 1990s. However, unlike Flair, Toyota was both a master technician and a high flyer, dazzling fans with her moonsaults, suicide dives, and diving headbutts off the top rope.

Born March 2, 1971, she began wrestling at the age of 16, making her debut in August 1987. She quickly began to stand out from her peers for her pacing, the depth of her moveset, and her incredible sense of timing, making last-minute kick-outs from pin attempts that kept fans on the edges of their seats. All Japan Women named her its Rookie of the Year in 1988.

"Before I came to test [try out] at AJW, I was a very shy girl,"

Toyota said in a 1987 interview with *Joshi Puroresu* magazine, shortly after her debut. "I didn't dare talk to anyone. But after discovering wrestling, everything changed."

If Toyota was shy in real life, it certainly didn't come across in the ring. She possessed a natural showmanship and an innate understanding of wrestling psychology. She also had the strength, balance, and agility to pull off an assortment of innovative and exciting power and aerial moves.

Toyota had a lengthy feud with Toshiyo Yamada, which culminated in a hair vs. hair match in August 1992. Toyota won the

*The Ric Flair of women's wrestling, Manami Toyota.*
KURT SCHIMMEL

match, but the storyline was that she had earned so much respect for her opponent that she did not want Yamada to have to lose her hair. Toyota had to be restrained, while Yamada did the honorable thing and adhered to the stipulations of the match, having her hair sheared off. That experience brought the two enemies together, and Toyota and Yamada began teaming, beating Aja Kong and Bison Kimura for the WWWA tag title in March 1992.

On April 11, 1993, Toyota and Yamada lost the tag belts to

Dynamite Kansai and Mayumi Ozaki in a best of three falls match that would be voted Match of the Year by readers of the *Wrestling Observer Newsletter*, the first time a women's match would earn that prestigious distinction in the history of the *Observer* awards since they were instituted in 1980. Two years later, she won the same award for a 60-minute draw against Kyoko Inoue. That match earned close to twice as many first-place votes as the next runner-up, the famed ladder match between Shawn Michaels and Razor Ramon. Toyota was also named Most Outstanding Wrestler of the Year for 1995, an award given based on workrate. It was the first — and only — time that award was given to a woman, as Toyota beat out the likes of Eddie Guerrero, Rey Mysterio, and Chris Benoit.

On March 26, 1995, Toyota arrived at the pinnacle of AJW, beating Aja Kong to win the WWWA championship in Yokohama. She lost the belt back to Kong three months later. On December 4, 1995, she won the title for a second time, beating Kansai in Tokyo. Her second WWWA title reign lasted a year, until it was ended by Inoue in a rematch of their classic 60-minute draw, which unified Inoue's All Pacific and IWA titles with the WWWA title.

Fans were treated to a dream match between two of the best female wrestlers of all time on November 28, 1998, when Toyota faced former Crush Gal Chigusa Nagayo, a match Nagayo won.

Toyota moved on to the GAEA promotion in 2002, rekindling classic rivalries with Yamada and Kansai and winning the GAEA title in October 2002. In 2007, she took a sabbatical from the ring after a tribute show held in her honor, where she wrestled in every match on the card.

In 2010, Toyota made her first appearance in the United States with a tour of the CHIKARA promotion. She defeated Daizee Haze in a singles bout in Baltimore, Maryland, then teamed with CHIKARA founder Mike Quackenbush to beat Claudio Castagnoli and Sara Del Rey, making Del Rey submit. She returned to CHIKARA in 2011 to compete in the annual King of Trios Tournament, teaming with Quackenbush and Jigsaw. She made subsequent returns to the company in December 2011 and September 2012, and made her UK debut in November 2016.

"Manami Toyota is maybe the most influential Joshi star in women's wrestling," Sara Del Rey told Diva Dirt in a 2011 interview. "She was one of the first women I saw doing things equally spectacular as the guys. You could tell she had a heart and a passion in the ring that was like no other. She presented herself with style, grace and a feminine beauty, but you also knew she could downright kick your butt. She is the perfect combination of everything people love about the sport and she appeals to everyone. There are million reasons why she is considered the best and none can be argued because she is."

## Aja Kong

*"God made the Devil just for fun.*
*But when he wanted the real thing,*
*he made Aja Kong."*

Those lyrics are from Aja Kong's entrance music and probably best define what kind of character Kong was. Simply put, Aja Kong was the harbinger of a new era in All Japan Women's Wrestling.

"Kong [was] a prime factor in the rebirth of the AJW promotion in 1990, in the wake of the end of the teenybopper era," Dave Meltzer wrote. "During the 1980s, AJW relied mainly on teenage girls for their audience, [led by young-girl-heroine drawing cards such as Chigusa Nagayo.] It was the appearance of the monstrous Kong and tag team partner Bison Kimura on the men's shows in 1990 and generally having the best matches on the show that caused the hardcore wrestling fans to have to respect AJW."

With her crushing high-angle back suplex, her wicked swinging backfist (later adopted by her tag team partner Awesome Kong), and her lethal brainbuster, Kong was a brutal striker with an explosive offense. One of the most decorated women in Japanese wrestling

*The evil Aja Kong.* DAVE PRAZAK/SHIMMER

history, she also was awarded the prestigious (and particularly rare for women's matches) distinction of five-star matches by Meltzer three times, two against legend Manami Toyota.

Born Erica Shishido on September 25, 1970, she was the daughter of an African-American U.S. serviceman and a Japanese woman, a mixed-race child in a nation where interracial children are a rarity. She enrolled in the All Japan Women's dojo and graduated in 1986, wrestling her first match that summer. She stood 5'5" tall and weighed 220 pounds, making her much larger than most other Japanese females. Given her size and unique look, she debuted as a monster heel in the mold of Dump Matsumoto. It was only normal that she debuted as a member of Matsumoto's evil stable Gokuaku Domei ("Atrocious Alliance").

Following Matsumoto's retirement, Kong focused on tag team wrestling. She and Grizzly Awamoto won the World Women's Wrestling Association tag team title in December 1989, but the team stayed together only a few months. Kong then partnered with Bison Kimura, adopting the team name of Jungle Jack. The duo won the WWWA tag belts on two occasions.

In November 1992, Kong finally managed to defeat Bull Nakano to claim the WWWA championship. Her first reign as WWWA champion lasted two and a half years. She also had a two-month reign in 1995.

In 1995, she traveled to America where she debuted for the WWF. At the 1995 Survivor Series, Kong teamed with Bertha Faye (Monster Ripper), Tomoko Watanabe, and Lioness Asuka to face Alundra Blayze, Kyoko Inoue, Sakie Hasegawa, and Chaparita Asari. Kong singlehandedly eliminated each member of the babyface team, ending with Blayze, whom she dispatched with her trademark spinning backfist. That win made Kong the top contender for the WWE women's title, but the title shot against Blayze never occurred as Blayze was released from the company the following month and the women's division put on ice.

Kong returned to Japan, where she competed in HUSTLE and All Japan Women. In 1997, she announced she was leaving AJW and founded a new promotion called Hyper Visual Fighting ARSION (usually referred to simply as ARSION). She reigned as Queen of ARSION champion from August 1999 until December 2000, when she dropped the title to Ayako Hamada.

She continued to compete as a freelancer in the 2000s and made a couple appearances in the United States, facing Sara Del Rey at a CHIKARA event in December 2011 and making a surprise appearance at SHIMMER in April 2015 for a retirement farewell send-off for Tomoka Nakagawa.

"My first worship was when I was 20 and it still is my hero in wrestling. It's Aja Kong, because she's awesome and she wrestles like every woman I think should — it's a fight, and I love it. She's amazing, she's the best. I'd definitely say top three greatest women of all time," said Del Rey.

Kong's impact in Japan cannot be overstated; several of her mannerisms and set-up moves were even copied by American Leon White when he developed the Big Van Vader character in Japan in the late 1980s.

"Aja Kong is a huge star in Japan, not just a wrestling star, but someone you see on TV all the time — on game shows, morning talk shows, afternoon studio shows, early evening news and gossip shows, and late night comedy talk shows," said author and journalist Fumi Saito. "She can be scary, funny, witty, and sometimes smart and serious. She has a special ability to connect with an audience that transcends wrestling."

## Megumi Kudo

In the mid-1990s, the Philadelphia-based Extreme Championship Wrestling rose up as an underground alternative to the WWF and WCW. ECW built a passionate cult following based on its unique blend of violent matches, risqué storylines, and diverse competition. It was a promotion where hardcore brawlers like the Sandman and New Jack could coexist with high-flying luchadors like Rey Mysterio Jr. and Psicosis, and mat technicians like Dean Malenko and Chris Benoit.

ECW never featured a women's division, although it was infamous for its signature catfights, which announcer Joey Styles called with glee. Francine, Dawn Marie, Tammy "Sunny" Sytch, and Beulah McGillicutty and their panty-revealing pull-aparts were staples of ECW shows.

Future WWE women's champions Jazz and Lita (as Danny Doring's valet, Miss Congeniality) got their start in ECW, and Luna Vachon was brought in for a feud with Stevie Richards, so ECW occasionally presented women's wrestling as more than a peep show, but those instances were few and far between.

As ECW was taking root in America, a similar promotion was gaining ground in Japan. Atsushi Onita founded Frontier Martial-Arts Wrestling in 1989. Onita's group popularized bizarre hardcore matches such as exploding barbed-wire death matches and bouts featuring weapons such as barbed-wire-wrapped baseball bats and sickles.

Unlike ECW, FMW prominently featured its women's division, which was centered around a petite young woman named Megumi Kudo.

Kudo was born on September 20, 1969. She played basketball during high school and enrolled in the All Japan Women's dojo in 1986 at the age of 16. Despite her athleticism, Kudo was not a natural wrestler, and she was slow to adapt to the rigors of All Japan Women's grueling training. She was released from All Japan Women in 1988 and found work as a kindergarten teacher. But the lure of the ring proved strong, and in 1990, she joined Atsushi's renegade FMW promotion.

Kudo was a beauty in a world of brawlers, madmen, and masochists. With her looks and her strong work ethic, Kudo quickly became the centerpiece of FMW's women's division, which also included Combat Toyoda, Shark Tsuchiya, and Crusher Maedomari. Kudo captured the FMW women's title six times from 1991 until her retirement in 1997.

*Hardcore wrestling was also for women, at least for Megumi Kudo.* GEORGE NAPOLITANO

Kudo became famous for wrestling in brutal death matches, including a classic electrified barbed-wire death match against Toyoda. In her very last match, she won the title for the last time against Tsuchiya in a no-ropes 200V double hell, double barbed-wire barricade, double landmine, glass crush death match in front of 16,000 fans before vacating it in her retirement ceremony on June 13. In those matches, charges would go off when a wrestler touched the electrified wire or when they landed on boards rigged with explosives outside the ring.

Kudo was an expert at selling, especially in hardcore matches. She was thrown around the ring like a rag doll, whipped into barbed wire, and even blown up (or, at least, been made to look as if she had been blown up via some impressive pyrotechnics and smoke bombs). Bloody and battered but unbowed, Kudo always rallied back for more. In many ways, her unbreakable underdog persona embodied the very essence of FMW.

Kudo is also credited with innovating the Kudo driver, also known as "da cop killa," used by Homicide. Kudo positioned a bowed opponent's head on the back of her tailbone, reached back and hooked her arms, and turned into her opponent, lifting the opponent upside-down on her back. Kudo then dropped to her buttocks, bringing the opponent crashing down, seemingly unprotected on the top of their head. It was a visually stunning move, especially when Kudo used it against larger, heavier opponents like Toyoda and Tsuchiya. Cheerleader Melissa later adopted the move as a tribute to Kudo.

Kudo branched out into other forms of entertainment, releasing a music album in 1992 and appearing as a young mother forced to try her hand at wrestling to pay the bills in the 1992 movie *A Human Murder Weapon*. She retired in 1997 and married wrestler Bad Boy Hido in 1998. She dabbled in broadcasting, working as a wrestling color commentator and as the host of a weekly radio show. Although her wrestling career lasted only about 10 years, Kudo was a dynamic figure in one of the most innovative promotions of its era and was a pioneer as a woman competing in hardcore matches.

### Monster Ripper

To fans in Japan, Mexico, and Puerto Rico, she was known as Monster Ripper, a feared face-painted behemoth. Fans in Western Canada knew her as Rhonda Singh, a bruising powerhouse with a devastating gorilla press body slam. And to WWF fans in 1995, she was known as Bertha Faye, a colorful comedy wrestler who was able to wrest the WWF women's title away from Alundra Blayze in 1995.

Born Rhonda Ann Sing in Calgary, Alberta, on February 21, 1961, she regularly attended Stampede Wrestling events as a child and dreamed of becoming a wrestler. As a teenager, she went to the same high school as Bret and Owen Hart and she repeatedly tried to approach the Hart family to inquire about becoming a wrestler, but between scheduling conflicts and the fact that Stampede wasn't regularly promoting women's wrestling, her requests fell on deaf ears.

While on a family trip to Hawaii, she saw a broadcast of All Japan Women's wrestling on television, and she

*She was Monster Ripper in Japan, but in Calgary she was Rhonda Singh.* MIKE LANO

became convinced that wrestling was what she wanted to do in life.

"I was in Hawaii on vacation and zapping through the channels [when] I stumbled on Japanese women's wrestling," she told SLAM! Wrestling. "They were hitting each other with chairs and everything! It was an all-girl company and I thought it was the coolest thing. It sparked my interest."

So she wrote to Mildred Burke after finding an advertisement for Burke's school in a magazine. At the age of 17, she moved from Alberta to Encino, California, to train with Burke. She was Burke's last student.

Sing was 5'8" and her weight fluctuated between 180 and 280 pounds — possibly higher toward the end of her career. Her size made her a marketable commodity in Japan, and she made her first tour to Japan during her rookie year in 1979. Dubbed Monster Ripper, she was cast as a juggernaut brawler. She made an immediate impact in All Japan, winning the WWWA championship twice within a year of debuting for the company.

"Some of the Japanese girls came to L.A. to train and scout some talent. [Mildred] Burke was the only U.S. trainer having women go over to Japan at the time," she told SLAM! Wrestling. "They were saying, 'Hey! A fat girl! We like her.' That was in November, and by January I was main eventing in Japan. I could tie my boots and do a backdrop. I was pretty limited."

For Dave Meltzer, Sing was on top of her game at that time. "During this period, Singh was considered the number one woman wrestler in the world, as she held the world title in Japan and Mexico at the same time, which were the two markets that featured women's wrestling at a time when it was in bad shape in the U.S," said Meltzer, explaining Sing's place in Japanese wrestling history.

As she was an inexperienced *gaijin* newcomer to Japan, several of her opponents took liberties, hitting her with cheap shots and sandbagging her in matches, leaving her disappointed and frustrated. The Dynamite Kid encouraged her to fight back and taught her that the best way to earn respect was to show her toughness. Once she learned that lesson, she quickly became one of All Japan Women's top commodities.

"[After that] when a well-known woman wrestler bullied one of the young, new girls, Rhonda put her in her place, which gained her respect from the boys," wrote Bret Hart in a SLAM! Wrestling column.

Because of many factors, she was also often called the female version of Terry Gordy. "The two were the same age, Singh being born about eight weeks before Gordy," said Meltzer. "They were huge kids who broke into wrestling very young, known for being agile with wrestling skill despite their size. Both used the power bomb as a finisher, years before such a move even had a name, and popularized the move in Japan; actually Ripper popularized the move in women's wrestling before Gordy did in All Japan, where American wrestlers who toured Japan discovered it."

In the late 1980s, Sing returned to Canada, wrestling for the Stampede promotion she grew up watching. She took on the name Rhonda Singh (plans to pair her with resident heel Gama Singh never materialized). She was recognized as the first Stampede Wrestling women's champion, by virtue of having scored a win over Wendi Richter prior to her Stampede debut.

She moved on to Puerto Rico, where she captured the World Wrestling Council women's title five times from 1987 to 1991, and worked also for AAA in Mexico in the early 1990s, her size making her one of the biggest heels there. She was a powerhouse brawler who flattened opponents with her gorilla press slam, sit-out powerbomb, avalanche, and seated senton.

In 1995, she was signed by the WWF to help fill out the women's division. By that point, her weight had ballooned upwards of 300 pounds. Instead of casting her as the brawling juggernaut, the WWF recast her as Bertha Faye, an obese comedy wrestler hailing from Walls, Georgia. It was a Vince Russo idea. She was paired with diminutive manager Harvey Wippleman to complete the sideshow "fat lady/twerp" archetype. The WWF forbade her from using the power moves that had made Monster Ripper an international attraction. Instead, her character was set as pure comic relief — the fat lady straight out of the Georgia trailer park.

She defeated Blayze for the women's title at SummerSlam 1995 but lost the belt back to Blayze two months later. She left the promotion in 1996. According to Sing, the original booking plan had her and Bull Nakano vying for the championship. "We had big heat in Japan, so this is what they wanted to do. Madusa [Blayze] was going away, and she was getting new boobs and a new nose. For three months, it was going to be Nakano and I. She was going to drop the belt to me. Madusa was going to come back after a while, we'd add a few more girls and make it a legitimate women's division."

Those plans never came to pass. Instead, she went back to Japan and made some appearances in WCW, where she portrayed an overweight Nitro Girls wannabe named Beef. Again, she was played as comic relief, a far cry from the monster heel she had portrayed for most of her career.

"She was very tough in the ring," said Susan Green. "Of course it's hard when someone is 280, 290 pounds to have any leverage against them. But she was dedicated, she might have been that big, but she was solid."

She retired from wrestling in 2000 and took a job providing care to people with disabilities. She died on July 27, 2001, of a heart attack at the age of 40.

## Reggie Bennett

In some ways, Reggie Bennett was the prototype for Chyna and any other big, powerful American women wrestlers who followed in her footsteps.

She was born on January 24, 1961, in San Diego, one of nine roughhousing siblings. As a teenager, she developed an interest in powerlifting and eventually moved to Venice, California, the epicenter of the bodybuilding universe in the 1980s.

In an interview with the website Dirty Dirty Sheets, she said she had never seen a pro wrestling match until she actually wrestled in her first match. "Mando Guerrero was training my now ex-husband for a wrestling movie. He asked me if I wanted to make some money with my body. At the time, I was a bodybuilder and I thought he was propositioning me," she said. "There was a big show going on in Hawaii and then [traveling] down the coast of California and they needed a girl to be in a 10-woman battle royal because they were one short. Mando taught me how to get over the top rope and that's all I really knew."

Following that tour, Guerrero sent Bennett and fellow bodybuilder Terri Power (who became Tori in WWF) to former Olympian Brad

Rheingans to continue their training in Minnesota, where they trained under Rheingans and Denise Storm. She signed with the fledgling Ladies Professional Wrestling Association and became one of the company's featured stars. At 5'8" and 249 pounds of muscle, she stood out from the pack.

As luck would have it, she landed a vitamin drink commercial that played in Japan, and the commercial proved to be a sensation. Bennett became an overnight celebrity, and once All Japan Women found out she was a wrestler, they brought her into the fold. Bennett

*Reggie Bennett was used as a monster heel in Japan.* MIKE LANO

joined AJW in 1994 and quickly became their biggest *gaijin* star. She was the first American monster in the company.

On May 15, 1995, she defeated Manami Toyota to win the IWA women's title in Niigata, Japan. She would hold that title until December 4, 1995, when she lost the belt to All Pacific champion Takako Inoue in a title vs. title match. She won the All Pacific title on June 22, 1996, winning a tournament for the vacant title.

Bennett also did a bit of acting, including a small part in the Sylvester Stallone film *Over the Top*. She met Terry Funk on set and developed a friendship with the Funker. Thanks in part to that friendship, she was invited to make a surprise appearance at the end of ECW's first pay-per-view, Barely Legal in 1996, where she joined Raven's Flock in a beatdown of Funk after Funk upset Raven for the ECW title. But there were no long-term goals for Bennett in ECW, and she moved on to the new ARSION promotion in Japan in 1997.

"[ARSION] was fresh," she said. "The idea of pushing submission and 'ultimate' style fighting appealed to me. I had already done an ultimate tournament and placed third, and that was done one month after dislocating my collarbone from my sternum."

Bennett retired from wrestling in 2001, wrestling Manami Toyota in her retirement match.

## SUPER WOMAN, GREAT WAR (BIG EGG WRESTLING UNIVERSE)

All Japan Women proved that women's wrestling could be a draw on its own merits, as opposed to being a novelty draw in men's events. In 1994, AJW decided to find out just how many fans they could draw by producing the biggest, most star-studded women's wrestling event of all time.

Strong from two very lucrative years, the time was right to try the biggest venue in Japan, the Tokyo Dome.

So on November 20, 1994, All Japan Women partnered with GAEA Japan, JWP Joshi Puroresu, Ladies Legend Pro Wrestling, and FMW to present a women's wrestling supercard at the Tokyo Dome. The event was called AJW Doumu Super Woman Great War but became known colloquially as Big Egg Wrestling Universe, a reference to the egg-shaped Tokyo Dome and the interpromotional, universal feel of the event.

Even WWF women's champion Alundra Blayze was signed on to defend her championship against Bull Nakano in a featured bout.

*The biggest women's wrestling show ever.* KURT SCHIMMEL COLLECTION

The event also featured a handful of male wrestlers (including the Great Sasuke, Jinsei "Hakushi" Shinaki, and Super Delfin) and male midget wrestlers, as well as female amateur wrestlers, kickboxers, and shoot fighters, but mainly, it was about women's wrestling.

Promoted as the biggest card in the history of women's wrestling, the 23-bout mega-card drew an announced attendance of 32,500 fans for a ridiculous gate of $4 million.

"That show sold more merchandise than this past year's WrestleMania [WrestleMania 25]," Dave Meltzer wrote in 2009. "They did $612,000 just in program sales. The program was equivalent to the program the NFL would put together for the Super Bowl, and something no other pro wrestling promotion in history has ever come close to producing. Most of the crowd stayed for a show that lasted ten hours [beginning at 2 p.m., ending at 11:56 p.m.], featured a 60-piece marching band, [and] a parade of wrestlers representing 11 different flag-carrying federations that looked like a scaled down version of the Olympic Games opening ceremony."

In some ways, this supercard was All Japan Women's swan song. The company had hit its prime in the 1980s with the Beauty Pair and the Crush Gals. All Japan's success prompted other women's promotions to get in on the act, creating a nationwide boom period for joshi wrestling in the early 1990s that culminated in a series of interpromotional events between several promotions. But by 1994, the boom period was already dying out.

"This event was aimed more towards a more casual movie-going and concert-going audience," said Japanese wrestling journalist and author Fumi Saito. "Since it was in the Tokyo Dome, it gave people the feeling it was a big, historical event."

The card featured an eight-woman interpromotional tournament to determine the top women's wrestler in Japan. It was also advertised as the retirement of Akira Hokuto, one of the most respected female wrestlers of all time. "If you were a serious wrestling fan, you *had to be* there. People felt that way about her," Saito said.

"The special effects of the ring entrances were something only the Pride promotion years later could approximate," wrote Meltzer, who attended the event. "There was not just the pyro and pinwheel fireworks, but laser light shows corresponding to the music of the entrance, and with the lasers also making the faces of the biggest stars in a light show on the Tokyo Dome roof. The entrances made it appear wrestlers were entering in cages on space ships [actually brought in by hidden lowered cranes from backstage, but the visual effect with steam coming from the stage to the bottom of the entrance vehicle looked like ships levitating in midair], in giant balloons, with acrobatic Ninjas and amidst a parade of Harley Davidson motorcycles. Every match had its own corporate sponsor. It was one of the greatest pro wrestling shows in history at that point in time."

But although the 10-hour spectacle was a financial success and a massive one-of-a-kind undertaking, some experts felt it was overblown, a perfect example of too much of a good thing.

"I was sitting in the commentary booth for over eight hours. By the time the night ended, my brain was not working very well," Saito said. "The Tokyo Dome gave the event this big historical feeling and they all tried to do too much in the ring. At the end of the night, people ended up not remembering a whole lot of what they were watching."

Still, with a lineup including the likes of Chigusa Nagayo, Reggie Bennett, Shinobu Kandori, Bison Kimura, Jaguar Yokota, Lioness Asuka, Combat Toyoda, Akira Hokuto, Aja Kong, Manami Toyota, Dynamite Kansai, Megumi Kudo, Cutie Suzuki, Bull Nakano, and Alundra Blayze and because of the magnitude of the show, it will be remembered as the biggest women's show of all-time, something that might never be matched.

★ ★ ★

## Ayako Hamada

A second-generation star, Ayako Hamada has thrilled audiences in Japan, Mexico, and the United States ever since her debut in 1998. Born Ayako Valentina Hamada Villarreal on February 14, 1981, she is

*Ayako Hamada also made a name for herself with SHIMMER.* DAVE PRAZAK/SHIMMER

the daughter of Gran Hamada, a pioneer of Japanese wrestling in his own right, who had a good career in both Japan and Mexico. That's why his two daughters — Ayako's sister, Xochitl, also wrestles and became the AAA's first Reina de Reinas champion in 1999 — were born and raised in Mexico. At the age of 17, Hamada wrestled her first match for Japan's ARSION promotion, winning the Twin Star of ARSION (tag team) title less than a year after her pro debut.

At the age of 19, she defeated joshi legend Aja Kong to win the Queen of ARSION championship. She left ARSION in 2001 and defeated Momoe Nakanashi to win the WWWA title in May 2003 in Yokohama. She eventually lost that title to Amazing Kong, beginning a rivalry that would flare up repeatedly in the United States over the next few years. A year later, she defeated Miss Janeth, dubbed the Sherri Martel of Mexico, to win the UWA women's title. In January 2004, she captured the All Asia Athletes women's title, then she turned her sights to her native Mexico, where she wrestled for the AAA promotion where she would be a regular in 2007 and 2008.

After making her mark in Japan and Mexico, she was able to

showcase her talent when she signed with TNA as a highly touted newcomer. A feud with Alissa Flash culminated in a rare women's Falls Count Anywhere bout in October 2009, which Hamada won. She formed a tag team with Kong and won the TNA Knockouts tag title in January 2010. She was stripped of the tag title two months later when Kong was fired by TNA. Hamada won the title a second time with Taylor Wilde in August 2010 but vacated the title when she chose to leave TNA at the end of 2010. Unfortunately, she was rarely given that opportunity to shine on the national stage in TNA, which was a major reason behind her decision to leave that company.

In the meantime, Hamada established herself as title contender and a huge crowd favorite in SHIMMER. Her bouts against Cheerleader Melissa, Sara Del Rey, Madison Eagles, and Kana (Asuka) are widely considered to be some of the greatest matches in SHIMMER history.

In 2012, Hamada was named Wrestler of the Year by the women's wrestling website Ringbelles.

"All of my 10 favorite matches I've seen this year, there's six of her. That's six out of eight she did at SHIMMER, and six of them are in my top ten favorites," said former NCW Femmes Fatales promoter Stephane Bruyere, who presented Hamada with the award. "She's just amazing. She's the best right now. When we talk about quality of matches, there's nobody that can top what she can do."

Upon her return to Japan in 2011, she signed with Pro Wrestling Wave, where she captured the Wave title once and the tag team title three times (with Yuu Yamagata). Although her time on the national stage in the United States was brief, Hamada is without a doubt a proven star internationally.

# MEXICO

Women's wrestling was never as popular in Mexico as it was in Japan. Yet, because professional wrestling was always highly thought of, the country had some very popular luchadoras over the years. But in recent years, the women's scene has evolved, and women wrestlers are now better positioned on cards. Current Mexican star Dulce Garcia believes WWE's women's revolution has something to do with that. "American companies like Lucha Underground and WWE are putting emphasis on women's wrestling, and that's driving the girls in Mexico to be the best they can be and push themselves," she says. "The women are showing that they are able to be in the main event and entertain the fans. They're waiting for a female Luchador to be picked up by WWE."

## Irma Gonzalez

Trained by two Mexican wrestling legends in Gori Guerrero and Tarzan Lopez, Irma Gonzalez wrestled in six different decades, something very few wrestlers, male or female, have ever managed. Born Irma Morales Munoz in Cuernavaca, Morelos, on August 20, 1936, she started her career on her 19th birthday. One of the first national women's champions in her home country, she wrestled for all the big offices in Mexico. Known also under monikers such as Rosa Blanca and La Novia del Santo ("Santo's girlfriend"), she also won tag team titles with her daughter, Irma Aguilar. Gonzalez was a big star from in 1950s and wrestled in Los Angeles as well. She performed in many hair vs. hair matches, and although she wasn't wrestling on a regular basis by then, Dona Irma took her official retirement in 2004.

## Lola Gonzalez

Also trained by Gori Guerrero, Lola Gonzalez was to a certain extent the babyface version of the Fabulous Moolah in Mexico. In the early 1990s, she was responsible for booking the luchadoras in Mexico. Born Maria Dolores Gonzalez on March 2, 1959, in Ciudad Juarez, she had started her career in 1975. Nicknamed Lola La Grande, she was at one point in her career the most popular *técnica* in Mexican women's wrestling and the biggest star of that era. She won the UWA world women's title on multiple occasions and wrestled in many hair vs.

hair and hair vs. mask matches. At the time, UWA was using female wrestlers much better than EMLL, where women would be used in opening matches. In fact, in Mexico City, women's wrestling gained respect with the rise of Gonzalez and Pantera Surena. Gonzalez also traveled quite a bit, working in Japan in the 1980s, as well as in Calgary and Dallas. In June 1992, CMLL created its first women's title. Gonzalez lost the best of three falls match against Bull Nakano in the first show in Mexico's history to be headlined by women.

## Lady Apache

Born Sandra Calderon on June 26, 1970, Lady Apache is one of the most prolific female wrestlers in Lucha Libre and one of Mexico's biggest stars. Raised in Mexico City, she wrestled her first match on her 16th birthday in June 1986. She married her trainer, wrestler Gran Apache (Mario Balbuena Gonzalez), and took the name Lady Apache in his honor. She became stepmother to Apache's two daughters, Fabiola and Mariella, who went on to wrestle as Faby Apache and Mari Apache, respectively.

Calderon and Gonzalez divorced, and she eventually married Jesus Alvarado Nieves, who wrestled under the name Brazo de Oro ("Arm of Gold"). Brazo de Oro was a major player in the CMLL promotion, eventually becoming the booker, and Lady Apache became one of CMLL's top stars.

In November 1996, she won a four-woman tournament to win the vacant CMLL women's title, which had been vacated when champion Reina Jubuki left to wrestle for WCW. Lady Apache held the title for three months until losing the belt to Mariko Yoshida in Tokyo, Japan, marking the first time the CMLL women's title had changed hands outside of Mexico.

She regained the title in May 1999 and held it for more than a year before leaving CMLL to join the rival AAA promotion, again resulting in the championship being declared vacant.

In February 2001, she won the annual Reina de Reinas ("Queen of Queens") tournament promoted by AAA in Veracruz, Mexico, winning

*Lady Apache (left) with Reina Jubuki (Akira Hokuto).*
MIKE LANO

a four-way bout against Miss Janeth, Tiffany, and Alda Moreno in the finals. She won that tournament a second time in February 2004.

She also won the Mexican national women's title on two occasions, in 2002 and 2004, and won the World Wrestling Association women's title in 2014.

She divorced Nieves and married a third time, this time settling down with Edgar Luna Pozos, who wrestled as Electroshock. She and Electroshock won the AAA World Mixed Tag Team title in 2003 at TripleMania XI. The duo won the title by winning a four-team elimination bout against Chessman and Tiffany, El Brazo (her former brother-in-law) and Martha Villalobos, and Gran Apache (her ex-husband) and Faby Apache (her stepdaughter). In 2016, she teamed with Faby and Mari and won the women's division of AAA's World Cup tournament.

In a 30-year career, Lady Apache has wrestled for every major promotion in Mexico and represented Lucha Libre internationally. "Sandra is one of the sweetest people I have ever met outside of the ring; she presents herself with humility and class," said Jennifer Blake, a Canadian-born wrestler who spent several years wrestling in AAA. "She is known as one of the greatest women wrestlers in Mexico and a legend of women's wrestling there. I met her earlier on in my career and she told me I was good, but that I needed to lay it in harder. Years later I saw her again and she told me how much I had improved and that I had gotten really good. I was very appreciative of her advice and praise. It really meant a lot to me coming from such a legend in the sport."

## La Diabolica

The most well-known masked luchadora in Mexico, she started her career at 21 years old in 1986. Known as a *ruda* (heel) character, she won both the national women's title and the CMLL women's title in 1993, becoming the promotion's third women's champion. She lost the title the following year against Akira Hokuto's alter ego in Mexico, Reina Jubuki. There was little work for women in Mexico in the second part of the 1990s. When Lady Apache left the promotion in 2000 for lack of work, La Diabolica was awarded the title, but a year or two later, she left for the same reasons, frustrated at her lack of opponents. She joined AAA and has split her time between there and the Mexican indie scene since. Believed to have been born on September 28, 1965, La Diabolica's real name isn't known, as is the case with almost all of the masked Mexican wrestlers.

## Sarah Stock

Sarah Stock was ready for a change, so she packed up her bags and moved 1,854 miles from her hometown to chase her wrestling dreams in Monterrey, Mexico. Little did she know she would resuscitate women's wrestling within the oldest wrestling promotion in the world.

Born in Winnipeg, Manitoba, on March 4, 1979, she grew up playing soccer, horseback riding, and running cross-country. She earned her bachelor's degree in chemistry at the University of Manitoba. She also trained in Muay Thai kickboxing before beginning her wrestling training with her local promotion, Top Rope Championship Wrestling. After little more than a month of training, she had her first match in February 2002. She began competing throughout Canada, including

*From Canada to Mexico, Sarah Stock.* DAVE PRAZAK/SHIMMER

stints in the Canadian Maritimes, but with the dearth of female opponents, she typically wrestled against men.

By 2003, she was looking to test herself against new opposition, so she moved to Mexico despite being unable to speak Spanish. There, she adopted a mask and took on the persona Dark Angel.

From 1999 to 2003, CMLL cut down on women's wrestling, using only a few local women, or joshis when they were coming to the country. That changed when Stock arrived.

"In 2003, they stopped booking women until Dark Angel came to Mexico and [journalist] Ernesto Ocampo kept putting her on magazine covers," recalled Dave Meltzer. "Finally, on July 15, 2005, the promotion booked La Amapola and Dark Angel vs. Marcela and Lady Apache as an experiment, and they got a huge reaction and people threw money in the ring, so they've been regulars ever since." La Amapola holds the record for the longest CMLL world women's title reign, while Marcela's four championships are the most in the company's history. Interestingly enough, Stock never won the title. She won the Lucha Libre Femenil Juvenil title in October 2003 and made occasional trips back to the

United States, wrestling for Ring of Honor, Ohio Valley Wrestling, and Samoan Afa's World Xtreme Wrestling, which was promoting women's wrestling with the institution of its annual Women's Elite 8 tournament.

Dark Angel was forced to unmask after a loss to Princesa Sujei in April 2004. She left the LLF promotion and flirted with Asistencia Asesoria y Administracion before signing with the rival Consejo Mundial de Lucha Libre promotion, which was building a new women's division. She remained based in CMLL for most of the next 10 years, as the company gave her the freedom to embark on multiple tours of Japan, the United States, and Canada.

"It was always a goal to wrestle full time, and this is one of the only places I could do that," said Stock. "All wrestling is respected there, whether you are a midget or a woman or a man."

She participated in the tournament to crown the first SHIMMER champion in 2007, defeating future champions Cheerleader Melissa and MsChif before falling to the eventual winner, Sara Del Rey.

Recommended by Mike Tenay, Stock debuted in TNA as Sarita in 2009. She teamed with fellow Canadian Taylor Wilde to win a tournament to become the first Knockouts tag team champions, although that championship was scrapped a couple years later. After she and Wilde had dropped the belts to Awesome Kong and Ayako Hamada, Sarita turned heel, eventually aligning with Hernandez, Anarquia, and Rosita to form the stable Mexican American (ironically enough, Stock was neither of those things). She had a second run as Knockouts tag champion, winning the belts with Rosita in 2012. That year, she also suffered a bout of Bell's palsy, which caused temporary facial paralysis. To hide the malady, she wore a "protective" mask, claiming a facial injury.

In January 2013, it was announced that Stock had left TNA. She turned up in Japan, winning the Wonder of Stardom championship in April 2013 and holding it six months before losing the belt to Act Yasukawa.

In 2015, as part of a turnover of their women's division, she accepted a backstage job with WWE, working alongside her old

SHIMMER nemesis Del Rey as a trainer for NXT, the company's developmental system. She wrestled her farewell bout in CMLL on September 18, 2015, defeating Princesa Sugehit in front of 14,300 fans at the Arena Mexico in Mexico City, on a card headlined by Atlantis vs. La Sombra.

"Since joining CMLL in 2005, the women have had a steady stream of work with really great female wrestlers and matches on the most important cards. There is so much quality in terms of the women and their wrestling. The public is very knowledgeable and appreciates and respects great wrestling above anything else. It has been a wonderful place to work, train and learn," Stock said to the *Miami Herald*.

Stock, who most probably influenced other Canadians like Jennifer Blake and Taya Valkyrie (who's also working for *Lucha Underground*) to have careers in Mexico, was a respected and well-traveled competitor who constantly sought out new challenges and consistently delivered excellent matches in the ring. With her international knowledge and experience, she has become an invaluable resource to the WWE developmental system.

## Sexy Star

She wrestles "for every girl out there who needs a hero, because every woman is sexy and every woman is a star."

The Mexican-born *luchadora enmascarada* Sexy Star was introduced to American audiences in 2014 when she appeared on the premier episode of *Lucha Underground* on the El Rey Network. Representing the spirit of female empowerment, she was presented as a woman who took up wrestling and martial arts after surviving an abusive relationship and depression. Through her mask, she hides her own identity while representing the fighting spirit and perseverance of women everywhere. "It's not just a character. This is what I believe. This is why I wrestle. This is my personal motto. I narrowed my story down to these words," she explained.

Equal parts inspirational underdog and mysterious sex symbol,

Sexy Star has become a fan favorite in both her native Mexico and the United States, appearing in the Latin American version of *ESPN: The Body* magazine. Born Dulce Garcia Rivas in Monterrey on September 20, 1982, she made her wrestling debut in August 2006, wrestling under the name Dulce Poly. Within four months of her debut, she captured both the Federacion Internacional de Lucha Libre mixed tag title (with her trainer Humberto Garza Jr.) and the FILL women's title.

In 2007, she jumped to the Asistencia Asesoria y Administracion promotion, where she adopted the name Sexy Star and would remain until April 2016.

*"Sexy Star" Dulce Garcia.* PAT LAPRADE

With her signature blonde hair and daredevil ring style, Sexy Star quickly became one of Mexico's most recognizable wrestling women. She captured the AAA Reina de Reinas title twice and had notable rivalries with Faby Apache, exotico Pimpinela Escarlata, and Super Fly. She was presented as a viable challenger for male wrestlers, especially in *Lucha Underground*. During the filming of the third season in April 2016, she won the main *Lucha Underground* title in an Aztec warfare match (a kind of battle royal match), only to lose it at the next day's taping to Johnny Mundo. A few months later, she unmasked at a boxing show in Mexico City. In the process, she also left AAA. Now working under her real name, Dulce Garcia made her SHIMMER debut in November 2016 against LuFisto. Although it was reported that she planned to retire, that was never the case.

"I never said that I'm going to quit wrestling. It's something I have a passion for. It's something I wanted to do, and once I set my mind to doing something, I do it. I might get knocked down but I always get back up and try again."

Nevertheless, her popularity, and the fact that she's significantly smaller than most of her male opponents, helped make her a role model to young girls throughout North America.

# UNITED KINGDOM

From Sue Brittain to Paige, there have been many female wrestlers coming from the U.K. In the 1980s and 1990s, Klondyke Kate was considered one of the best heels in England, wrestling for more than 30 years. Scotland's Kay Lee Ray and Northern Ireland's Rhia O'Reilly wrestle for SHIMMER and SHINE, Nikki Cross (Nikki Storm) is performing with NXT, while Wale's Nixon Newell could very well be the next to follow in Cross' footsteps. But none of these women can be compared to Sweet Saraya.

### Saraya Knight

With a mouth that could make a longshoreman blush, a blatant disdain for authority, and an affinity for kicking people (both men and women) in the groin, "sweet" isn't necessarily the first adjective that comes to mind when describing Saraya Knight. To use her own words, she's "a nasty, vicious, horrible bitch" . . . at least in wrestling.

The mother of Paige (as well as son Zak and stepson Roy, who wrestle as the U.K. Hooligans), Saraya was born Julia Hamer on October 19, 1971, in Penzance, Cornwall, England.

She ran away from home at 15 to escape physical abuse from her mother and stepfather and lived on the streets. "I took whatever I could fit in one kit bag and walked out the door. No money, no nothing," she said. Life on the streets was miserable; she was raped and struggled with addiction, finding food and shelter wherever she was able. She said she channeled some of those experiences to help her cultivate her heel persona.

In desperation, she decided to leave town and try to start a new life in a new environment. She found work in Norwich as a live-in

*"Sweet" Saraya Knight.* DAVE PRAZAK/SHIMMER

chef at a holiday camp in 1990, hitchhiking the 12-hour trip to the camp. That's where she met wrestler and promoter Ricky Knight (real name Ian Bevis), winning his heart by sneaking him an extra chicken breast from the kitchen. The two began dating, and she left the kitchen to tour with Ricky, becoming his manager, Sweet Saraya. She immediately began training to become a wrestler herself.

"My trainers were tough and they could fight. There was never a girl that had come out of England that could be classed as a bloke in wrestling. Princess Paula was a tough cookie, but she was a female worker. Klondyke Kate, Busty Keegan, Julie Starr, Tracey Kemp — all these girls that were out there were very feminine. . . . There wasn't any girls that went out there and wrestled in the masculine way. So they taught me how to fight by kicking the living shit out of me."

Wrestling was a family business for the Knights, who operated the World Association of Wrestling promotion and ran regular holiday camp shows around Norwich. In addition to wrestling, Saraya was involved in all facets of the company, from promoting to training.

In 2007, a freak injury nearly spelled the end of her career and simultaneously launched one of her most storied rivalries. Saraya and Cheerleader Melissa were brawling outside the ring when Melissa threw Saraya into a cluster of steel chairs. Saraya came down on a soda can, the jagged edge of which ripped through her knee and severed a tendon. The injury sidelined Saraya for eight months before she was able to return to the ring.

In 2011, she made her U.S. debut with SHIMMER along with her daughter, who was wrestling as Britani Knight. Coincidentally, the duo was managed by Rebecca Knox, who would reunite with Britani four years later in WWE: Britani as Paige and Knox as Becky Lynch.

Saraya quickly found a niche in SHIMMER and settled into a den mother role with the crew backstage, although her personality inside the ring was far from motherly. With her brawling tactics and a unique submission game cultivated on the British circuit, she was completely unlike anyone else on the U.S. independent scene. In October 2011, Saraya turned on her daughter, blaming her for their losing streak as a team, leading to a violent no-DQ bout, which Britani won.

Talking about how her mother influenced her ring psychology, Britani told Steve Austin on his podcast about her mother giving her real punches, before adding: "You're rushing too much, you need to slow down!"

Britani moved on to WWE. While happy for the opportunity presenting itself for her daughter, Saraya admits she had mixed emotions at the time.

"You've got to understand. She isn't just my daughter. She's my best friend. We traveled everywhere together. All of a sudden she's gone, at age 19, off to WWE," Saraya told *Pro Wrestling Illustrated* in a 2014 interview. "I was alone and I was wondering if my career was over. I was quite fearful. I was doing well in SHIMMER and other places, and I thought maybe they just wanted me because they wanted her. I'm older than the rest of the girls and have a different style. Maybe they won't want me anymore."

As it turned out, the exact opposite was the case. Saraya was pushed as SHIMMER's top heel, eventually winning the SHIMMER title from her archrival Cheerleader Melissa in March 2012. She held that title for more than a year until she finally relinquished it to Melissa in a steel cage match in April 2013. That same year, she was ranked number three in the PWI's Female 50. While still competing in her native England and for SHIMMER, she also wrestles for SHINE in Florida. In November 2016, that same style of hers made her a baby-face for the first time since debuting for SHIMMER.

She and her family were featured in a documentary titled *The Wrestlers: Fighting with My Family* produced by England's Channel 4 in 2012. A natural heel in the ring — she could create riots in a heartbeat — she is respected, admired, and beloved by her peers on both sides of the Atlantic. Aside from wrestling, she's in charge on Bellatrix, an all-female promotion in England, and trains the next generation of women wrestlers coming from the U.K.

"She's despicable, she's cheating, she's sneaky, she's vicious, she's calculating, and she's taking her time. I wanted to give her a shout out. She's awesome," said Stone Cold.

# AUSTRALIA

Many Australians have found success in pro wrestling: Sherrie Sinatra and Amy Action in the past, and Emma, Kellie Skater, Shazza McEnzie, Billie Kay, and Peyton Royce in recent years. But only one woman can actually claim to be one of the reasons why.

## Madison Eagles

A native of Sydney, Australia, Madison Eagles has soared all over the wrestling world, collecting championships, praise, and accolades everywhere she lands.

"Madison Eagles is everything a female professional wrestler should be, and is someone who I'm extremely proud to have as SHIMMER champion," said SHIMMER promoter Dave Prazak in 2016. "Madison is a top flight female athlete in every sense of the term. Be it title defenses at SHIMMER against women like Cheerleader Melissa, Ayako Hamada, Mercedes Martinez, MsChif, and Jessie McKay, or facing legends like Manami Toyota in CHIKARA, Madison delivers every time she steps into a wrestling ring."

Born Alexandra Ford on June 5, 1984, she enrolled in the International Wrestling Australia school in 2001. At 6'1", she stood out above the class. She started out playing the bodyguard of wrestler A.J. Freely before wrestling her first match in November 2001.

In 2003, she traveled to the United States for a WWE tryout and put in time training at Ohio Valley Wrestling. She wrestled a few matches on the U.S. independent circuit before returning home to Australia. There, she established a wrestling school and then the all-female Pro Wrestling Women's Alliance in 2007, the first one of the sort in Australia.

"I just wanted to get the girls to do something they had never done before, which is travelling and working with girls they had never worked before," Eagles explained.

In addition to becoming one of the focal points — and eventual champion — of PWWA, Eagles took an active role in training new students, becoming a mentor to the likes of Kellie Skater, Shazza McEnzie, Peyton Royce (K.C. Cassidy), and Billie Kay (Jessie McKay). Skater actually became the first PWWA champion in June 2008 and wound up becoming a regular in Japan and for SHIMMER.

"Being a mother, I never feel jealousy when I see someone I've trained do well. It's more like I'm very proud and really happy," said Eagles. "I'm proud that they were able to do what they wanted, whether it was Jessie and K.C. getting to NXT, Skater wanting to wrestle in

Japan or Shazza coming to SHIMMER."

In 2008, Eagles debuted with SHIMMER, teaming with her protégé, McKay, as the Pink Ladies. But with her hard-hitting style, technical mastery, physical size, and international experience, Eagles quickly moved into singles contention, merging as a top contender for the SHIMMER championship. In April 2010, Eagles defeated MsChif to win the SHIMMER title, which she would hold until October 2011, losing the belt to Cheerleader Melissa.

By virtue of her showing in SHIMMER, Eagles was named number one in

*Madison Eagles won the SHIMMER title twice.*
DAVE PRAZAK/SHIMMER

the 2011 PWI Female 50 ranking, becoming the first non-WWE- or TNA-affiliated talent to top the list.

While based in Australia, she completed tours of the United States, Canada, and Japan, pausing her wrestling long enough to have three children but still managing to quickly return to the ring each time. In October 2014, a feud against her "best frenemy" Nicole Matthews ignited in SHIMMER when Matthews threw a fireball in Eagles face, en route to winning the SHIMMER title in a four-way elimination match also involving Eagles, Matthews, Athena, and champion Cheerleader Melissa.

In October 2015, Eagles won the SHIMMER title a second time, defeating Matthews in a no-DQ bout. She admitted the feeling of winning the title for the second time was different from the feeling of winning it in 2010. "The first time, if I did a poor job, they could just take the belt off me. This time, it's like, 'We know you can do a good job.' There's a lot more pressure this time." A knee injury shortened her second reign; she lost the title in June 2016. Still trying to get as many Australian woman wrestlers as she can ready for big opportunities, she trains Charli Evans and Jessica Troy, who, along with Toni Storm, are considered the best prospects coming from the land down under.

"She's the most influential woman Australia's wrestling has ever seen," praised McEnzie. "She's freaking superwoman!"

# DAVE PRAZAK'S CRAZY IDEA
## *SHIMMER*

In the late 1980s and 1990s, a few women's promotions were established, such as the Ladies Professional Wrestling Association and the Professional Girl Wrestling Association, but neither had staying power. In November 2005, a unique women's wrestling promotion held its first event in a small Eagles Club in the Chicago suburb of Berwyn, Illinois, and it would prove to be the most influential women's promotion in the United States.

Dubbed SHIMMER in honor of the Veruca Salt song "Shimmer Like a Girl," the promotion was the brainchild of Dave Prazak, a Chicago-based wrestling manager and announcer. Prazak had appeared as a manager in IWA Mid-South and Full Impact Pro Wrestling and had managed several prominent wrestlers, including C.M. Punk, Colt Cabana, Adam Pearce, and many others. In his role as a manager, he had feuded with several women on the independent scene and had developed a considerable network of contacts.

In 2003, Prazak took on booking duties for IWA Mid-South's promoter Ian Rotten and began booking the company's women's division, which was centered around Rotten's pupil, Mickie Knuckles.

"I was the one that would call up Lacey or Rain or Traci Brooks or whoever at the time and arrange for them to be there," Prazak said in a 2015 interview on the *PWI Podcast*. "Daizee Haze, MsChif, and Mercedes Martinez were all part of it as well, and eventually Sara Del Rey and Cheerleader Melissa. We had the building blocks in place to do an all-women's show."

In mid-2004, IWA Mid-South presented a women's show to crown its first women's champion. On May 20, 2004, Lacey defeated Martinez and Haze in a three-way match in the finals of the Volcano Girls tournament (another Veruca Salt reference) to win the IWA Mid-South women's title.

Subsequent women's events were planned but never occurred because of financial issues. Prazak eventually split with Rotten and looked to promote a women's show on his own.

"I had a plan to do, essentially, some IWA Mid-South women's division events, perhaps a DVD series of the women's shows, and to do a format where we tape two shows in one day just to get the most out of the plane tickets and gas prices involved," Prazak said. "I left IWA and I had all of these plans, so it was either try to do it myself or completely abandon the idea of having anything to do with women's wrestling. So I decided to give it shot."

Prazak turned to Allison Danger, who was working with him in Ring of Honor, and asked her if she wanted to get involved. Danger quickly agreed to get on board. Veteran Lexie Fyfe joined the roster and eventually assumed a backstage role, assisting Prazak, helping as an agent, and providing feedback to the wrestlers after their matches.

"We didn't know if it would work," Danger said. "I remember going over the booking stuff. We knew from the first day that we were going to get Sara [Del Rey] and Mercedes [Martinez] and bring them together because they were the top of the indies. Other matches looked like they could have been great or they could have been style clashes that just didn't work."

*Dave Prazak with Tomoka Nakagawa and Daizee Haze.* DAVE PRAZAK/SHIMMER

On November 6, 2005, SHIMMER taped its first two DVDs at the Berwyn Eagles Club. This time, a men's match was the special novelty match, as the show kicked off with a battle royal featuring Jimmy Jacobs, Claudio Castagnoli (Cesaro in WWE), Austin Aries, Delirious, and others.

"I made sure when I was doing commentary on the first two DVDs that we didn't reference future shows, because who knew if there were going to be future shows," Prazak said. "We drew maybe 70 people for that show."

While the walk-up was weak, the DVDs proved to be immensely popular. "Immediately, there was a huge demand to buy the thing," Prazak said. "ROH [a promotion that also relied heavily on DVD sales for revenue] said the DVD was selling more rapidly than anything they had released on their website since Samoa Joe versus Kenta Kobashi. It's still a niche product. You're only going to draw a few hundred fans to a live event. But there's a worldwide audience willing to watch the product after the fact on video."

"SHIMMER is very important for my career, but mostly SHIMMER is important for the world of female wrestling," said Cheerleader Melissa. "For me especially, it gave me the opportunity of being the best wrestler that I can possibly be and to work with other top talent that I would've never ever normally got to work with under normal circumstances. SHIMMER also helped the development of Cheerleader Melissa, especially character-wise. So I do owe a lot of my career to SHIMMER."

The success of SHIMMER also helped inspire other women's promotions, including Women Superstars Uncensored in New Jersey, SHINE in Florida, Bellatrix in England, and NCW Femmes Fatales in Montreal. The rise of women's wrestling on the independents began to change the perception of women's wrestling in general. With WWE showcasing models and TNA featuring three-minute women's matches as filler on national television, SHIMMER helped show audiences that women could wrestle competitive and exciting 10-, 15-, and 20-minute-plus matches and could still attract a paying audience.

"We helped open the eyes of independent wrestling promoters to the idea of having the women on their shows in a match that was more than the first match after intermission that goes for five minutes, the popcorn match," Prazak said. "Actually having the female wrestlers on the card in a key spot, having a lengthy match that actually mattered and utilizing that talent for more than just putting them on a poster because they look good. If we had a hand in opening up more opportunities for the wrestlers on other cards during the subsequent years, then fantastic. Then we actually contributed something to the wrestling industry. Then it was all worth it. All the headaches and sleepless nights of taping weekends were worth it."

In October 2015, SHIMMER celebrated its 10th anniversary with the tapings of DVD Volumes 78 and 79. Over its first 10 years, SHIMMER has grown to feature female wrestlers from all over the world, including Japan, the United Kingdom, and Australia, as well as throughout the United States and Canada. Several women moved on from SHIMMER to fame and fortune in WWE, including Beth Phoenix (who wrestled at the first DVD tapings), Natalya Neidhart (Natalya), Britani Knight (Paige) and Davina Rose (Bayley). Others, like Athena (Ember Moon) and Mary Dobson, started with NXT, while Courtney Rush (Rosemary), Cherry Bomb (Allie), and Allysin Kay (Sienna) all work for TNA. And the next ones to make the jump to either of those promotions could very well be the likes of Candice LeRae, Kimber Lee, Nicole Savoy, or Evie.

Without a doubt, a case could be made that the first shots of the 2015 WWE Women's Revolution were actually fired at the Berwyn Eagles Club a decade before.

# THE WOMEN OF THE INDEPENDENTS

With women's wrestling stagnating on the national stage in the post-Stratus era, a number of talented women began capturing attention on the independent circuit, and their work helped to take women's wrestling to new heights.

### Allison Danger

The first time Cathy Corino walked into the ring, she was a last-minute substitute, volunteering for a valet spot in an independent show. By the time she hung up her boots because of injuries 13 years later, she had become one of the most influential female wrestlers of her generation and a cofounder of a promotion that launched the careers of several women who went on to worldwide acclaim.

Born March 31, 1977, in Winnipeg, Manitoba, Corino grew up in Trappe, Pennsylvania, just outside of Philadelphia. An athlete through childhood, she played hockey, field hockey, and softball and ran track. Her first exposure to wrestling came through her brother, Steve, who was a huge fan growing up. Steve went on to become a professional wrestler, debuting in 1994 and going on to find fame in ECW, the NWA, and Ring of Honor.

Cathy became friends with members of the ECW roster through Steve. When the Sandman's wife and usual valet was unable to attend an event in Reading, Pennsylvania, in May 2000, Cathy was asked to fill in and accompany the Singapore cane–wielding hardcore hero to the ring.

*SHIMMER co-founder Allison Danger.* DAVE PRAZAK/SHIMMER

It was an experience that changed her life. "It's so hard to say what it is, but there's this feeling you get when you walk through that curtain and the music is going, the lights are going, people are yelling. It's intoxicating," Corino said. Right there, I was hooked. I knew this was for me. From that very first time, it felt like home."

She began training under Mike Kehner and Rapid Fire Maldonado in Boyerton, Pennsylvania, and made her debut as a wrestler under the ring name Allison Danger. In 2003, Danger joined ROH as the valet for several characters, including the Christopher Street Connection and Christopher Daniels's stable, the Prophecy, one of the top acts in ROH. Danger said she learned a valuable lesson working with Daniels.

"He told me to work on my game face," Danger said. "He said he could look at my face and see everything that was going on in my mind — whether I was happy or sad or nervous or whatever. When that happens, the fans can tell when you're nervous. That's when you lose control. The people aren't supposed to control us; we control them. We play on their emotions. They don't get to play on ours."

She eventually split with the Prophecy and launched into a feud against former Prophecy members B.J. Whitmer and Dan Maff.

In addition to valeting, Danger was actively wrestling outside ROH, including a tour of Japan and subsequent tours of Europe. On her travels, she came upon a traditional Japanese Noh mask, an ivory white face with an implacable expression. Perhaps as a reminder of Daniels's advice, she began wearing it to the ring.

"I never fit that typical Diva, sex kitten aspect of wrestling. Once I got to a point in my career where I realized that's not me and stopped trying to fit that mold, I started to think what are some of the coolest things that set people apart?" Danger said. "I saw that mask, and I thought how creepy would that be? How it would look under the lights. My music hits, I come through, and it's that face they see. Everything is dark and the lights hit that face. That's going to draw people in in a way that I normally couldn't, getting that creepiness factor. When I realized I couldn't be the sex symbol or the buxom blonde, I realized I had to celebrate what made me different, and what made me different will make me interesting and will make me marketable."

In the fall of 2005, Danger received a call from Dave Prazak, who was looking to expand his Volcano Girls events from IWA Mid-South into a stand-alone women's promotion he called SHIMMER. Both Prazak and Danger had ties in ROH; between them, they had a network of talented female wrestlers at their disposal. Danger took the offer.

"I wanted to branch out into other parts of wrestling, other than competing and valeting," Danger said. "We didn't know if it would work. Now, here we are 10 years later, and SHIMMER is still going strong."

Danger competed at the first SHIMMER event, defeating Beth Phoenix on November 6, 2005. In addition to her backstage duties of helping book and organize the show, Danger continued to compete and remained a cornerstone of the promotion.

Her dream of wrestling for WWE never materialized. "I was told straight out to get my tits done. Lose 20 pounds and get my tits done.

Then WWE would be interested in me," she said. "It was never anything demeaning or anything insulting. They were just being honest with me, and I respected them for it. At that time, that's what WWE was looking for — less athletic women and more models. That's what they wanted. I was not that girl."

While others may have gone in for the breast augmentation surgery, Corino chose not to. "I felt like, for me, there would always be that dark cloud of 'Did I get here because I was talented or did I get here because I dropped the six grand on a boob job?' I needed to know, for me, that I made it because I was talented," she said.

In addition to wrestling for SHIMMER, Danger competed on the independent circuit, winning the World Xtreme Wrestling tag team title (with Alere Little Feather), the Pro Wrestling World-1 women's title, and the International Catch Wrestling Association women's title, among others.

However, Corino's in-ring career would come to a premature end. In January 2013, she suffered a stroke. Doctors found lesions on her brain, likely exacerbated by years of bumps and headshots. The brain injuries were potentially life threatening. Having had a baby girl just a couple years earlier, the decision was simple. She retired from wrestling in April 2013.

Corino says she still suffers effects from her wrestling career. She actively encourages younger wrestlers to be aware of the dangers of concussions.

"I'm going to be 40 years old and it's hard for me to get out of bed some days. I don't remember walking without a limp. The other day, I went to get into a car and couldn't figure out why it was locked. The driver of the car looked at me and I realized I was at the wrong car. I have these little blips where my speech gets a little messed up. I forget where I parked my car," she said.

"I didn't have medical insurance for most of my career. When I got concussions, [the thought] was once you feel better get back in there. I didn't want to miss time on the road. Now I'm paying the price for it. Now my brain is mush. Last night, I couldn't walk up a flight of stairs to tuck my daughter into bed because my right leg went out on me. I have piriformis syndrome [a condition where the piriformis muscle behind the buttocks causes pressure on the sciatic nerve]. I actually have to get my ass Botoxed to release it, to paralyze it, so I can start moving pain-free."

Ironically, the athletic, fast-moving style that Danger helped popularize on the independents and in SHIMMER became fashionable in WWE after Danger retired because of health issues. Now an RPM indoor cycling instructor, Corino currently lives with her husband, Marco Jaggi (who wrestled under the name Ares) and their daughter, Kendall Grace. She remains active with SHIMMER, where she serves as co-booker and default den mother to the roster.

She said she still wonders about her legacy in wrestling now that her in-ring days have ended.

"I want to hope that I helped put the current style of wrestling on the map, that I was a part of it. Since I retired one of the things I struggle with to this day is the feeling that wrestling has passed me by and that I've been forgotten. That's one of the hardest things for me to deal with, to wonder if I did this all in vain. Then I go to SHIMMER and these other shows and I have these young girls who come up to me and say, 'You're why I do this, I still watch your tapes.' And I realize, oh man, even after everything is done, I still have the ability to touch the occasional person. That's such a good feeling."


## Mercedes Martinez

Mercedes Martinez's career has been marked by her dedication to her craft and her refusal to compromise her ideals and values. The tattoo she bears on her midsection concisely sums up her mentality: "Only God Can Judge Me."

"Mercedes Martinez, the wrestler, is not far from who I am in real life," said Martinez. "I speak my mind. I don't sugar-coat things. My style has never changed in 16 years. Strong style, technical wrestling. That's who I am and that's what I want people to see from me."

*"The Latina Sensation" Mercedes Martinez.*
DAVE PRAZAK/SHIMMER

Born Jasmine Benitez on November 17, 1980, in Waterbury, Connecticut in the shadow of WWF headquarters in Stamford, she was a wrestling fan from childhood and was captivated by the larger-than-life personalities of Hulk Hogan, Randy Savage, and the Big Bossman. "I was the middle child out of five kids," she said. "I watched wrestling with my uncle and my brothers. Wrestling was big with them. Growing up, I followed it. I roughhoused with my brothers and wrestled in the backyard with them and the neighbors. Of course, I never for a moment thought that I was going to be a professional wrestler."

Somewhat surprisingly for a woman who has eschewed the T&A approach to women's wrestling, she became a fan of *GLOW* in the late 1980s, even though the terms "strong style" or "technical" could never be applied to the *Gorgeous Ladies of Wrestling*. But, for Martinez, it was empowering to see women given characters like the men and promoted on television. A star basketball player in high school, she went on to play collegiately at Teikyo Post University, where she studied criminal justice, but an injury forced her off of the hardwood. That's when she heard about Jason Knight's pro wrestling school that had recently opened nearby. "I started training to try to get back into shape [for basketball]," she said. "Wrestling just fell into my lap. I guess I was pretty good at it."

So good, in fact, that she wrestled her first match barely one month after beginning her training in 2000. She caught the bug and left basketball for wrestling. Knight gave her the ring name Mercedes Martinez. "Honestly, I don't think he really gave it much thought," she said. "He basically said Mercedes was a luxury car and not a lot of people could see it, so it was something they wanted. 'Now, you are Mercedes; something people will want to see and want to get, but can only see from afar.' Here's your name, now go out there and work, that's all there was to it."

She competed in promotions throughout New England, including Sheldon Goldberg's New England Championship Wrestling and Ian Rotten's IWA Mid-South. SHIMMER promoter Dave Prazak was impressed with what he saw and brought Martinez in to headline SHIMMER's first event, facing Sara Del Rey in 2005. Martinez and Del Rey wrestled a 20-minute draw. Ring of Honor brought her in as part of the Vulture Squad stable, starting a rivalry with Lacey.

In 2006, Martinez was brought in for a look by WWE, wrestling Victoria in her tryout match. "I was told to revamp myself," she said, in reference to the feedback the WWE agents provided following that match. "My style was too aggressive for them — too hardcore, too strong-style. I had to tone it down and we could go from there. I didn't want to water down myself and be something they wanted me to be when I knew what I was capable of at that time."

So Martinez said thanks but no thanks and went back to the independents. "I don't regret turning them down because what they wanted wasn't right for me," she said. "If what's going on now [a greater emphasis on athleticism and workrate] had happened 10 years ago, I believe I would have been there."

Sean McCaffrey had purchased Women Superstars Uncensored and was looking to restructure the company. He brought in Martinez as one of his top attractions and also as booker. One of her most memorable bouts in WSU was a 71-minute bout against Angel Orsini in 2009, a match that originally had been conceived as a 30-minute Iron Woman match. "Iron Women's matches at that time were usually 30 minutes. We thought, we can do that, that's easy. Let's give the fans something they haven't seen, something that's never been done. We ended up going more than 70 minutes," she said. "At that time, there hadn't been anything like it. We were only supposed to go a little more than an hour. We went out there and beat the hell out of each other and let it all out. When you have the crowd behind you and you have enough gas in the tank, you just keep going until you can't go any more." In 2011, she beat her own record when she went 73 minutes against Lexxus (Alexxis Nevaeh) in what is considered the longest match in women's wrestling history.

Martinez has been one of the most decorated women on the indie circuit, winning such titles as the IWA Mid-South women's title, the IndyGurlz Australia title, the NCW Femmes Fatales title, the WSU title (twice), and the World Xtreme Wrestling women's title (four times). In 2011, she was named number two in the PWI Female 50, behind Cheerleader Melissa.

In 2014, she quietly retired from wrestling but returned in a big way in 2016, winning the SHIMMER title for the very first time against Madison Eagles. On November 12, she lost it to Kellie Skater, only to win it back the following night, making her a rare, two-time SHIMMER champion.

"Her work, talent and attitude always pushed the promoters to give her an important role in the company," said former NCW Femmes Fatales promoter Stephane Bruyere. "What she did for WSU is huge. She helped bring notoriety to the company and was the source of a few partnerships, including with Femmes Fatales. She's one of the best female wrestlers, if not the best, who was never signed by one of the main wrestling companies."

## Malia Hosaka

Malia Hosaka may be the most well-traveled female wrestler of the past 30 years . . . and not just because she works as a flight attendant outside of the ring.

Hosaka has competed in just about every major promotion in the

United States over the past 30 years and has made tours of Europe, Japan, Egypt, Turkey, Guam, Puerto Rico, and Uzbekistan, to name a few. Although she was billed as hailing from Osaka, Japan, she was born on October 7, 1969, in Honolulu, Hawaii, her heritage being half Japanese and half American.

Some women took up wrestling because they were fans as kids. Hosaka not only was not a fan, she actively disliked wrestling . . . at first. "My dad was a huge fan. I hated it. I thought it was the stupidest thing on TV," she said. "I watched a match between the Missing Link and Bugsy McGraw and I laughed my ass off. I told my dad that anybody could do that. He said, 'I bet you couldn't.' And I said 'I bet I could.'"

*Former NWA world women's champion Malia Hosaka.* MALIA HOSAKA COLLECTION

She went to train primarily under the legendary Killer Kowalski, and two months before her 18th birthday, she wrestled in her first match. After working for the LPWA, FMA in Japan, and ECW, she defeated Debbie Combs in 1996 for the NWA women's title, only to lose it back to Combs the following day. She also had the opportunity to wrestle against greats such as Leilani Kai and Luna Vachon, both of whom made a lasting impact on her career.

"Luna taught me to take every crazy bump that was out there, mostly by giving it to me," Hosaka said. "But she knew what she was doing. She protected me. She would say, 'We're going in the stands' and I would just follow her. I trusted her. She taught me, no matter where you go, how to protect yourself in taking the bumps and giving the fans your all.

"Leilani would not give me the start of the match. The referee would come over to pat me down and say, 'Leilani said to go dropkick her,' so I'd run across the ring and here we go. They taught me to learn to listen on the fly and to feed to them."

When WCW decided to build a women's division, Hosaka was brought in for matches against Kai, Madusa, and Akira Hokuto. "What I was told when I was there was that Madusa really wanted the Japanese girls in there to work with. She didn't think there were any American girls out there worth working with, and she was all about Japan, Japan, Japan," Hosaka said. "I think I was a way for them to bring in a Japanese girl without the expense of bringing in someone from a Japanese company."

In 1999, she got the shot of a lifetime: an offer from the WWF. She debuted on the June 28, 1999, edition of *Monday Night Raw* as a ringside fan who answered an open challenge from Ivory, the women's champion. It was supposed to be the start of a major underdog storyline, but it never got off the ground.

She went back to the indies but briefly resurfaced in TNA in 2003. In 2006, she debuted in SHIMMER, where she teamed with fellow veteran Lexie Fyfe as the Experience. When she left SHIMMER, a pair of herniated discs in her back made her consider retirement. "The doctor said one more bad fall and I'm paralyzed," she said. "Brandi Wine told me to get back in the ring because I was still riding dirt bikes and flipping over the handlebars. She said, if you can do that, you can get back in the ring, and I need a tag team partner."

Hosaka returned and teamed with Wine to win the SHINE tag team title in 2014, one of more than a dozen independent titles she has collected in her three decades in the game. Still active, Hosaka admits that her candor has cost her some opportunities, but she makes no apologies. "I made enemies. Definitely. I don't play politics," she said. "If you give me a horrible match, I'm going to tell you it's a horrible match."

## Lexie Fyfe

"If I hadn't ended up as a wrestler, I would probably have gone into musical theater."

For Lexie Fyfe, the appeal of pro wrestling lies in the blend of athleticism and theater. For an athlete and an extrovert like Fyfe, the wrestling ring presented a natural stage. Born May 30, 1969, Mary Beth Bentley grew up in Denville, New Jersey, and attended Elon College in Elon, North Carolina. She was introduced to the world of independent wrestling by a coworker who was training to become a wrestler and working as a valet under the name Brandi Wine. Brandi invited Bentley to a show that changed her life.

"I have never been a shy person, and I'm usually the person at the party who's doing the goofiest stuff or talking the most," she said. "At the same time, I liked to lift weights and ride mountain bikes, so wrestling kind of combined both of those elements for me."

Bentley enrolled in Ken Spence's wrestling school in Winston-Salem in April 1995, making her pro debut later that year. She continued training under Spence for about a year, then continued her training at OMEGA Championship Wrestling with Matt and Jeff Hardy. There, she learned more about the psychology behind a solid wrestling match.

She also made several visits to Johnny Rodz's wrestling school in New York to add more variety to her training. She supplemented her wrestling income with bartending jobs that could accommodate her unorthodox schedule. Known as the Foxy Lady, her signature move was "the attitude adjuster," a version of the TKO cutter.

Fyfe wrestled actively from 1995 until 2010, when she took time off from the ring to have a child. She won the Professional Girl Wrestling Association title in 2001 and the NWA women's title in 2005. She also held several other independent championships in the Mid-Atlantic region. One of her frequent rivals was Leilani Kai, who became one of her mentors.

*One of the most well-respected vets on the indie scene, Lexie Fyfe.* DAVE PRAZAK/SHIMMER

"Leilani Kai probably had the most impact on my early career, as far as helping me become the wrestler that I ended up being," she said. "She taught me so much in my early days. I wouldn't have grown like I did without her."

Fyfe was part of the first SHIMMER taping in November 2005 (she defeated Christie Ricci). She formed a tag team with Malia Hosaka known as the Experience; the team was positioned as the wily veterans on the roster. In addition to competing, Fyfe also took on a backstage role in SHIMMER, working as an agent, coach, and adviser. At most tapings, she's positioned in front of a monitor backstage. After every match, the wrestlers go to Lexie for feedback, suggestions, and a critique of their matches. It's an indication of the respect Fyfe was given by her peers.

On April 21, 2008, Fyfe landed one of the most unique gigs of her wrestling career. She appeared on *WWE Raw* as Hillary Clinton and wrestled "Barack Obama" (portrayed by wrestler Deon Davis) in a match spoofing the Democratic primary, the McMahons being well known Republicans.

In 2004, she and her husband created SLAMmin Promotions, an

online wrestling promotion where fans were able to download matches or to order custom matches featuring an array of female wrestlers.

When asked about sex appeal in women's wrestling, Fyfe again compares wrestling to theater and other forms of popular entertainment.

"I think sexuality does play a role in mainstream wrestling for the casual fans. They see a sexy-looking chick and might stick around for the match whether the wrestling is good or not. I think the more hardcore fans or 'pure' wrestling fans don't care about it as much," Fyfe said. "That being said, it helps if you look good and are in shape, whether you are a male or female wrestler, unless you find a gimmick that fits your look. Remember, it is theater. You need to treat it as such."

When SHINE began operations in 2012, Fyfe became a babyface authority figure in the company. She assists backstage and helps the wrestlers coordinate their travel in and out of Tampa, where she lives and where SHINE is based.

"I had 15 years active, followed by five more years [and counting] in other facets of the business. It's hard to pick one greatest memory," Fyfe said. "I still remember walking through the curtains for the first time. I had some wonderful times on the military tours I did, meeting and entertaining the soldiers. And the first time I got out in front of a crowd of more than 1,000 people and got them all to boo me. That was an awesome feeling."

## THE WORLD OF CUSTOMS

Women's wrestling has been described as a niche product, but like any niche product, it attracts its share of superfans and passionate devotees.

Some of these dedicated followers take their fandom to the next level through the trend of custom wrestling, where fans can play pro wrestling booker and order custom-made matches featuring their choice of women competing in a match the buyer can help lay out.

The scope and variety of custom matches is expansive, ranging from fetish-style catfight companies to companies that present only trained pro wrestlers competing in traditional matches. The fetish companies usually have no connections to the wrestling business, utilizing models and amateurs in matches designed purely to arouse the viewer.

However, companies like SLAMminLadies, run by Lexie Fyfe and her husband, avoid the fetish market and offer traditional matches, filmed inside a ring in a studio without fans. "We are not a catfighting or bikini wrestling site. There are plenty of those who are happy to cater to that style and do a good job of it. Please do not bother to ask us," reads a disclaimer on the SLAMminLadies website.

Customers can provide an outline of a match and select the wrestlers they would like. They may also request specific moves, gear (e.g., traditional wrestling gear, barefoot, or one-piece bathing suits), and other details; the wrestlers have the ability to agree to do the match or turn it down. Matches are taped, and the customers are sent a one-of-a-kind DVD of a match they have laid out, allowing them to play booker and create their own dream matches.

Custom matches can be a lucrative enterprise for women at the independent level. Custom matches also typically feature fewer high-risk bumps than matches performed in front of an audience, so they are usually safer and less physically demanding, allowing wrestlers to tape several custom bouts during the course of one day.

The cost depends on the length of the match requested, whether it is a singles match or tag team match, whether the match includes a referee, and other factors. Prices can vary between $100 and $600 per match for SLAMminLadies custom orders.

Although privately produced custom matches date back more than 70 years, custom matches are frequently misunderstood, according to Fyfe, especially because of their interactive nature, the overall secrecy that surrounds them (being privately taped and custom-made for the buyer), and the customer's ability to request that matches include fetishized content (such as wrestlers competing barefoot or matches heavy on hair-pulling or kicks to the groin, for example).

"I think there is still a stigma attached to customs, although it has become more accepted over the years," Fyfe said. "Most people don't realize that custom wrestling started back in the Mildred Burke days. There are 8 mm films of the matches she produced still out there. After that, it did become a little more fetish-oriented with a lot of catfighting companies opening up. When I broke into the business in the mid-1990s, there was a mixture of both. You had to know what companies to work with and who to stay away from.

"I pride myself in the fact that SLAMminLadies is a very pro style company," she said. "I think that almost everyone has a positive experience with us and feels comfortable working here. It started out as just a way to make some extra money on the road after the influx of women wrestlers caused the pay to go downhill. It blossomed into a decent business, so I've stuck with it."

For Mia Yim, customs are a good way to earn extra money, and they aren't a seedy business like some people might assume. "I do customs for the money," Yim said. "It's easy and less strenuous than actual shows. We also have a lot of fun with it, as we can joke around with each other.

"Customs get a bad rep because there are plenty of sketchy custom companies," she continued. "I've been asked to do bikini customs or bedroom stuff, which I always turn down. People judge and I have to explain what real customs are, but it doesn't bother me. I know what I'm doing and I always say no when [someone asks for] something that I'm not comfortable with."

★ ★ ★

###  Cheerleader Melissa

Wrestling has always been close to Melissa Anderson's heart. She grew up watching her father, Doug Anderson, perform, and she knew it was something she wanted to try. Born August 17, 1982, she attended high school in Palmdale, California, and joined the school's soccer and wrestling teams. When her father's tag team partner, Bill Anderson (unrelated, although she has always considered him her uncle), opened a wrestling school in San Bernardino, she felt compelled to get in the ring and give it a try, beginning her training at age 15.

"I liked it right away," she said. "At the time, I didn't think that I'd be able to travel the world doing it. I just liked the athleticism of wrestling, the fact that it was a contact sport and you could come off the ropes and fly. And I had grown up watching my dad and uncle do it. It was only natural that I would love it."

She wrestled her first match in August 1999, balancing her school work with training and wrestling shows on the weekends. She became a manager, working with Shannon and Shane Ballard, who were using a hockey-themed gimmick based on the Hanson Brothers from the movie *Slap Shot*. Melissa became their cheerleader, and "Cheerleader Melissa" was born. "I thought it would be for a short period of time," she said. "I realized very quickly that in the field of sports entertainment, that the name Melissa wasn't marketable — it wasn't catchy and not getting people's attention at all. So I had to suck it up and dig out my skirt again and go 'Damn!' because I really thought it would only be a phase and it sure backfired on me."

She worked around California with the Ballards, including a stint in All Pro Wrestling, where she received additional coaching from Christopher Daniels and Daniel Bryan. In 2002, she was invited to tour Japan with the ARSION promotion. On her 20th birthday, she was given the honor of wrestling against legendary Japanese wrestler Lioness Asuka. Being put in the ring with such a well-respected veteran demonstrated that the ARSION matchmakers respected Melissa's talent.

"From the very beginning of my training, I made a point to move around the ring like the guys. Footwork, the bumps, everything," Melissa said. "I wanted to pay attention to the little details. I learned that wrestling isn't just about the execution of the move, but it's also about what you do before and after the move, too. All of that matters."

That attention to detail was appreciated in Japan and began to attract attention in the United States, as well. In 2004, the Cauliflower Alley Club awarded her its Future Legend award, a sign that the insiders in the CAC expected big things from the California cheerleader.

She became a staple of ChickFight, which started as an eight-woman tournament presented by APW and grew into a stand-alone women's promotion. She won the tournament in 2006 and 2007. ChickFight closed in 2008 but was resurrected for a 2015 ChickFight tournament featuring SHIMMER talent. Melissa again advanced to a three-way finals bout that saw Kay Lee Ray defeat her and Evie.

With ChickFight attracting attention on the West Coast, Melissa joined SHIMMER when the company opened in 2005. She competed in the first 60 SHIMMER

*2013 PWI Female 50's #1 wrestler, Cheerleader Melissa.*
GILDA PASQUIL/SHIMMER

events; she was forced to settle for a run-in at Volume 61 after being sent to the hospital for stitches after a match against LuFisto earlier in the day. Frustrated at being unable to compete in the later tapings, she sped from the hospital back to the Berwyn Eagles Club, arriving just in time to surprise the fans with a run-in during the main event, joining Mercedes Martinez for a beatdown of LuFisto.

Melissa became the first two-time SHIMMER champion, winning the title in October 2011 and regaining it in April 2013. She was named number one in the 2013 PWI Female 50, which deemed her the top woman wrestler in the world for that year.

While Melissa made her name on the independents and internationally, she also flirted with both WWE and TNA. In 2005, she was penciled in to debut as an Arabic character in a stable with Muhammad Hassan and Khosrow Daivari, but the storyline was abruptly dropped, largely because of sensitivities following Islamic terrorist attacks in London in July 2005. In 2008, she debuted in TNA in a similar role, wearing a niqab and billed as Raisha Saeed, the manager of Awesome Kong. As Saeed, Melissa wrestled occasionally, but she mostly served as Kong's manager and mouthpiece.

Signing an accomplished wrestler and putting her in a mostly non-wrestling role was a curious decision. Taking a woman as attractive as Melissa and covering her head to toe in a burka simply made no sense whatsoever. Eventually, someone at TNA realized that. Since Melissa was doing so well in her role as Saeed, they wanted her to continue, but they asked her to do double duty. Melissa debuted a new persona, Alissa Flash, in 2009. Wearing stylized face paint as a tribute to Sherri Martel, Flash was a new inception of the Melissa character, but after a wild feud with Ayako Hamada, she was rarely used. Frustrated with the experience, Melissa requested her release from TNA in 2010.

"My time in TNA was a really good learning experience," she said. "It was my first time consistently working for a large company on television [she had previously wrestled dark matches for both WWE and TNA]. When you get out of training, you don't necessarily learn about things like maintaining and protecting an image or TV time and commercial breaks. I got to learn and understand those things in TNA."

In 2014, she was named president of Stardom's American branch and put in charge of booking American talent for the Japanese promotion. In her work with Stardom, she has had many conversations with the Stardom commissioner, Madusa Miceli, a person Melissa considers a kindred spirit.

"When I talk to Madusa, I sometimes feel like I'm talking to a version of myself from the future. We've had so many of the same experiences," she said. "When she worked for some of the bigger companies, she would struggle because she had trained in Japan with that style. She would wrestle and the men would be pissed that they had to follow her. I was like, 'Oh God, you too?'"

In 2016, she joined *Lucha Underground* as the masked Mariposa. Even though the promotion falls into the same pattern as TNA as far as putting her under a hood, she is excited for what the future holds. "*Lucha Underground* is breaking all sorts of rules and breaking new ground for females," she said. "I think we're on the verge of a huge breakthrough in women's wrestling across the board, in WWE, in *Lucha Underground*, in TNA. I just wish . . . damn, why didn't this happen a few years ago when I was a few years younger!"

Even with so many fans throughout the world, her biggest is probably her dad.

"She's done more than I ever came close to doing," said Doug Anderson. "She's more talented than I was and more gutsy. The wrestler in me is a little bit envious, but the daddy is really proud."

## LuFisto

Once she's done with wrestling, LuFisto will be remembered as one of the better female talents of the past 20 years never to be signed by one of the main wrestling organizations. There may be reasons for that, but her workrate, her wrestling skills, her presence, her understanding of the business, and her passion are not among them.

Through her work in Nashville for promoter Bert Prentice, she had talks with WCW in 2000, even being invited to a show in Kitchener, Ontario. But so much was going on with WCW at that moment that it didn't go any further. In 2009, in the midst of the upcoming TNA Knockout Tag Team championship tournament, she was in talks with Terry Taylor and very close to being signed when Hulk Hogan and Eric Bischoff came on the scene and, simply put, weren't enthusiastic about her. "I had heard that I wasn't looking enough like the Beautiful People," LuFisto said.

She also celebrated her 15th year in pro wrestling by having a tryout with TNA on June 23, 2012. She tried to enter both TNA's Gut Check

*LuFisto knocked down the Ontario Athletic Commission in 2006.* GILDA PASQUIL/SHIMMER

challenge and the most recent version of WWE's *Tough Enough,* both without success even though she was one of the most popular wrestlers in fan voting. Nevertheless, she had and still has an international career, something not everyone can put on their resume.

Born Geneviève Goulet in Sorel, Quebec, on February 15, 1980, her interest in wrestling was sparked when she saw performers like Bull Nakano, Manami Toyota, and Akira Hokuto on tape. But Goulet had an idol in Montreal too. "It was Luna Vachon, because of her look, how solid she was in the ring and her way of involving the crowd. She was a heel, but I loved her!" After having been coached by Pierre Marchessault and Patrick Lewis, she met former local wrestler Lise Raymond. "Mulling over that today, I can say that meeting her was more than crucial. Lise Raymond told me to stand tall, fight for my ideas and never to allow the wrestlers who didn't want women in their world demean me. She even told me that it was better to be a bitch and secure one's spot than to get along with them, that wrestling's a cut-throat profession and that I should always keep my head held high in order to be considered a serious wrestler," she relates.

This is exactly what Goulet did. Under the name Precious Lucy at first, and later under the name LuFisto, she's wrestled across the

Montreal territory, Ontario, British Columbia, the United States, Mexico, Europe, and Japan. After having adopted a very popular extreme style in the late 1990s and early 2000s, the wrestler, who was then nicknamed the First Lady of Hardcore, was rewarded for her choice. She was invited to participate in some extreme wrestling shows in Mexico for Lucha Libre Femenil. Moreover, in 2003 she went to Japan for a two-month tour, training with the likes of Sara Del Rey and Kana.

"I didn't intend to do extreme wrestling. I was given the opportunity to do it in a match and I saw it as a way of trying new things and challenging my own limits. I also wanted to prove, one more time, that girls were capable of being as good at this as the guys were. Finally it allowed me to make a name for myself, be different and contribute a new style to female wrestling," relates the wrestler, who has been coached over the years by Len Shelley and the Proulx brothers, as well.

"She's worked hard to get where she is," noted WWE's Kevin Owens. A regular with SHIMMER and SHINE, LuFisto has also worked for most of the biggest independent federations in the United States, including CZW, PWG, WSU, and ROH. In 2014, she was voted fifth in the PWI Female 50, her highest ranking to date. In Quebec she's considered almost a demi-goddess by other female wrestlers. Many among them chose to become wrestlers because of her, and they are often awestruck when they get to work with their hero. Furthermore, Goulet has taken many young women from Quebec, the rest of Canada, and from the U.S. under her wing over the years and helped them improve and develop. She's also very popular with the Quebec media and is seen by many experts as the best female wrestler to come from Montreal after Vivian and Luna Vachon. "When I discovered LuFisto . . . she was wrestling for CZW, blood pouring out of her beautiful face, no fear in her eyes. I was mesmerized by her strength, ability, and passion," wrote Ontario independent wrestler Kaitlin Diemond in a SLAM! Wrestling column. Now residing in the United States, Goulet wrestles all over North America and is in charge of Rogue Women's Warriors in Stevens, Pennsylvania.

# THE BATTLE OF THE SEXES: MEN VS. WOMEN

On September 20, 1973, in Houston, Texas, 30,472 fans were at the Astrodome that Thursday night and 90 million more were in front of their TVs to watch a tennis match, but not your average match. The number two female player in the world, 29-year-old Billie Jean King, was facing a former number one male player, 55-year-old Bobby Riggs.

The Battle of the Sexes was on. After falling behind in the first set, King rallied and, against all odds (literally since many bookies in Las Vegas lost tons of money), won in three straight sets. The proof was there: women could actually compete with — and even beat — men in a sporting event.

Seven years later, on Thanksgiving Day, 1980, in Atlanta, Georgia, a capacity crowd of 12,000 people at the Omni witnessed something most thought they would never see: a tag match between two men and two women. Not your regular mixed tag, either; two women were pitted against two men as part of a tag team tournament.

"On the surface, I wasn't crazy about it, but I came up with an idea that I thought might draw some money," booker Ole Anderson said in his 2003 autobiography. "It was an idea similar to the tennis match between Billie Jean King and Bobby Riggs in 1973. . . . I used that as an example. I was just trying to create a little interest."

Men vs. women in pro wrestling had existed forever. It was present at the end of the 19th century and in the first part of the 20th century, before women were banned from wrestling in several states. But the 1980 match was the first to gain so much publicity in the modern era. Several other promoters were strongly against it and made sure Anderson knew they didn't like it.

"When Verne [Gagne] heard that I put the girls in the tournament with the men, he was really ticked off at me," Anderson wrote. "He called and said, 'Boy, talk about exposing the business. How in the hell can the girls wrestle with the men?" But Ole wouldn't back down.

The match would see Steve O and Jerry Roberts (Jacques Rougeau Jr.) against the team of Joyce Grable and Judy Martin. The most experienced worker there was Grable, who was 27 and had been wrestling for many years. Martin was in her first year, while Steve O and Rougeau had only a few years of experience between the two of them. The match was announced in October and was allowed some time on television in order to promote it. In an interview with Jeff Leen, Grable recalled having fun during interviews.

"I would say, 'Every time you men walk in a courtroom, we women take everything you make, we get everything you worked your life for.' All the men just hated me. I loved it."

The same enthusiasm wasn't shared on the men's side, especially by Rougeau, who really didn't want to do the match but was forced by Ole.

"I definitely didn't like the idea of wrestling against girls," Rougeau recalled. "I'm sure I didn't like the idea because where do you want me to put my hands? Where would you want me to put my hands on her? Can't touch her ass, can't touch her, you know, so, no. I'm just trying to think — if she grabs a headlock on you, you've got her tits in your face."

Thanks to the buildup and the novelty of it, the crowd was really excited for the match the night of the show. As far as the match itself, plenty of false finishes and good wrestling made it exciting to watch. The men won the match, but everyone was pleased afterward, including Rougeau.

"When he treated us as equals, we could really get out there and wrestle. That's when he saw, well, goodness, they can wrestle," said Martin.

The level of respect had grown between the two teams, and a rematch was scheduled for Christmas Day in Columbus, Georgia, which was even better than the first one because of the newly developed trust the four individuals had for each other. Even in losing, Grable and Martin were praised for their performance and gained a lot of respect from their peers, both men and women.

Ole's crazy idea of a wrestling version of the Battle of the Sexes had paid off. However, men against women didn't become a regular act after that. Seen as a gimmick match, it worked in small doses, like any novelty. Twenty-three years later, the same year that Trish Stratus and Lita wrestled against Chris Jericho and Christian on a WWE PPV, a young woman from Sorel, Quebec, would become a pioneer in her own right by pinning down an entire athletic commission for her rights to wrestle men.

In April 2003, Geneviève Goulet, under her wrestling name of LuFisto, was scheduled in Toronto, Ontario, for an inter-gender hardcore tag team match. But some time before it, she got an email letting her know her appearance had been canceled. Why? Because another promoter had filed a complaint to the Ontario Athletic Commission, which had a clause that women couldn't wrestle men, even if by then it was pretty much known that wrestling was sports entertainment. Even WWE had presented some mixed matches in Ontario.

Since there weren't many women wrestling in her native province of Quebec when she first started, Goulet had wrestled all her life against men and developed a good reputation for those matches. Years earlier, she had left Jacques Rougeau's promotion because, not surprisingly, he didn't want her to wrestle men. So Goulet retaliated with a complaint to the Ontario Human Rights Commission.

"From the first moment I spoke with a representative at the OHRC, I received nothing but unconditional support for my cause," Goulet said. They saw what I saw, that the regulation in question was a violation of my human rights, based on my gender. I filled out the necessary paperwork and it was time to take down that regulation."

On May 10, 2006, she won the fight and also changed everything. The OAC decided not only to change its ruling but also to deregulate professional wrestling altogether.

"It's been something we've been considering for a while. There's been a lot of requests from promoters for de-regulation," OAC commissioner Ken Hayashi said to SLAM! "The bottom line is there were no real health and safety regulations [to oversee], that's the main thrust of this office. Wrestling is choreographed, pre-arranged. I think we are the only jurisdiction in Canada that still regulates it.

*Judy Martin wrestled in a Battle of the Sexes match in 1980.* WRESTLING REVUE ARCHIVES/WWW.WRESTLINGREVUE.COM

It was just a matter of time and that time has come; we no longer regulate professional wrestling."

Even if the decision wasn't based exclusively on her complaint, Goulet's protest was the straw that broke the camel's back. Goulet had pinned the OAC for the three count. On December 12, 2012, LuFisto became the first woman in Canada to win the main title of a major promotion when she won the NSPW title, the premier promotion in Quebec. Almost two years later, British Columbia's Nicole Matthews followed her path by winning the ECCW title.

Wrestling needs to be believable in its stories and in its matches, but it also needs to be larger than life. Women are not and should not be seen the same way now as they may have been 50 years ago, where even a match between the Fabulous Moolah and Lou Thesz would have been unthinkable. If a 5'5" guy (like Rey Mysterio) can win a world title, a woman should be entitled to win matches over men. A woman doesn't need to look like Chyna or Jazz to accomplish that feat. In an era where size has never been so meaningless, one would think that gender wouldn't matter either.

As a promoter, Elite Canadian Championship Wrestling's Scotty Mac wanted to keep his options open and not be trapped in time with an old-school mentality.

"The wrestling business has changed leaps and bounds since Moolah and Thesz. I'm not going to resist change. I'm going to embrace change. If wrestling is evolving then I'm going to evolve," said Mac.

Other promotions have also made women the focal point. Pro Wrestling Guerrilla in California has used 5'2" Candice LeRae against men and put her over. She became one of the most popular wrestlers there. *Lucha Underground* has been using Ivelisse, Sexy Star, and Mariposa against men. We can almost say they have an intergender division, something previously unheard of. Absolute Intense Wrestling even did a Battle of the Sexes show, with all matches being a woman against a man, and Acclaim Pro Wrestling based in Ottawa, Ontario, has put all of its titles on women. Strong from the test run they had done with Sara Del Rey in 2012, CHIKARA became the first big independent promotion to put its title on a woman, when Kimber Lee became the Grand Champion in 2015.

"I'm a big advocate for inter-gender matches. You need to take it from a different perspective. If I'm wrestling a guy about my size, I can wrestle toe to toe with him. I train as hard you know," said Kimber Lee. "But if I'm wrestling a guy that is way bigger than me, I'm gonna approach it from a different angle. The psychology will be different, and it has to be done right."

Michael Langan, a regular CHIKARA fan, described how women are booked there and the effects on the crowd:

"CHIKARA goes out of its way to present Kimber Lee, Heidi Lovelace, and any other female that comes through the company as just wrestlers. In the year plus that Kimber Lee has been on shows, my wife and I have personally seen a huge increase in young little girls coming to the shows. They leave with smiles, and the general execution of her rise has been so perfectly handled that a crowd at the old ECW arena [which tends to be the most adult crowd at CHIKARA shows] behaved like 5-year-olds at the finish."

And it seems to have worked out for them. Since then, CHIKARA has followed up with Lovelace winning the title over Lee and with four all-women teams in its annual King of Trios tournament, one of them winning it.

In a world where there's more men than women, it's inevitable that female wrestlers are going to train and wrestle men at some point. For a lot of women, it's a way for them to get better because they can do stuff they can't do with another woman.

"I've learned how to fight from underneath and be an underdog, which is something I never really experience fighting other females," explained Nicole Matthews.

Long gone are the days when Andy Kaufman would beat up a woman as a comedy act onstage and proclaim himself the Inter-Gender Wrestling Champion of the World. The intolerance toward domestic violence in sports, with men now being suspended or even fired as soon as it goes public, has made some people change their minds on inter-gender matches, especially the TV people.

"TV stations here are very negative about inter-gender matches," said Dave Meltzer. "AXS thought about not airing a match from New Japan where Maria gets punched by Doc Gallows. Since the footage of Ray Rice punching his girlfriend aired, the TV stations don't see this the same way. If it would only be highspots I wouldn't bother, but since it's stomping and punching, that's what they are against and that's what *Lucha Underground* does. I don't mind Candice LeRae in PWG in front of 400 fans. But a growing promotion can't do that."

It didn't stop *Lucha Underground* from putting its main title on Sexy Star, and although women in the crowd loved her winning the title, and a lot of guys did too, many of the regulars were furious at the finish. In an interview on the MMM show, Lucha Underground's Executive Producer Eric Van Wagenen explained his decision, saying that they didn't have enough money in the first season to bring in a lot of women, and if they didn't do inter-gender matches, they'd just have Sexy Star vs. Ivelisse matches. AAA in Mexico had the same kind of reaction when Faby and Mari Apache wrestled against two male wrestlers, the highest profile inter-gender match ever in Mexico City. Fans were complaining, saying it would kill the promotion's credibility and believability. For Kimber Lee, gender shouldn't change anyone's thinking. "I still stand with it. If we agree to get in a ring across from a man, it's a fair game. Because no longer are we men and women, we are wrestlers at that point."

Stephanie Bell, who wrestles as Jade in TNA and who said publicly that she once was a victim of domestic abuse in a relationship with a male wrestler, thinks inter-gender wrestling has a place in wrestling's realm. "I love inter-gender wrestling, as long as there is an actual story behind it and not just a spot fest. Wrestling in the ring is both for entertainment and consensual. Once it's brought back home, that's where a line is crossed."

As in the real world, there are still a lot of double standards in wrestling between men and women: The way they're portrayed, the way they're sold, the merchandise they're going to sell — many things are different. "Girls are expected to look fresh as a daisy where a guy tries to get all sweaty before he goes to wrestle," said Lee. "That being said, a man will show his abs on a picture, because that's what the girls wanna see."

Wrestling is an act, it's a physical theater. If Catwoman, Wonder Woman, or Batgirl can beat up men in a fantasy world, why can't a female wrestler beat a man in a scripted world? "At the end of the day, wrestling should be entertaining," concluded Matthews. "Sometimes to be the most entertaining, a company needs to break some barriers and do something that other companies around them may not be doing."

★ ★ ★

##  MsChif

In October 2010, Rachel Collins Frobel was profiled on the PBS series *The Secret Life of Scientists and Engineers*, where her dual life as a geneticist and a wrestling banshee-demon was featured, something you don't see every day in the wrestling realm.

Billed as hailing from "the Inferno" and "the Edge of the Netherworld," her wrestling persona is an emerald banshee with a piercing scream and a superhuman ability to absorb punishment. In her life outside the ring, she works as a genetics scientist at a microbiology laboratory, about as far removed from the wrestling world as possible. But it was a day at the lab that inspired her to chase her childhood dream of becoming a wrestler.

"I wanted something fun in life, that's really what it was," she said. "One day, a secretary in the office asked me, 'If you could do something — anything — fun in your life, what would it be?' I said I would learn to wrestle. And that's when I decided to do it."

Born in St. Louis, Missouri, the girl who grew up to become MsChif began training with Gateway Championship Wrestling in 2000. There were only two female students in the class, and the other girl left wrestling after two shows. "I think it was a good way to learn, looking back," she said. "When I started, [the guys] saw how hard I was training. After just a couple sessions, I was already surpassing the other girl, who had been training almost a year."

Her background in dance, gymnastics, and martial arts helped her training, particularly her flexibility.

She made her wrestling debut in July 2001 and wrestled inter-gender matches against male opponents most of the time, until Daizee Haze came on the scene. Haze and MsChif worked well together, and the two were paired up in matches all over the Midwest independents.

In January 2007, MsChif became the 18th woman to be recognized as NWA women's champion, winning the title from Christie Ricci in Lebanon, Tennessee. Although the NWA — and the NWA women's title — had fallen off in terms of prestige and prominence, MsChif was honored to wear the historic championship belt.

"[NWA promoter] Ed Chuman really wanted to kick up the women's division and get it out into the spotlight," MsChif said. "It was a really exciting time. Unfortunately, several of the NWA promotions didn't have a lot of money and weren't willing to invest in women's wrestling. It never took off quite the way Ed wanted."

On April 26, 2008, MsChif defeated Sara Del Rey to become the second SHIMMER champion. She simultaneously held the NWA women's, NWA Midwest women's, and SHIMMER championship, an accomplishment that earned her national attention. *Pro Wrestling Illustrated* ranked her as number four in the 2009 PWI Female 50.

With her matches against Serena Deeb, Wesna Busic, LuFisto, Amazing Kong, Sarah Stock, and Madison Eagles, MsChif helped raise the bar for women's wrestling in the independents. She also scored bookings for Ring of Honor, which featured women's matches only on rare occasions. Much like the male wrestlers she had trained with, MsChif was earning respect from all corners — from the fans, her peers, and the media. She went on to tour Japan twice, which she considers one of the top highlights of her career.

On July 4, 2013, she married wrestler Michael Elgin, and that's when she began wrestling with the idea of starting a family.

"I had been wrestling for 12 or 13 years by that point. How long

*Scientist during the day, MsChif at night.* <small>MATHIEU SAGE</small>

are you going to be wrestling anyway, especially the girls who tend to retire sooner? I started to see my matches going a bit downhill from where they used to be. That's when I started thinking, if I want to have this little guy, this is a good time to do it."

She took a sabbatical from wrestling and gave birth to a baby boy in September 2015, but she isn't ready to officially announce her retirement yet. "I'd like to come back and wrestle a bit more some day. I haven't closed the door on anything yet," she said.

## THE CANADIAN NINJAS:
### *Portia Perez and Nicole Matthews*

Portia Perez and Nicole Matthews grew up in different parts of Canada, but both girls shared the dream of becoming professional wrestlers. They both accomplished that dream and — together — became one of the most successful and influential female tag teams of the 2000s.

Both Perez (born Jenna Grattan) and Matthews (born Lindsay Duncan) were born in 1987. Perez grew up in Brockville, Ontario, outside of Ottawa, while Matthews grew up in Coquitlam, British Columbia. Both discovered wrestling at a young age.

Perez began training to wrestle while still in high school and made her pro debut at age 16. At a petite 5'3" and with a baby face that looked even younger than her 16 years, she didn't look like the prototypical wrestler, but she stood out from the crowd and made a positive impression. When Perez wrestled as a heel, she perfectly played the role of the bratty little sister.

"I lived over an hour from the wrestling school where I was trained, and I wasn't old enough to drive when I first started," Perez said. "My dad, my mom, and my older sister drove me to every training session and every show until I was old enough to drive. I really couldn't have asked for a more supportive family."

Matthews swam and played volleyball in high school and began training to wrestle after graduation. She had her first match in February 2006 after training under Michelle Starr, Scotty Mac, and Vance Nevada. By 2007, Matthews had captured her first championship, winning the ECCW SuperGirls title with a win over Nattie "Natalya" Neidhart and Veronika Vice.

While Matthews was gaining steam in B.C., Perez was traveling throughout Canada, the Northeastern United States, and the Midwest. She debuted with SHIMMER on May 21, 2006, losing a pre-show match. But Perez's charisma and determination were apparent right away, and she was invited back for subsequent DVD tapings, becoming a regular member of the roster and ultimately becoming one of the linchpins of the promotion.

In October 2007, Matthews was brought into SHIMMER and paired with Perez. The two adopted the name the Canadian Ninjas — an ironic name as there was decidedly nothing ninja-esque about either of them.

For Matthews, simply being invited to compete for SHIMMER was a dream come true.

"Honestly, my only initial goal was to wrestle for SHIMMER. At the time, there wasn't really any feasible way for a female wrestler who looked like me to get signed with WWE, and I wasn't exactly interested in working that style. I wanted to be a great wrestler, and that's it," she said.

The Canadian Ninjas had an instant rapport. Their natural chemistry resonated with fans, and even though they were heels, they were heels the fans loved to hate.

Nicole Matthews and Portia Perez, the Canadian Ninjas. DAVE PRAZAK/SHIMMER

On May 3, 2009, the Ninjas took the SHIMMER tag team title with a win over the Ohio Girls (Ashley Lane and Nevaeh) to become the second SHIMMER tag champions. Perez and Matthews kept the title for nearly two years until finally losing to Hiroyo Matsumoto and Misaki Ohata in March 2011. They became the first two-time tag champions in SHIMMER history when they regained the belts in July 2012 in Montreal.

Both women said their friendship was the key ingredient that made their tag team work and gave them staying power.

"I think the biggest factor is the lack of egos between us," Perez said. "There is absolutely no way you are going to function as a team if you can't put your egos aside. You need to be able to share the spotlight and work towards showcasing your teammate as well as yourself."

Although they wrestled as a tag team, Perez and Matthews also competed in singles bouts, a lot of times with the partner who wasn't wrestling standing at ringside and causing distractions. Perez, representing the angry young upstart, had a violent feud with SHIMMER cofounder Allison Danger that lasted until just recently.

As far as Matthews goes, 2014 was her year as a singles competitor. On August 23, she won the ECCW title, a men's title she would lose and win back a second time the following year. Less than two months later, on October 10, 2014, Matthews scored a huge singles victory, winning a fatal four-way elimination match for the SHIMMER championship over champion Cheerleader Melissa, Madison Eagles, and Athena, thanks in part to an assist by Perez. The match came down to Matthews and Eagles. Perez distracted the referee so Matthews could throw a fireball into Eagles's face, allowing her to win the match and claim the vacant title.

The woman who had dreamed of making the SHIMMER roster had become the standard-bearer.

In October 2015, Perez made an announcement that she was retiring because of injuries, at only 27. The fans jeered; it was just another heel tactic from a woman who made rule breaking a form of art. But it was true. Perez wrestled her final match on October 11, 2015, teaming with Matthews, Lacey, and Kimber Lee against Madison Eagles, Daizee Haze, Lexie Fyfe, and Kellie Skater. Perez received a standing ovation from the fans — and the SHIMMER locker room — after the match. When given the mic for a retirement speech, she simply said to the live crowd: "I hate you all. Now I'm leaving!" in a truly Portia Perez fashion only she could deliver. The day before, Matthews had lost her title to Eagles.

"Truthfully, I knew my wrestling career was on borrowed time for a couple of years," she said. "It started in 2011, when I separated my shoulder for the first time. I separated my shoulder on a Sunday, and by Wednesday, I thought there was something seriously wrong with my neck. For the next year or so, my shoulder would separate every now and then. Over time, the lack of soft tissue support in the right side of my upper body led to more and more strain being put on bones and other ligaments and tendons. In the end, cervical discs had been affected and I was dealing with a lot of nerve compression and related issues."

Wrestling allowed Perez to see the world. Over the course of her career, she wrestled in 15 countries, 7 Canadian provinces, and more than 25 states. "Some of my best memories were just the absurd happenings that are unique to travelling with a bunch of professional wrestlers," she said. Matthews got to travel too, working for REINA in Japan as well as for PWWA in Australia.

As singles competitors and as a tandem, the Canadian Ninjas were a cornerstone of SHIMMER and two of the promotion's most decorated and respected stars.

"I never could have asked for a better partner, and to be able to tag team with one of my best friends for eight years was a fantastic time," Matthews said. Matthews is still wrestling as a single competitor, while Perez transitioned from the ring to SHIMMER booking duties.

## Jessicka Havok

According to Jessicka Havok, TNA president Dixie Carter never knew quite what to make of the Havok Death Machine.

"One of the writers let slip when I was in Japan that [Dixie] didn't understand my look or my character and didn't believe I was pretty enough to be a Knockout," Havok said. "But I didn't let it bother me because that's not why I was hired. I was hired to wreak havoc on the Knockouts division, not to become one of them."

Born in Canton, Ohio, Jessica Cricks made her wrestling debut in 2004. She caught the wrestling bug at the age of nine when she became a fan of "Stone Cold" Steve Austin. By the time she was 16, she had made up her mind that she wanted to follow in Austin's footsteps and become a wrestler herself.

At slightly over 6 feet tall in her wrestling boots, she towered over most of the other wrestlers, both male and female. She made her pro debut in 2004 and spent the next few years wrestling around the Ohio independent scene, a hotbed for female wrestling with names like

Sassy Stephie, Hailey Hatred, Neveah, and Madison Rayne all being natives of the Buckeye State.

In 2009, she began wrestling for the all-female Women Superstars Uncensored promotion in Philadelphia. She formed a team with Hatred, and the two won the WSU tag team title in the summer of 2009.

The Havok character evolved through the subsequent years. Cricks experimented with different influences, changing her look but never straying from her extremely physical, stiff style. She added a customized light-up gas mask and black gear decorated with studs and other accessories, looking like a postapocalyptic version of DC Comics' Harley Quinn, and she called on other inspirations — including comic books, video games, and horror movies — to keep her look and persona fresh.

In March 2012, she put her WSU Spirit title on the line in a title vs. title match against WSU champion Mercedes Martinez and won the title, becoming a dual champion. That win, and the fact she was part of a cool stable named the Midwest Militia with Stephie and Allysin Kay, launched Havok to a new level. She went on a winning streak that carried over into Combat Zone Wrestling, SHIMMER, and other promotions. She was ranked number four in the 2013 PWI Female 50.

After leaving WSU, she debuted in TNA Wrestling in September 2014, after several weeks of hype videos heralding her arrival. She immediately set her sights on champion Gail Kim and captured Kim's title just weeks after her debut.

Despite that initial success, Havok's TNA run was brief, as she lost the title three days later (or 49 days, on TV) when Taryn Terrell pinned Kim in a three-way match. TNA was indeed taping television weeks — or sometimes months — in advance of airing and not running live events. Although she was on TNA television, Havok went months without wrestling for the company, finally officially acknowledging that she had left the company in late July 2015.

Havok's hard-hitting style and unique look and presence helped her built a dedicated fan base, but she didn't have the standard body

*"The Havok Death Machine" Jessicka Havok.* RICKY HAVLIK

type for women wrestlers in the 2000s. The focus on her "look" as opposed to her work took time to get used to.

"When I first got into wrestling, I didn't think that I had anything wrong with my body," she said. "I never as a kid growing up thought that I was fat or anything like that. It was when I started training to wrestle that the people that I trained with would tell me that I needed to lose weight. That actually really hurt me, a lot more than I would have liked to admit probably. But the longer I stayed in wrestling, the more I realized that I don't really have to be like anyone else. I think it helps me that I'm not a cookie-cutter model. Wherever I go to wrestle — whether the people know me or not — I get a reaction. My character is very important to me. I take it very, very seriously."

And this is something that many of her peers understand and agree with, including ring veteran LuFisto. "When I look at Jessicka Havok,

I see strength, a will-power to succeed despite the odds, a woman that isn't afraid to speak her mind and one that dares to be different. Everywhere she goes, she captivates the attention of everyone that is watching. Definitely one of my favorite opponents of the past years."

## Santana Garrett

The other girls on the cheerleading team just couldn't understand Santana Garrett's passion for wrestling.

"I remember being in middle school and telling my friends I had been at pro wrestling practice with my dad, and that I was going to be a wrestler and start training. They just couldn't understand it," she said. "I feel like they didn't really accept it until I started becoming successful in it."

Born on May 22, 1988, in Ocala, Florida, Garrett began training with her father, "TNT" Kenny G., and wrestler Chasyn Rance (and under the watchful eyes of Scott Hall and Larry Zbyszko, who assisted at the school). She made her pro debut in 2009.

"My debut match was in Granite City, Illinois. Walking through that curtain for the first time, seeing my biggest fan — my dad — and my little brother there to cheer me on. That is a moment that I'll never, ever forget."

Garrett went all-in with wrestling, competing throughout the Florida independent circuit while continually attending training classes at least once a week.

After being used as a valet in TNA, Garrett made her debut with SHIMMER in 2012. The following year, she earned tryouts from NXT and TNA's developmental promotion, Ohio Valley Wrestling. She returned to TNA (which taped at Universal Studios in Orlando, near where she lived) in early 2013, this time as a wrestler. She adopted the ring name of Brittany and scored an upset win over Gail Kim in her debut match with the company. Brittany was the all-American underdog; it was a role that suited her to a tee.

But a couple months after her debut, Brittany's character underwent an edgier makeover. She developed a fascination with Madison

Rayne, telling her she loved her and heavily insinuating a lesbian attraction, heavily reminiscent of the angle Mickie James had worked with Trish Stratus in WWE in 2005–2006.

It was a storyline that left her feeling uneasy. "I do like the idea of a challenge, of taking on another persona that is far from what I am. It got a little risqué," she said. "I have a rule of thumb that I've always gone by. I never want to do anything that I'm not comfortable doing. If I can't watch it with my little brothers and my

*Second generation wrestler Santana Garrett.* DAVE PRAZAK/SHIMMER

dad, then I probably shouldn't be doing it."

The storyline never fully developed. Brittany had a heel turn and left TNA in December 2014.

Garrett attacked the independent circuit with renewed passion and had a career year in 2015. On February 7, 2015, she defeated Barbi Hayden to win the NWA women's championship. Two months later, she put the NWA championship on the line in a title vs. title match against SHINE champion Mia Yim. Garrett won that bout and took possession of two of the most prestigious women's titles on the indies. It proved to be the start of an undefeated streak that lasted almost 90 matches over the course of a 10-month span.

In October 2015, Garrett fulfilled a longtime dream and completed her first tour of Japan for Stardom. On November 23, she defeated Io Shirai in another title vs. title match to win the Wonder of Stardom championship, which she held for six months. Her NWA title defense was the first in the country since the heyday of Fabulous Moolah. All of that got her ranked number four in the *Pro Wrestling Illustrated* Female 50 of 2015. If 2015 wasn't good enough, she wrestled a few matches for NXT in 2016, trying to get a deal with WWE.

Garrett said she has seen a surge in the popularity of women's wrestling since she got her start. "When I started training, there were zero females in my wrestling classes in both of the schools I trained. Now, just at one school where I train, there are seven young, talented females who train with me," she said. "Women's wrestling is making a huge comeback. I'm very excited to see where it goes from here."

# NXT, the REVOLUTION, and the RETURN of the WOMEN'S TITLE

As late as 2012, when Sasha Banks was hired by WWE, their vision of women's wrestling was very different from what it is today. "When I first started, we were told to wrestle like Divas," Banks recalled on *WWE 24*. "No strikes, no hitting, pull the hair, catfights." Consequently, of all WWE's big-stage women's matches between 1988 and June 2013, only four had been given at least three stars by Dave Meltzer. But in the following years, that ratio would change quite a bit.

At the TLC PPV on December 15, 2013, Divas champion A.J. Lee and Natalya would have one of those matches. Although Natalya was praised for her performance, to her credit, it was Lee's second three-star match that year, the first one being against former partner Kaitlyn in what was the best women's match in WWE since Trish and Lita. Four months later, in Little Rock, Arkansas, during a *Main Event* taping, the tandem did it again, upping their game with an even better 14-minute match. Meltzer, who gave the match three and a half stars, wrote that it "was the best women's match on WWE TV in so long I can't even remember, and better than anything women's wise in WWE or TNA since the Gail Kim vs. Taryn Terrell matches."

Unfortunately, the company was unable to transfer that energy into WrestleMania that year, where a multiwoman match didn't place high in anyone's rankings. Although the situation wasn't constant on the main roster, down in Orlando, Florida, a number of women were starting to flourish.

Paul Levesque's brainchild, NXT, is the developmental territory of WWE. In February 2014, Levesque produced the first two-hour special to be presented on the WWE Network, NXT Arrival. Paige, the NXT women's champion and perhaps the first one to separate herself from the pack, wrestled Emma, who was caught in a comedy act with Santino on the main roster. They were given more time than usual for a women's match, and they had a good match. "For me I always felt like our Divas and women were underutilized. It was about treating them like the athletes they are," said Levesque on *WWE 24*.

Since Paige was called up to the main roster a few months later, she vacated the title and a tournament was held to crown the next champion. On May 29, 2014, NXT TakeOver would become a game changer. In the tournament final, Ashley Fliehr — better known as Charlotte, Ric Flair's daughter — was to face another competitor with wrestling in her genes, Natalya.

Charlotte won the match and the title, but that's secondary. In a show where Sami Zayn faced Tyler Breeze and Neville squared off with Tyson Kidd, Charlotte and Natalya, with Flair and Bret Hart in their respective corners, had the best match on the card, something completely unheard of by WWE standards.

"It came across as the epic women's match in modern WWE," wrote Meltzer, who gave the match a whopping four stars. "It was presented differently than any women's match, almost like a world title match, was given time and it was the performance of a career of Natalya to insiders. But it also was the breakout performance of Charlotte, who came across like a future superstar if the women's division in its future changes from models doing short matches to women wrestlers doing serious pro wrestling."

If WWE was still presenting Divas, NXT became the place to watch great women's wrestling. It didn't matter which male wrestler was on the show; at every NXT special since that night, a women's match has been one of the highlights at the end of the night.

Around the same time, a new phenomenon was the talk of the town in women's combat sport, and her name was Ronda Rousey. Between February 2013 and August 2015, she won her six UFC fights, totaling less than eight minutes in the Octagon. She was put in the main event of a PPV on her first night in with the company, something seen as a gutsy move at the time as it was also UFC's first women's fight ever. But UFC proved to be right. Her fight with Liz Carmouche drew 450,000 buys on PPV, destroying the previous record for a women's fight main-eventing a PPV, held by Laila Ali vs. Jacqui Frazier (respectively the daughters of Muhammad and Joe) in a boxing match in 2001 with more than 100,000 buys. Rousey would become one of UFC's biggest draws ever. She had the ability to connect with people, she was dominating her opponents, and she was presented as a star from the get-go. Rousey became in a way what any woman performing in combat sports wanted to be.

"It kills the out-of-date and stupid idea that women can't fight and cannot generate any attention from the public. She is the proof that good women fighting works," said LuFisto. "She's a great role model for all us women — and definitely, I feel like she's a huge part of the Divas' revolution too," added Paige.

Rousey's success and ability to draw is the reason McMahon and Levesque decided to put more emphasis on the women's division and to make a pitch for a revolution to begin in the WWE. So in the summer of 2015, they brought up Charlotte, Sasha Banks, and Becky Lynch all at the same time, with the idea of showcasing women to a degree the company had never done before. But if Levesque is the one in charge of NXT, the last word goes to his father-in-law when it comes to WWE. In a conference call for the NXT TakeOver: Respect show in October 2015, Levesque summed up Vince McMahon and his vision of women's wrestling: "Is there a different way that he wants to present it in his mind on the main roster, whatever, sure. That's where he is with it."

And that's probably why the concept never truly transferred from NXT fans to WWE fans. All the things that made those NXT matches so great, all the things that made Rousey a superstar — almost nothing of that was used at first for the women on the main roster. And even if there has been some change lately, still very few WWE events are main-evented by women.

Instead of letting the ones who could actually give a four-star performance work together, creative mingled the Divas and the wrestlers. Instead of letting personalities get over to create feuds, creative decided to play teacher, with Stephanie making teams on air like a high school teacher would do. Instead of letting the fans slowly witness the changes, seeing the upgrade in the workrate and the presentation and organically becoming fans of the product, creative pushed the "Divas Revolution" expression down their throats to the point the fans couldn't take it anymore and simply decided to reject the whole idea. At the end of the day, WWE wasn't willing to recognize Divas as wrestlers yet; the fact that the NXT title was called the women's title, while in WWE it was still called the Divas' title, expressed it the best.

# THE DEATH OF THE DIVAS TITLE

It took almost a year before WWE presented its women differently, when it was announced at WrestleMania 32 in Dallas, Texas, that the company had officially dropped the Divas title and the term *Diva* as Lita unveiled a new white championship belt with a bright red face plate (evocative of All Japan Women's signature red belt) and announced that the winner of the triple-threat match between Charlotte, Becky Lynch, and Sasha Banks would be recognized as *women's champion*.

The change in terminology was widely praised and was seen as a change in mentality, presenting female wrestlers as athletes as opposed to prima donnas. The "butterfly belt" could finally be retired and replaced with a belt that looked similar to the world title, and not an unnecessarily feminized knockoff.

Trish Stratus expressed her support of the change a couple weeks later when she spoke at the 2016 CAC Reunion. "As seven-time WWE women's champion, nothing makes me happier than seeing the women's title come back. Of course, if someone wins it seven times, we may need to revisit that statement," she said. "The new women's championship

*Lita, unveiling the new women's belt.* RICKY HAVLIK

signals the demise of the Divas championship. It's pretty well known that I was never really into the term *Diva*. I felt like, 'Hey, just call us what we are, women wrestlers.' I worked my whole career for the right to be called a woman wrestler."

Stephanie McMahon released a statement on the new designation. "This title belt represents the pinnacle of achievement, and that in WWE, it isn't about gender, race, or ethnicity — it is simply about being the best at what you do."

Not everyone felt the same though. "It's kind of like when you sell your first car and you're like, 'Oh, but I know you're beaten and ugly, but I want you!' That's how I feel about the Divas championship," said Nikki Bella.

Although the term *Divas* was kept for E!'s *Total Divas*, ring announcers are now saying that the following match is a "women's division match."

The three-way match was one of the most promoted acts for WrestleMania, to a level no other women's match had been before. Due to excitement over the new title, the match was considered the match of the night by the vast majority of fans, a first in 32 years. The fans celebrated as well the very next night, during a segment with Charlotte and all the other women on *Raw*, by chanting in unison "women's wrestling."

"Talking about a revolution sounds like a whisper, as the old song says. It was just about going out there and doing our thing — having stories where people get emotionally involved. It doesn't matter if we're women. It shouldn't matter; it's 2016," said Becky Lynch in an interview with *Sports Illustrated*.

A few months later, WWE decided to split its roster between *Raw* and *SmackDown*. With the women's champion exclusively wrestling on *Raw*, it was decided that *SmackDown* would have its own women's championship, and the first champion was crowned on September 11, 2016.

Women wrestlers definitely have a better role now in WWE than ever before. It's now safe to say that the women's matches are not the bathroom breaks they once were. Fans are more generous and pay more attention to them. Of course, the flip side is that with better matches come higher expectations. With so many women being hired and groomed, one can only think that higher-ups in the company are behind these women and will not let the division die as it did in the mid-'80s or the early '90s.

As far as NXT goes, it has become *the* place to be for women. Now a touring brand as well as a developmental promotion, NXT's women's matches are always among the most anticipated matches on the card. Although they are still hiring women from crossfit, body-building bikini, and cheerleading competitions, it's not unusual anymore to see many women who were weekend female warriors on the indies getting contracts or simply being invited to wrestle at tapings and such. Interestingly, in 2016, 30 percent of the NXT roster was made up of women, and they came from all over the world and from many different fields.

Australia had Billie Kay and Peyton Royce, Japan had Asuka, the U.K. had Nikki Cross (Nikki Storm), and the United States had Ember Moon (Athena). Fitness modeling had Alexa Bliss, cheerleading had Carmella, and bodybuilding had Dana Brooke. Even the second- and third-generation wrestlers were part of it. Nia Jax is Dwayne "The Rock" Johnson's cousin, and although they have not yet signed contracts with NXT, Tessa Blanchard (daughter of Tully, granddaughter of Joe, raised by Magnum T.A.) and Rachel Ellering (former Road Warriors and current NXT manager Paul Ellering's daughter) are often used by the promotion. And if at one point in time the ring was a dangerous place for a woman who didn't have a wrestling background, this time around, these women aren't rushed in the ring and are actually properly trained by Sara Amato and Sarah Stock. In the summer of 2016, Brooke, Jax, Carmella, and Bliss were all promoted to the main roster, leaving room for other young prospects like Mandy Rose and Liv Morgan. NXT and WWE have also influenced other wrestling promotions such as Ring of Honor, which had its first all-women's show in 2016 and is considering having a women's championship for the first time.

Many consider the rise of Charlotte, Banks, Lynch, and Bayley the start of what is now called the women's revolution. Others will mention Paige as the trendsetter, and some will say Natalya. At the end of the day, all these women deserve recognition as they have all stepped up to the plate when it was so important for them, and for the future of the division, to do so.

# CHARLOTTE FLAIR

The entire world knew Ashley Fliehr's father as the Man. What did that make her? The Daughter? The Little Girl? Maybe the Champion?

As it turned out, Ashley wanted to do more than ride along on the coattails of her celebrity dad, "The Nature Boy" Ric Flair. She had a few chapters she wanted to add to the Flair legacy herself.

The conventional wisdom regarding the Flair family was that Ric's youngest son, Reid, would be the one to follow in his father's Bruno Magli–wearing footsteps. A former AAU national champion in high school, Reid had trained under his father and Harley Race and had completed a tour of All Japan. He was being groomed for great things. But Reid was beset by legal problems and problems with drugs and alcohol. In March 2013, he was found dead of a heroin overdose in a Charlotte, NC, hotel room.

It was a tragic loss that devastated the family, one that largely overshadowed another important family development. Ashley, Ric's youngest daughter with his ex-wife, Elizabeth, had been signed to a WWE developmental contract. A standout volleyball player in high school, she had graduated from college and worked as a personal trainer. Although she was around wrestling her entire life, it wasn't until she was in her mid-20s that she considered trying it herself,

Wrestling as Charlotte (a nod to her hometown of Charlotte, North Carolina), she made her NXT television debut on July 17, 2013, just four months after Reid's passing.

"I grew up always playing sports, but never in a million years did I think that I would become a WWE Diva," she said in a 2015 interview on the *PWI Podcast*. "I was in Miami when the Four Horsemen were inducted [into the WWF Hall of Fame in 2012]. It was me, my little brother, Reid, and my dad, and we were sitting with [then director of talent relations] Johnny Laurinaitis at dinner. They were talking and joking, and they said, 'You know, Ash, you should really just give it a go.' At that point, I was just personal training and my little brother was an aspiring wrestler at the time. He was pretty much my motivation. I wanted to do it with him. So I said, 'Sure, why not?'"

She said her father wouldn't let her take the decision lightly, however. "He said, if you're going to do this, you have to put your whole heart into it," she recalled. "This is one huge opportunity and it's not easy."

Somewhat surprisingly, Flair didn't have a hand in training his daughter; all of her training came through WWE's developmental system and the Performance Center.

After nearly a year in NXT, she competed in — and won — an eight-woman tournament to fill the vacant NXT women's title.

As champion, she unveiled a new twist on an old favorite, adding a high back bridge to her father's signature figure-four leglock and dubbing it the figure-eight. She reigned as NXT women's champion for almost eight months until dropping the belt to Sasha Banks. She was voted the 2014 Rookie of the Year by *PWI* voters, becoming only the third female to attain that distinction (following Madusa Miceli in 1987 and Veda Scott in 2012). Ric Flair won the same award in 1975.

She was called up to the main roster in July 2015 as part of the Divas Revolution storyline, alongside Paige and Becky Lynch as Team PCB (Paige, Charlotte, and Becky). Flair defeated Nikki Bella to win the WWE Divas title at Night of Champions 2015, ending Bella's record-setting title reign.

She eventually parted with teammates Paige and Becky Lynch and adopted a more aggressive heel persona, taking on her father as her manager.

"She does stuff I could never do. She's that good of an athlete. They only come along once in a lifetime. She has the credentials," said Ric in an interview with *WrestleZone*, adding that none of his achievements was as rewarding for him as his daughter's success.

She entered her first WrestleMania in Dallas in 2016 as Divas champion and therefore will be listed in the record books as the last Divas champion. Her win over Banks and Lynch made her the first women's champion under the new regime of Levesque and Stephanie. After losing the title to Banks in July, she won it back a few weeks later. Because of the brand split, the title is now known as the *Raw* women's championship. Her combined Divas and women's title reign was the longest in WWE in over a decade. On October 3, 2016, she main-evented *Raw* alongside Sasha Banks in a four-star match. Banks won to regain the title, but just three weeks later, at the Hell in a Cell PPV, the Queen would take back her championship. The occasion would mark not only the first time that women would compete in a Hell in a Cell

*Charlotte, with her father "The Nature Boy" Ric Flair.* RICKY HAVLIK

match, but the first time that women would main-event a WWE PPV. Unfortunately, the decision for Banks and Flair to main-event was not made until the day before the event and therefore not promoted.

"The first women's main event on a WWE PPV show can only happen once, and can only be promoted once," argued Dave Meltzer. "It's a waste of a one-time opportunity, doing it without promoting it. Why waste the chance to hype a show as history-making by doing it at the last minute, rather than make a big deal about for a month? I would have been 100 percent for the idea if it was announced a month earlier. And even okay with if it was announced two weeks earlier. Historically, there was never one time, and quite frankly, this wasn't the case either, where a women's match was the most antic- ipated on any PPV. On this show, at least it was close." They then exchanged the title a couple of times, with Charlotte ending 2016 as champion. One can expect that this will probably not be the last meeting between the two champions.

Only three years after her first match, the reluctant Nature Girl has already secured her place in the WWE history books.

# SASHA BANKS

The embodiment of swagger, the BO$$ made her WWE TV debut on the July 13, 2015, edition of *Raw*, in a segment that officially launched the so-called Divas Revolution. But the fact of the matter is that Sasha Banks was part of a revolution that started months earlier in NXT, where she was earning praise and winning over fans with an impressive run as NXT women's champion.

Although she grew up in different parts of the country before finally settling in Boston, Massachusetts, Mercedes Kaestner-Varnado was actually born in Fairfield, California, on January 26, 1992.

A wrestling fan since childhood, she enrolled in the Chaotic Wrestling school in Woburn, Massachusetts, in 2010 and trained with Brian Fury, Brian Milonas, and Todd Smith. Impressed with her athleticism and drive, the school granted her a three-month scholarship to get started, and she was on her way.

"This has been my dream since I was 10," she told the website SportingNews.com in 2015. "I remember I started watching it and my mom came into the room and was like 'what is this? You cannot be watching this stuff.' She made me turn it off and I remember going to my little brother's room and turning it back on. I was just so interested in it and at that very moment, something clicked with me. Ever since then, I always knew that being in the WWE was the only dream I ever had and I've been chasing it ever since."

She made her pro debut in August 2010, wrestling as Mercedes K.V., and won the Chaotic Wrestling women's title in December 2011.

New England Championship Wrestling promoter Sheldon Goldberg said he vividly remembered when she wrestled for him in the summer of 2010.

"All of us who were working in the company at that time were struck by her beauty and by her level of physicality," Goldberg said. "I don't believe she had many matches at the time, but it was pretty evident that she was going to be something special. I specifically remember her entrance for her tag match at our 10-year anniversary show. As soon as she came through the curtain, people stopped what they were doing and took notice of her, and that is the hallmark of someone who was going to be a star. On top of that, she was immensely likable and unpretentious as a person, even though she looked like she just stepped out of a beauty magazine."

She participated in a WWE tryout in June 2012 and was signed to a developmental contract. She moved to Tampa to train at Florida Championship Wrestling.

She debuted under the name Sasha Banks in NXT in December 2012 and competed in the tournament to crown the inaugural NXT women's champion in June 2013, but she lost to Summer Rae in the opening round. In September 2013, she adopted a more aggressive, arrogant persona and dubbed herself the Boss (also stylized as the BO$$), wearing shades and gaudy jewelry and developing a rock star persona. The rock star swagger came naturally; she is a cousin of rapper Snoop Dogg. The gimmick clicked right away.

"My cousin took me to WrestleMania when I was 16 and I swear to God I thought I was going to get signed just because I was like, 'Can I meet Vince? Can I?' and, of course, nothing happened," Banks recalled on Chris Jericho's podcast.

In 2014, she competed in another tournament to fill the vacant women's title but was eliminated in the second round with a loss to Natalya. She finally won the title in February 2015 at NXT TakeOver: Rival, pinning champion Charlotte in a four-way match that also included Becky Lynch and Bayley. That would be the first of many four-plus-star matches she would have that year. Banks successfully defended the title against Charlotte, Lynch, and Alexa Bliss before losing the belt to Bayley at NXT TakeOver: Brooklyn in August 2015, a month after making her debut on the main roster.

In WWE, Banks was teamed with Naomi and Tamina Snuka as Team BAD (Beautiful and Dangerous) and placed in a three-team rivalry with Team Bella (the Bellas and Alicia Fox) and her old NXT rivals Team PCB. She returned to NXT to challenge Bayley for the title in October 2015 at NXT TakeOver: Respect. Banks and Bayley wrestled a 30-minute Iron Man match, where the wrestler who scored the most pinfalls or submissions in 30 minutes was declared the winner.

Bayley retained the title in a spectacular contest that was given the main event spot of the show. Because of all those accomplishments, Banks was voted Woman of the Year for 2015 by *PWI* readers.

"For the first time since 1984, WWE built a national broadcast around an advertised women's match as the main event," said Meltzer about their October match.

After competing in a high profile match at WrestleMania 32 in Dallas, Banks was given the biggest opportunity of her career on July 25, 2016. On the

*WWE Raw women's champion Sasha Banks.* BILL OTTEN

first *Raw* after the brand split, she defeated Charlotte to become the WWE women's champion. Although she lost the title a few weeks later because of back problems, this was an emotional moment for her. However, she was not the only one crying. Mick Foley wrote on his Facebook page, "In all my years I don't think I've ever seen a crowd this large line up outside the curtain to specifically congratulate one person. I have certainly never seen so many tears." Banks is as popular with the fans as she is behind the scenes. At *Raw* in Los Angeles on October 3, Banks regained the title as she and Charlotte performed in their best one-on-one match since their NXT days. It was quite fitting, since they were also main-eventing the show. The following week, Banks issued this statement: "I feel like I'm on top of the world right now," said Banks. "But it wasn't that long ago that I would watch women like Trish Stratus and Lita tear it down in the main-event and say to myself, 'I want to be like that.' Well my dreams came true last week when I faced Charlotte in the main-event of *Monday Night Raw*."

Three weeks later, in the main-event of Hell in a Cell, she lost the title to Charlotte. On November 28, Banks won the title back, once again in the main-event of *Monday Night Raw*, only to lose it one more time in the December PPV, making this rivalry the best in women's wrestling today and solidifying their legacy in WWE's history.

# BAYLEY

In 2015, California native Bayley defeated Sasha Banks to win the NXT women's title in a classic match before a capacity crowd of a little over 13,000 fans at the Barclays Center in Brooklyn. Six weeks later, she retained the title in the main event of NXT TakeOver: Respect, beating Banks 3-2 in a 30-minute Iron Man match; that match made history as it was voted Match of the Year for 2015 by readers of *Pro Wrestling Illustrated*, becoming the first women's match to earn that honor. Perhaps even more impressive is the fact that their previous encounter in Brooklyn was named first runner-up in the same category as well as being voted third-best match of the year by the *Wrestling Observer Newsletter*, the first time in 20 years that a women's match would rank that high and a first for a North American bout.

The match was also very well received by male wrestlers in the company. "It was so incredible to watch. It was just a really special moment. I had trouble keeping myself together," said Seth Rollins in WWE 24. "There was so much emotion in that match. And if you see grown men in tears watching a women's match for a championship, that's what this is all about," added Cesaro.

"I went to congratulate Bayley. It was a tough act to follow honestly," said Kevin Owens, who had the task of wrestling Finn Balor right after.

"The Brooklyn match was one of the greatest I've ever seen and there will be many more," said Paul "Triple H" Levesque in a conference call. "That was an amazing match by any standard, men, women, alien," said NXT's Samoa Joe.

No doubt about it, Banks and Bayley had clearly struck a chord with the fans. Bayley just can't hide her love for wrestling. "When I first started training, my trainer told me to stop smiling so much," she said in a 2015 interview with the *Miami Herald*. "It was just fun to me. I couldn't help it."

*It's Bayley!* BILL OTTEN

Her passion and demeanor have made NXT's resident "hugger" one of the most popular women in the sport. Bayley's appeal is easy to understand. Her bubbly, carefree demeanor, coupled with her enthusiasm, her willingness to greet and hug fans, and her infectious ring entrances (complete with wacky, waving inflatable tube men) set her apart from the pack and inspired some young fans to begin dressing like her (most notably Izzy, the Bayley superfan who became an institution at NXT tapings at Full Sail University in 2015).

Born Pamela Rose Martinez on June 15, 1989, she became a wrestling fan at the age of 10, inspired largely by Randy Savage. By age 13, she was attending local independent wrestling shows with Big Time

Wrestling in nearby Newark, California. A talented basketball player in high school, she decided against college and chose to try her hand as a pro wrestler instead, a decision that initially left her mother concerned. However, Pamela's determination and focus persuaded her mother to give her blessing.

She enrolled in Big Time Wrestling's school and trained under Jason Styles. She had her first match in April 2008 and adopted the name Davina Rose. She began competing throughout California and eventually landed in SHIMMER in 2011. There, she had an opportunity to wrestle with and against some of the top names on the indies at the time, including Serena Deeb, the Canadian Ninjas, Mercedes Martinez, and Cherry Bomb.

In December 2012 — barely four years after her first match — she was signed by WWE and began competing at NXT. She was presented as an innocent and naïve fangirl and quickly became a crowd favorite, being used mostly to put over other girls.

"Bayley is kind of contrary to every Diva conversation that had been had probably in the past 10 years when it comes to what we were looking for. And it's exactly why we brought her in," Levesque said on the WWE Network.

The turning point came in the spring of 2015, when Emma (returning to NXT after a run in WWE) slapped her in a backstage segment, accusing Bayley of being too goody-goody to ever become a serious wrestler. The refocused Bayley proceeded to beat Emma and defeat former NXT champion Charlotte to earn the title shot.

Her NXT title reign lasted a little over seven months, when she lost to Asuka in Dallas over WrestleMania weekend. Although she had made her main roster debut in July, teaming with Sasha Banks at the Battleground PPV, she had one more match to do in NXT. A year after her star-making performance, she wrestled Asuka at NXT TakeOver: Brooklyn II, losing one more time. But the loss didn't matter. For the fans, the message was clear: Bayley's time in NXT was over. Two days later, she made her official *Raw* debut, to one of the biggest reactions of the night.

Bayley says it has been easy to connect with her fans, including young girls like Izzy and others, because that's exactly what she used to be.

"Bayley is a dream chaser. She's grown up watching the product, wrestling," she told the *Miami Herald*, speaking in the third person about her wrestling persona. "She knows everyone, from top to bottom, all the history. She's been motivated since she was 10 years old and is finally here, trying to pursue the dream, live the dream to the fullest."

# BECKY LYNCH

SHIMMER founder Dave Prazak remembers the first time he saw footage of Rebecca Knox in action.

"Rebecca Knox was the first international talent [other than Canadians] that we brought in to SHIMMER," Prazak recalled. "She was a 19-year-old wrestling prodigy out of Ireland. I had gotten a DVD from Lexie Fyfe. It was a match in front of nobody, in a wrestling school. It was Rebecca versus Finn Balor, and I thought, 'Wow, she is a really good technical wrestler!' She was very good, and I dove into watching more matches of Rebecca Knox against different opponents."

Born Rebecca Quin on January 30, 1987, she grew up in Dublin, Ireland. She was active in horseback riding, swimming, and basketball as a child. When she was 15, she learned that a pro wrestling school was opening nearby in Bray, County Wicklow. Both she and her brother had been wrestling fans, so they stopped by the school to give it a look.

After meeting trainers Fergal Devitt (later known as Finn Balor in WWE) and Paul Tracey, both she and her brother decided to give wrestling a try, although neither expected wrestling to become a career. "Through school I wasn't thinking about becoming a professional wrestler. I was intent on becoming a solicitor," she told the *Dublin Herald* in 2013.

Rebecca stared training in June 2002 and wrestled her first match five months later under the name Rebecca Knox. She showed

*"The Lass Kicker" Becky Lynch.* PAT LAPRADE

immediate prom-
ise and flourished
under the guidance
of Devitt and Tracey.
She began accept-
ing bookings outside
of Ireland, including
in NWA-UK Ham-
merlock, furthering
her training at their
school.

By 2005, she was
competing through-
out Europe (including
the World Queens of
Chaos promotion in
France), Japan, and
Western Canada, win-
ning the first Super-
Girls championship
in British Columbia (a
title that would later
be held by Ivory, Nata-
lya, Emma, and Nicole
Matthews, among others). Her dreams of law school fell by the wayside
when she decided to drop out of school and concentrate on wrestling.

Prazak brought her into SHIMMER in February 2006; she beat
Allison Danger in her debut and went on to feud with Daizee Haze
in a pair of critically acclaimed matches. Knox was one of the top heels
in SHIMMER, and plans were made to schedule Haze and Knox in a
60-minute Iron Man match at an upcoming SHIMMER taping.

But with early success came early injuries. She had broken both
of her ankles at different times. Then, on a tour of Germany in
September 2006, she suffered a head injury during a match, opening

a nasty laceration that required stitches. After that match, she began experiencing severe headaches and vision problems. Doctors diagnosed the injury as potential cranial nerve damage.

At 19 years old, she decided it was time to walk away from wrestling. She took a sabbatical from the ring, during which she went to school for acting and took a job as a flight attendant. She dabbled in martial arts and SCUBA diving, and tried her hand at stunt work.

"Nothing captured my heart the way wrestling did," she told WWE.com in 2015. "I did all these things that were separating the aspects of wrestling and trying to make it fit."

She decided to ease herself back into wrestling. In March 2011, she returned to SHIMMER as a manager, managing the Knight Dynasty (Britani "Paige" and Saraya Knight).

She began training again and eventually earned a tryout with WWE, signing a developmental contract in 2013. She debuted as Becky Lynch, a high-stepping Irish dancer, in NXT in August 2013. Her character was retooled a bit and developed a steampunk look, including goggles and a steamy ring entrance with hidden pipes spewing steam into the entranceway. As it was for many women in NXT, 2015 was a crucial year for Lynch. At NXT TakeOver: Unstoppable, she offered up the performance of her career so far, in a losing effort against champion Sasha Banks. The next day at the NXT tapings, fans treated her like she was a big star.

She made her official debut on the main roster on the July 13 edition of *Monday Night Raw*, joining Team PCB (with Paige and Charlotte) in the Divas Revolution. By the end of 2015, the Lass Kicker was the top contender for the Divas title and one of the most popular females in WWE. A few months after WrestleMania 32, she was drafted by *SmackDown* and was more than happy about the turn of events. "When I was drafted to *Smackdown*, I was like, 'Hell yes, I'm going to captain this ship.'" And she did just that when on September 11, at the Backlash PPV, Lynch won a 6-way elimination match to become the very first *SmackDown* women's champion, a title she kept for three months before losing it to Alexa Bliss.

"You know when people say, 'When you know, you know?' I knew," Lynch told WWE.com. "It has been tough at times, but I've never been happier in my life. I just feel like this is what I'm meant to do."

# PAIGE

Although wrestling was the family business, Saraya-Jade Bevis had no interest in stepping into the ring as a young girl, according to her mother Julia (a.k.a. "Sweet" Saraya Knight).

"Saraya didn't want to wrestle. She wanted to be a zoologist," Julia said. "Her dad threw her in the deep end. One of the girls ain't turned up. We need you."

Saraya-Jade was 13 years old when her father, Ricky Knight, pressed her into service. Knight was promoting wrestling shows at holiday camps in Norwich, England. His daughter had played inside the ring and had watched enough wrestling to know the basics, so he had her fill in when another female wrestler no-showed.

Saraya-Jade never looked back.

Both her parents wrestled, as did two of her brothers (Zac and Roy), her sister, and her uncle. Even her grandfather was involved as a referee. She adopted the name Britani Knight and competed in her family's promotion, but she also spread her wings, competing throughout the United Kingdom and all over Europe, including tours of Germany, Norway, Belgium, and France. She regularly worked with her mother, both as tag team partners and as opponents, and won several European titles. She studied the tapes of her two heroes, Bull Nakano and Madusa, eventually copying Nakano's PTO as her finisher.

"I initially met Paige on my first visit to the U.K. She was 14 at the time and already a force to be reckoned with," Allison Danger said. "Not only did she have the ability and skill, but she also already had an in-ring maturity you don't see at that age. Her parents instilled a phenomenal work ethic into her and her brothers."

In March 2011, Britani and her mother, Saraya, debuted in SHIMMER as the Knight Dynasty, with Rebecca Knox (Becky

Lynch) as their manager. The Knights had undeniable chemistry, with Britani playing the cute and bratty daughter and Saraya in the role of the ass-kicking mom. The team became contenders for the tag team championship, but after they suffered a few losses, Saraya turned against her daughter, disowning her in the storyline and slapping her hard in the face. In October 2011, Britani beat her mother in an intense no-DQ grudge match.

"I always knew Paige would be a great fit for SHIMMER,

*"The Anti-Diva" Paige.* RICKY HAVLIK

it was just a matter of her being the right age for us to use her," Danger said. "Paige and Saraya Knight walked into our locker room and became family, not just coworkers. It was time for America to see what both of them were about, and I'm grateful that SHIMMER was where that happened."

WWE scouts had already taken notice. Her first tryout wasn't conclusive enough as Bevis portrayed someone she wasn't: a diva, sporting blonde hair and a spray tan. Six months later, she got another chance. She came out as herself, with black hair and not tanned at all. She and her brother Zac wrestled against one another, and they beat each other up. Officials had seen plenty, and she was signed to a WWE developmental contract in September 2011 and reported to Florida Championship Wrestling soon after her last SHIMMER match. Although she had just turned 19, she already had six years of experience and had wrestled all over the globe.

She debuted on FCW television in 2012, forming an alliance with Sofia Cortez (better known as Ivelisse) as the Anti-Diva Army, declaring war on the former models and pretty faces in the developmental system. After splitting from Cortez, she continued to be billed as the Anti-Diva and became something of an antihero for the fans. She had been bouncing bars when she was only 15 and therefore brought a tougher style to the women's division — or, as she says it herself, a "stiff but safe" style.

That year, she and her family were profiled in a U.K. documentary titled *The Wrestlers: Fighting with My Family*, which showcased her start with WWE.

On June 20, 2013, Paige became the first NXT women's champion, winning an eight-woman tournament to claim the title. She scored wins over Tamina Snuka and Alicia Fox to advance to the finals, where she beat Emma.

She made her WWE debut the night after WrestleMania 30, coming out to the ring to congratulate Divas champion A.J. Lee for retaining her title in a 14-woman invitational bout. Lee took offense, claiming Paige was trying to steal her moment in the spotlight, and challenged Paige to a match. Paige won the subsequent bout in 1:20, becoming the second female to win a championship in her WWE debut (Gail Kim was the first, in 2003).

She lost the butterfly belt back to Lee in June 2014, then regained it with a win over Lee at SummerSlam. She was ranked number one that year in the PWI Female 50. She also joined the cast of the E! reality show *Total Divas* in October 2014 and brought the ratings up from the previous season.

In 2015, she was a major part of the Divas Revolution in WWE, where she was paired with Charlotte and Becky Lynch. A couple of months after making her WrestleMania debut in Dallas as part of the 10-woman tag team match, she was sidelined with a back and shoulder injury. In the fall of 2016, she underwent a neck surgery, and has yet to make a comeback. At only 24, the best is yet to come for her. "One day, I want to make it into the WWE Hall of Fame," concluded Paige.

# EMMA

Sometimes, a dance fad comes on the scene and becomes a cultural phenomenon overnight. We have seen the *Whip, Nae Nae*, the Macarena, Vogue-ing, Fandango-ing ... and, for a brief period in 2013, there was the Emma-Lution.

Emma's awkward, arm-pumping dance became a sensation in NXT in 2013. When her entrance music hit, the fans at Full Sail University would join in in unison, pumping their arms arrhythmically. It didn't matter that it was a silly dance; Emma had the charisma to make it work. She was over.

Tenille Dashwood had come a long way in a short period of time. Born in Melbourne, Australia, on March 1, 1989, she was introduced to wrestling when she was eight years old by her older brother. She became a fan of Steve Austin and Trish Stratus and began to explore the independent scene in her native Australia. At the age of 13, she was front and center for WWE's Global Warming Tour when it touched down in Melbourne in 2002, where she met Stratus face to face.

She began doing some ring crew work for Pro Wrestling Women's Alliance in Australia at the age of 16 before deciding to move to Western Canada to train at Lance Storm's Storm Wrestling Academy in Calgary. She wrestled her first match in 2007, then returned to Australia in 2008. For the next few years, she balanced an impressive travel schedule, bouncing between Australia, the Vancouver-based Extreme Canadian Championship Wrestling, and the U.S. independents, including SHIMMER.

In 2010, her globe-trotting had caught the attention of WWE scouts, and she was offered a developmental contract. She opted for surgery to correct chronic issues with her shoulder first, then reported to Florida Championship Wrestling in 2012, becoming the first

*Tenille, before she became Emma.* DAVE PRAZAK/SHIMMER

female Aussie wrestler to be signed by WWE.

"To me that was all I ever cared about. For anyone who's growing up like me as a big wrestling fan I'd encourage them to give it a shot," she said in an interview.

Now, with her quirky little dance, Emma appeared to be one of WWE's rising stars. Unfortunately, the little things that get over in front of 400 superfans at Full Sail University don't always translate to arenas seating upwards of 10,000 people. Emma debuted on the main WWE roster in January 2014, seated at ringside as a fan of Santino Marella. Eventually, Marella invited her into the ring for a dance-off against Summer Rae, where Emma debuted her arm-extending dance. She was paired with Marella for the first half of 2014, wrestling mixed tag bouts against Fandango and Summer Rae.

Emma never got over in WWE the way she did in NXT. When Marella announced his retirement, she was left without a storyline.

In January 2015, she was sent back down to NXT for repackaging. She turned heel and began working with new signees and younger talent, including Bayley, Asuka, and Dana Brooke. At the NXT TakeOver: London in December 2015, she had an incredible match with Asuka, showing what she could really do in a ring. She returned to the main roster in time for WrestleMania 32. She was then teamed with Dana Brooke, her tag team partner from NXT. But bad luck struck when she got a back injury and needed surgery. Upon returning to the main roster, fans were shown vignettes of her, teasing a new name, Emmaline. An incredibly fit competitor with experience that belies her youth, she is a versatile wrestler with plenty of potential for years to come.

# ASUKA

For knowledgeable joshi fans, the sight of Kanako Urai standing beside Ric Flair and Sgt. Slaughter at NXT TakeOver: Brooklyn on August 22, 2015, was simply shocking.

Urai, known professionally as Kana, certainly didn't fit the WWE mold. At 5'3" and 137 pounds, and just a few weeks before her 34th birthday (an age where many women are looking to retire rather than to sign a WWE developmental deal), Kana didn't look the part. She wasn't a former model, a reality show contestant, or a cute young ingénue from the indie scene. She was known as a bona fide ass-kicker and a strong-style specialist from the All Japan Women tradition. She was the polar opposite of the then-reigning WWE Divas champion, Nikki Bella.

But looks and style aside, there was another major reason why it was surreal to see Kana on a WWE broadcast. After all, this was a woman who shook up the women's wrestling scene in Japan, writing a scathing editorial that came to be known as "the Kana Manifesto," clearly outlining everything she believed was wrong with women's wrestling. Kana had a reputation for being outspoken and controversial; seeing her in the corporate-friendly context of WWE was jarring.

Urai was born on September 26, 1981, in Osaka, Japan. She studied at the Osaka University of Arts Junior College and worked as a graphic designer, but she was drawn to wrestling because of her appreciation of wrestlers such as Keiji "The Great Muta" Mutoh, Minoru Suzuki, and Akira Maeda.

She made her wrestling debut in 2004 in the all-female AtoZ promotion but stepped away from the ring because of illness in 2006. She returned to the ring in September 2007 as a freelancer, wrestling for several independent promotions including Ice Ribbon, Joshi Puroresu, and Pro Wrestling Zero 1, among others.

But Kana was discouraged by what she saw on the independent scene. As a wrestler who was inspired by the stiff, athletic, and realistic-looking contests en vogue in men's wrestling, she was appalled by the stylized, image-first approach to women's wrestling that was in fashion at the time.

In 2010, she wrote an article for *Weekly Pro Wrestling* recommending certain changes be made to wrestling. Her five main suggestions were:

- Conduct an audit of every joshi wrestler and dismiss the ones who were substandard.
- Encourage other women to leave the business if they cannot develop their own persona or character.
- Expand the expectations of joshi wrestling to include different styles of wrestling, like the men's game.
- Squelch negativity and encourage an atmosphere of mutual respect.
- Eliminate obviously fake-looking moves.

The Kana Manifesto ruffled feathers throughout the Japanese women's wrestling world and established Kana as *persona non grata* on the joshi scene.

"The actual suggestions are all sensible, but the issue wasn't as much with the suggestions as the Japanese mentality at this 'rookie' wrestler with a reputation for being overly stiff in the ring telling all the joshi veterans and the promoters what they needed to do to fix the entire scene," said the late Stewart Allen, cofounder of the U.K.-based Ringbelles.com website, in a 2014 email interview. "They didn't think she had the seniority or respect to be making those demands."

The Manifesto helped establish Kana as a heel in Japan, and she made the most of the animosity by becoming the top female in the

*One of Japan's best woman wrestlers, Asuka.* ERIC SALOTTOLO

SMASH promotion, run by Yoshihiro Tajiri. She joined the Shirai sisters, Io and Mia, to form a heel stable, the Triple Tails, which lasted 15 months. Io would end up being one of the best and most popular joshis, winning the Tokyo Sports award for best female wrestler in 2015 and 2016 and wrestling for *Lucha Underground*. Dubbing herself Sekai no Kana ("World Famous Kana"), Kana won a tournament to become the first SMASH women's champion on September 8, 2011.

The following month, Kana made her first tour of the United States, debuting in SHIMMER in October 2011. Kana got the superstar treatment, beating Mia Yim in her SHIMMER debut and scoring a huge win over former SHIMMER champion Sara Del Rey in her second match in the promotion. With her wicked roundhouse kicks, intense spinning backfists, and superb submission game (including the crossface chickenwing, the cross armbar, and the dragon sleeper) — as well as her trademark face paint, which she regularly changed and modified — Kana immediately became a crowd favorite in SHIMMER and remained one of the promotion's top attractions and title contenders from 2011 through 2014.

Within a week of her appearance on NXT TakeOver: Brooklyn, WWE made the official announcement that Kana had signed with the company. In the press conference held in Japan, Urai said she felt she had done everything she could do in Japan and that WWE was the final goal of her career. She made her in-ring debut in NXT at TakeOver: Respect, under the ring name Asuka, honoring one of the best joshis ever, Lioness Asuka. Even though she's a fan of the American culture, her English needs to improve. That being said, fans quickly discovered that Asuka didn't need to talk to be over. Her looks and her mannerisms are plenty enough to get her meaning across, something that only the best can get away with. On April 1, 2016, Asuka defeated Bayley to capture the NXT women's title in a featured bout at NXT TakeOver: Dallas over WrestleMania weekend. Exactly three months later, she returned to Japan for the first time since joining NXT, keeping her title against Natalya. Since then, she has also successfully defended her title against Bayley and Mickie James.

For Dave Meltzer, Asuka is without a doubt a rare talent. "She's the only woman on the roster with the Brock Lesnar feel to her like she's legit. And the crowd chanted 'Asuka's gonna kill you' from the start. She may be the best worker in WWE, man or woman," he concluded.

# SARA AMATO

Mainstream wrestling fans may not know the name Sara Amato, but they're certainly familiar with her work.

In her role as assistant head coach at NXT, Amato has had a hand in helping to train some of WWE's most popular female wrestlers of recent years. In fact, she's so good at what she does that she now trains not only women but men as well. The WWE gig is just deserts for Amato, who — as Sara Del Rey — forged a reputation as one of the most respected and admired female wrestlers on the independent circuit in the 2000s.

"They call her the Queen of Wrestling, and deservedly so," said Cheerleader Melissa, who wrestled against, and alongside, Del Rey in SHIMMER. Born November 13, 1980, Amato grew up in California and enrolled in the All Pro Wrestling boot camp in Hayward, California, in 2001. At 5'10" and about 150 pounds, she had the physical size needed for the ring, but she struggled initially with training and was forced to

*NXT trainer Sara "Del Rey" Amato.* DAVE PRAZAK/SHIMMER

work harder to master the craft. She trained under Donovan Morgan and Mike Modest, and later under Bryan Danielson.

One year after she made her pro debut, she was accepted for a tour with ARSION in Japan. The opportunity proved to be a tremendous learning experience. "I trained with guys for years, but it was when I went to Japan and worked with a group of all females that my technique was really fine-tuned," she told *VICE* in a 2015 interview. "There wasn't a safety net." She was particularly impressed with Aja Kong and modeled herself after Kong's hard-hitting combat style.

She returned to the United States, completed a tour of Mexico, and then settled in on the independents. She wrestled in the first SHIMMER event in November 2005, battling Mercedes Martinez in a 20-minute draw. In 2007, she won a 16-woman tournament to be crowned the first SHIMMER champion. She held that title for one year until losing it to MsChif.

She also appeared in Ring of Honor and in CHIKARA, where in 2010, she wrestled a personal dream match, teaming with Claudio Castagnoli (Cesaro in WWE) to face Manami Toyota and Mike Quackenbush in a mixed tag bout. The next year, CHIKARA brought in Del Rey's hero, Aja Kong, as well as Tsubasa Kuragaki and Ayako Hamada; Del Rey scored wins over all three Japanese imports.

In 2012, by virtue of her wins against male wrestlers such as Castagnoli and El Generico (Sami Zayn in WWE), *Pro Wrestling Illustrated* ranked her number 430 in the PWI 500, a rarity for females.

In July 2012, she signed with WWE, not as an active wrestler but as a coach. If it was a surprise for many fans out there, it was Sara's dream job all along.

"Training has always been my one true passion; it's what I really love about pro wrestling. I thought I had unique experiences and perspectives to share with the women in NXT. WWE agreed, and here I am," she told *VICE*.

"You can have all the knowledge in the world, but it's useless if you can't explain it," Triple H told *VICE*. "That's what makes Sara special: She can feel it, but she's also able to articulate that feeling."

Del Rey's sterling reputation from the independents has helped inspire the women who train under her in NXT. "She had succeeded at the highest level, and now she was paving the way as WWE's first female coach," said Charlotte. "I just wanted to work incredibly hard for her."

# STEPHANIE MCMAHON

*Holding the Future
of Women's Wrestling
in Her Hands*

The McMahon family has been a major powerbroker in wrestling for generations, even if Jess and Vince Sr. never came close to lacing up the boots and getting in the ring themselves. That wouldn't be the case with the next generations of McMahons.

Vincent Kennedy McMahon was the first to cross over from promoter to wrestler, starting his active career in the spring of 1998 during his ongoing feud with "Stone Cold" Steve Austin. He would end up winning the Royal Rumble and the WWF championship. His son, Shane, followed his path at the end of 1998, winning the European title and showing some impressive skills. The following year, Vince's little girl, Stephanie, joined them. Like her brother and father, she would wear some gold, winning the women's title on one occasion.

Although she will not be remembered for her wrestling career, Stephanie grew up in wrestling's most powerful family and has

*She still got it: Stephanie McMahon defeats Brie Bella.* R.P. STRICKLAND

become one of the most important and influential people in the history of the sport.

Born September 24, 1976, in Hartford, Connecticut, she first appeared on the national stage as a child, modeling T-shirts in the catalogue in *WWF Magazine* without being credited as being the boss's daughter. After she earned her degree in communications from Boston University in 1998, she started working for her dad as an account executive.

The following year, at the suggestion of then-booker Vince Russo, she became part of a storyline in which she was abducted by the Undertaker. She soon became a regular in the cast of *Monday Night Raw* by having an on-screen relationship with Test and then one with Triple H, which led to the two of them getting married in real life.

It was during the McMahon–Helmsley era that she wrestled the most. She won the women's title on *SmackDown* when she defeated Jacqueline on March 28, 2000, in her very first singles match. She kept the belt for five months before dropping it to Lita in the main event of *Raw* with the Rock as special guest referee. As a character, she was playing a very credible spoiled-brat rich girl who couldn't take no for an answer. She was a character the fans loved to hate.

She then moved on to a feud with Trish Stratus. At the No Mercy PPV in 2003, she wrestled her own father in a controversial hardcore match. Six days later, she married Paul Levesque (Triple H), with whom she has since had three daughters.

She came back to the ring at SummerSlam 2014 in a high-profile match with Brie Bella. Fans in Los Angeles were really into McMahon's comeback in the ring, and after a well-executed DDT and neck snapper, they erupted with a "You still got it" chant.

"For someone who is not a trained wrestler and hasn't done a match in a decade, she was out there without gimmicks and did a very solid looking match," wrote Dave Meltzer.

"It was a very proud moment for me. I worked incredibly hard for it," McMahon said in an interview. "When I came back from the ring and I walked backstage, I ran into my children and my mother, who were all clapping and chanting, 'You still got it.' It was something I will never forget."

Aside from wrestling, McMahon has been a regular character since 2013, when she and Triple H christened themselves the Authority, playing an exaggerated heelish version of their real-life roles in the office. After overseeing the creative side of the business for close to a decade, she became WWE's chief brand officer, on top of being one of the owners of the company as the McMahon family owns a large part of the business. In 2016, *Ad Age* magazine named her one of the 30 most powerful women in sports. Behind the scenes and even on air, Stephanie turns more and more into her father, to the point that Shane calls her "the Vincess."

# RONDA ROUSEY:
## The Biggest Prospect Who's Not Even a Wrestler Yet

Since the heyday of Billy Wolfe and Mildred Burke, there's never been a better time for a woman to become a pro wrestler, thanks to another power couple — Triple H and Stephanie. That being said, the women's division could use a name to bring it into mainstream circles. Coming off the 2016 Summer Olympics, some people think that the very first American gold medalist in freestyle wrestling, Helen Maroulis, could be the one. "Maroulis was the potential star coming out of the competition," wrote Dave Meltzer. "There will only be one 'first American women's gold medalist' in history. She has a good look and comes off well on television, and can be marketed greatly." However, Maroulis might defend her title in 2020, making her a long shot for WWE at this time. Others think UFC fighter and *Dancing with the Stars* contestant Paige Van Zandt, who's a WWE fan and has said she would love to do wrestling one day, could be it. Yet, the answer could in fact be a mixture of both of these women's strengths — a UFC fighter, Olympic medalist, and the woman who actually most influenced the revolution that women's wrestling is having.

Ronda Rousey and her friends, calling themselves the Four Horsewomen, are known to be huge wrestling fans. One of them, Shayna Baszler, has already made the transition from MMA to pro wrestling, making her SHIMMER debut in June 2016 having already had a try-out with WWE. Rousey has been seen several times at WWE and Pro Wrestling Guerrilla events. She was invited into the ring by the Rock for an altercation with Stephanie McMahon at WrestleMania 31, adding fuel to the rumors that she will one day compete for WWE. Her loss to Holly Holm in November 2015 might also be the something that pushes her away from the Octagon and into the squared circle. As she enters her 30s, pro wrestling could offer greater stability than the UFC.

"I'm ready. I've seen NXT, I remember Nattie and Charlotte's match for the title. Nattie was actually training with the original Four Horsewomen to get ready for that fight," she told *Rolling Stone* a few days before her fight with Holm. "I have so many obligations, but I really want to find a way to make it happen. I'm a huge fan of wrestling, and I would like to see the position of women in the sport continue to improve, so if I can be a part of it, great."

"I'm really encouraged by the progress I've seen with what they're doing with the women in WWE, but I feel like there's a lot more that can be done," said the 2008 Olympic bronze medalist in judo. "They're doing some of it now, too. I'm really excited that they've brought up all these great women from NXT, who are all different from the normal mold they would use for the Divas division. I'm not going to take credit for anything, but I definitely want to be part of it as much as I can."

Rousey might have what it takes to provide a fresh spark and help take the women's division to the next level.

*UFC's Ronda Rousey could very well be the future of women's wrestling.* COURTESY OF WORLD WRESTLING ENTERTAINMENT, INC.

## WHAT DOES *the* FUTURE HOLD?

Although WWE has not had a female star of Rousey's scope yet, McMahon is dedicated to finding the right formula to make it happen.

"Women play an integral role in WWE, both in the corporate side as well as on television. There's a lot of girl power at WWE. And we're proud of it," McMahon told *Good Morning America*'s Amy Robach. "We embraced our fans who asked us to do more with our female performers, to feature them as athletes, to give them more meaningful

*The future of women's wrestling could be in Stephanie's hands.* RICKY HAVLIK

characters and storylines. They're not just eye candy, we want more. And we are doing everything we can to super serve that need." As a testament to that, at a WWE try-out in September 2016, 19 women were featured — the largest number of female prospects ever invited.

As far as Trish Stratus is concerned, Stephanie is the main reason women's wrestling has been show-cased that much in recent years.

"There would have been no career, there would have been no opportunity, there would have been no revamping of the women's division if Stephanie wasn't behind it all," Stratus said. "She is always supportive of showcasing a strong, powerful woman. There would have been no division and none of the women would have got the push that we needed or the encouragement we needed without her."

Like it or not, in the wrestling world, WWE is the one setting the trends for the mainstream audience. And even if the company has made use of its female talent better than ever before, there's still room for far better and more exciting things. As of this writing, WWE's plan is to have a women's tournament on NXT and a weekly WWE Network show, pretty much like the Cruiserweight Classic. But what could be next? An all-female promotion like MMA's Invicta on the

WWE Network? An all-female Royal Rumble match? Or, why not, a women's match headlining WrestleMania. With Ronda Rousey's popularity and the ratings success that other women's combat sports athletes like Holly Holm and Cris Cyborg have enjoyed, Dave Meltzer argued that WWE should model itself after MMA. "There's never been a better time for women in combat sports and WWE needs to see what is working with MMA and apply it in a scripted environment."

In her unpublished autobiography, Mildred Burke wrote that restoring the status of women would revive the entire sport. And that's exactly what Stephanie McMahon seems to be doing. The future of women's wrestling might very well be in her hands.

# Selected Bibliography

Dave Meltzer's *Wrestling Observer Newsletter*, the *Wall Street Journal* of professional wrestling and mixed martial arts, was instrumental to us. Stu Saks's *Pro Wrestling Illustrated*, the longest running pro wrestling magazine in the United States, was also a good source of information. Ruth Leitman's film *Lipstick and Dynamite, Piss and Vinegar: The First Ladies of Wrestling*, the best film ever done on the subject, gave us great insights on a number of women wrestlers. The WWE Network, pro wrestling's premier streaming service, gave us the opportunity to watch or re-watch so many women's matches from the last 30-plus years.

In addition to those sources, the following books and websites were valuable references during the creation of *Sisterhood of the Squared Circle*.

Anderson, Ole, and Scott Teal. *Inside Out: How Corporate America Destroyed Professional Wrestling*. Crowbar Press, 2003.

Apter, Bill. *Is Wrestling Fixed? I Didn't Know It Was Broken: From Photo Shoots and Sensational Stories to the WWE Network, Bill Apter's Incredible Pro Wrestling Journey*. ECW Press, 2015.

Assael, Shaun, and Mike Mooneyham. *Sex, Lies, and Headlocks: The Real Story of Vince McMahon and World Wrestling Entertainment*. Broadway Books, 2004.

Banner, Penny, and Gerry Hostetler. *Banner Days: Autobiography of the First A.W.A. Women's World Wrestling Champion Penny Banner (1954–1977)*. Flying Mare Publication, 2004.

Blassie, Classy Freddie, and Keith Elliot Greenberg. *"Classy" Freddie Blassie: Listen, You Pencil Neck Geeks*. Pocket Books, 2003.

Brody, Howard. *Swimming With Piranhas: Surviving the Politics of Professional Wrestling*. ECW Press, 2009.

Chyna and Michael Angeli. *Chyna, the 9th Wonder of the World: If They Only Knew*. HarperCollins, 2001.

Dumas, Amy, and Michael Krugman. *Lita: A Less Traveled R.O.A.D. — The Reality of Amy Dumas*. Pocket Books, 2003.

Ellison, Lillian, and Larry Platt. *The Fabulous Moolah: First Goddess of the Squared Circle*. HarperCollins, 2002.

Flair, Ric, Keith Elliot Greenberg, and Mark Madden. *To Be the Man*. Pocket Books, 2004.

Hart, Gary, and Philip Varriale. *My Life in Wrestling . . . With a Little Help From My Friends*. Gean Publishing, 2009.

Hébert, Bertrand, and Pat Laprade. *Mad Dogs, Midgets and Screw Jobs: The Untold Story of How Montreal Shaped the World of Wrestling.* ECW Press, 2013.

Holly, Bob, and Ross Williams, *The Hardcore Truth: The Bob Holly Story.* ECW Press, 2013.

Hornbaker, Tim. *Capitol Revolution: The Rise of the McMahon Wrestling Empire.* ECW Press, 2015.

Hornbaker, Tim. *National Wrestling Alliance: The Untold Story of the Monopoly That Strangled Pro Wrestling.* ECW Press, 2007.

Jares, Joe. *Whatever Happened to Gorgeous George?: The Blood and Ballyhoo of Professional Wrestling.* Prentice Hall, 1974.

Jennings, L.A. *She's a Knockout!: A History of Women in Fighting Sports.* Rowman & Littlefield, 2014.

Leen, Jeff. *The Queen of the Ring: Sex, Muscles, Diamonds and the Making of an American Legend.* Grove/Atlantic, Inc., 2009.

Leiker, Ken, and Mark Vancil. *World Wrestling Entertainment Unscripted.* Pocket Books, 2003.

McCoy, Heath. *Pain and Passion: The History of Stampede Wrestling.* CanWest Books, 2005.

Molinaro, John F., Jeff Marek, and Dave Meltzer. *Top 100 Pro Wrestlers of All Time.* Winding Stair Press, 2002.

Oliver, Greg. *Pro Wrestling Hall of Fame: The Canadians.* ECW Press, 2003.

Patterson, Pat, and Bertrand Hébert. *Accepted: How the First Gay Superstar Changed WWE*. ECW Press, 2016.

Piper, Roddy, and Robert Picarello. *In the Pit with Piper*. Berkley Boulevard, 2002.

Thesz, Lou, and Kit Bauman. *Hooker: An Authentic Wrestler's Adventures Inside the Bizarre World of Professional Wrestling*. Lou Thesz, 1995.

Cagematch
www.cagematch.net

Diva Dirt
www.diva-dirt.com

FSC Club
www.fscclub.com

G.L.O.R.Y. Wrestling
www.glorywrestling.com

Highspots
www.highspots.com

History of WWE
www.thehistoryofwwe.com

Kayfabe Memories
www.kayfabememories.com

LadySports Online
www.ladysports.com

Online World of Wrestling
www.onlineworldofwrestling.com

Ringbelles
www.ringbelles.com

SLAM! Wrestling
http://slam.canoe.ca/Slam/Wrestling

Smithsonian
www.smithsonianmag.com

Wrestlezone
www.wrestlezone.com

Wrestling Classics
www.wrestlingclassics.com

Wrestling Title Histories
www.wrestling-titles.com

Wrestling Observer
www.f4wonline.com

WWE
www.wwe.com

# *Acknowledgments*

## PAT LAPRADE

When I began watching wrestling more than 30 years ago, I couldn't necessarily describe myself as a fan of women's wrestling — I was just a wrestling fan, period. At least that was true until I started working with Kim Leduc (former wrestler Paul Leduc's daughter), Gen "LuFisto" Goulet and Gen "Sweet Cherrie" Lacasse on the launch of the ALF, Montreal's first all-women's promotion. I discovered a product so unique and so full of potential. That was a decade ago. Since then, I have also been part of NCW Femmes Fatales and helped out at the SHIMMER shows I attend. And my affinity for women's wrestling has just kept growing.

I'd like to thank Kim and both Gens for including me in their team right from the beginning. I'd like to thank also Stephane Bruyere for opening the doors of both Femmes Fatales and SHIMMER to me. A huge thank you also goes to Greg Oliver, who has become a mentor to me in so many ways. Thanks to my partner in crime, Bertrand Hebert, for advising me and being there when I needed him. And finally, thanks to my mom, my family, and my friends, who put up with me talking about wrestling (and women's wrestling) . . . all the time.

## DAN MURPHY

Shortly after ECW Press greenlighted this book, I had an upheaval in my personal life that left me in a deep depression. Writing requires long hours alone with your thoughts, and alone with my thoughts and emotions was the last place I wanted to be. Working on this book gave me a purpose during a time when it was difficult to get up out of bed. I found inspiration in the stories of these women — performers who found the courage to chase their dreams, to defy expectations, and to entertain fans around the world.

I used to carry a quote by Teddy Roosevelt in my wallet: "Far better is it to dare mighty things, to win glorious triumphs, even though checkered by failure than to rank with those poor spirits who neither enjoy much nor suffer much, because they live in a grey twilight that knows not victory nor defeat." The women in this book did that, they dared mighty things. Their courage and perseverance inspired me when I needed it most.

In my 20 years writing for *Pro Wrestling Illustrated*, I have had the privilege of meeting and befriending many wrestlers. I logged a lot of miles driving with my friend Laura (Cherry Bomb) Dennis and other women back and forth to SHIMMER shows. I understand the sacrifices women wrestlers make to follow their dream: the injuries, the travel, the friends, family, and boyfriends who question: "When are you going to give up this silly wrestling thing and settle down?" I'm honored to be able to tell their stories.

# DAN AND PAT

The idea for the book was first discussed while we were doing time-keeping duty for a SHIMMER show in the fall of 2014. Accordingly, we would like to thank Dave Prazak for letting us be a part of his creation. We would also like to thank the following people: Michael Holmes, Crissy Calhoun and all the team at ECW Press for believing in this idea and for their wonderful work; Greg Oliver, Dave Meltzer and Vance Nevada for sharing all of their files about women's wrestling; Jamie Melissa Hemmings for all the interviews she let us access; the Cauliflower Alley Club and the Professional Wrestling Hall of Fame for their always appreciated collaboration; Yan O'Cain for all the work he did on pictures (you're so gifted, man!); and every person interviewed for the book: your input, big or small, was very much appreciated. And last but not least, all the photographers who contributed to the book: thank you for helping to give life to our stories.

This book is dedicated to the dreamers. It's a recognition of the sacrifices and struggles that are inherent in the strange business of professional wrestling. To every woman included in this book — and all others who have done so much to compete, to entertain and to dare mighty things — *thank you.*

*Authors Dan and Pat with Mayu Iwatani and Io Shirai at the CAC.* YAN O'CAIN